Educational Supervision in Social Work

Educational Supervision in Social Work

*A Task-Centered Model for Field Instruction
and Staff Development*

Jonathan Caspi
William J. Reid

COLUMBIA UNIVERSITY PRESS   NEW YORK

COLUMBIA UNIVERSITY PRESS
Publishers Since 1893
New York Chichester, West Sussex
Copyright © 2002 Columbia University Press

Library of Congress Cataloging-in-Publication Data

Caspi, Jonathan.
      Educational supervision in social work : a task-centered model for field instruc-
tion and staff development / Jonathan Caspi, William J. Reid.
      p.   cm.
      Includes bibliographical references and index.
      ISBN 0–231–10852–4 (cloth) — ISBN 0–231–10853–2 (paper)
      1. Social work education. 2. Social service—Field work. 3. Social workers—
In-service training. 4. Social workers—Supervision of. I. Reid, William James,
1928–

HV11 .C335 2002
361.3'071—dc21   2002019663

⊗

Columbia University Press books
are printed on permanent and durable acid-free paper.
Printed in the United States of America

c 10 9 8 7 6 5 4 3 2 1
p 10 9 8 7 6 5 4 3 2 1

Contents

Preface   *ix*

1   A New Model of Educational Supervision   1

2   A History of Educational Supervision in Social Work   31

3   Principles of Effective Instruction   55

4   The Supervisory Relationship   96

5   The Person of the Supervisor   126

6   Preparing for Supervision Beginnings and Endings   156

7   The Development and Basic Principles of TCS   172

8   The Social and Direct Teaching Functions of TCS   182

9   Target Goals   211

10   Tasks, Obstacles, and Contracting   242

11   Task Review   276

12   Applications of TCS   289

Appendix: TCS Guidelines   *305*

References   *313*

Name Index   *329*

Subject Index   *335*

Preface

This book puts forth a task-centered model for educational supervision, which we hope will be a useful contribution to supervision practices. It provides clear steps for systematic articulation and attainment of educational objectives. There is an abundance of information on principles associated with quality educational supervision in the literature. However, this body of knowledge is usually not organized into coherent models of supervision. The Task-Centered Model for Educational Supervision (TCS) incorporates these principles and systematically puts them into action.

Undergraduate and graduate programs in social work, education, psychology, and counseling have learning objectives that their students must achieve during their internships in order to successfully complete the degree. Although it seems as though most students do attain these goals, it is often unclear how. Supervision practices vary widely, occurring behind closed doors and out of the view of the school. Too often, supervision focuses on case dynamics without explicit links to learning. TCS methodically ties case considerations to educational goals. Program administrators, supervisors, and students appreciate knowing how educational objectives are to be assessed and achieved.

This book should be of primary interest to field instructors, agency supervisors, and field education directors. It may also be helpful to field interns, social workers in staff positions, and supervisors from other disciplines (e.g., counseling, education, psychology). In addition to presenting TCS, the book provides in-depth information about all aspects of educational supervision, including principles associated with quality instruction and effective supervisory relationships. Therefore, it can be used as a text in courses or seminars on educational supervision and field instruction. Finally, this book and TCS should appeal to those interested in furthering the development of quality instructional supervision, such as researchers, field directors, and agency administrators.

We would like to express our thanks to the people who contributed to this effort. Dr. Anne E. Fortune's invaluable feedback helped make the book much clearer than it would otherwise have been. We are grateful to Leslie Kriesel for her thoughtful and flawless copyediting. Bonnie Kenaley's help with the index is much appreciated. We wish to thank the many students, practitioners, and colleagues whose cases and ideas became a part of the book. Finally, we are indebted to our families. Without their support and encouragement, this work would not have been possible.

J.C.
W.J.R.

Educational Supervision in Social Work

1   A New Model of Educational Supervision

You picked up this book because you have an interest in educational supervision—teaching interns in field practica, training staff, or assisting the ongoing professional development of social work clinicians. If you are like many staff supervisors, field instructors, and clinical consultants, you are looking for a book that helps you *do* supervision. Much literature on this subject provides helpful theoretical principles of effective supervision but gives little direction about how to apply them in practice. Additionally, because these principles often address different aspects of the encounter, it can be challenging to work them into a coherent model of supervisory practice. The lack of comprehensive educational supervision models further complicates this endeavor.

This lack provides the central rationale for this book, which presents the Task-Centered Model for Educational Supervision (TCS). As you will see, TCS offers strategies and steps for "how to do" educational supervision. It systematically puts principles of effective supervision into practice. In particular, TCS outlines an ordered series of discrete activities that occur within and between supervision meetings, for the continuous attainment of learning and practice objectives.

The first section of the book, chapters 2 through 6, presents an overview of the nature, history, and principles of educational supervision. These chapters provide the context and foundation for understanding and implementing the model. At the center of the supervisory process is the relationship between the supervisor and the supervisee. Strategies for building and maintaining productive and open relationships are reviewed. The supervisor must take the lead in developing the relationship and has a great impact on the success of the encounter. However, the person of the supervisor has received little attention, so it is considered in some depth.

TCS is presented in chapters 7 to 11. Illustrative vignettes show how the model looks in action. The book concludes with discussion of the various applications and uses of the model and a chapter on the application of the model in various educational and practice environments.

A Note About the Development of TCS

TCS was originally developed for educating social work students during their practicum experiences (Caspi and Reid 1998). Therefore, both the model and this book primarily focus and draw upon social work field instruction practices, concepts, and literature. Because its central function is supervisee learning, field instruction knowledge provides a solid foundation for educational supervision practice. Though it was developed as a field instruction model, TCS procedures and principles have clear applications for educational supervision with staff, with peers, and in consultation arrangements. Thus, we offer this book for those engaged in educational supervision of any type. If you would like to get an overview of TCS at this time, refer to the appendix, which provides the model's guidelines.

The objective of this chapter is to briefly introduce you to educational supervision and TCS. It begins by discussing the nature of educational supervision and clarifying terms used in this book. Then it provides a summary of TCS and a vignette of a typical TCS supervision meeting—a look at the model in action. This chapter concludes with an overview of the remainder of the book.

What Is Educational Supervision?

Supervision can be defined as the overseeing of another's work with sanctioned authority to monitor and direct performance, to ensure satisfactory performance (which includes client safety). How this is accomplished and what this entails widely differ among supervision arrangements. Processes vary according to whether or not supervisees are staff, student interns, peers, or people who have contracted for clinical consultation.

Supervision has been conceptualized to consist of three primary functions: educational, administrative, and supportive (Kadushin 1992). Although quality supervision is considered to involve active implementation of all three functions, one is often given greater emphasis over the others. Which function takes priority often fluctuates during work with an individual supervisee, even within individual supervision conferences. However, the nature of the encounter is defined by which function is consistantly emphasized throughout, reflecting its overarching objective.

In educational supervision the focus of the encounter is supervisee learning. Knowledge and skill development take priority over administrative and supportive tasks. This is in contrast to administrative supervision, which is concerned with management of supervisee work, with a primary focus on meeting agency requirements (e.g., number in caseload, rate of intakes or discharges, meeting client goals). The learning needs of the supervisee are considered to be less important than the functional needs of the agency. Moreover, administrative supervision of staff may not include any educational activities. Planned learning in such arrangements is by choice, not a requirement. In order to engage in educational supervision with staff, the supervisee must first discuss it openly to clarify the primary purpose of the encounter.

Quality supervision includes support for supervisees, who commonly experience strong affective reactions to their work. Supervisors are responsible for helping with supervisee frustrations, attending to concerns, "sustaining worker morale . . . and giving supervisees a sense of worth as professionals" (Kadushin 1992:19). Support is necessary when a supervisee's affective responses are at the fore, particularly when they impede the ability to engage in administrative or educational activities. Attention to the emotional aspects of the supervisee's experience can be critical in ensuring productive job performance and preventing burnout.

This book is about educational supervision. While much consideration is given to the supportive function and some to administrative responsibilities (e.g., evaluation), principles and methods for attainment of learning objectives are paid the greatest attention. Indeed, TCS was designed as a model for addressing the educational function of supervision of interns and staff.

Clarification of Terms

In the human services, various terminology is used to describe different aspects of the supervisory encounter. For purposes of clarification, the most commonly used terms in the book are discussed here.

Intern

The term "intern" is used in this book primarily to refer to students completing agency-based experiential educational requirements in human service programs. Interns usually provide direct service under the supervision of an agency employee (or, less commonly, a school faculty member). In addition to "supervisor," these employees are referred to by a variety of terms when in their supervisory role, including "field instructor," "practicum instructor," "field teacher," "site supervisor," "mentor," "preceptor," and "cooperating teacher." Note how most of these emphasize the educational function of the encounter.

Staff

The term "staff" refers to workers, paid or volunteer, who are not at the agency because of school or program requirements. These include workers with and without professional degrees. While those with degrees usually have more training than nondegree staff, both engage in similar educational supervision processes, although they teach skills at different levels.

Consultation

Supervision arrangements that are privately contracted for (i.e., outside the agency domain) are referred to here as "consultation." Consultation is distinguished from supervision by the fact that consultants do not usually have sanctioned authority over the supervisee. Instead, the worker or intern hires the consultant, often without the knowledge of the agency. In references to consultation arrangements, the supervisory pair consists of the "consultant" (the one providing the supervision) and the "consultee" (the one receiving supervision). For a more in-depth discussion of consultation, see chapter 11.

TCS

Although TCS is described in great depth in the latter half of this book, we introduce the model at the start with a brief overview. This is followed by a "case" presentation of a supervision meeting, which is intended to bring the model to life and illustrate how its procedures look in practice.

Overview of TCS

TCS offers a set of steps for the supervisor and supervisee to follow during and between supervision meetings. These steps were designed to assist the supervisory pair in systematically articulating and attaining learning and practice objectives, and putting into practice the features commonly associated with effective educational supervision (these features are discussed in depth in chapter 3). TCS provides a road map for conducting the educational supervision meeting. These steps are offered as guidelines to be used flexibly, not as a rigidly prescribed series of activities.

Outline of the TCS Sequence

Beginning phase (from initial meeting until completion of first contract)
Social stage
Explaining supervision and TCS
Educational stage
Target goals stage
Identifying, prioritizing, and selecting tasks
Anticipating and negotiating potential obstacles
Contracting
Middle and ending phases (from completion of first contract through final encounter)
Social stage
Task review
Educational stage
Target goals stage
Identifying, prioritizing, and selecting tasks
Anticipating and negotiating potential obstacles
Contracting

The Three TCS Phases

As you can see, the model is organized into three overarching phases: beginning, middle, and ending. The beginning phase is brief and concludes at the completion of the first contract. It contains a step specifically to inform supervisees about the social work supervision process and TCS procedures (which includes supervisors copying the guidelines included in the appendix and sharing them with supervisees). The sequence of steps carried out during the middle phase is used the most, since that phase runs from the first contract until the end of the supervisory encounter. It is also the phase depicted in the full illustrative vignette later in this chapter. The ending phase follows the same sequence as the middle phase. However, since the end of supervision represents a unique time in the encounter, educational work focuses on issues that commonly arise during termination (see chapter 5 for a discussion of these issues).

TCS Process

The TCS process essentially entails the selection of supervision objectives and the formulation of tasks to achieve them. During each meeting, supervisees and supervisors collaboratively identify learning and practice objectives for immediate, targeted work. These objectives are evaluated, prioritized in order of perceived importance, and formulated as "target goals." Actions, or tasks, for attaining target goals are then selected. Prior to finalizing the selection of tasks, potential obstacles to theur implementation are considered. This step involves asking supervisees to predict problems they might encounter when attempting to carry out the selected tasks. Its purpose is to promote successful task implementation and consideration of possible consequences of proposed intervention activities. The supervisory pair may change, modify, or keep selected tasks with "backup plans" for handling obstacles in case they arise. At the end of each meeting, the supervisor and supervisee review the selection of target goals and tasks, and mutually agree to them in the form of a contract. The supervisee then implements the agreed-upon tasks, typically in work with cases.

At the start of the next supervision meeting, task implementation and target goal attainment are evaluated. If target goals have been successfully attained, the supervisee and supervisor select new ones. If not, existing goals are kept for continued work or modified based upon the evaluative discussion. The process of continually identifying goals, tasks, and obstacles and then implementing, reviewing, and evaluating tasks represents the major activities of TCS, carried out during each supervision meeting and direct encounter.

TCS was also designed to address the affective components of supervision. Each meeting begins with a "social" period to assist the transition into supervision activities, provide support, and tend to the supervisory relationship. Because supervisees often experience intense feelings during their work with cases and in supervision, this step ensures that the supervisor takes time to address them. This demonstrates to supervisees that their supervisors care about them (and not just their performances) and prepares both to actively engage in the instrumental work of supervision.

Another important step of TCS, the educational stage, includes time specifically set aside for direct instruction. Supervisees typically have many questions, and this step allows for supervisors to provide requested information and share their practice knowledge. It occurs near the start of each supervision meeting, and naturally segues into the focused work of identifying and working toward objectives.

A TCS Supervision Meeting: The Model in Action

Although we include many illustrative vignettes and brief narratives of supervision meeting dialogue throughout the book, we thought it helpful to introduce the model with an example of an entire TCS meeting. In the following vignette, you will be able to observe the model's steps and its systematic process of articulating and working toward clear learning and practice objectives. As you read the vignette, please refer to the "Outline of the TCS Sequence" provided earlier for a list of the model's steps. It may be helpful in orienting you. Because in-depth discussions of each stage are provided later in this book, only brief explanations of steps and the supervisor's actions are given here. (For a descriptive overview, with explanations of each step, please refer to the appendix).

The following is a narrative of a TCS supervision meeting between a social work graduate intern and her field instructor (i.e., educational supervisor). The intern is working in an outpatient mental health agency and is learning how to provide traditional therapeutic intervention (e.g., one-hour, weekly meetings in the agency office) to individual clients. In this case, the intern has met the client only once and successfully performed an intake but is now unsure about how to proceed.

The supervisory pair have met only a few times and are beginning to make clinical decisions regarding cases. The case at the center of the following supervisory meeting involves a client who is a white, middle-class woman in her early fifties. She has sought treatment wishing to learn how to handle chronic back pain she has been suffering with for the past year. In this vignette the supervisor,

Lottie, and the intern, Sara, utilize TCS to guide their supervisory process, set practice and educational goals for the supervisee, and develop strategies to assist the client. They have already completed the first TCS contract and are now following the middle phase sequence of the model. As stated earlier, this phase constitutes the majority of interaction in TCS supervision; we selected a session that was most typical of the process to demonstrate the model.

An Illustrative Vignette of a TCS Meeting

Each supervision meeting begins with the social stage. The duration is usually brief (about five minutes of a one-hour meeting, although it may last longer depending upon need). The social stage generally consists of welcoming sequences and "small talk" to help make the transition from outside interests to supervision activities. It may include discussion of affective reactions to supervision and practice. Addressing supervisee anxiety first can help maximize focus on the instrumental functions of supervision (developing learning objectives, formulating interventions to be carried out with clients).

> LOTTIE (SUPERVISOR): Good afternoon! How are you doing?
> SARA (INTERN): Okay, I guess. (sounding a little dejected)
> LOTTIE: Wow! Your enthusiasm is overwhelming! (using humorous sarcasm—they both laugh)
> SARA: Sorry.
> LOTTIE: Well, what's up? (inquiring about what is troubling Sara before moving on to instrumental functions of supervision meeting)
> SARA: I am looking for a new apartment, and I thought I had one. But just before supervision, I got a call from the landlord telling me that the tenant decided not to move out. So now I don't know what I am going to do.
> LOTTIE: That's very disappointing!

During the social stage, supervisors utilize social work engagement skills, including validation, empathy, reflective clarifying, and supportive statements, to address supervisee affective reactions. Because supervision is not therapy, "uncovering" questions and interpretations are avoided. The objective is to support the supervisee and help reduce anxiety that may impede the work of supervision. The social stage also teaches the use of these skills through modeling. In this situation, Lottie uses, and models, the skill of empathy.

SARA: It is! And it was such a nice place. Now I don't know what I am going to do!

LOTTIE: It really is very frustrating, not knowing what to do. Do you have to be out of your current apartment by the end of the month?

SARA: Well, no . . . but I really hate it!

The two continue to talk about the apartment situation for a few minutes. Lottie notes that Sara's anxiety about the situation remains high and begins to wonder how well Sara will be able to attend to the work of supervision.

LOTTIE: You are really feeling very overwhelmed by this.

SARA: Yes, I just want it resolved.

LOTTIE: Let me ask you a question. Would it be better for you if we rescheduled this meeting for later in the day, or even the week, so that you can go take care of the apartment situation? I am worried that it will be difficult for you to concentrate on what we have to do here if you are thinking about apartments.

SARA: No. I am here now . . . and there is not much I can do about the apartment at this minute. But thanks for asking. I can focus on our work, don't worry. (She smiles.)

As demonstrated, questioning an anxious supervisee about their ability to attend to supervision is an effective technique for handling stress that might impede the process. It acknowledges the stress (rather than trying to work around it) and challenges the supervisee to make a decision about how to handle it. In addition, questioning forces the supervisee to be self-reflective and self-evaluative—important skills for practicing good social work. Once the stress is openly discussed, the chances that it will remain an obstacle to supervision are greatly lessened.

LOTTIE: Good. Just so you know, if you have major things going on that make it difficult for you to attend to supervision, please let me know and we can try to work around them.

SARA: Thanks! It's a relief to know that. Shall we get down to business?

LOTTIE: Sure. Let's take out the TCS guidelines. I have found that it is helpful to have them out during supervisory meetings until they become second nature.

We recommend that supervisors copy a set of the guidelines (in the appendix) for their supervisees so that both can take part in directing the process. In addition, learning the steps of systematically setting discrete goals and formulating tasks to achieve them are important skills for lifelong learning and autonomous practice.

> SARA: Sounds good. (They each look at their copy of the guidelines.) Hey! It looks like we just did the social stage! (She laughs.) So the next step is the task review.
>
> LOTTIE: Yes. So, how did you do with the implementation of your contracted tasks?
>
> SARA: Well, I met with the new intake we discussed last week . . . and I really felt anxious afterward. I have no idea how to help her.
>
> LOTTIE: It sounds like you left feeling a bit overwhelmed.
>
> SARA: Definitely! I left thinking, "I am not a doctor, I don't know how to get your pain to stop!"
>
> LOTTIE: Sometimes, at first, it is not always apparent how we can be helpful, but after some discussion, things become clearer. That's what supervision is for—to help you learn things about practice that are new, to enable you to learn ways of solving such puzzles. Okay, before we figure out what to do with this client, let's review what you did with her this past week. (Note how the supervisor keeps the focus on the task review stage and does not follow Sara's lead to problem-solve the case. Had they jumped into "what to do," they would have neglected to review and evaluate Sara's work.) What tasks did we select for work with this client? (The two pull out their written contracts to review.)
>
> SARA: Let's see. Well, we only selected two target goals this week because I don't yet have that many cases. Both target goals were specifically related to this case. The tasks for first one, "Explore the problem," were to clearly identify the problem that has brought her to seek therapy, explore the client's perception of the cause of the problem, and explore what she has already attempted to solve it for herself. We decided on these tasks because it was my first meeting with her. We thought it important that I make sure I truly understand what her problem is all about.
>
> LOTTIE: Right! This target goal emerged from our discussion about performing clinical assessments. And the second target goal and set of tasks?

SARA: We also decided that because I am just learning how to do counseling, I should master basic communication skills: actively use reflection and clarification, respond to expressions of strong feeling with empathy, and admit it when I don't understand client remarks and request more information. We kept this last one from the week before . . . because the first time we met I pretended to understand her when I really did not. (She smiles, a little embarrassed.)

LOTTIE: Yes, I remember. (She returns the smile.) They are both good target goals and appropriate to the steps we felt you should take in the case. If you remember, they also correspond to learning objectives outlined on your school's evaluation form—learning how to employ communication skills such as reflection and clarification, and learning the process of problem identification and exploration—how to perform assessments. So, how did it go? Let's start with the first. What did you discover was the problem?

SARA: When I asked her, she said it was to "stop being in pain all the time." I have no idea how to do this!

LOTTIE: You are worried that you cannot help her?

SARA: Yes.

LOTTIE: That is a common fear of new, and *old*, social workers! (They laugh.) Okay, so she wants help with the pain. Did she say what she would like from her work with you?

SARA: Well, just that she wants to stop feeling the serious pain in her back.

LOTTIE: Has she been to see a doctor?

SARA: I asked that. She says she has and that the doctor says it's "all in her head," which is why she is here.

LOTTIE: Sometimes doctors miss things. Has she consulted with more than one?

SARA: I don't know. I will ask her next time. But can it really be "all in her head"?

Following is the contract Sara and Lottie completed the week before the meeting presented here. It lists the target goals and tasks discussed throughout this vignette. A second contract with the target goals and tasks formulated during this supervisory meeting is provided at the end of the vignette.

DATE: *Sept. 20*

CONTRACT

A. Target Goals

List in order of priority the goals (up to three) that you and the student agreed to work on. Identify each goal in a single word or phrase. Include the date the goal was first formulated. On the line below each identified target goal, provide the related practice or educational objective.

GOAL #1: *Explore the problem* date form. *Sept. 20*
>   Related practice or educational objective: *Perform complete assessments*

GOAL #2: *Successfully implement basic communication skills* date form *Sept. 20*
>   Related practice or educational objective: *Master communication skills*

GOAL #3: _____ date form. _____
>   Related practice or educational objective: _____

B. Prioritization Processes

>   √ a. student agreed on selection and priorities of goals
>   __ b. student disagreed on selection and priorities of goals
>   If "b" was checked, explain disagreement (use back if necessary)

C. Task Formulation

List three tasks the student will do to achieve each target goal:

GOAL #1
task #1: *clearly identify the problem that has brought her to seek therapy*
task #2: *explore the client's perception of the cause of the problem*
task #3: *explore what she has already attempted to solve it for herself*

GOAL #2
task #1: *actively use reflection and clarification*
task #2: *respond to expressions of strong feeling with empathy*
task #3: *admit when don't understand client remarks and request more info*

GOAL #3
task #1: _____
task #2: _____
task #3: _____

D. Were potential obstacles to task implementation considered?
   Circle one: (Yes) No

List any additional agreements (e.g., time limits): *Goals #1 and #2 will be completed in one week*

The task review process often raises new questions for supervisees. It provides many natural opportunities to segue into the next step, the educational stage, in which the supervisor spends a few minutes sharing information on a subject the supervisee has asked about. If this occurs before all the tasks have been reviewed, the supervisory pair tend to jump into the educational stage and then return to the task review. It is not unusual for the discussion to switch between the task review and the educational stage a number of times before moving on to the target goals stage. Here, Lottie takes the opportunity to quickly answer Sara's question and then returns to the task review process.

LOTTIE: When, after thorough medical examination, no biological or physical source for the pain can be identified, it is referred to as "psychosomatic." Do you know what this means? (It is good practice for the supervisor to ask the supervisee whether or not they have knowledge about a subject before teaching about it. There is little less appetizing to a supervisee than being lectured on a topic they already know well!)

SARA: No, not really.

LOTTIE: Simply stated, this means that after medical doctors have ruled out biological causes, they may conclude that the only remaining logical source for the pain is psychological in nature. This does not mean that the pain is false. The person really feels it—it is a real pain. Therefore, it is important when you work with people who have been told their pain is psychosomatic to take them seriously and seek effective ways to manage the pain.

SARA: How do you do that—help manage the pain?

LOTTIE: Well, that depends. We'll get to that, perhaps during our discussion of next week's target goals and tasks. Let's continue reviewing what you did, and what you discovered in your meeting with her. It sounds like you got a pretty good beginning idea of her problem. It is often helpful to narrow the focus of a person's complaint by learning more about it. What does she make of the "it's all in your head" diagnosis?

SARA: She said that at first she didn't believe it, but now she thinks it's probably true. She says that she has many stresses in her life and that all the stress may be hurting her back.

LOTTIE: That brings us to your second task of "exploring the client's perception of the cause of the problem." She thinks it is related to all the stress in her life?

SARA: Yes, she wonders if she removes all the stress, maybe the pain will stop.

LOTTIE: She is "carrying a lot of weight" around?

SARA: (Laughs.) That's a good way to put it. It seems like she is having trouble in almost every aspect of her life—her marriage, her job, her kids, her parents—and now she is stressed because she feels the pain keeps her from being able to fix these things.

LOTTIE: That is a lot to deal with!

SARA: Yes. I also asked her about what kinds of things might have happened in her childhood that she might have repressed and are now coming out as back pain.

LOTTIE: (A little surprised by Sara's change of focus.) Sometimes it is helpful to explore childhood experiences, but what made you jump from all her current stressors to exploring her past?

SARA: Well, I guess I assumed that when it's "in your head" that it's probably related to something from childhood. I have heard stories about people uncovering something they forgot and being released from their pain almost magically.

LOTTIE: Yes, I have heard those stories too, and sometimes this probably happens. So it sounds like you were trying out an intervention of sorts.

SARA: What do you mean?

LOTTIE: You were asking her about her childhood in hopes that she might remember something she had forgotten, have a cathartic moment, and be forever released from the pain.

SARA: Yes, I guess so. (She smiles.)

LOTTIE: How did it go? (Although Lottie already strongly suspects the client was not spontaneously cured by becoming suddenly aware of childhood events, she does not want to make any immediate assumptions or embarrass Sara. It is a good strategy to avoid giving supervisees the impression that their early attempts at interventions are "silly." It is more helpful to challenge the supervisee to think about and evaluate their behaviors critically, without the supervisor's negative judgment.)

SARA: Well, she mentioned a few events that she is still upset about, but she denies any abuse in the family. I don't think I know how to ask the right questions.

LOTTIE: Maybe. It does take some time to learn how to uncover feelings about events that happened a long time ago. It also takes some skill to learn how to relate past events to present situations. Although I am sure it happens, it is rarely so simple that recalling a particular event will be the cure. If only it were. . . . But I do think it is good to ask questions about potential areas of stress in order to complete a thorough assessment of her situation.

SARA: So I'm on the right track?

LOTTIE: To be honest, I don't know yet. You have moved fairly quickly into trying out interventions. I like to take more time exploring the situation and formulating a thorough assessment before trying to intervene. I find that a solid assessment tells me what issues are most necessary to address. I guess I am curious whether or not you think you avoided further discussion of all her current stresses in favor of exploring her past?

SARA: There was just so much going on for her. I thought if I could release her from her back pain she could deal better with all of those things.

LOTTIE: Interesting! And this is probably the case. If she had less pain, she might feel less stress. But perhaps it could go the other way around—dealing better with her stresses may serve to reduce her pain. You said earlier that *she* thought all her stress was causing her pain, so why not follow her lead and focus on reducing her stress?

Note that while the supervisor takes a collaborative stance, she still provides direction for the intern, who is a very novice practitioner. As the intern develops greater knowledge and skill, the supervisor will reduce the level of direction, increasingly challenging the intern to direct her own learning and practice.

SARA: You're right! That does make sense. But I don't even know where to begin—and she doesn't either.

LOTTIE: It does seem overwhelming right now. But it sounds like you actively implemented the first task of identifying the problem, and at least began the second of discovering her perception of its causes. How do you think you did with it?

SARA: Well, I actually think I did pretty well. But I understand it more clearly after talking about it just now. As I said, I am not sure what to do, but I think I have a clear idea of the problem that brought her in. She has a lot of things causing her stress, which is aggravating her back pain. I guess the next step would be to find out about more about the different things causing her stress?

LOTTIE: That makes sense. It might be useful to discover which is causing her the *most* stress and perhaps begin your exploration there. I agree that you did a nice job of completing the first task. You now have a clearer picture of what brought her in and how to proceed. Using the task implementation rating form, how would you rate your implementation? (The task implementation rating form can be found in chapter 11.)

The supervisee rates their success completing each task on a scale from 1 (not done) to 4 (fully done). While the determination of the rating is initiated by the supervisee's own assessment, the supervisor shares in the process. The result is a mutual understanding of the supervisee's performance. The process of rating task performance serves multiple purposes (also taken up in detail in chapter 11). Its primary purpose is to provide a mechanism for ongoing mutual evaluation of the supervisee's work.

SARA: I think I would rate it a 3.

LOTTIE: Why? How did you come up with that score?

While the rating itself is interesting, it is particularly helpful to explore the supervisee's thinking behind it. In other words, it is important to learn about the criteria the supervisee uses in judging their work. Perhaps not surprisingly, we have discovered that occasionally supervisees will rate their work high, but when asked to explain how they determined that they did well with the task, describe criteria that demonstrate they did not truly understand it. One example of this is an intern who rated his performance of the task involving employing empathy as a 4. When asked what he did that would make it a 4, he said that he "repeated everything back to the client," which showed he clearly did not understand the concept of empathy. Exploring task ratings is useful in evaluating supervisees' conceptual abilities.

SARA: When I first came in I would have scored it a 4 because I thought I did it really well. But after talking, I can see that I have a general idea of what brought the client in, but now I need to find out more specifically about her stressors. Now I would rate it a 3—that I mostly completed the task. But there is still a little more to do.

LOTTIE: I agree. I think I would rate it exactly the same. That's a really good score for a first go at it! Have you ever attempted problem identification before?

SARA: No. This is the first client I have ever seen. (She is smiling.)

LOTTIE: Well, a nice job! Perhaps we could remember the need to further explore the client's problems when we are thinking of tasks for next week, later in this meeting.

SARA: Sounds good.

LOTTIE: How did you rate the second task, inquiring about the cause of the problem?

SARA: I think the same. Again, I now know a little about her multiple stressors, but I don't think I know enough about how she perceives each one. For example, I don't know which are causing her the most problems.

LOTTIE: Well, I am not so sure I would agree with that score. You know she has many stressors—that's true—but you did not really learn from her what she thinks is causing them, other than her back pain. We only have a beginning theory relating stress and back pain, and need to learn more.

SARA: That's interesting. I think you are right. I did not think of it that way. I will have to ask more about her perception of each stressor when I see her next. I guess I would rate it a 2 . . . that's pretty bad.

LOTTIE: No, I don't see it as bad. In fact, I think that is pretty good for a first go at it. Remember, you are here to learn. You are not expected to be able to do everything perfectly the first time, or even the second or third time, out. You are learning new skills. Think: if you were playing tennis, you would not expect to be able to serve perfectly in the beginning. It takes time and practice. You are off to a very good start!

SARA: Thanks!

LOTTIE: What about the third task, "Explore what she has already attempted to do to solve the problem"? We have not talked about that yet. How did that go?

SARA: Well, I did not get to do that one yet—we ran out of time. We got so busy talking about her back pain and all the different stressors, and her childhood, that I never asked about what she has been tried to do about it.

LOTTIE: Okay. That happens. Frequently, we have areas we want to explore at the beginning of a session but get onto other things. However, I thought this task was a good one—if you know what she has tried, you can learn about what has worked and can try to build on those things. You can also avoid suggesting things she has already tried.

SARA: Yes, I hate when people do that to me! (They laugh.) I guess I will try that task again next week. It seems like a logical next step anyway.

LOTTIE: Good idea. How about the second target goal and tasks related to communication skills?

The pair repeat the task review and task implementation rating processes with work done related to the second target goal. As three target goals, each with three discrete tasks, are typically selected for work each week, the task review entails examining and rating implementation of up to nine tasks. The educational stage typically follows. Because Lottie and Sara have already engaged in didactic instruction (i.e., the educational stage), they decide to move directly to the next step of the TCS model, the target goal stage.

LOTTIE: You have done a nice job with your tasks! Since you agree that we have already done the work of the educational stage, the next step is for us to select target goals. We can select three new ones, keep some from last week, or keep all from last week. It depends upon your learning needs, but it also depends upon your case needs.

SARA: Mmm. . . . Well, let's review each of the target goals from last week, and I can better evaluate what I think I should do next.

LOTTIE: Sounds good. Your first one was related to problem exploration. A few things to think about: Do you feel you attained that goal? Do you feel competent enough about this skill that you could do it on your own with other cases—without it being specifically contracted? Does the case call for you to do more right now? During our earlier conversation, it sounded like you felt more exploration was needed.

SARA: Yes, I think so. I would like to keep this target goal because I think I don't know enough about the problem.

LOTTIE: Okay, so we will keep that one.

SARA: I also think it would be good to keep the goal of problem exploration because I need to practice it with other clients. I am having
some difficulty with another case and I now wonder if it is because I
still do not have a good idea of the problem. Can we talk about that
case? I was kind of hoping we could.

LOTTIE: Absolutely.

As you can see, case discussion occurs throughout each meeting in TCS
supervision. However, the target goals stage is a natural place for discussion
of new cases and cases supervisees have questions about. Here, the supervisory pair enter into an in-depth discussion of another case. Lottie helps Sara
consider "next steps" and develop strategies in the form of target goals and
tasks.

SARA: As you know, I am working with Mrs. Jackson. She is the
woman with two young children who is having trouble with her
younger daughter. She is about four years old. I tried to do the same
tasks—you know, the ones related to problem exploration—that I did
with the case we were just talking about, but I don't think I did them
correctly.

LOTTIE: Okay, tell me what happened.

SARA: Well, we talked a lot about how her daughter was behaving.
She has been trying to bite her mother!

LOTTIE: Oh, no. What's going on that a four-year-old would behave
this way?

SARA: I asked why she was trying to bite her mother, but she just
shrugged. Her mom says it's because her ex-husband is turning her
daughter against her.

LOTTIE: Sadly, we often hear such things.

SARA: She says whenever her daughter returns home from a weekend
with her dad, she is out of control.

Lottie continues to explore the situation with Sara. It fairly quickly
becomes clear that Sara attempted to learn as much about the situation as possible, using the tasks she had selected for the prior case. However, this case dif-
fered in a number of ways, including involving young children as clients, parenting issues, and divorce. How practitioners explore various situations
depends upon the conceptual framework they use to understand case dynam-

ics. Lottie, who held a family systems perspective, wanted to learn more about the family's process of interactions—particularly as it involved the young girl. She was less interested in the mother's perception of "why" the daughter was behaving badly. Sara was unfamiliar with concepts such as family process, and the pair returned briefly to the educational stage. Once Sara had some background in family systems, she decided she wanted to keep the goal of problem exploration but modify the tasks she had selected the previous week.

SARA: Wow! That discussion of family systems really helped. I have a much clearer idea of next steps for this case. I did not know what I was going to do with a four-year-old who will not, or cannot, talk to me. But asking about how things escalate gives me somewhere to go. I need to continue problem exploration, but now I want to find out about the series of events that occurs when the daughter becomes so angry. I also want to learn more about whether or not the daughter is being triangulated into her parents' conflict.

LOTTIE: That makes a lot of sense to me. Should we include this as a target goal?

SARA: Wouldn't this be the same target goal of exploring the problem? I want to try some different kinds of questions, but I think it is the same target goal. Can I choose that goal twice?

LOTTIE: Yes, both target goals relate to problem exploration and the larger objective of performing assessments, but I think one has more to do with family dynamics and the other about exploring problems with the individual as the focus of attention. So I guess I see them as variations of the same target goal. But you certainly could choose the same target goal more than once, as long as the tasks are different so they represent different learning and practice activities.

SARA: I see the difference in focus. I guess I would like to choose problem exploration twice. Perhaps one can be "explore family dynamics" and the other could be the same one I had last week, with the focus on the individual?

LOTTIE: Sounds good to me! I like the way you partialized the broader objective of problem exploration into target goals that represent different aspects of this process. Each will have you doing different tasks.

Note that Lottie has moved the discussion into the next TCS stage, identifying, prioritizing, and selecting tasks. Typically, the supervisor will work

with the supervisee to identify and select three target goals before considering tasks. However, some prefer to identify tasks for target goals as they are
being discussed. We have found that both approaches work well. In addition,
it may be determined by the supervisory pair that they will only focus on two
target goals, or even one, for the week. The model was developed to be used
flexibly. If selected target goals are particularly demanding, it may make
sense to choose less than three during a particular week.

> SARA: Yes. I was thinking perhaps I could try tasks like "ask which
> problem is the one causing the most stress," and "ask about how often
> and when the problem takes place" for the first case. And I could try
> the tasks "explore the sequence of events that occurs when daughter
> becomes angry" and "inquire whether or not the mother and her ex-
> husband are having ongoing, open discussions regarding parenting
> issues" for the second case—with Mrs. Jackson.
> LOTTIE: Those all sound very good! Let's write them down before we
> forget them.

A centerpiece of TCS is the weekly contract. All target goals and tasks are
written on a TCS contract in order to ensure clarity and to establish mutual
agreement on the work to be done before the next supervision meeting.
Although TCS was designed so that the last step in the supervision meeting
sequence would be the contracting stage, we have found that some prefer to
write down the target goals and tasks as they are selected.

> SARA: Okay. Shall we write them on the contract?
> LOTTIE: No, let's wait until we get to that stage. After we select the
> tasks we will consider potential obstacles to successful implementa-
> tion. I have found that tasks often need to be changed or modified
> after a review of potential obstacles—which means the original tasks
> have to be erased or scratched out, leaving a messy contract. But I do
> think we should write them down on another sheet of paper.
> SARA: Okay.

They note the discussed target goals and tasks on an available legal pad.
Lottie then asks Sara if she is ready to select the third target goal. After
reviewing her work with a target goal she worked on the past week, "successfully employ basic communication skills," they decided that Sara would
begin work on a new target goal. Although Sara felt she needed to continue

to improve her communication skills, they both felt that she could work on those with each case and did not need to maintain this objective as an overt target goal. Sara wanted to discuss another case she had begun to work with, and this led to selecting a new target goal and the tasks to attain it (taken up later in this vignette). They then move into the next TCS stage, anticipating and negotiating potential obstacles.

LOTTIE: Okay, you have done a very nice job thinking of areas of learning you would like to address using target goals. You have also formulated some sensible-sounding tasks. However, the next stage involves trying to think of things that could get in the way of successful task implementation. As I said earlier, we may discover we need to change or alter some of the tasks we selected.

SARA: Okay. The tasks for the first target goal are "ask which problem is the one causing the most stress," "ask about how often and when the problem takes place," and then one we are keeping from last week, "explore what she has already attempted to do to solve it for herself." So I am supposed to think of what could happen to keep these from going well?

LOTTIE: Correct.

SARA: Well . . . I don't really see how anything could mess up the first one. It's pretty straightforward.

LOTTIE: What if she (the client) is unable to rank the things causing her stress, that is, tell you which is the *most* stressful? She may think they are all equally stressful.

SARA: I guess so, but in my conversation with her she seemed to be more focused on some things than others. I really don't think that will be a problem.

LOTTIE: Good. You are probably right. I only asked if that could happen to have you think ahead about various possibilities.

SARA: It is true that I did not consider that. The second task about how often and when the problem occurs . . . I think this one may have some obstacles. She may not know how often her pain occurs or exactly when. She may not keep track of those things.

LOTTIE: Excellent point! What would you do if she didn't know the answer to your questions about how often and when?

SARA: I guess I could have her write down each time she is in pain and note the time, like on a chart.

LOTTIE: That's a great idea. So I don't think you need to modify this task. However, thinking about potential obstacles has you more ready with a backup plan if she is unable to respond to your inquiry.

SARA: Yes, that does feel better.

LOTTIE: Mm . . . one other thing to consider: she may not be able to write things down when she is in severe pain.

SARA: I had not thought of that. Maybe I should talk with her about that, because I would not want her to agree to do the chart if she were truly unable.

LOTTIE: That makes sense. And what will you do if she says she will not be able to complete it when she is in pain?

SARA: I guess I will ask if there are other ways she could keep track of pain episodes, by memory, or having another person in the house help her.

LOTTIE: Both of those ideas sound reasonable. What about the third task? Do you see any potential obstacles?

SARA: I don't think so. I think she can tell me what kinds of things she has tried in the past to try to fix the situation. For example, she said she has gone for a doctor's examination and mentioned yoga, but I don't remember if she tried it or just thought about it. I think this task is pretty straightforward too.

LOTTIE: Okay.

SARA: I am just worried that she has tried everything I could think of and I'll have nothing left to offer.

LOTTIE: Oh, so you are seeing obstacles to helping her with ideas, but not to the task of asking her about what she has done?

SARA: Yes. I can ask about it, but then I don't know that I will be able to help.

LOTTIE: Yes, you entered into this profession because you wanted to be helpful. (They both laugh.) Perhaps during your discussion of the many things in her life that are causing her stress you will better understand how to help. You are worried about what to do, but lack enough information to intervene properly.

SARA: Okay. One step at a time.

LOTTIE: I am glad you raised it, because your anxiety about what to do after you carry out the task can be an obstacle to carrying out the task itself. For example, you may ask the question (do the task) and then not be able to properly attend to the answers.

SARA: I could see that happening! (She smiles.) But I don't think it will, now that we have talked about it. I better understand that I can be more effective if I focus on gathering information before trying to help.

LOTTIE: I think you will find that by asking these questions, you will be helping.

Lottie and Sara continue to consider potential obstacles to each task. Upon doing this, they determine that one of the tasks for the third target goal needs to be modified. The goal relates to Mark, one of Sara's other clients, a man in his early thirties struggling with depression.

LOTTIE: The second task for your upcoming meeting with Mark is "teach client how to correct distorted thoughts."

SARA: Yes. Like we discussed before, in one of my classes we have been learning about cognitive-behavioral therapy. The instructor says it is one of the best approaches for depression.

LOTTIE: It is true that you have done a nice job of formulating an assessment in this case. Mark does seem to be quite down and has some of the features of depression. Can you see any potential obstacles to successful implementation of this task?

SARA: No, not really.

LOTTIE: I think it is a good task, but perhaps premature in your work with Mark. I see a couple of potential problems for you to think about in regard to trying this task out now. First, you will have to determine whether or not he is experiencing distorted thoughts, and in what ways they emerge. It is likely that he is experiencing distorted thinking, but some exploration of the details, his internal dialogues, would shed more light on his situation. Second, most people do not actively attend to their thoughts. In other words, their thoughts are invisible to them and happen "automatically," sort of like breathing. Most people don't pay close attention to their breathing. I think before he can correct his thoughts, you may have to help him recognize his thought patterns. Third, before he can correct a distortion, he needs to be able to identify it as such. Most people don't recognize when their perceptions are flawed, but rather believe their thoughts to be the truth. Typically, once we have helped clients attend to their internal dialogue, the next step is to teach them to question whether or not their thoughts are accurate . . . and *then* to correct them.

SARA: Wow! I guess I really jumped ahead in this situation. It seems as though I am always leaping ahead to trying to help rather than focusing on gathering assessment information. I guess I have to slow down and learn how to do that.

LOTTIE: That is something most new practitioners do—jump ahead to interventions. I am glad you recognized your tendency to do that. It will help when we discuss potential obstacles to future tasks.

Note that the process of partializing tasks often reflects the order of how practice is carried out (e.g., performing assessments before attempting interventions). By breaking down practice in this way, supervisees learn how to thoughtfully proceed in their work, developing self-awareness regarding their practice.

LOTTIE: So, shall we modify this task?

SARA: Yes, I see now how I jumped ahead. I would like to change the task and try to explore his thoughts with him. I would like to find out what kinds of things he is telling himself regarding things that seem to be getting him down.

LOTTIE: You mean you would like to help him identify his negative thoughts?

SARA: Yes. Perhaps the task could be to "ask Mark about what he tells himself in regard to his girlfriend." It seems like his relationship is the thing he is most upset about now.

LOTTIE: That sounds good. I like its specificity. Can you anticipate any potential obstacles to carrying this task out successfully?

The two enter into a brief conversation about potential obstacles and determine that no major obstacles seem to be present for this task.

The final step of TCS is contracting. As stated earlier, at the end of each session the supervisor and supervisee complete a TCS contract that clearly articulates the target goals and tasks to be completed by the next meeting. Target goal and task selections are reviewed and added to the contract. This promotes clarity of expectations. The contract is then duplicated (usually using a copy machine), and each leaves the supervision meeting with a copy in hand. Here, Lottie segues into the contracting stage and brings the meeting to a close.

LOTTIE: Okay. We are getting near the end of our meeting. We now need to complete the contract. We have already completed two of the three target goals and the tasks that accompany them. Let's add the third, the target goal that emerged when we were reviewing Mark's situation.

SARA: Well, I think we said the third target goal was something like "implement cognitive-behavioral assessment of depression."

LOTTIE: Yes, that's correct. As currently stated, it is a rather broad goal. We may need to keep this one for a few weeks and incrementally add assessment areas in the form of tasks. It is interesting how all three target goals have to do with the broad learning objective of performing assessments, but each addresses a different part of that activity. Let's write that target goal on the contract. One of the areas you on which you will be evaluated is being able to work from multiple practice orientations. I believe we are addressing this objective with this contract. Each target goal has you performing assessments from different perspectives!

SARA: Hey, that's interesting! I would not have thought of that. I am glad you raised evaluation criteria with me. I can now see how we can meet them.

LOTTIE: Yes, by working incrementally on each evaluation criterion, we will be sure to address them all by the time we have to formally evaluate your work.

SARA: That's very reassuring!

LOTTIE: The tasks, as I have them written on this legal pad, for this last target goal are "administer the Beck Depression Inventory" and "educate the client about the principles of cognitive-behavioral therapy"—I think you said you were going to give him a handout you got in class?

SARA: Yes.

LOTTIE: And "ask Mark about what he tells himself in regard to his girlfriend," the one modified task we just discussed. Does this sound right?

SARA: Yes, that's it. I am happy to have these tasks. They really provide a focus for my work. I feel like I know exactly what I am supposed to do when I meet with each client. Having the contract is great. I can read it just before I go into a meeting to remind me what we discussed in supervision.

LOTTIE: That's great! Just remember to also listen to the client. You have to be careful that your learning agenda to complete tasks does not get in the way of hearing clients and attending to their needs.

SARA: I think the contracts help me do that. If I did not have them, I think I would feel overwhelmed by how much I would have to think about—and be even more likely to miss what the client is saying. I think the contracts and tasks help me relax and stay more focused so I can make the client's agenda primary.

LOTTIE: That's wonderful. You really seem to be making a great start! And you really seem to be tuned in to the advantages offered by TCS.

SARA: Thanks! Are we meeting the same time next week?

LOTTIE: Yes, let's hold this day and time in our schedules to meet every week. Let me make a copy of the completed contract. Don't forget to take a task implementation rating form for this week.

SARA: Okay. Oh, I just remembered that you said I should suggest that my client with the back pain get a second opinion. Should I add that as a task?

LOTTIE: It's a good thing you remembered. That's really up to you. You already have three tasks selected for your work with her. You can add it as a fourth, or if you think you can just remember it on your own, you can do it that way.

SARA: I think I will write it at the bottom of the contract, just so I don't forget.

LOTTIE: Okay. Good luck this week.

What follows is the completed contract from this supervision meeting. Sara will now implement the selected tasks in her work with cases. She will also rate her task performance on the task implementation rating form. When she returns the following week, she and Lottie will follow the same series of steps outlined in the above vignette. This sequence will guide the process of educational supervision throughout their encounter. Because Sara's work is continually reviewed, when it is formally evaluated (i.e., graded for school), they should both be clear about how she has performed—which areas she has succeeded in, which need more work, and which have yet to be addressed.

DATE: *Sept. 27*

CONTRACT

A. Target Goals

List in order of priority the goals (up to three) that you and the student agreed to work on. Identify goals in a single word or phrase. Include the date the goal was first formulated. On the line below each identified target goal, provide the related practice or educational objective.

GOAL #1: *Explore the problem* date form. *Sept. 20*
     Related practice or educational objective: *Perform complete assessments*

GOAL #2: *Explore family dynamics* date form. *Sept. 27*
     Related practice or educational objective: *Perform complete assessments*

GOAL #3: *Implement cog-beh assessment of depression* date form. *Sept. 27*
     Related practice or educational objective: *Perform assessments from varying practice perspectives*

B.   Prioritization Processes

     √ a. student agreed on selection and priorities of goals
     __ b. student disagreed on selection and priorities of goals
     If "b" was checked, explain disagreement (use back if necessary).

C.   Task Formulation

List three tasks the student will do to achieve each target goal:

GOAL #1

task #1: *ask which problem is the one causing the most stress*
task #2: *ask about how often and when the problem takes place*
task #3: *explore what she has already attempted to solve it for herself*

GOAL #2

task #1: *explore the sequence of events that occurs when daughter becomes angry*
task #2: *inquire whether or not the mother and her ex-husband are having ongoing, open discussions regarding parenting issues*
task #3: _____

GOAL #3

task #1: *educate the client about the principles of cognitive-behavioral therapy*
task #2: *ask Mark about what he tells himself in regard to his girlfriend*
task #3: *administer the Beck Depression Inventory*

D.   Were potential obstacles to task implementation considered?
   Circle one: (Yes) No

List any additional agreements (e.g., time limits): *Ask back pain client if she has sought a second doctor's opinion.*

The above vignette offers a look at TCS in action. As each supervisory pair or group utilizes the model, there will be slight variations in how it is implemented, reflecting process preferences or adaptations to the practice environment. The model is intended to be used flexibly in order to be applicable in a wide array of supervisory arrangements. Because it does not prescribe a set of learning objectives but a process to systematically attain learning and practice objectives, TCS can be utilized in almost every educational supervision environment.

Overview of the Book

This book is organized into two parts. The first section examines various aspects of the supervisory encounter in order to give context for the presentation of TCS. Illustrative vignettes are provided throughout this and the second section in order to demonstrate described principles and procedures in action. Chapter 1 provided a brief introduction to educational supervision and to TCS. Chapter 2 provides a history of educational supervision (i.e., field instruction) in social work, and an overview of a variety of existing approaches. Chapter 3 consolidates and organizes a vast body of knowledge regarding effective instructional practices in supervision. This chapter provides useful information for ensuring productive supervisory practice. TCS was designed to systematically put these principles into operation during its implementation, so this background will give greater meaning to TCS activities. The central role of the supervisory relationship in quality educational encounters is considered in depth in chapter 4. Chapter 5 continues exploration into a facet of this relationship that has great impact on supervisee learning but has been largely unexplored: the person of the supervisor. In particular, supervisor anxiety, self-awareness, and conscious use of self are considered. Chapter 6 begins discussion of the supervisory process and presents information for preparing for both the start and end of the encounter, prior to the initial meeting. While it may seem strange that the finish of the encounter will be discussed before the first meeting has taken place, considering endings early in the process promotes handling of this stage. Additionally, the activities discussed in chapter 6 help supervisors to prepare for implementation of TCS.

The second section presents TCS and its discrete and organized series of procedures for systematic attainment of learning and practice objectives.

Chapter 7 discusses the development considerations that went into building TCS and presents its basic principles. This overview is intended to foster a more in-depth understanding of the model and its origins. Chapter 8 begins the presentation of the model's sequence. The initial steps, which include the social and educational functions of the model, are described. Chapter 9 introduces the task planning and implementation sequence (TPIS), which follows. The sequence begins with the target goals stage and entails generating, prioritizing, and selecting partialized learning and practice objectives for immediate work. Chapter 10 continues the presentation of TPIS and describes the next set of TCS stages: generating tasks, anticipating potential obstacles to task implementation, task selection, and contracting. Tasks represent the activities the supervisee carries out toward attainment of selected target goals. After contracting, the supervisee implements these agreed-upon tasks in work with cases between supervision meetings. At the subsequent meeting, implementation success is reviewed in a step called "task review," which is presented in chapter 11. Chapter 12 examines the application of TCS in a variety of settings and for a range of purposes, and concludes the book. An appendix provides a set of guidelines for implementation of the model. We hope that these guidelines will be copied and given to supervisees so that they will be better able to understand and participate in their own learning during supervision.

2　A History of Educational Supervision in Social Work

To understand the purpose and utility of TCS, it is important to consider it within the historical and contemporary contexts of educational supervision. This chapter provides a historical overview of educational supervision in social work and considers ways in which various approaches relate to TCS.

Educational supervision existed prior to formal, school-based social work education (George 1982). As the training of new social workers became formalized in academic settings, the experiential learning process was maintained and became known as "field instruction" (discussed in depth later in this chapter). Social workers not in formal degree-granting programs typically learned on the job, under the direction of a supervisor. While these two arrangements, academic and on-the-job training, remain, approaches to field instruction have changed throughout social work's history.

A Brief History of Approaches to Field Instruction

Note: In this book, the terms "approach" and "model" refer to different constructs. While both represent an organized set of principles for supervision, approaches are general, contextual, and broad-based considerations for supervision, while models offer specific, discrete, step-by-step guidelines that direct the process of supervision. While approaches tend to emphasize theoretical procedures, models offer concrete ones.

Although field education has enjoyed periods of greater and lesser status during the history of social work education (Schneck 1991a), it has been a long-standing tradition that professional learning must include an experiential component in addition to academic study. The various approaches to field education are, for the most part, connected to specific periods in the history of social work education. Each emphasizes a different mode of learning (e.g., direct practice, cognitive development, psychoemotional growth, linking academic and experiential information, self-directed discovery) and gives general procedures for instruction. The approaches presented below represent common categorizations of field instruction types. However, note that none provides coherent guidelines. These include the apprenticeship, academic, therapeutic, articulated, and andragogical (adult learners) approaches.

The Apprenticeship Approach

In the early days of the profession, in the latter half of the nineteenth century, the primary method of teaching and learning was the apprenticeship approach (Jenkins and Sheafor 1982), which involved "doing in the field under the direction of others who had learned in the same way" (George 1982:37). A more experienced worker demonstrated professional behaviors that the learner attempted to emulate (Jenkins and Sheafor 1982). The experienced worker then provided immediate feedback about the learner's performance (Bogo and Vayda 1998). The message underlying instruction was "learn to do as I do." The primary teaching strategy was demonstrating and modeling skills, behaviors, and attitudes required to perform in the position of an agency social worker.

Although this type of teaching is currently used, it is usually in conjunction with other approaches (Shafer 1982). Observation of an expert worker by various methods (e.g., sitting in on and/or participating in a session, viewing through a one-way mirror, examining audiotapes or videotapes) is the primary mode of learning (Shafer 1982). While the apprenticeship approach offers a teaching-learning process, it does not provide guidelines that inform a systematic series of organized activities.

The Academic Approach

As education became formalized during the early part of the twentieth century and training programs and schools of social work flourished, so did an emphasis on academic learning. The academic approach reflected a move toward classroom-based education, and deemphasized learning in the field practicum (Jenkins and Sheafor 1982). The focus was on cognitive development of practitioners, which involved acquiring a foundation of general knowledge or "commonalities" (Fortune 1994). The purpose of the field practicum, when utilized, was to apply this knowledge to practice. Because the focus was on classroom education, little attention was given to developing guidelines for field practicum activities.

Therapeutic and Growth Approaches

The profession's emphasis on psychoanalytic thinking in the 1920s and 1930s generated a focus on both personal and professional growth as a central facet of field instruction (Bogo 1983; Kilpatrick 1991). The therapeutic approach (George 1982), also referred to as the growth model (Bogo and Vayda 1998; Wijnberg and Schwartz 1977), and the clinical treatment method (Shafer 1982) focused on the supervisee's anxiety and transference problems that would emerge in the supervisory relationship (Webb 1983). It often became difficult to distinguish whether the goal of supervision was educational or therapeutic (George 1982). Controversy developed around whether professional development required "personality growth" (Fortune 1994). A major criticism of the therapeutic approach concerned the tendency to become more focused on uncovering the supervisee's personal "stuff" than on educational goals. Due to such criticism and later supervisee reports finding this supervisory style "objectionable" (Rosenblatt and Mayer 1975), the therapeutic approach has been largely abandoned.

The Articulated Approach

The 1940s through the 1960s was a period of attempting to strengthen the quality of field instruction (Kilpatrick 1991). There were efforts to develop consistent guidelines and procedures for schools of social work.

Among the needs identified was a clear articulation of "learning activities between class and field" (George 1982:52). In the field, supervisees were acquiring information in largely unstructured and idiosyncratic ways. Moreover, there was little attempt to connect and integrate the various sources of information (e.g., agency experience, field instructor, classroom). This led to a push, from the 1960s through the present, to develop an articulated approach (Jenkins and Sheafor 1982) that clearly and systematically links academic and field learning.

At present, most schools attempt to use an articulated approach, but there is much concern that a successful linking of classroom and field is not being consistently achieved (Bogo and Power 1992; Raskin 1994; Tolson and Kopp 1988). This may not be a realistic approach in today's economy, which does not permit the investment of time needed to achieve a systematic and sequenced integration (Bogo and Vayda 1998; Tolson and Kopp 1988). However, such linking of class and field work remains a desirable goal (Raskin 1994; Wodarski, Feit, and Green 1995). While creative approaches have been specifically developed for this purpose (Collins and Bogo 1986; Rabin, Savaya, and Frank 1994), most have not been designed to fit into traditional one-to-one concurrent practicum arrangements. (For an exception, see Vayda and Bogo 1991.)

Andragogical Approaches

In the past thirty years, social work field education has promoted the use of adult learning principles (Knowles 1972; Kolb 1984) as an area for exploration and incorporation (Brannon 1985; Clancy 1985; Davenport and Davenport 1988; Fox and Zischka 1989; Gelfand et al. 1975; Lowy 1983; Marshack and Glassman 1991; Wijnberg and Schwartz 1977). Such principles have been applied to field instruction approaches (Manis 1979; Wijnberg and Schwartz 1977; Wilson 1981). They promote procedures that include learner-directed objectives, build an egalitarian supervisory relationship, value and draw upon past experiences, and focus on problem-solving immediate challenges (rather than subject-centered learning).

The trend toward adoption of adult learning principles has most recently been complemented by feminist teaching approaches (Dore 1994; Lazzari 1991), which promote similar values and principles but recognize and emphasize the role of power in the supervisory relationship.

Contemporary Field Instruction

Presently, field instruction continues to be a requirement of all social work programs that issue the bachelor's or master's degree in social work. Student field activities commonly entail providing social service to clients two or three days each week, under the direct, one-to-one guidance of a field instructor. This is usually done concurrently with coursework. These common structural features of modern field education make what is considered to be the "traditional approach" to field instruction (Hale 1969; Rothman and Jones 1971), which is described later in this chapter.

The focus of most contemporary field instruction is on case problem-solving and planning activities. While the educational function is emphasized, the process is largely driven by the needs of the supervisee's cases. Learning activities typically emerge from consideration of how to intervene. This results in a rather idiosyncratic process in which learning objectives are addressed according to case demands. Indeed, it is largely unknown whether or not field interns are actively working toward and achieving educational objectives—although it is commonly accepted that this is occurring.

Nevertheless, "There is general consensus that field instruction is the most significant, most productive, most memorable component of social work education" (Kadushin 1991:11). Social work students and alumni view the field practicum as the most valuable part of their training (Gizynski 1978). In fact, students almost unanimously select it as their most beneficial course (Raskin 1989c). Furthermore, the field experience has been found to have the most important impact on the development of student social work practice (Tolson and Kopp 1988).

Concern About the Development of Field Instruction

Despite the favorable feedback about field instruction, concerns about its development remain. Although field instruction is commonly accepted and often referred to as a "core" or "central" component of social work education, it does not receive the same attention as the rest of the curriculum in terms of research and systematic development (Ellison 1994; Raskin 1989a; Shatz 1989; Sheafor and Jenkins 1982; Smith 1981). Shatz (1989) offers possible explanations for this, including the difficulty in selecting and operationalizing outcome variables, field directors' lack of time and knowledge of research methodology, and the "lack of academic recognition and reward of field experience as equivalent in status and rigor to traditional coursework" (xxv). Raskin (1994) adds that empirical studies may require utilizing modified practicum arrangements that schools fear implementing due to accreditation concerns.

Field instruction largely goes on behind closed doors. Little research has been done to uncover what occurs behind those doors. Indeed, not much is known about what works and what does not in field instruction (Shatz 1989), or about which behaviors are most successful in achieving objectives of professional competence and identity (Rotholz and Werk 1984). Perhaps this partly explains why students perceive field work as not only the part of their education that gives them "the most excitement and pleasure" but also the experience that causes them "the most struggle and pain" (Shatz 1989:xxvi).

Looking for a Model That Guides the Practice of Field Instruction?

Despite the criticism that the social work practicum does not receive adequate attention from educators, a substantial body of field education literature does exist. Although a broad range of topics are discussed, as Rich (1993) contends about supervision, field instruction literature also lacks a uniform or concise body of knowledge, and is "largely haphazard" (137). Although a significant amount of information is available, it has not been adequately organized for the practice of field instruction (Schneck 1991c). We have attempted to address this problem by pulling together the principles of effective educational supervision into a single chapter (see chapter 3).

Although field instruction is recognized as a distinct "branch of social work practice" with its own knowledge, values, and skills (Bogo and Vayda 1998; Eisikovits and Guttman 1983), there are few practice models for field instruction. Social workers have available many practice approaches (e.g., psychodynamic, cognitive-behavioral, solution-focused) that offer guiding principles for work with clients (Dorfman 1998; Turner 1996). Indeed, these approaches help practitioners make decisions about "what to do" with cases, promoting consistency of practice and positive outcomes. For the purposes of illustration, imagine for a minute that these practice approaches do not exist and are not available to guide clinical decision making. Instead, practitioners base their clinical approach on their own experiences as clients in treatment. If clinical practice were carried out in this way, there would be great concern about client welfare—it is a rather frightening scenario! Essentially, the equivalent has been occurring in social work practicum instruction. While much attention has been given to developing solid treatment models, little has been paid to models for the practice of educational supervision. Field instruction lacks a well-articulated model that is grounded in current theory (Saari 1989).

Lack of a Model

An extensive review of social work field education literature demonstrates a marked lack of coherent models that provide instructors and students with discrete procedures for field instruction (Caspi 1997). What does exist are program designs and approaches that emphasize different modes of learning that "developed largely without a guiding conceptual framework and tested theory" (Shatz 1989:xxvi). In addition, principles are frequently put forth regarding what should occur between the field instructor and the student to optimize learning; however, there is little that guides the interactive dimensions of the field instructor-student relationship toward achievement of learning goals. In short, social work field education has been working without a well-articulated model that informs the *process* of field instruction. Indeed, the need for field instruction designs that are effective and provide supervisors with direction and confidence has been repeatedly voiced (Raskin 1989; Shatz 1989).

Accountability and Quality Concerns

The lack of a field instruction practice model raises concerns about accountability and quality of education. Field supervisors mostly rely on their own experiences as supervisees in forming their approach. Knowing this, it is not difficult to see why educators have noted a lack of quality field instructors (Kaplan 1988; Larsen and Hepworth 1982; Webb 1983) and suggest that field instruction "typically is varied, uneven, and unsystematic" (Larsen and Hepworth 1982:50). It can be argued that this is related to the lack of a coherent, well-defined model for the practice of field instruction.

Unstructured educational procedures raise concerns about how supervisees meet learning objectives. Rotholz and Werk (1984) posit three main objectives for student supervision: socialization, development of social work skills, and development of professional judgment (18). Although overarching objectives may be addressed, there is little knowledge about how this happens and to what extent they are actually being achieved. Furthermore, field instructors are responsible for monitoring intern practices and ensuring quality service to clients. Lack of systematic procedures for doing this raises additional concerns about client welfare.

Although there is no research known to the authors that links field instructor behaviors and client experiences, it has been shown that field instructor skills and abilities affect student satisfaction (Alperin 1998; Fortune et al. 1985) and practicum success (Abramson and Fortune 1990), both of which are factors in the provision of quality client treatment. Therefore, "it is essential that some direction be offered as to the best techniques to use" to achieve educational goals in the practicum (Rotholz and Werk 1984:18).

Dimensions of Field Instruction: Structure, Content, Process

Field instruction operations occur on multiple levels, including selection of practicum objectives, how these objectives are to be met, and when, where, and in what context the field instructor and supervisee will meet. The various dimensions of field work can be broken down into three categories that must be considered in order to give context and meaning to TCS: structure, content, and process. What follows is an overview of existing approaches that address specific facets of the field instruction encounter within each category. A variety of approaches provide structure, inform content, and direct process. With a few exceptions, most are designed to address aspects of only one of these areas..

Structure

"Structure" refers to the fixed arrangements in which the process of field instruction occurs: the time, place, number of participants, and frequency of meetings—essentially the when, where, who, and how much of supervision. The most common structure is the traditional approach (Rothman and

Jones 1971), which consists of one field instructor and one student meeting face to face for one hour each week. This typically occurs concurrently with coursework. The duration of each field instruction relationship is one school year. Alternative structures have also been utilized in the field. For example, in group approaches, multiple students receive supervision together, and in "secondary supervision," two field instructors work together to supervise one student (Marshack and Glassman 1991). A more in-depth look at traditional and alternative approaches follows.

The Traditional Approach

The traditional approach (Rothman and Jones 1971), also called the tutorial method (Raskin 1989; Shafer 1982; Watson 1973) and the singular field instruction model (Henry 1975), permeates almost the entire history of social work field education and continues to be the most often used structure for practicum teaching. Rothman and Jones (1971) outline the components of the traditional approach (48–49):

- Upon entering graduate school, the student is immediately placed in an agency.
- At the agency, the student begins direct practice, where he or she is able to apply theories learned in the classroom and try out new knowledge.
- Field instruction occurs (usually) within the context of a one-to-one relationship with (usually) an agency employee who has greater practice knowledge and skill. This person is most commonly referred to as the student's field instructor or supervisor.
- Field instruction sessions usually occur weekly.
- Process recordings of supervisee-led sessions with clients are provided by the student for reflective analysis with the field instructor. The recordings usually include supervisees' emotional and cognitive reactions to events in the session and their own behaviors.
- The student is responsible for assignments, often in the form of carrying a caseload.
- In the second year of graduate education, the student is usually placed in a different setting and in a different field of practice.
- Field instructors are assisted by school faculty (field liaisons), orientations, seminars, workshops, and conferences.

- The field instructor is usually assigned "quasi-faculty" status, and often is responsible for giving the student a grade for her or his performance.

DeJong (1975), McClelland (1991), and Hale (1969) also present the central features of the traditional model. They add the following characteristics to those presented above:

- Field instruction is focused on development of skills in one method of practice.
- Concurrent placement and classroom activities occur throughout the student's entire graduate education.
- The planning of learning experiences is tied to agency function and caseload needs.
- The placement is in one agency (per school year).
- Role identification with the field instructor and a tutorial approach are the central methods of teaching.
- The student is often expected to perform in a similar capacity to an employee, in a work role.

Alternative Structural Approaches

Although the traditional approach remains the most common structural arrangement, the assumptions that underlie it have been challenged, and models promoting alternative structures can be found in the literature. These can be considered "innovations in field designs" (Schneck et al. 1991).

Block Placements

At present, concurrent placement is the most frequently employed structure for field programs. However, block placement arrangements, in which the student engages in field and classroom activities at separate times of the year, have been utilized with some frequency (Kilpatrick, Turner, and Holland 1994). Although the timing of the classroom-field relationship is altered, other aspects of the traditional approach remain the same. While concurrent placements are considered preferable because they are more effective at enhancing students' conceptual learning of practice (Fortune 1994), block placements may be more expedient in some situations. For example, using block placements may be a creative and necessary way to increase the number of available placement agencies in rural settings (DeJong 1975).

Delayed-Entry Approach

The delayed-entry approach entails delaying the concurrent classroom-field structure for a number of weeks in order to prepare new (e.g., first-year master's level) students with some knowledge prior to entering the field (and beginning a concurrent, traditional placement). Although there seem to be no significant differences in student skill development outcomes between delayed-entry and concurrent approaches (Gordon and Gordon 1989), a proposed advantage of the delayed-entry model is that it provides students with an understanding of their work within an overarching perspective of the social welfare system (Grossman and Barth 1991). The finding that skills learned prior to entering the field are difficult to transfer to actual clinical work (Gordon and Gordon 1989) is consistent with other alternative curriculum structures that set out to prepare students for field work. For example, it has been suggested that skills developed in classroom and laboratory settings are not necessarily transferred to actual practice situations (Collins and Bogo 1986; Gordon and Gordon 1989; Tolson and Kopp 1988). However, some structural approaches have been developed to address this issue (Collins and Bogo 1986; Rabin, Savaya, and Frank 1994)

Group Approaches

Another assumption of the traditional model that has been challenged is the one-to-one relationship as the prime teaching-learning arrangement. Group field instruction is a commonly used alternative (Shafer 1982) and typically involves two or more students meeting together with one field instructor, although multiple supervisors can also utilized. In the group, students use each other as resources for learning and support. A benefit of group supervision is the opportunity for students to learn how to conceptualize practice by having to critique and provide thoughtful feedback about other students' work. It has been suggested that some group structures are preferable to individual arrangements (Parihar 1983; Mayers 1970). Although group field instruction has been used with some frequency as an adjunct to individual supervisory meetings, group approaches have only recently been offered as a primary modality for practicum education (Kaplan 1988; Lammert and Hagen 1975; Mayers 1970).

Task, Secondary, and Team Approaches

Marshack and Glassman (1991) question the traditional placement structure of one student to one instructor in today's economy of shrinking resources and increasing field instructor turnover. Instead, they promote the consideration of both group and task supervision models. "Task supervision," also referred to as "secondary supervision" and "team teaching" (Shafer 1982), entails a student working with a designated field instructor, who retains the "overall control of student assignment and evaluation processes" (92), and a second person, a task supervisor. The task supervisor also has teaching functions, and is often used when the designated field instructor does not possess expertise in a practice area the student is learning (91). A survey of field instructors conducted in 1983 reported that approximately one third utilized secondary supervision (Marshack 1986).

Field Units and Centers

A number of educators employ the use of field units in their program designs (Lammert and Hagen 1975; Norberg and Schneck 1991; Pilcher and Shamley 1986). The field unit has been defined as "three or more students placed in the same agency who work closely together and share resources, including supervision" (Conklin and Borecki 1991:122). Similar to teaching and training centers that employ school faculty (Knappe 1975), these units are often headed by a faculty field instructor, which enhances the link between school and field learning. Although primarily phased out in the 1970s and 1980s due to resource difficulties, the faculty-supervised field unit has recently been promoted as a valuable teaching model that should be considered for reinstatement (Conklin and Borecki 1991). In the meantime, field units continue to be utilized, but with agency supervisors.

Another alternative structure is the "field instruction center" (Henry 1975). This typically consists of a group of agencies located within close proximity to each other. Students are given assignments in two or more agencies in order to gain diverse learning opportunities in generic social work. Experiencing multiple agencies throughout the school year differs from the traditional approach, where the student remains in one agency. While it is likely that multiple agencies offer opportunities for more breadth of knowledge, remaining in one should provide greater expertise in a focused area.

Structure and TCS

Although a moderate number of structural designs exist, it is likely that new alternative structures will be offered in response to decreasing resources for field instruction and demands for improved practicum education. As you will see, TCS avoids prescribing a particular structure. Instead, it was developed to be adaptable and usable in a wide variety of structural contexts and program designs.

Content

Content refers to the educational objectives that are to be worked toward during the field instruction encounter; it reflects the focus of discussion. Identifying objectives that include the skills and content that must be mastered in order to become a competent social worker is of great interest to the profession (Pilcher 1982; Bogo 1983). A number of competency-based (Collins and Bogo 1986; Larsen 1980; Pilcher 1982), universal learning objectives for microlevel practice (Dore, Epstein, and Herrerias 1992), and core content (Fortune 1994) models have been developed. Objectives pose a challenge to outlining a core set of knowledge and skills for learning: they frequently differ from school to school, among agencies, according to geographical location, and with each supervisee's individual needs. Furthermore, some warn that a "preconception of rigid learning goals is especially serious . . . because it closes out discovery of self and the recognition of the unexpected" in practice (Judah 1982:146). How and to what degree learning objectives should be defined has been a topic of debate in social work education (Hamilton and Else 1983).

Presently, schools of social work usually indicate a core set of skills and knowledge that students should achieve during their field placements (Gray, Alperin, and Wik 1989). "There is, theoretically, no outside limit to what students *may* learn, but there is a minimum they *must* learn, and this must be specified somewhere" (Judah 1982:146). This body of knowledge and skills can usually be found in a school's field placement evaluation instrument, which reflects the school's curriculum objectives (see sample learning objectives below). In work settings, they may be spelled out in job descriptions as well as on evaluation forms. These objectives "are of primary importance in determining student learning tasks" (Dea, Grist, and Myli 1982:238). However, the professional standards regarding what specific skills and content must be learned, at what point in the supervisee's development, tend to be stated in global terms (Kilpatrick 1991).

Sample Learning Objectives
Communication skills:
can communicate ideas clearly
utilizes listening skills with clients
uses empathy appropriately
attends to client's nonverbal behaviors
recognizes impact of own nonverbal behaviors on client
able to facilitate communication between group members

Assessment skills:
integrates knowledge of life-cycle development
utilizes multiple sources of data in formulating assessment
can organize information from various sources' incoherent assessment
integrates issues related to diversity and oppression when formulating
    assessment
considers biological, psychological, and environmental factors in for-
    mulating assessment
can clearly identify the problem for focus of work

While stating learning objectives in global terms allows for flexibility and innovation, objectives that are explicitly established and in behavioral terms provide clear expectations against which progress can be assessed more definitively (Pilcher 1982). If objectives are not explicitly defined, it can become unclear what is being evaluated. For example, a learning objective stated as "performs family assessments" does not make clear to the supervisee or the supervisor whether this refers to assessing support, interactional patterns, child abuse, or underlying marital conflict—to name only a few examples. A supervisee might do quite well with one of these areas and not the others. Thus, it is helpful to break down global learning objectives into discrete parts.

Content at Various Levels of Learning

Of special concern in field education is developing a clearer articulation of objectives at various levels of learning. It has been suggested that the core sets of skills and knowledge currently being taught and learned at the undergraduate and graduate levels are not so different (Fortune 1994; Kilpatrick 1991; Munson 1987). This is of concern for field instruction because supervisors need to be able to distinguish between the learning needs of undergraduate and graduate students (Curiel and Rosenthal 1987). Fortune (1994) presents a comprehensive content and skills model that explicates the competencies for social work practice at three levels of education.

Beyond Core Content

Some educators feel that there are areas of social work practice that call for mastery of skills and knowledge beyond the core content. They offer content approaches and models that put forth objectives for particular practice settings. In general, these goals do not replace but are added to the core learning objectives and individual student goals. The models include competencies designed for students learning social administration (Carroll and McCuan 1975; Neugeboren 1971; Patti 1980), community-oriented practice (Lammert and Hagen 1975; Rothman and Jones 1971), and health services (Bogo and Taylor 1990), and for undergraduate students placed in a psychiatric setting (Dawson 1975). Other content approaches are offered to enhance specific clinical practice: skill building for empathic responding (Laughlin 1978), assessment of children (Zayas 1989), prevention (Tendler and Metzger 1978), research (Gantt et al. 1991; Grossman 1980; Mokuau and Ewalt 1993; Pilcher and Shamley 1986; Rabin 1985), administration (Neugeboren 1988; Patti 1980), group work (Glassman and Kates 1988), working with the chronically suicidal outpatient (Lynch 1987), and termination (McCroy, Freeman, and Logan 1986; Wall 1994).

Content and TCS

Social work scholars and practitioners will undoubtedly continue to propose and debate new learning objectives and practice competencies. TCS does not prescribe content, but rather outlines procedures for achieving them, for the following reasons.

First, social work is highly diversified in terms of practice orientations and systems levels of intervention. Therefore, core objectives for one field of practice will require different learning goals than for another. For example, students in community organization or administration "tracks" need to master different sets of knowledge and skills than do students specializing in family treatment or group work.

Second, interns and staff begin supervision with varied degrees of previous experience, knowledge, and skill. Some are highly sophisticated from the start and require different learning objectives than novice practitioners.

Third, different practice settings require greater attention to some skills than others. For example, supervisees working in crisis centers must learn different skills (e.g., stabilizing client functioning, referral), than those in longer-term settings (e.g., uncovering unrecognized anxieties, marital counseling).

Fourth, as discussed earlier, having a predetermined core set of objectives raises concerns about incorporating a supervisee-directed learning experience (Abramson and Fortune 1990) and about recognizing unexpected subjective reactions (Judah 1982).

Fifth, schools of social work have individualized mission statements and curriculum objectives, which reflect their particular educational orientation and values.

Sixth, deciding on the content for supervision is often complicated by multiple sources of input. Supervisees' educational objectives not only reflect those outlined by the school but also include personal goals, field instructor input, agency needs, and availability of learning opportunities.

Finally, approaches already exist that, to varying degrees, outline practicum competencies for social work education (Fortune 1994; Dea, Grist, and Myli 1982; Pilcher 1982; Schneck 1991b; Wilson 1981). Therefore, TCS was developed to offer strategies for addressing this complex and idiosyncratic dimension of educational supervision, rather than to outline learning or practice objectives.

Process

While content represents what needs to be learned, process refers to how objectives are met. Process is the "progressive phases and course of teaching activity through which teaching and learning objectives are achieved" (Siporin 1982:178). It "implies a series of gradual steps moving toward particular events over time" (Lowy 1983:56). Hence, process refers to how supervisors and supervisees interact with each other in order to complete the tasks of the encounter—i.e., how they *do* supervision.

Unfortunately, few models offer a comprehensive process for doing supervision. Most of what is available is in the form of guiding principles that maximize learning or inform teaching. The following section reviews these approaches, then takes a brief look at methods that provide guidelines for dealing with discrete aspects of the encounter. This is followed by an examination of modifications to clinical intervention models for the purpose of guiding the educational supervision process. The section ends with a review of process approaches that have utilized task-centered procedures for supervision.

A Word About Learning- and Teaching-Centered Approaches

Educational process can be conceptualized as involving two separate facets: teaching and learning. Although this distinction is not always clear due to the interdependent and reciprocal nature of the instructional encounter, it is helpful to consider these components separately because most field instruction approaches emphasize one more than the other. The approaches are organized here by their emphasis.

Learner-Focused Process Approaches

A number of learner-focused process approaches have been offered. In them, supervisors follow principles aimed at maximizing the learning experience of the adult supervisee. Most adult learning approaches incorporate andragogical principles (Knowles 1970). Although first introduced in the early 1970s, andragogy is still considered to be "state of the art" in adult education.

Andragogical Approaches

Andragogy is the process of helping adults learn, as opposed to pedagogy, which is defined as "the art and science of teaching children" (Knowles 1970:38). Although it is unclear whether andragogy is a theory of teaching or learning, or simply principles of sensible practice (Kramer and Wrenn 1994), it promotes the consideration of adult learning processes and offers direction for teaching adult students. Andragogical approaches emphasize a relationship between supervisees and field instructors that is more collaborative and egalitarian than previous educational supervision models (Bogo and Vayda 1998). The supervisor is seen less as a transmitter of knowledge and instead adopts the roles of facilitator, resource person, and guide as he or she assists the student through a process of "self discovery" (Knowles 1972). In these approaches, supervisors take on the role of guide because adult students are viewed as being capable of directing their own course of learning. Hence, self-directed selection of learning objectives and activities by supervisees is promoted, and occurs through a collaborative process of negotiation with supervisors. Equal, and often greater, responsibility is placed on supervisees for determining the arrangement and focus of their learning. In addition, they are viewed as having an "accumulation of a unique set of life experiences" (Clancy 1985:77) that are of value and should be drawn upon. It is suggested that due to the egalitarian nature of the supervisory relationship, there is more openness and trust, resulting in a safe and fertile learning environment (Manis 1979).

In recent years, a few approaches that inform the teaching-learning process have integrated andragogy and other adult learning theories. Knowles

(1972:39) was the first to present a teaching "design" based on principles of andragogy, but it was not specifically designed for educational supervision. Although field instruction approaches that promote adult learning principles do exist (Marshack and Glassman 1991; Schneck 1991b; Wijnberg and Schwartz 1977; Wilson 1981), only one model that explicitly incorporates the principles of andragogy (Knappe 1975) and just a few that do so for the educational supervision of staff (Brannon 1985; Clancy 1985; Gelfand et al. 1975; Lowy 1983) are known to the authors.

Additional Adult-Sensitive Learning Approaches

While andragogical principles seem to underlie many field instruction approaches, other adult-sensitive learning approaches are available. For example, Wijnberg and Schwartz (1977) present a "role systems" approach that incorporates principles similar to those of andragogy, combining them with Parsonian social system theory. Both Bogo and Vayda (1998) and Raschick et al. (1998) offer models of field instruction based on the learning theories of David Kolb (1984). Eisikovits and Guttman (1983) put forth a supervision approach that incorporates John Dewey's (1938) experiential learning continuum.

Adult Learning Principles and TCS

Models that incorporate adult learning principles help supervisors respond to supervisees' needs. However, little instruction is available on how to systematically use these principles in supervisory practice. In other words, these principles have not, for the most part, been made operational. TCS does operationalize andragogical principles through its prescribed sequence of activities.

Approaches That Offer Strategies for Teaching

Models that incorporate adult learning principles are valuable to supervisors because they provide frameworks for responding to supervisee *learning* needs. In comparison, *teaching* approaches are helpful in that they offer supervisors strategies for conveying new information, developing supervisee skills, and handling challenging aspects of the instructional encounter.

Only a limited number of field instruction approaches provide strategies for the teaching component of the teaching-learning encounter (Larsen 1980; Manis 1979; Pettes 1979; Schneck 1991b; Shulman 1994; St. John 1975; Webb 1983; Wilson 1981). Of these, two also outline learning content

(Schneck 1991b; Wilson 1981). Although some of these approaches put forth general guiding principles for "doing" field instruction (Webb 1993; Wilson 1981), only two offer discrete procedures for attainment of practicum objectives (Larsen 1980; Manis 1979). The competency-based/task-centered approach (Larsen 1980) is the only existing model that offers empirical evidence of effectiveness. In addition, it is the only one that offers discrete steps for achieving practicum competencies and informs the within-supervision meeting sequence. Supervisees of this approach performed at higher levels of competence and had more confidence in their skills than those taught by traditional approaches, which "varied from instructor to instructor . . . , was less systematic, less task-focused, more global, and more focused on case dynamics than on student performance and skill level" (Larsen and Hepworth 1982:53). Although this field instruction model has never received further development, it clearly supports using task-centered procedures for the practice of educational supervision.

Just to Clarify

Pettes (1979) offers a "task-centered approach" for staff and student supervision. Although it is referred to as such, it does not incorporate the procedures and principles of the task-centered practice model (Reid 1992). Instead, it presents supervisors with tasks for preparing for and working with supervisees. Hence, the approach provides a helpful and comprehensive "menu" of possible supervisor tasks but not a systematic process by which these strategies are structured, defined, or selected. The supervisory tasks presented in Pettes's approach are important, complement student tasks, and can easily be integrated into a model that offers a process, such as one using procedures of task-centered practice—e.g., TCS.

Feminist Pedagogy

A recent complement to andragogy is feminist pedagogy, which focuses more on the teaching component of the supervisory encounter. Feminist pedagogy is primarily concerned with how power is utilized in teaching relationships, and it offers principles for modeling that are empowering rather than inhibiting.

Pedagogical techniques (e.g., lecture, assigned reading, instructor-selected learning objectives) continue to be actively used in social work education and are recognized as important elements in teaching (Kramer and Wrenn 1994). In fact, the technique of didactic explanation has been identified as central to student satisfaction in the field (Fortune and Abramson 1993; Ellison 1994). However, traditional pedagogical relationships have recently been viewed as a potential threat to a productive learning experience (Cramer 1995). Characterized as a "banking" approach in which experts "deposit knowledge into the empty vaults of students" (Cramer 1995), traditional pedagogy implies a rigid and authoritarian hierarchy, ignores learners' past experiences, and avoids involving student input into their own education. Indeed, instructors have greater power than students, which can inhibit rather than encourage learning (Fox and Zischka 1989). Since supervisees often mimic their supervisors' professional behaviors, modeling inhibiting rather than empowering uses of power risks supervisees' learning to use authority in this way when working with clients. (See chapters 3 and 4 for more discussion on attending to power in the educational supervision relationship.)

Because pedagogical strategies are recognized as important but raise concerns related to power, educators have recently applied concepts of feminism to pedagogical principles in what is called "feminist pedagogy" (Cramer 1995; Dore 1994; Lazzari 1991). A central goal of feminist pedagogy is learner empowerment (Lazzari 1991). This approach posits that instructors can model productive use of relational power. For example, the instructional relationship should be collaborative (as opposed to directive), giving the learner opportunities for legitimate participation in their education, even for challenging the teacher's knowledge (Dore 1994). In addition, the relationship should be a situation where subjective and intuitive knowledge is validated, all participants experience growth (Dore 1994), and the strengths of both are emphasized (Lazzari 1991). By modeling authority in this way, instructors demonstrate to their students ways to use power in other (e.g., practitioner-client) relationships.

While principles of feminist pedagogy have been proceduralized for use in the social work classroom (Cramer 1995), they have not been made operational for educational supervision. Indeed, feminist pedagogy seems to be in its beginning stages of development, and has only received limited attention for field instruction (Lazzari 1991). Yet its principles hold great potential to guide the practice of educational supervision. Indeed, a major consideration in the development of TCS was to put these principles into operation.

A Blended Teaching Approach

Kramer and Wrenn (1994) offer a classroom teaching approach that blends andragogy and traditional pedagogy. Such blending makes sense and offers promise for educational supervision. Although self-directed learning goals are important, supervisees often do not possess the knowledge to select appropriate goals. It is not realistic to expect that supervisees, particularly new ones, can completely self-direct their learning, and it is probably unfair to expect them to do so. Traditional pedagogical techniques are often necessary. However, because strict traditional pedagogy raises concerns about power in the educational relationship, consideration of feminist pedagogy in the blending of andragogical and traditional approaches seems important.

Approaches for Challenging Aspects of the Instructional Encounter

Some aspects of the educational supervision encounter are more challenging than others. For example, linking classroom and field knowledge is recognized as important but is often difficult to systematically accomplish because of the "considerable investment of time of faculty and practicum instructors" to sequentially integrate class and field curricula (Tolson and Kopp 1988:133). A handful of approaches address this and other challenging aspects of the educational supervision encounter. These include linking class and field learning (Collins and Bogo 1986; Rabin, Savaya, and Frank 1994; Tolson and Kopp 1988; Vayda and Bogo 1991), developing learning agreements (Hamilton and Else 1983; Wilson 1981), providing feedback (Freeman 1985; Fox and Zischka 1989; Kadushin 1992; Latting 1992), handling student emotional reactions (Catalano 1985; Grossman, Levine-Jordano, and Shearer 1990; Wilson 1981), and attending to issues of human diversity (Benavides, Lynch, and Velasquez 1980; Berkun 1984; Gladstein and Mailick 1986; Manoleas and Carrillo 1991; McCroy et al. 1986a).

TCS and Process

As TCS is presented, you will note that adult learning principles, feminist pedagogy, and direct instruction are all incorporated into the model's principles and operationalized in its procedures. In addition, the model was developed to be flexible so that approaches that address challenging aspects of the instructional encounter can be utilized as needed without interrupting the overall TCS process.

Modifying Practice Models for Educational Supervision

Given the lack of comprehensive models for the practice of field education, it is not a surprise that supervisors have looked to existing clinical treatment approaches for direction. While this limits providing education and raises concerns about "therapizing" supervisees, with appropriate modification practice models can offer direction for supervisors.

Efforts to apply professional knowledge and skill to the educational process are not uncommon (Mishne 1983). It can be argued that practice models' applicability to education is questionable because they have been developed for healing rather than teaching. However, many practitioner skills are useful in educational supervision, including the ability to create positive relationships, use of self (e.g., modeling behaviors), strategies for problem solving and achieving goals, helping others develop self-awareness, dealing with anxiety, contracting, and appreciating human diversity. In fact, educators have argued convincingly that supervision and therapy are isomorphic—that the supervisory relationship is similar to the therapist-client relationship (Haley 1976; Kahn 1979; Norman 1987; Storm and Heath 1985). "Both require a good relationship between a more knowledgeable 'expert' and a learner" (Kahn 1979:520). The activities carried out in both systems are also similar (Shulman 1994). Reid (1984) describes both processes as involving "a group of persons (two or more) . . . faced with a problem in the functioning of a social system" (116), who work together toward resolution of the difficulty. The group could be "a practitioner and troubled family members . . . or a supervisor and supervisee" (116).

Hence, with proper attention to modification, clinical models can have powerful application to supervision. Storm and Heath (1985) "encourage supervisors to consciously adapt and use their therapy theories as *models* [italics theirs] for supervision" (88) and add that they have "seen structural, strategic, and structural-functional therapy theories applied successfully to supervision" (95). Other approaches have used theories of sibling position to construct a "systemic" model of supervision (Zimmerman, Collins, and Bach, 1986), and principles of Gestalt therapies for supervision (Serok and Urda 1987). It is important in the process of converting clinical models into supervision approaches that the focus remain on the education and practice behaviors of the supervisee, and not shift to his or her personality. In other words, supervisors should take care not to "therapize" the supervisee. In addition, educational supervisors must learn skills beyond those they already possess as clinicians. For example, they must learn to instruct, identify learning needs and educational objectives, conceptually translate theory into practice, and evaluate performance.

However, the approach of adapting a clinical practice model for the practice of educational supervision has great potential. Although models have been developed that draw upon practice knowledge (Kaplan 1988; Halgin 1985/1986; Tolson 1987; Webb 1983), they do not represent direct adaptations of clinical models. The models that do (Basso 1987; Larsen 1980) are all modifications of the task-centered practice model (Reid and Epstein 1972; Reid 1992). Furthermore, studies suggest support for this approach (Larsen and Hepworth 1982; Stuyvesant 1980), and the development of TCS.

Support for Adaptation of the Task-Centered Practice Model

Perhaps more support exists for adapting task-centered procedures for the purpose of educational supervision than for any other existing practice model. Larsen's (1980) competency-based/task-centered approach (CBTC) is perhaps the first of this type of adaptation. CBTC demonstrated empirical evidence of effectiveness. Students supervised with CBTC performed at a significantly higher level, reported greater confidence in employing skills, and perceived more assistance from their supervisors than did a comparison group supervised by a traditional, case-focused approach (Larsen and Hepworth 1982). Another study comparing supervisors who actively used a CBTC manual with those who did not indicated that CBTC supervisors reported higher levels of classroom-field integration than the comparison group (Stuyvesant 1980). Although both studies used small samples, they support task-centered procedures for educational supervision.

Task-centered supervision procedures have been utilized on other occasions as well. Kaplan (1988) offers a group model for field instruction that incorporates task-centered group practice principles. Tolson (1987) and Basso (1987) both examined features of practicum instruction that used task-centered procedures. However, the supervision approaches discussed in these reports were not the focus of the research.

Parihar's (1984) task-centered model for management in human services used task-centered structure, procedures, and technologies to guide problem-solving activities between administrators and staff. Both found the model to be "considerably helpful" (98). The successful application of task-centered practice principles to an administrative supervision situation demonstrates the flexibility and power of the technologies the model offers.

Finally, the task-centered practice model was adapted for the development of TCS. An evaluation of a pilot test of the model demonstrated strong support for its continued development, testing, and application (Caspi 1997).

3 Principles of Effective Instruction

This chapter provides an overview of principles commonly associated witheffective fieldinstruction. The purpose of reviewing these features is threefold. First, it familiarizes the reader with what elements are considered important for maximizing the educational experience. Second, it helps to give meaning to the power and utility of the Task-Centered Model for Supervision (TCS). How TCS addresses these principles and aids in promoting a positive supervisory relationship will be demonstrated throughout this book. Third, understanding principles of effective instruction is critical for forming a productive supervisory relationship. We posit that the development and maintenance of such a relationship can be achieved through systematic implementation of these principles. Because of its centrality to supervision, the supervisory relationship is considered in depth in the following chapter.

Learning Is Best When . . .

Despite the lack of a coherent and systematic model for educational supervision, the social work literature does put forth a common (albeit unstructured) group of principles for effective supervision. These essentially offer considerations for maximizing student learning, outlining certain circumstances in which "learning is best." These principles have been organized here and outlined below. A discussion of each follows. TCS was designed to systematically address each of these principles, as is demonstrated through the presentation of the model in subsequent chapters.

Learning is best when it . . .

- is partialized
- has direction
- is clearly structured
- involves feedback
- incorporates adult learning principles (e.g., andragogy)
- incorporates concepts of feminist pedagogy
- attends to power in the supervisory relationship
- utilizes contracting
- attends to preferred learning style
- offers a range of opportunities
- links clinical encounters to learning goals
- links classroom and field
- recognizes the supervisor as role model
- attends to parallel process
- recognizes supervision as a developmental process
- balances autonomy and dependence
- is supported by the environment
- attends to supervisee affective experiences
- attends to the supervisory relationship

Is Partialized

Students must begin to master much knowledge and many necessary skills in their school experience. They frequently begin their practica having few, if any, of these skills, yet they are required to provide "full" treatment early in their first semester. This demand can feel overwhelming to students, who are anxious they are "not doing what they are supposed to," and to field instructors, who "experience pressure about the totality of what needs to be taught" (Matorin 1979:153). Imagine asking a person who has never before played basketball to join in a competitive game. For many social work students, this is, metaphorically, what they are being asked to do (or *believe* that they are being asked to do, although it may not be what the supervisor actually expects). It makes sense to learn the many skills individually and incrementally—to focus first on how to dribble the ball, then how to pass it, shoot it, and so on, successively—rather than attempting to learn all of these things simultaneously.

Partializing learning, which involves breaking objectives "down into small manageable parts" (Wilson 1981:27), can be an effective way to reduce student anxiety. Focusing on and developing competence in a limited number of skills at a time enables the student to use them as a foundation on which to build (Kadushin 1992). "By gradually mastering one skill at a time, students gain increasing confidence that counteracts the sense of discouragement they typically experience when they mistakenly believe that they are expected to gain immediate expertise in every respect" (Larsen and Hepworth 1982:56).

Giving graded task assignments (Reid 1978), initially selecting relatively easy-to-accomplish tasks and then slowly increasing the complexity with the completion of each, is a feature of the task-centered approach. Educators concur that when learning is partialized the student "won't be tested to the limits of his ability right away and can experience some success" (Wilson 1981:26). TCS is formulated to identify and work on only a few skills at one time, and in progressive fashion.

Has Direction

Learning is best when it has a clear focus—when the learner and teacher have a mutual understanding of the purpose of the learning encounter. Clearly articulated target goals and activities for attaining them provide direction for the supervisory process. Conversely, confusion about or lack of target goals can lead to haphazard, unsatisfactory, and potentially unproductive practicum experiences. Lack of well-defined goals risks a supervisory process consisting of idiosyncratic and disconnected meetings that are more focused on case handling than supervisee learning. This type of supervision is referred to here as the "case of the week" (CW) approach.

Case of the Week

The CW approach involves supervisees bringing to each meeting the case that is currently causing them the greatest anxiety. The supervisory pair then work together to problem-solve the immediate clinical issue. The following week the supervisee may raise a new case that needs immediate attention, and there is little, if any, follow-up or connection to the prior week's discussion. This continues throughout the supervisory encounter.

Case problem solving is central to educational supervision, and has been identified as what supervisors and supervisees spend the most time on during sessions (Basso 1987). However, in the CW approach, there is generally little discussion of how practice strategies relate to learning objectives, and the supervision meetings are not linked by any content. Each week may involve a different case, often without an explicit linking to prior supervision meetings or to learning. As expressed by one student being supervised by such an approach, "We spend one week on one thing, and the next week another thing is at the center of attention." Such supervision is haphazard and without direction.

Is Clearly Structured

Structure has been found to be beneficial to the supervision process (Freeman 1993): it provides clarity of expectations, roles, and activities that will be undertaken. It is helpful to supervisors and supervisees to know when meetings will take place, who will be involved, how long they will last, and what should occur during and between encounters. As put by one student supervised by a structured approach (TCS), "I knew what to expect for each supervision. Each session was similar and simple to follow." Knowing what to expect from and during supervision is helpful in reducing anxiety (Freeman 1993). Similarly, it is helpful to include arrangements for back-up or emergency situations (e.g., client crisis), particularly if the supervisor is not available. Providing structure for such times is also reassuring.

A clear structure also helps provide direction to the learning process. A clear outline of *how* learning objectives are to be achieved helps supervisees feel more confident that they will be attained. Unfortunately, practicum instruction (Larsen and Hepworth 1982:112) and clinical supervision of staff are typically unstructured. An increasingly used, and worrisome, version of unstructured supervision is the type that is received "on the fly."

Supervision on the Fly

While it is important that the supervision process be consistent and supported (e.g., regularly scheduled meetings, no frequent interruptions or changes), many supervisors are frustrated by busy schedules and lack of time for supervision (Kadushin 1974; Rothholz and Werk 1984; Shulman 1993; Strom 1991). Indeed, some settings restrict the supervisor's ability to be available for uninterrupted supervision. As a result, "supervision on the fly" is becoming more common. This entails the supervisee "grabbing" the supervisor on a "catch-as-can" basis (e.g., stopping the supervisor in the hall on the way to a meeting). Usually this results in a rushed discussion of a case or administrative issue that is rarely done in collaborative fashion. Such an approach raises anxiety for supervisees, who are unsure whether or not they will get a chance to discuss their cases, and frustrates supervisors, who feel pressed to give quick and directive responses without opportunity for discussion. It also impedes the utilization of a collaborative framework. These encounters are rarely focused, do not address learning goals, and do not promote an open and trusting supervisory relationship. As will be discussed later in this book, TCS can be used to facilitate on-the-fly supervision. Nevertheless, such an approach should be used sparingly (e.g., in emergency situations), and efforts to find time for more appropriate supervision should be made.

Involves Feedback

Supervisees learn best when they receive feedback about their performance. They need to know what they are doing well and what areas need improvement (Kadushin 1992). Effective feedback is important for clarifying expectations and distinguishing between desired behavior and actual performance (Latting 1992). How is one to improve their skills without it? Feedback is an important teaching tool, albeit not an easy one to implement. Supervisees want explicit and direct information about their performance (Kadushin 1992; Munson 1993). However, they have reported that they receive an inadequate amount of critical feedback (Kadushin 1974; Latting 1992). Indeed, giving feedback can be quite difficult, particularly when it involves corrective or negative evaluations. Supervisors often struggle with how to tell a supervisee that they are not doing something well. In turn, it is difficult for many supervisees to accept such feedback (Munson 1993; Kaiser 1997). Fortunately, there are available methods for giving feedback in a productive way (Freeman 1985; Kadushin 1992; Latting 1992; Shulman 1993). From these and other sources (Caspi 1997; Munson 1993), we have assembled seven principles for effective feedback: it 1) is *ongoing*, 2) focuses on *specific* behaviors, 3) is *timely*, 4) includes *positive* appraisals, 5) attends to *affective responses*, 6) includes *supervisee input*, and 7) is *evaluated for quality*.

If you want someone to "swallow" something (particularly if does not appear appetizing), you better make it tasty! By implementing these strategies, supervisors will be better able to couch feedback so that supervisees can hear and accept it.

Ongoing

Feedback should not be something that occurs sporadically. Instead, it should be an ongoing process. Receiving feedback about performance only during formal evaluations can be highly problematic, as field instruction evaluations commonly take place only two or three times during the entire course of the practicum, and staff evaluations typically occur annually. Not knowing for long periods of time about their performance causes students anxiety about whether they are on track and in good standing with the supervisor. Being unsure about which parts of their performance are going well and which aspects need improvement makes it difficult to know how to improve practice, and whether or not the learner is moving toward educational goals. It is not uncommon for a supervisee to mistakenly interpret a supervisor's lack of feedback as tacit approval. Unexpected evaluation often results in conflict over the supervisor's assessment. Ongoing feedback is helpful in preparing for formal evaluations—if the supervisee and supervisor have been critiquing performance all along, there should be few surprises.

About Specific Behaviors

It is important that feedback relate to a *certain action* that took place in a *particular situation*, rather than being global in nature. For example, it would not be particularly helpful for a supervisor to tell a supervisee that he was "not good with anxious children." This global evaluation would likely leave the supervisee wondering what exactly it was that he did to inspire that evaluation, and it does not suggest any clear avenue for addressing the identified problem. An additional drawback of global feedback is that it can be perceived as a comment about a personal defect rather than a critique of professional performance.

Nonspecific feedback is difficult to interpret, and puts the onus on the supervisee to either infer meaning or challenge the supervisor to be more specific—something many students do not feel is safe to do. In contrast, feedback about specific behaviors allows the student to do something about them. Global evaluations (e.g., labels) do not. For example, what can be done about "not good with anxious children"? Until specific unfavorable behaviors or attitudes with such children are identified, not much.

Labeling as Nonspecific Feedback

Unfortunately, much feedback takes the form of labeling supervisees. "Too passive," "resistant to learning," "afraid of the elderly," "supportive," and "passive-aggressive" are a few examples of labels the authors have heard supervisors use to describe their supervisees. Efforts should be made to avoid this form of nonspecific feedback. For example, Tom, a supervisor, told Jill, his supervisee, that she was "too directive." Jill found this label confusing. Was she always "too directive"? Were there situations in which she *should* be directive? What specifically did Tom observe that led him to this conclusion? What was she doing that could be considered "directive"? Was offering suggestions to clients acceptable? Was she too directive with adults as well as children?

As can be seen, Jill was left with many questions about this feedback. There was little she could do to change her practice without more specific guidance from Tom (should she feel safe to request it). Furthermore, such feedback can lower supervisees' confidence about their overall practice. For Jill, it would be difficult to respond to any client without wondering if she were being overly directive.

Timely

Feedback should be given as soon as possible after the interaction of concern has taken place (Freeman 1985; Kadushin 1992; Latting 1992). If much time has gone by between the behavior and the feedback, it is likely the supervisee will be confused about which of many past behaviors the supervisor is referring to. In addition, such feedback is often seen as outdated (i.e., something the student no longer does). A potential problem of delayed feedback is the supervisee feeling that the supervisor has selectively chosen events to support his or her sense of the supervisee (e.g., during a formal evaluation). For example, some supervisors will recall and critique previously undiscussed examples of students' behavior as a way to override them in a power struggle. This is most likely to occur in a supervisory relationship that does not include processes of ongoing and immediate feedback, as can be seen in the following scenario:

> Ellen and her supervisor Jane met once each week for supervision. The encounter entailed Ellen's reporting on the status of each client to Jane, who focused on client progress. Rarely was Ellen's work critiqued. During her annual evaluation, Jane marked Ellen low on an item called "works well as a member of the treatment team." Caught by surprise, Ellen asked why she was rated this way. Jane stated that she had noticed times when Ellen had not included the team in making case decisions. Ellen, confused and becoming defensive, demanded examples of this. Jane, also becoming defensive and feeling her authority was being challenged, responded by saying, "Remember Mr. Smith's case and how you told him of his care plan before the whole team discussed it?" Ellen replied that Mr. Smith's case was a one-time occurrence, that it involved unique circumstances, and that it had taken place over four months before. She added that because Jane had not commented on the behavior at the time, she had concluded it was acceptable for her to make independent decisions about such cases.
>
> Both Ellen and Jane were frustrated by this encounter. Ellen felt the feedback to be unfair and outdated, and Jane felt that Ellen did not accept her criticism. Discussing a behavior close to the time the event takes place can go a long way toward clarifying expectations. The supervisee then has the opportunity to work on and improve performance prior to the formal evaluation. Probably the most problematic aspect of delaying feedback is that it negatively affects the supervisory relationship.

Positive

It would be difficult to overemphasize the importance of positive feedback. Supervisees engage in many activities that they do well, and it is important that they be recognized (Kadushin 1992). Complimenting behaviors can go a long way to boost confidence and motivation and reduce burnout. Indeed, the desire to perform well is often enhanced through extrinsic rewards such as supervisor praise (Latting 1992). Because part of the supervisor's role is to critically examine the supervisee's performance with the aim of improved practice, supervisors should take care not to lose sight of things the supervisee is doing well. Identified strengths can serve as a foundation on which to build. Positive feedback can boost confidence and increase motivation to continue building upon strengths and taking risks to improve work in new areas. For example, Jane felt that she did not perform well during a particular client interview. With her supervisor, Beth, she was able to talk about what had not gone well and also identify some positive things she had done. Jane was able to see that the interview was not a total failure. Beth's positive feedback motivated Jane to continue to implement the identified productive behaviors in her next clinical interview, while also trying out new behaviors to overcome her previous difficulties.

Furthermore, when sharing particularly critical feedback, it is helpful to also share positive evaluations. This can be helpful in reducing feelings of failure. For example, rather than saying, "You filled out these forms all wrong," it might be more helpful to say, "You did a nice job getting these forms filled out so quickly. However, it looks like you are experiencing some confusion about how to answer certain questions. Why don't we take a few minutes to go over them?" The same criteria for giving feedback discussed above—that it be ongoing, immediate, and about specific behaviors—apply to giving positive feedback.

Although combining negative and positive feedback can be helpful with particularly difficult critiques of practice, supervisors should take care not to make this "marriage" of feedback regular practice. A common approach to giving negative feedback is using the "sandwich technique," in which critical comments are embedded between two positive ones. One consequence of this strategy is that the supervisee learns to expect negative feedback when positive evaluations are given. Essentially, they wait for the "but . . . " (e.g. "You have done a great job with Ms. Jones, *but* your forgot to complete her intake forms") and begin to ignore the positive statements (Shulman 1993). For the most part, we recommend that supervisors let positive and corrective evaluations stand on their own, and consistently strive to achieve an appropriate balance between the two.

Complimenting Difficult Supervisees

With some supervisees, it is difficult to identify areas for positive feedback. Typically, such difficulty reflects either a deteriorated supervisory relationship or a supervisee who is emotionally unprepared for the demands of social work practice. Novice supervisees, who initially may make many mistakes, still offer areas for praise. For example, it is almost always possible to comment on the supervisee's good intentions, even when their resultant behaviors were clinically inappropriate.

Severely deteriorated supervisory relationships frequently entail lack of mutual respect and efforts to undermine each other's competence. In addition, supervisors of "difficult" supervisees are frequently worried that complimenting will give the wrong impression—that the supervisee is doing well. It is possible to improve such relationships through mutual exploration of how the relationship deteriorated, and by giving positive feedback. As in work with difficult clients, supervisors should make efforts to identify areas that are going well in order to reengage the supervisee in the supervision process.

Occasionally, supervisors encounter people who are not cut out for the social work profession. Such individuals are typically well intentioned but unprepared for the rigors of working with human suffering. It is not always easy to distinguish between problematic supervisee behaviors caused by a poor supervisory relationship and those due to being overwhelmed by professional practice. Supervisees who are encountering difficulties in working with others may attempt to conceal this from their supervisors and thus act in ways that seem rebellious and inappropriate. Students are not always open about their fears of failing. It is, again, helpful to compliment struggling supervisees on things they may be doing well, even if these areas seem small. Supervisees who are not able to handle clinical work should be counseled out of direct practice. However, identifying strengths in other areas of social work (e.g., research or policy) can be useful for redirecting the supervisee in a way that does not discount all previous efforts and leaves self-esteem still somewhat intact.

Attends to Affective Responses

Supervisory feedback can refer to many facets of the supervisee's work focusing on the supervisee's behaviors, attitudes, or affective responses. Supervisors attend more to what supervisees are *doing* with cases or how they are *thinking* about their clinical work than to how they are *feeling*. While this is expected, it is important to remember that practitioners often experience intense emotional reactions to clients, environmental constraints, and even their supervisors!

There is evidence that supervisors do not actively attend to supervisees' emotional experiences (Siddle and Wilson 1984), despite suggestions that such attention is important (Baker and Smith 1987; Caspi 1997; Ellison 1994; Fortune and Abramson 1993; Norman 1987). In addition, provision of support is recognized as a central feature of supervisory practice (Kadushin 1992; Shulman 1993). It is helpful to address supervisees' affective responses, particularly when their behaviors suggest high emotional intensity (or a significant lack of emotional intensity when the situation would seem to demand it—e.g., no apparent reaction to hearing of a client's suicide). Feedback related to affective experiences generally takes two forms: sharing with supervisees observations and interpretations of their behaviors (e.g., "You sound angry at Ms. Jones."); and exploring feelings through questioning ("It sounds like you did many things with Mr. Thomas. At the time, how were you feeling about the way he was reacting to you?").

Giving feedback about affective responses in the form of questions is recommended. Supervisees frequently respond negatively to interpretations of particularly intense feelings. Using questions to address affective responses may be less threatening, as supervisees can disclose emotional material at what they feel is the appropriate time. Furthermore, exploration through questions promotes skills of self-inquiry (Munson 1993), and practitioner self-awareness is recognized as a central feature in deliberate and ethical practice (Atwood 1986; Hepworth and Larsen 1990; Kadushin 1992).

The following example illustrates the benefits of addressing intense emotional responses, which include reduced anxiety, enhanced self-awareness, and a source for problem-solving cases.

One day Jill walked into her supervisor's office exclaiming, "This client is not doing any better despite my best efforts!" Anne, the supervisor, could have responded to this statement in many ways. She could have asked about what Jill has *done* with the case. Anne could also have inquired about how Jill *viewed* the situation (e.g., how she thought about the case in formulating her assessment and interventions). But, because of the emotional intensity behind Jill's statement, Anne decided to acknowledge Jill's strong feelings. She responded, "You sound frustrated and angry." Jill said that she was, indeed, very frustrated. Further exploring Jill's feelings through the use of questioning, Anne inquired, "What part of working with this client is so frustrating?"

Jill replied, "He is stubborn and resistive. He says that he will try new things and then never does—he takes no responsibility for changing!" Upon hearing herself say this out loud, Jill said, "I guess my expectations for this client are unrealistic. Perhaps I should reevaluate my goals."

Anne replied, "We all want our clients to improve quickly, but that is our agenda; the client may not be ready to move. Often, when we are frustrated, it is because our own agenda is not being realized."

Jill thanked Anne for letting her voice her frustrations. She also wondered whether or not the client was also frustrated, and planned to address this with him in their next meeting. Jill was able to give herself feedback about her practice (e.g., reevaluate expectations, explore client's experience with treatment) as a result of exploring her affective response to the client. In addition, she benefited from increased self-awareness, and what it might mean for her when she is frustrated with a client in the future.

Note that by attending to Jill's emotional response and by giving her an opportunity to "vent" her feelings, Anne helped Jill to separate from her feelings and more clearly consider case dynamics and her role in the treatment process.

One area of potential emotional intensity is the supervisory relationship. Supervisees have emotional reactions to their supervisors, and particularly to their supervisors' feedback. Despite the fact that most feedback is given with the supervisee's best interests in mind, they are occasionally unhappy with the critiques. It is not uncommon for supervisees to hide such reactions from their supervisors. This can become an obstacle to productive supervision meetings—if a supervisee does not like their supervisor's critique, they may be less receptive to future feedback or teachings. When giving critical feedback, it is important to watch for cues (e.g., nonverbal behaviors) that suggest a strong emotional reaction. It is also important to check in with the supervisee by asking for their reactions to the encounter, particularly if such cues are identified. Inviting supervisees to participate in the feedback process is important.

Includes Supervisee Input

Feedback should not be linear and unidirectional, flowing solely from supervisor to supervisee. Instead, it should be a mutual process in which both share in the evaluation of performance. "Effective feedback should be a process of sharing ideas rather than giving . . . answers" (Kadushin 1992:166). It is helpful for supervisors to take the lead and check in with supervisees about their perceptions of feedback. For many supervisees, it may be the first time they have been invited to respond to an authority, and therefore they may be hesitant to share reactions openly. It is vital that supervisors take care to model openness and nondefensiveness—particularly since this is what they are asking of the supervisee (Latting 1992)! Furthermore, some supervisees may have heard such invitations before, only to be chastised when they have disagreed with their supervisors (Shulman 1993). It can at times be difficult to accept supervisee feedback, but demonstrating openness serves as an opportunity to model professional use of self and nondefensiveness (Latting 1992; Shulman 1993).

Additionally, feedback should not come only from the supervisor. Supervisees should be invited to evaluate their own behaviors and share the evaluation with the supervisor. Assessing one's behaviors is an important professional skill (Atwood 1986; Norman 1987).

Purposeful Questioning As a Feedback Strategy

As briefly discussed earlier in relation to addressing affective responses, an effective strategy for giving feedback while simultaneously challenging supervisees to self-reflect is purposeful questioning. This is a method of giving feedback that invites supervisee response by couching critiques in the form of questions. Supervisees usually appreciate critical feedback, experiencing it as helpful for improving practice; however, they prefer their supervisors to raise issues for examination through questions (Caspi 1997). They tend to view questions as less directive, confrontational, and punitive. Additionally, supervisees appreciate that their supervisor is guiding them to think about aspects of case dynamics that they have not yet considered. This approach reduces defensiveness and increases openness to feedback. Alternative ideas for clinical work that emerge from the supervisee (triggered by the supervisor's questions) increase feelings of competence and motivation to accept and try different behaviors.

Formulating purposeful questions also helps supervisees to critically examine their clinical work, promoting a process of self-discovery and self-assessment skills (Munson 1993). The following scenarios of Bill and his supervisor illustrate the difference between direct, critical feedback (#1) and the use of questioning to address the same issue (#2).

Scenario #1

BILL: ... and then I said to her, "If you do your homework, then we can play a game together." That didn't seem to work either.

SUPERVISOR: I think the reason your client, Amy [age 8], ignored your attempt to help her with her homework was that you have not established clear rules for your relationship with her. In addition, you have not considered what *she* expects to do with you. You now seem just like another authority figure telling her what to do. She will not trust you or believe that you are different as long as you try to get her to do what *you* want her to do.

BILL: But I think I have been engaging her. I mean ... I spent the past two weeks playing games with her! She seems to like me. She is always asking the teacher when I will be coming to visit with her. She is really stubborn!

Although the supervisor's feedback offers some legitimate ideas for Bill to consider, it rules out Bill's perception of why Amy refuses to do the homework with him. Furthermore, Bill is not challenged to do the conceptual work of trying to assess the situation for himself. As you can see, he already feels that he has done engagement work, and he is made defensive and frustrated by the supervisor's feedback. One area in which Bill has developed feelings of competence is in building relationships with clients. Receiving critical feedback about his ability to do this is particularly difficult and results in a defensive response. Note the parallel process here: Bill's not including Amy in the clinical process is replicated by the supervisor's not including Bill in the supervisory process. Bill's work with Amy may be a reflection of the way in which the supervisor is working with him.

Scenario #2

BILL: ... and then I said to her, "If you do your homework, then we can play a game together." That didn't seem to work either.

SUPERVISOR: Sounds like you feel stuck with Amy. Do you think this has something to do with the rules you have established for your relationship with her, in terms of what you will do together?

Note that the question is not a neutral one. The supervisor is indirectly giving feedback by guiding Bill to consider his relationship to Amy.

BILL: Well, I have been trying to make her feel safe with me—we have been playing games for the past two weeks. But I think that it is important that we begin making progress on her math difficulties. I thought that by now she would be more willing to accept work from me. I wonder if I have moved too fast here?

Note that Bill does not respond defensively to the supervisor's suggestion, but instead uses it as a point for exploration.

SUPERVISOR: Do you think she was surprised that you changed your approach with her—that you had established your time together was about playing games, and now it is about doing homework?

Again, the supervisor uses a question to direct Bill's consideration of the case as a problem of relationship rules. At the same time, formulating this feedback as a question allows Bill more freedom to disagree with the supervisor's assessment than if it had been given as a statement (e.g., "You changed the rules on Amy and caught her off guard").

BILL: Yes. I guess she was caught off guard and maybe a little angry with me that I changed the rules so suddenly.

In scenario #2, Bill's supervisor gives him feedback by gently suggesting—through the use of questioning—areas for Bill to consider in evaluating his situation. As a result, Bill is challenged and able to identify a potential practice obstacle. Supervisees are more likely to develop self-awareness and self-assessment skillls through a continued process of feedback in the form of purposeful questioning than through the sole use of direct feedback, which essentially presents students with "answers" without challenging them to come up with their own.

Evaluating the Quality of Feedback

Supervisors should try to evaluate the quality of their feedback and learn whether or not it was helpful. Feedback can generally be evaluated on two levels: its usefulness for solving clinical problems and its value for improving practitioner skill. One method of evaluation is to review the supervisee's application of feedback received in a subsequent supervision meeting. The following vignette illustrates this process:

> Mary, a supervisor, shared with Tom, a new staff member, that his interaction with Ms. Jones involved him asking a nonstop string of questions, thus restricting this client's ability to voice her own needs. Tom accepted this feedback and stated that he would change his approach with this client and use more open-ended questions. Mary added that Tom should try to allow Ms. Jones more time to respond as well. At the following supervision meeting, Mary and Tom were able to discuss the usefulness of Mary's feedback by reviewing how Tom put it into action with Ms. Jones. Tom reported that by implementing the suggestions from supervision, he was better able to identify the problem Ms. Jones wanted to ameliorate and then was able to start treatment in that area. Furthermore, he reported that he could think of other situations in which he needed to alter his behavior to allow more time for client input. Hence, Mary's feedback can be evaluated as helpful for improving both client treatment and Tom's skill as a practitioner.

It is important to remember that although feedback can be evaluated on two levels, it may prove useful on one level and not the other. For example, feedback can be valuable for addressing supervisee skill even when it does not help with case progress. If the client in the above vignette had not responded to Tom's change in behavior, the feedback could have been evaluated as useful for promoting worker performance, but not useful in helping resolve the clinical issues in this case.Then the supervisor and supervisee could have explored why the feedback was not clinically useful. The lack of client response might have been due to a variety of causes, including Tom's improper application of the feedback, additional unidentified clinical considerations, or case dynamics not originally having been accurately assessed.

In turn, feedback may be evaluated as useful for addressing clinical issues but not helpful for improving supervisee practice. This generally occurs when supervisor feedback is either given or received without a thorough understanding of why it has been suggested. For example, Tom could have implemented the use of open-ended questions and allowed more time for clients to respond without understanding why he should do these things. He would then have been unlikely to integrate these skills and know when to use them in other situations. One method of maximizing the potential for feedback to be valuable for practitioner skill development is to explicitly link it to learning objectives.

Link Feedback to Learning Objectives

Feedback is most effective when it is tied directly to learning. There are two levels at which this linkage can occur. First, when supervisors give feedback they should also clearly articulate what they hope supervisees will learn from it (Kadushin 1992). Second, the supervisory pair should discuss how this new information (i.e., feedback) ties into the student's learning objectives. This second level is particularly important when using learning objectives as measures for formal evaluation.

In our experience, feedback is usually focused on case problem solving and not tied to the supervisee's learning. As a result, students often leave supervision with strategies for working with a particular client but with little understanding of how these strategies are linked to target learning objectives. The following vignette illustrates this phenomenon.

> Ashley presented a case to her supervisor, Hattie, which involved a six-year-old boy who was having behavior problems at school. Ashley had been using a "diversion technique" when the boy started to act up that involved interrupting his tantrums by giving him toys to play with. Although the technique was effective, Hattie gave Ashley feedback that "more could be done." She explained that Ashley's approach served to stop the problem behavior when it occurred but did little to prevent it. Hattie then suggested that Ashley construct a behavior chart with the boy, in which he would be awarded stickers each time he went for part of the day without any problems. When the chart was full of stickers, he should be taken out for ice cream as a reward. Ashley was excited about the idea and left the supervision meeting planning to implement it the next day.

Although Ashley may have had a general understanding of why this intervention approach is helpful, the lack of discussion about how its implementation relates to her learning is problematic. Hattie's suggestion was presented without examination of the context in which it was developed. There was no discussion of what theories underlie the technique or how it related to Ashley's knowledge of child development. Furthermore, how the case dynamics and proposed intervention were linked to Ashley's learning objectives were not considered. Essentially, Ashley left supervision with a behavior to implement but with little understanding of the strategy, why her supervisor selected it, or how it fit into her existing knowledge of interventions. She probably could not answer the following questions: Why is this strategy an effective one to use in this case? Is this same technique appropriate for twelve-year-olds? What information led Hattie to formulate the intervention the way she did (e.g., why not mark an "X" on the chart for each bad behavior, with the child losing privileges when the chart is filled?)? Why does Hattie expect that this child will be able to go for any time without acting out? Ashley has been given a tool without much discussion of its various applications, and if it does not work, she likely will not know why. This is not uncommon. Because supervision generally focuses on case problem solving, the focus is usually on what will benefit clients—without explicit consideration of how it benefits supervisees.

Linking learning to feedback aids the formal evaluation process. For example, at the time of Ashley's evaluation, it is likely that both Ashley and her supervisor will have difficulty identifying progress on learning objectives. They will need to "go back in time" and, from memory, reconstruct how implementation of various behaviors related to competencies. Furthermore, it would have been highly beneficial for Hattie to have shared what she would like Ashley to learn from the feedback, rather than remaining focused only on the benefits for the client.

The Art of Feedback—Selecting Areas for Critique

The above principles describe how to implement effective feedback, but it is also critical for supervisors to consider which aspects of supervisee performance should be critiqued. There are, at any time, multiple areas that can be evaluated and commented upon, but giving feedback about each one at every opportunity is neither economical nor productive. Supervisors "need to be selective in terms of the amount that a person can absorb" (Kadushin 1992:166). A sensible guideline for selecting areas to critique is to evaluate which feedback will be most useful to the supervisee. The operating agenda for giving feedback should be to meet the needs of the supervisee, not the supervisor. Feedback that is not useful to the supervisee will, in turn, not be helpful for the client. As a reminder, it is often necessary to explain the relevance of feedback in order to make its usefulness clear.

Latting (1992) offers thoughtful guidelines for deciding whether or not to give corrective feedback. She directs supervisors to assess their standing as credible before giving feedback, and to take care that it is only given if the purpose is to help—not to pretend the aim is to be helpful when the supervisor's true intention is to express aggression or justify unfair decisions. Additionally, she encourages supervisors to attend to the receiver's willingness to accept the corrective critique and ability to take action to improve the behavior. Feedback about past behaviors that supervisees cannot do anything about is not particularly helpful. Instead, corrective feedback should be "directed toward future improvement . . . with an emphasis on skill building rather than fault finding" (Latting 1992:426).

Knowing what to critique is challenging and can be considered one of the more artful aspects of supervisory practice. However, steps can be taken to optimize the process, as outlined in the above principles. Furthermore, we encourage supervisors to take time to attend to supervisees' responses and to ask for supervisees' input about their preferences in terms of receiving feedback. One strategy is to ask students, "What kind of feedback are you looking for?" or "How can I be of help?" Allowing supervisees to share what type of feedback they are seeking can greatly increase receptivity, clarify expectations, and assist in the selection of feedback process. Furthermore, by asking supervisees their preferences, supervisors can learn how to design a feedback process that it is most useful to each student.

Incorporates Adult Learning Principles

Social work education involves teaching adults, so integration of adult learning principles is helpful. As discussed in the previous chapter, one set of learning principles frequently put forth for guiding adult education is andragogy (Knowles 1970). Andragogy assumes that as people mature they become less dependent and more self-directed, have more experiences to build and draw upon, are more interested in and motivated by what they need to learn than what they ought to learn, and develop a more problem-solving orientation, in contrast to children, who have a subject-centered orientation and prefer collaborative instructional relationships.

Indeed, there is some indication that andragogical approaches are preferable to pedagogical, or child-centered, methods, particularly for women (Davenport and Davenport 1988). This has important implications for social work education, as approximately 80 percent of M.S.W. students are female (Sowers-Hoag and Harrison 1991). However, studies also "question the belief that older learners automatically become more andragogical and that younger learners must be pedagogically-inclined" (Davenport and Davenport 1988:84). Older learners are more likely to have experienced traditional pedagogy throughout their lives, and may not be prepared to share in the direction of their learning. On the other hand, younger supervisees may have had more past opportunities to take responsibility for their learning, and experience traditional methods as objectionable. Supervisors using andragogy as a guiding approach should openly share and discuss its appropriateness with the learner.

It is possible that supervisees become more andragogical in their orientation as they learn more. Beginning students and staff may need their supervisor to direct the educational process until they develop the knowledge and security needed for self-direction. In addition, many novice supervisees do not possess enough information to be able to select their own learning objectives. As they learn more, they are more able to identify what they need and want to work on. Indeed, some may initially prefer pedagogical approaches and move toward andragogical approaches as they progress through their programs of study. Therefore, supervisors should be able to perform pedagogical functions without infantilizing adult students. Recent literature on feminist pedagogy holds promise for addressing these concerns (taken up later in this chapter).

The learning theories of Kolb (1984) and Dewey (1938) have also been helpful in considering approaches for adult education. Since the introduction of adult learning to social work education, the importance of involving adults in the direction of their own education, within a collaborative teacher-student relationship, has been consistently emphasized.

Self-Directed Learning

Because adult learning is motivated by purpose (Knowles 1970), adults enter into formal education with many self-defined goals (e.g., obtaining a professional degree, preparing to work with a particular population). Furthermore, adult learners are not "empty vessels" waiting to be filled with the supervisor's great wisdom (Cramer 1995); they have prior experience, a working base of knowledge, and ideas about what they would like (or need) to learn. Rather than assuming that the supervisee knows little, the supervisor should try to identify what is known that can be used to build upon, and what gaps in knowledge and skills exist that need to be filled (Munson 1993). Because adult learners often have particular objectives in mind, a sensible goal is to help them learn how to access the knowledge they need. This reduces dependency on present and future supervisors for their learning and practice needs. Finally, acquiring self-directed learning skills promotes their ability to engage in autonomous practice.

Incorporates Principles of Feminist Pedagogy and Attends to Power

As discussed in the previous chapter, feminist pedagogy applies principles of feminism to the field of teaching. This approach is only in its beginning stages of development, but its principles hold great potential for guiding the practice of field instruction (Lazzari 1991), social work education (Cramer 1995; Dore 1994), and staff supervision. At the center of feminist pedagogy is its attention to power and how it is used by the person with greater power (i.e., the supervisor).

Educational supervision, and particularly field instruction, involves processes of evaluation and therefore is inherently a teacher-learner relationship in which there is an imbalance of power (Hamilton and Else 1983; Jacobs 1991; Johnston, Rooney, and Reitmeir 1991; Manis 1979). As previously stated, a danger of this type of relationship is that it may inhibit rather than empower learning (Fox and Zischka 1989). An example of a disempowering relationship is one in which a supervisor tells supervisees what to do, when, and how; little input from the supervisee is allowed; and any deviations are punished. This authoritarian arrangement clearly says to the supervisee, "I am the one with power. I control you. You are not perceived as competent." A further danger of this type of approach is that it "teaches" supervisees (by example) how to use authority in relationships where they have the power. Such behaviors could potentially be carried over into their interactions with clients.

A central goal of feminist pedagogy for students is empowerment. Although a formal hierarchy exists, the educational relationship should be collaborative, with the student free to challenge the teacher, subjective and intuitive knowledge validated, and authority modeled so that it promotes validation and empowerment (Dore 1994). Authority, in this case, involves "sharing" power—giving the supervisee responsibility and power to direct their own learning. The adult learner's knowledge and creativity are validated and utilized. If given the chance, people often formulate unique and innovative strategies for achieving goals. By giving the supervisee room to develop and try out ideas, the supervisor gains opportunities to expand their own problem-solving repertoire. Thus, shared power has the benefit of promoting the growth of all participants in the educational encounter (Dore 1994; Lazzari 1991).

Experiencing an empowering relationship (in which power is shared) firsthand has additional benefits. First, it enables the student to learn, *in vivo*, behaviors for constructing empowering relationships in their work with clients. Second, the student experiences self-determination, a central value of social work (Hepworth and Larsen 1990), as the "receiver" in a helping relationship.. Third, by developing techniques for self-directed learning and self-supervision, the supervisee is empowered to become an independent learner, preparing for autonomous practice. One approach for helping supervisees develop such techniques is to help them integrate a supervision framework (e.g., TCS) that directs a learning process.

Utilizes Contracting

Contracting is recognized as a beneficial tool for providing direction and clarifying expectations for supervision (Fox and Zischka 1989; Kaiser 1997; Reid and Epstein 1972). The contract is an agreement between participants engaging in a joint activity (e.g., supervision) that generally spells out how that activity is to be carried out, roles and responsibilities of the participants, and objectives of the encounter. Contracts vary in their level of explicitness and formality (Kaiser 1997). Nevertheless, articulating processes and goals for supervision helps to clarify expectations and give focus to supervision, and thereby reduces anxiety about the process (Fox and Zischka 1989).

In social work, contracting has referred to a number of different components of the supervisory process. For example, it is common that at the start of the encounter the supervisor and supervisee outline its structural arrangements—e.g., who will meet, where, when, how often, for how long, and role expectations (Kaiser 1997). Another common approach, "sessional contracting," involves coming to an agreement about the agenda for each supervision meeting (Shulman 1993). Typically, agenda setting occurs at the start of the supervision conference and allows supervisees the opportunity to raise issues that are most pressing for them at the time. A third use of contracting, employed more in student internships than in staff supervision, is the "learning agreement" (Thomlison et al. 1996), which spells out broadly defined objectives to be accomplished during the practicum. Educational objectives are commonly developed at the start, and attaining them is meant to become the focus of supervision—although there is some question whether or not this indeed happens. When students begin clinical work, they often become more concerned with solving client problems than their own education. Their learning objectives become "lost" until progress is reviewed at the time of the formal evaluation. "Goal-oriented" contracting is a helpful method for keeping the educational component of supervision at the fore (Fox and Zischka 1989).

Goal-Oriented Contracting

In this approach, goals for supervision become the focus of the encounter (Fox and Zischka 1989). Goals are selected for immediate work, and activities (i.e., tasks) to be performed to attain them are outlined. For the most part, these activities are implemented by the supervisee during clinical sessions with clients. Timelines are established for when goals should be achieved and contracts reviewed. Although variations exist, we believe goal-oriented contracts should be utilized at each supervision meeting. Accordingly, progress with goals and tasks can be reviewed at later meetings.

Developing learning goals at each supervision conference focuses the supervisory process, which centers around education. It forces a systematic rather than haphazard educational method, as well as partialization and incremental learning practices. In addition, formulation of activities to address the goals provides a concrete means for monitoring progress and performing evaluations (Fox and Zischka 1989). Spelling out goals focuses not only learning and supervision processes but also work with clients. Supervisees often feel overwhelmed by the complexity of cases and unsure which issue to address first. As one intern put it, "Sometimes I forget what I am supposed to do with a client, and having the contract keeps me on track." Another added that the "contract helps me know what I am doing so I don't feel lost." Having formulated discrete goal-based strategies for working with cases, supervisees are clear about how to proceed, and their anxiety about clinical work is reduced.

Contracting each supervision meeting (typically weekly) aids in clarifying expectations. In addition, this process outlines performance standards for the supervisee—ones they have had a role in defining. They know clearly which tasks they have agreed to carry out, and that they will be questioned about these activities when they return to supervision. It is helpful if goals and their respective tasks are articulated as specifically as possible. Supervisees like to know for what they will be held accountable, and feel that the contract serves to protect them as well. As one supervisee stated, "It [contracting] is a better way of covering yourself because you know that you said 'that,' and you all agreed on it, so there's no going back about the whole thing." The written (versus oral) contract is particularly helpful in this regard.

Written vs. Oral Contracts

A contract can be either a verbal or a written agreement. Verbal agreements are less time-consuming, and some supervisees might find written contracts to be restrictive and legalistic. Therefore, the supervisory pair should discuss the appropriateness of the written contract before using it. Other than these two considerations, we feel the written contract has advantages over the oral form.It provides a record of what was agreed to. Having goals and expectations documented make them more "real," and helps to minimize "games and hidden agendas that frequently accompany the [supervision]" (Fox and Zischka 1989:110). As one supervisee put it, "[The contract] could be done orally, but having a written contract I think is better because, you know, it means that you can't get out of it. You can't say, 'well, I don't remember,' because you have it written."

As stated earlier, many supervisees experience anxiety about performing up to their supervisor's expectations. Having a formally constructed, written contract can help reduce anxiety related to accountability—students can refer to the document in order to know what is expected of them. The contract helps minimize problems related to memory (e.g., conflicts with supervisors about what was agreed to). It is not uncommon for supervisees to forget the specifics of what they discussed in the meeting by the time they are facing their client. The written contract can help "remind" them of what they planned to do. We found that students often review their contracts just prior to meeting with clients for this purpose. Students reported that this reduced their anxiety about the clinical encounter, because, as one student put it, "I clearly knew what I was supposed to do." This type of presession review helped give focus and served as a mechanism to actively link supervision content to practice behaviors.

Additionally, the written contract helps to demonstrate the process of attaining target goals. At the start of supervision, particularly in student internships, students are aware that certain competencies must be acquired but may be unsure how. By articulating learning objectives and activities on weekly written contracts, students can clearly see how to work toward target goals. Furthermore, this process is beneficial in showing how particular actions relate to certain goals. The contract forces students to link theory to practice, making the leap from conceptual concepts (goals) to the activities (tasks) to attain them.

Finally, written contracts can be reviewed at the time of the evaluation in order to assess which performance areas have been explicitly addressed, which have not, and what progress has been made toward learning goals. Having a collection of written contracts assists the evaluation process because the supervisor and supervisee do not have to rely on memory about selected goals and learning progress.

Collaboration and Power

Contracting is intended to be a collaborative process between the supervisor and the supervisee. True collaboration mobilizes the learner as an active participant in outlining educational objectives and in defining the process of supervision. Such a process is congruent with adult learning principles (Knowles 1972). Although collaboration suggests equal power in the decision-making process, this is obviously not the case. The supervisor has formal authority over the supervisee, and the relationship is highly evaluative in nature. The supervisor ultimately has final say in decisions, and contracting is a process in which the power dynamic is very present. Indeed, it can become a supervisor-driven process if the supervisor is not careful to develop a safe and collaborative relationship with the supervisee. When students feel they have no authentic say about what should be on the contract, their participation is likely to be artificial (e.g., sharing ideas they know the supervisor wants to hear, not what they feel needs to be discussed).

How supervisors use their power during contracting is important. Supervisees learn clinical skills such as contracting by observing how their supervisors implement them during supervision (Shulman 1993). Supervisees may replicate the supervisory power dynamic when they are in positions of power—contracting with clients.

Contracts are a particularly beneficial tool for supervisees in relationships where the supervisor clearly demonstrates that they are in the power (e.g., authoritarian) position. When supervisees are in a vulnerable, one-down position, they are particularly concerned about satisfying their supervisors' expectations. Therefore, clearly articulated expectations can reduce their confusion and anxiety. Supervisors' anxiety about supervisee performance can also be reduced through explicitly spelled out expectations. Indeed, there are times when collaboratively oriented supervisors feel that particular supervisees, perhaps novice or untrustworthy, need greater direction.

The aim of contracting is to achieve mutual agreement through a collaborative process. However, when agreement or collaboration is not attainable, *mutual understanding* can help reduce anxiety and supervisory conflict (Kaiser 1997).

Attends to Preferred Learning Style

Learning can be optimized by attending to the supervisee's preferred style (Kadushin 1992). Learning style refers to the way in which an individual integrates new information. It is widely acknowledged that learners incorporate and organize knowledge in different ways (Fox and Guild 1987). While the ability to learn through a variety of processes is considered to be most effective (Kolb 1985), individuals favor particular ways of dealing with new experiences and information. For example, some learn better by reading about an issue before attempting to work with it, while others prefer to experience the issue firsthand and analyze it later. There is substantial evidence that students more readily integrate and remember new material when taught through their preferred learning style (Dunn 1982; Gardiner 1989).

Learning styles have been conceptualized in many ways (Fox and Guild 1987), mostoften by preferences for behavioral, cognitive, or affective processing. Additionally, conceptualizations organize the handling of new experiences according to preferences for abstract or concrete and sequential or random learning processes (Kolb 1985). (For more on learning style see Bogo and Vayda 1998 and Sweitzer and King 1999.)

It has been suggested that supervisors should work to construct an environment that is most "in sync" with the supervisee's preferred learning style (Fox and Guild 1987; Van Soest and Kruzich 1994). This entails working to "match" the supervisory process to the supervisee. This raises two distinct issues. The first relates to supervisors' need to be aware of their own preferred learning styles in order to avoid imposing a learning process that reflects their own favored mode and not their students' (Brown and Bourne 1996). This places supervisees in a potentially problematic position: simultaneously being evaluated on their learning but unable to utilize learning skills upon which they rely,and therefore risking negative evaluations (e.g., being labeled "resistant" or "not getting it" by the supervisor). Supervisors should take care to examine whether or not supervisory problems are related to learning style (Van Soest and Kruzich 1994).

The second matching issue is whether or not efforts should be made to always accommodate the supervisee's preferred learning style. This can be considered a developmental question. Educators recommend matching the student's preferred styleas helpful in the beginning of the supervisory relationship, but it may not be as the supervisee develops (Van Soest and Kruzich 1994). At the start of the supervisory relationship it is important to build a safe learning environment; however, learning is most effective, and the supervisee is a more powerful learner, if multiple learning styles can be utilized (Kolb 1985; Van Soest and Kruzich 1994). Supervisors should challenge advanced students with learning assignments that force the development of new skills. For example, it is necessary for the well-rounded practitioner to be both conceptual and intuitive. The supervisee who relies on intuition can benefit from challenges to become more conceptual. In turn, the cognitively oriented learner will be a more "whole" practitioner by developing skills of intuition.

There is a pragmatic reason for forcing the acquisition of multiple learning styles: social work practice necessitates it. Clients present practitioners with "new information" throughout the clinical relationship. The clinical world cannot always be constructed to fit the supervisee's preferred style of organizing new information. Practitioners who are not adept at integrating information in multiple ways are likely to miss valuable clinical data. A critical goal of supervision is to develop the well-rounded practitioner. Attending to learning styles is a valuable strategy for working toward this objective.

Each person brings to supervision her or his unique learning preferences, and therefore, supervision methods and styles should be individualized (Davenport and Davenport 1988; Fox and Guild 1987; Kadushin 1992). Knowledge of learning styles makes it "truly possible 'to start where the worker is' in designing the most individualized instructive method for doing effective work" (Fox and Guild 1987:77). We recommend that supervisors raise (and explain if needed) the concept of preferred learning styles and ask supervisees how they learn best. This should be an ongoing process in which the supervisor and supervisee assess what is and is not working in terms of the supervisee's learning.

Offers a Range of Learning Opportunities

Educational supervision works best when there are multiple opportunities for learning (Alperin 1998; Showers 1988) and diverse assignments (Fortune and Abramson 1993; Fortune et al. 1985; Raskin 1982). Supervisees particularly appreciate the chance to experience a range of assignments, to work with multiple populations and social problems, and to use a variety of practice methods (e.g., psychodynamic, cognitive, brief solution-focus) and modalities (e.g., individual, family, group, community organization). The student in an agency that treats only one social condition (e.g., substance abuse, sexual abuse) and has rigid rules about which methods are to be used will likely be less satisfied than the student in an agency that offers choices. For example, one study showed that expansion of learning opportunities through multiple supervisors was linked to greater satisfaction with the practicum (Alperin 1998).

Perhaps most important, supervisees want their learning assignments and opportunities to be relevant to their educational and practice objectives (Alperin 1998) and career goals (Showers 1988). Prior to accepting someone for placement or hire, it is necessary to evaluate whether or not an agency can offer the range and type of learning experiences they want. Being involved in the selection and of learning assignments is also meaningful to supervisees. Having input into the formulation of learning assignments increases their satisfaction (Fortune et al. 1985).

Links Clinical Encounters to Learning Goals

Much supervision time is dedicated to case exploration and problem solving (Basso 1987). When clinical encounters are not explicitly linked to learning objectives, supervision becomes the "case of the week" approach, and the educational focus is lost. Although learning does occur in this type of supervision, it is not systematic. Furthermore, when learning goals are not at the fore of the supervisory process, the unspoken message to the supervisee is that their learning is not a central concern. Hence, case assessment and planning should be consistently and directly linked to learning goals.

Links Classroom and Field

In student supervision, linking classroom and field work is an important but challenging task. Indeed, tying together and integrating classroom and practicum experiences has been repeatedly identified as a desirable goal (Sheafor and Jenkins 1982; Walden and Brown 1985; Vayda and Bogo 1991), but a seemingly elusive one (Raskin 1994; Jenkins and Sheafor 1982). Abstract classroom and textbook knowledge can be difficult for students to apply in actual practice situations, and in turn, it is not always clear how clinical encounters connect to ideas discussed in the classroom. The common approach to linking the two areas is class assignments through which students apply course content to field experiences. Additionally, some supervisors review students' course syllabi in order to try to match learning goals. While these efforts to link classroom and field experiences are helpful, they are almost never systematic.

The challenge of linking classroom and practicum education is complicated by two issues: they take place in different physical settings and they involve distinct learning processes. Because class and field work occur in separate environments, they typically focus on different areas of learning, and unfortunately, there is often not active communication between the instructor and supervisor. At times, classroom learning does not have immediate relevance for the student, or issues may come up in supervision that have not been addressed in the classroom. For example, instructors commonly raise the clinical concept of "termination" at the end of the semester. However, students often encounter many endings with clients prior to the end of the school term.

Classroom learning tends to emphasize cognitive development through the provision of abstract theoretical information, which students learn to apply in order to make sense of clinical phenomena—a deductive process (Jenkins and Sheafor 1982). In contrast, field learning is an experiential exercise in which students are challenged to consider how collected, disparate pieces of information relate to practice theory—an inductive process (Jenkins and Sheafor 1982). Supervisees are challenged to develop both inductive and deductive skills. As discussed earlier, learners may demonstrate a preference for one approach over the other. However, challenging and assisting them to develop both is likely to produce a better rounded learner and practitioner.

At present, most schools use an articulated approach (Jenkins and Sheafor 1982), which attempts to actively connect classroom and field, but there is much concern that successful linking is not being consistently achieved (Bogo and Power 1992; Raskin 1994; Tolson and Kopp 1988). This may not be a realistic approach in today's economy, which does not permit the investment of time needed to produce a systematic and sequenced integration of classroom and field (Bogo and Vayda 1998; Tolson and Kopp 1988). For example, it has been suggested that more systematic integration of the two areas can be attained through the use of faculty practicum instructors (DeJong 1975; Lammert and Hagen 1975). However, using school faculty to perform field instruction duties is generally considered financially costly for the university.

The successful integration of classroom and field education requires clearly defined learning goals that are agreeable to both school faculty and field supervisors (Jenkins and Sheafor 1982). The use of weekly contracting in the field, including school-defined objectives, holds promise as a cost-effective, straightforward method (Caspi 1997). Nevertheless, the systematic linking of classroom and field work remains a desirable but challenging goal in student supervision (Sheafor and Jenkins 1982; Raskin 1994).

Recognizes the Supervisor as Role Model

The supervisor should be recognized as a role model. Supervisees watch their supervisors carefully (Munson 1993), observing how they interact with staff, with clients, and with the supervisees themselves. They not only observe their supervisors' behaviors but also imitate them. It is not uncommon for supervisees to follow their supervisor's lead and use similar behaviors with other staff and, perhaps to a greater degree, with clients. Therefore, supervisors must take care to deliberately model professional and appropriate behaviors.

Many authors suggest that a central role for the supervisor is that of a role model (Bogo 1993), and supervisors themselves perceive this to be an important supervisory function (Freeman and Hansen 1995). How they interact with supervisees provides cues about professional social work behaviors. By observing their supervisor's "professional behaviors and attitudes . . . students learn experientially about relationship theory and skill" (Bogo 1993:32), knowledge they can use in their client relationships. Additionally, the supervisee "learns such skills as contracting, tuning-in, empathy, confrontation, dealing with authority, and so forth, as much by his or her interacting with the supervisor as by examining his or her own practice with clients" (Beless 1993). Supervisors can also model professional behaviors through role plays and demonstrations of how to use graphic materials such as genograms and ecomaps.

Because supervisees closely monitor and imitate their supervisors' behaviors, it is especially important that supervisors are aware of their actions and able to model professional behaviors, particularly sensitive handling of inherent hierarchical issues during the formation and maintenance of a productive relationship (Beless 1993). When they are in the practitioner role, supervisees are in the power position, and they must develop skills in handling such relationships. An ideal opportunity to demonstrate these skills is during the evaluation process, when supervision hierarchy is most visible.

Because the supervisory and clinical relationships are quite similar in regard to process, how supervisors interact with supervisees and clients teaches the supervisee how to interact with their own clients. The two relationships are interdependent; what occurs in one has direct impact on what occurs in the other—even covert and undiscussed behaviors (e.g., emotional reactions). The dynamics of the clinical relationship can also be mirrored in the supervisory setting. The idea that the relationships are interdependent and often mirror each other is recognized and referred to in the literature as "parallel process."

Attends to Parallel Process

The supervisory and clinical relationships are alike (Arlow 1963; Haley 1976; Kahn 1979; Reid 1984; Storm and Heath 1985). The concept of parallel process, however, is not simply the idea that the two relationships are similar but that they are linked (Kadushin 1992). Parallel process means that what is occurring in one relationship happens because of what is occurring in the other.

Specifically, parallel process refers to "the simultaneous emergence of similar emotional difficulties in the relationship between social worker and client, social worker and supervisor, and postulates a link between these two relationships, whereby emotions generated in one are acted out in the other" (Kahn 1979:521). The traditional view of parallel process has a psychodynamic orientation and emphasizes the influence of the client's emotional world (i.e., transference) on the supervisory relationship (Kahn 1979;

Wall 1994). The supervisee's countertransferential reactions are of particular interest. In the traditional view, supervisees may unconsciously respond to a client's emotional struggle by acting it out with their supervisor. Thus, the feelings triggered in the supervisor give diagnostic insights about what is occurring between the supervisee and the client.

It is the supervisor's task to identify when parallel process is operating so that it can be addressed. Cues include atypical supervisee behaviors, an impasse in the supervisory relationship, and in particular, instances when usual exploration of case dynamics is strained (Kahn 1979). After parallel process has been identified, the supervisor should bring it to the supervisee's attention at the time it occurs, discuss it openly with the aim of understanding and resolving it, and evaluate the effect on the supervisee's work with the client (Kahn 1979).

In the traditional view, parallel process begins with the client and is followed by a series of reciprocal influences (e.g., the supervisor's reaction to the supervisee being reenacted by the supervisee with the client). More current perspectives take a broader view of the concept and emphasize interactional processes that can start with any of the participants (Shulman 1993; Wall 1994). Reflecting this view, we strongly encourage supervisors to consider their own role in the origin of parallel process. After all, it is the supervisor who holds the greatest power and thereby is most able to influence the relationships. For example, a client who is not responding to treatment can be labeled "resistant" by a frustrated practitioner. The practitioner may then reenact the dynamic by not responding to the supervisor's suggestions (e.g., by saying each has been tried and failed), causing frustration in the supervisor. An alternate view should be considered: that the client's resistance is a reaction to the supervisee's taking a directive (rather than client-centered) stance—one modeled by the directive supervisor. Supervisors and supervisees should be careful to avoid blaming the client for impasses.

Attending to and addressing parallel process in supervision provides an excellent opportunity for students and supervisors to learn more about themselves and their clients (Wall 1994), and to improve their practice. During supervision meetings, supervisees can discover *in vivo* what the client may be experiencing, hence gaining insight about how to address clinical difficulties. In turn, by observing supervisees' behaviors, supervisors can learn about how their own behaviors contribute to the process (and to supervisory difficulties). Furthermore, because supervisory and clinical processes are analogous, the supervisor can teach clinical behaviors to the supervisee by implementing them in the supervisory relationship. For example, Shulman (1993) promotes employing clinical techniques such as tuning in, confrontation, moving from general to specific, and reaching into silences for supervision, for the purposes of teaching those skills and for conducting productive supervision. This reflects the importance of supervisors as role models whose behaviors will likely be implemented by supervisees in clinical encounters.

Recognizes Supervision As a Developmental Process

As supervision progresses, supervisees grow. Their focus and needs change. Indeed, supervisee growth has been conceptualized in terms of stages of development (Collins 1993; Dawson 1975; Hess 1986; Kadushin 1992; Kerson 1994; Reynolds 1942; Saari 1989). Supervisees are considered to "move through a series of identifiable, characteristic stages" as they learn to be, or mature as, social workers (Kadushin 1992:214). This challenges supervisors to alter their approaches in response to the supervisee's changing needs (Bogo 1983; Hess 1986; Kadushin 1992; Walther and Mason 1994).

In the beginning stages of development, supervisees need much direction. They typically are in need of much information about the agency, its policies and procedures, and methods of treatment. They may also require direction about how to perform basic clinical functions. Therefore, the supervisor has to be highly directive and provide didactic instruction (Kadushin 1992). Furthermore, new supervisees typically have unrealistic expectations about their abilities to change clients. As they learn about their limitations, they will need the supervisor to provide support.

As students progress, their dependency on their supervisors for direction decreases. The supervisory relationship becomes less hierarchical and more egalitarian, and the supervisor is challenged to take a more reactive than directive stance (Kadushin 1992). As supervisees develop, they become more open to self-examination and self-discovery, and more able to engage in autonomous practice. In short, the developmental process involves the supervisee changing from a highly dependent, internally focused neophyte into an autonomous, client-centered practitioner (Dawson 1975; Kadushin 1992). In turn, the supervisor must move from a highly directive, instructional, and structured approach to one that is flexible, involves the sharing and exploration of ideas, and allows the supervisee to be self-directed.

Being able to modify one's approach to match the supervisee's is a challenging aspect of providing educational supervision. The supervisor must be able to assess where the supervisee is in their development, and attempt to adjust their approach accordingly. This is not an easy task. Supervisors have preferred ways of operating, and supervisees may desire an approach that does not fit with their developmental level. For example, we have encountered new students who assess themselves as being able to operate independently, and therefore suggest they want little supervisor involvement. Conversely, we have worked with seasoned practitioners who initially indicate they need a great deal of direction. In both situations, the supervisor is in a quandary: should he or she take the supervisee's desired supervision approach, or an approach in line with the supervisee's developmental level?

The degree of supervisor direction and student autonomy should be evaluated collaboratively as the supervisory relationship progresses. It is important to remember that not only the student but also the supervisor and the supervisory relationship go through stages of development (Hess 1986). Indeed, the characteristics, demands, and issues of the supervisory relationship differ according to its beginning, middle, or end stage. Ideally, as the supervisor and supervisee become more familiar with each other, trust develops, allowing a deeper exploration of the supervisee's work and increasingly open discussion of supervision issues.

It is helpful to recognize supervision as a developmental process for additional reasons. Supervisors familiar with this process are better able to normalize particular supervisee experiences. For example, it is common for students who are close to graduation to have anxiety about their ability to obtain and perform in future jobs. Sensitivity to such stages is helpful in creating and maintaining a positive supervisory relationship, as illustrated in the following vignette:

> Barbara felt that Wendy had been performing well at her work and in supervision until the first week in January. At that time, Wendy seemed to withdraw from supervision and showed less motivation for practicum-related activities. When Barbara asked her about the change in her behavior, Wendy was reluctant to talk about it, saying, "I am just sad that the holiday is over." Barbara, who had been supervising graduate practicum students for many years, suspected that Wendy might be going through a developmental phase that she had encountered with many of her previous students. Barbara had observed that many students in their first year of practicum experience

a period of ambivalence about their choice to enter social work. This usually occurs soon after the school's winter break, when the student has had time away from the chaos of the first semester and can reflect upon their experiences. Indeed, a sign for Barbara that this might be the problem was the timing of Wendy's "motivational dip."

Drawing upon her knowledge of student development, Barbara said to Wendy, "Many of my students have told me that at about this time of the year they experience mixed feelings about their choice to be in graduate school, and whether or not social work is truly for them." She then asked, "I was wondering if perhaps you were having some of those feelings as well?" Wendy, thinking her supervisor was just about the most intuitive person alive, answered that indeed she had been struggling with feelings of ambivalence, and was not ready to "jump back in" until she had sorted it out. Barbara replied, "I think it is quite normal to experience some ambivalence about a major life choice, particularly now, after you have had some time to try it out." Wendy was relieved to hear that what she had thought was a personal crisis about a career choice was in fact something quite common for first-year students.

This discussion substantially reduced Wendy's anxiety and increased her motivation for supervision. She also appreciated her supervisor's sensitivity to her developmental struggle, and that Barbara had not negatively evaluated her. Barbara also noted that Wendy was more open about sharing her practicum and school-related anxieties.

Consideration of student behaviors in the context of their development can help to minimize problematic supervisory encounters. Furthermore, it enables supervisors to use relationship-building skills such as tuning in and normalizing students' affective responses.

Finally, attending to developmental process is helpful in performing evaluations. Supervisors and supervisees often question if the supervisee is "where they should be." Being able to assess progress is important for determining the approach the supervisor should take to establish an appropriate balance between student autonomy and dependence.

Balances Autonomy and Dependence

A constant question for supervisors involves determining to what degree a supervisee can perform autonomously. Supervisees also struggle with this issue, wanting to be both independent of and able to rely on the supervisor (Reynolds 1942). The question is complex because it involves issues of competence, approval, and authority. Supervisees want to appear competent and be approved of by their supervisor (i.e., authority figure), and may act overly independent or dependent. It is not uncommon for new supervisees to try to impress their supervisors by trying to act independently.

The balance of autonomy and dependence should be carefully negotiated by the supervisor and supervisee with the aim of reaching a mutually agreed-upon structure. This balance should be evaluated throughout the supervisory encounter, because as students develop, their needs for direction change.

While the issue is quite complex, the following simple rule can be helpful: It is easier to let out than to draw in the reins. This unflattering metaphor aside, consider what happens when a supervisor and supervisee agree to a fairly autonomous position for the supervisee, and performance is poor. This necessitates increased structure and supervisor involvement. Furthermore, the supervisor is forced to place greater restrictions on the supervisee's independence—something that runs opposite to student development and progress. In short, it is experienced as a punishment.

Now consider the opposite scenario. A supervisor and supervisee agree to an arrangement in which their is a high level of structure, supervisor involvement, and supervisee dependence, and the supervisee's performance is good. This means that the supervisory pair can modify the arrangement to allow more autonomy—something that is consistent with supervisee development. In this case, the change in the relationship in terms of autonomy and dependence is for positive reasons. It always feels better to move forward than to go backward, for both the supervisor and the supervisee.

Is Supported by the Environment

Educational supervision does not occur in a vacuum. The learning environment extends beyond the supervisory relationship and occurs within contextual considerations that include the agency, the community, the law, relationships to other agencies, external funding and accrediting bodies, and, in student supervision, the school (Kerson 1994). In order for educational supervision to be most effective, it must be supported by these various systems. Outside of the supervisory relationship, the agency provides the most immediate environment for supervision, and thus has great impact on its success. This is particularly true in supervision of student interns.

An agency that serves as a host site for field interns must be committed to the educational process (Selig 1982). First, the agency must view the intern as a learner, not inexpensive staff. The priority should be the student's needs, not the agency's. This is not to say that agencies do not benefit from having student interns. Field placements provide valuable growth experiences for agency staff. Often the best way to improve one's own practice is by having to teach it to another. Supervising an intern is also a good opportunity to become more connected with the school, have interaction with faculty, and learn about new developments in the field. Additionally, some prestige is associated with taking on supervisory functions. Furthermore, interns do provide services, contribute fresh ways of looking at agency and client population issues, and often initiate new programs (e.g., therapy groups, agency flyers).

This said, agencies should remember that practicum activities require a large investment of time. Staff serving as student supervisors must be prepared to meet with students a minimum of one hour each week for individual conferences, field questions outside the scheduled supervision meetings, complete paperwork and review process recordings, perform formal evaluations, and for many, attend school-based seminars—all highly time-consuming tasks.

Agency administrators must be prepared to provide the necessary resources to serve as a practicum site. Staff workload is a serious consideration. Although the practice is uncommon, staff asked to supervise interns should be allowed to modify their schedules to accommodate such activities. Typically, agencies ask already overwhelmed staff to add field instruction duties to their busy schedules. Instead, it is best if the agency can support reductions in caseload to allow for proper supervision of a student.

Support for field educational activities should be secured from the staff prior to agreeing to take interns. If staff are not welcoming, the student and the agency will suffer. It is unfair to put a student in the position of having to negotiate an unfriendly system where learning takes a backseat to survival. Interns should not be taken on without the awareness of agency staff (Shulman 1993).

The agency must see itself as a teaching center where multiple opportunities for learning are provided. This may mean a diversity of clinical assignments such as providing counseling with individuals, families, and groups;

exposure to a variety of populations diverse in terms of age, ethnicity, sexual orientation and gender; and the opportunity to engage in policy-formulation activities such as lobbying for legislation or reviewing child-placement protocol.

Finally, the agency should ensure that the physical structures are in place for hosting a field intern. Office space is often limited and consideration of where a student can see clients, do paperwork, and make phone calls is important. Disruption to staff, particularly when it involves an infringement of space, is likely to result in resentment toward the student, the field instructor, and the agency.

Attends to Supervisee Affective Experiences

Educational supervision is most effective when it is supportive and attends to supervisee affective experiences. Indeed, provision of support is considered a major supervisory function (Kadushin 1992). As discussed in the section on feedback, supervision is carried out by human beings who experience a wide range of emotional reactions to various aspects of the encounter. Therefore, it is important that affective experiences be acknowledged and that the supervisor be able to give support.

There seems to be some confusion regarding the degree to which supervisors are providing support. While there is indication that instructors are actively doing this (Johnston, Rooney, and Reitmeir 1991), there is also evidence that they have a "tendency . . . to neglect the emotive aspects of student learning" (Siddle and Wilson 1984:11). This is of concern because research suggests that socioemotional factors (i.e., emotional support) are of greater influence than task-related aspects (e.g., supervisor's practice knowledge and ability to train the student) on student satisfaction with the supervisor (Baker and Smith 1987). Furthermore, a positive instructional relationship based on the supervisor's availability and provision of emotional support has been found to advance student learning and increase satisfaction (Fortune and Abramson 1993). In turn, unsupportive supervision has been found to be offensive to students (Rosenblatt and Mayer 1975).

Taking time to give support and address supervisee anxiety has a number of benefits. First, it sends the message to supervisees that their supervisors are genuinely concerned about their welfare. This is crucial in building a safe, trusting, and open learning environment. Second, it lets supervisees know that discussing affective responses is acceptable. Much can be learned about social work practice through discussion of affective responses—e.g., self awareness. Third, when their anxiety becomes too high, supervisees are no longer able to do the work at hand, including attending to the supervisory conference. Indeed, overwhelming anxiety interferes with learning (Rompf, Royse, and Dhooper 1993). Addressing anxiety is helpful in reducing it to a manageable level. Fourth, by giving support, supervisors can model this behavior and demonstrate effective ways to reduce anxiety.

Giving support should not be confused with "hand-holding" or "spoon-feeding" (Matorin 1979:152). Supervisees encounter many uncomfortable moments in which they experience anxiety about carrying out certain actions with clients (e.g., confronting a parent about child abuse, asking about sexual abuse history). New social workers are particularly prone to this type of anxiety because they often feel they do not possess appropriate clinical sophistication. However, they should not be automatically released from taking a stress-producing action simply because they fear it. Provision of support includes making performance demands (Matorin 1979) while attending to and supporting affective responses (Norman 1987).

The process of confronting fears and carrying out difficult clinical tasks is necessary for developing skills and feeling competent as a practitioner. Protecting supervisees from challenging encounters essentially disables them. It conveys that they are not capable of handling difficult tasks and creates unnecessary dependency on the supervisor. Indeed, such an approach prevents supervisees from learning to handle difficult situations on their own and becoming autonomous practitioners.

However, there are times when giving support may mean temporarily intervening on the supervisee's behalf. Some clinical situations are so complex or "high risk" that they far surpass the new social worker's ability to handle them independently. After careful consideration of the situation, supervisors and supervisees should together develop a plan of intervention. Even if they decide that the supervisor will temporarily take over the case, the supervisee should remain involved in treatment planning in order to learn how the supervisor intends to address the situation. Supervisors can intervene on a few different levels. Two examples include offering support by being present for the clinical encounter but not taking charge of it, and conducting the session with the supervisee observing.

It is not uncommon for cases to raise personal issues for supervisees that hamper their ability to perform clinical functions. It is important that supervisors separate anxiety about not having the skill to perform a task from stress related to personal history. Supervisors can demonstrate support by normalizing and validating personal reactions to clinical work, by helping the supervisee to separate client issues from their own, by helping the supervisee to consider strategies for working with the issue (e.g., using self-talk to get through difficult encounters), and by being open to changing practitioners, if necessary. A particularly helpful show of support is remaining flexible about the supervisee's work schedule. Some personal matters are temporary (e.g., personal crises) and no longer interfere after a brief period of time has passed. The following example illustrates this point:

> Erin came to supervision looking quite agitated. When her supervisor, Dan, asked her what was wrong, she responded that she was having some difficulties at home, but that she was "okay" and was anxious to discuss a case. Dan, taking Erin's lead, asked about the case. During their discussion, it was obvious to Dan that Erin was having difficulty staying focused. He shared this observation with her, and she agreed. She then started crying and said that her father had just had a major heart attack and was in the hospital. Demonstrating support, Dan responded to her with empathy and offered to reschedule the supervision meeting so that she could join her father in the hospital. At first, Erin refused, saying that it would "not be professional" to allow personal matters to interfere with her work. Dan normalized her reaction by saying, "It would be difficult for anyone to attend to supervision during such a stressful time. It may be unreasonable to think that we can actually shut off personal crises when we come to work. We can meet another time when you are in a better place. Right now I think it is important for you to be with your father." Erin was very relieved, and said that she wanted to make up the time she would be missing. She also shared at a later meeting that Dan's understanding and flexibility greatly strengthened her feelings about her job. She said that at her last agency, employees were penalized for any absences—even family losses.

To have continued the supervision meeting under such circumstances would have been useless and potentially damaging. Erin and Dan would simply have been pretending to be engaged in supervision activities, when Erin's attention was clearly elsewhere. The process would have been inauthentic, and neither would benefited from it. Furthermore, Erin's lack of focus could have led to problematic clinical encounters, and eventually to negative evaluations of performance. In sum, it is important to remember that supervisees are human, experience strong emotional reactions to both professional and personal experiences, and often need support from their supervisors.

Attends to the Supervisory Relationship

Perhaps the most important feature of effective educational supervision is a positive supervisory relationship. Indeed, this is considered to be at the center of the educational process in supervision (Bogo 1993; Lowy 1983; Manis 1979; Nisivoccia 1990; Norman 1987; Siporin 1982). It is within this relationship that the supervisee takes risks associated with learning, including trying out new behaviors, asking questions, revealing vulnerabilities, sharing mistakes, seeking evaluation of performance, remaining open to critical feedback, opening up to new ways of knowing, and becoming self-aware. In order to take these risks, supervisees must trust their supervisors (Kaiser 1997). Learning is most productive when the supervisory relationship is good. In turn, a bad supervisory relationship will likely result in low motivation for learning, games of power (Hawthorne 1975; Kadushin 1968), and lack of respect for information given or received by the participants. Therefore, it is critical that both the supervisor and the supervisee strive to create a productive learning experience through responsible and respectful behaviors and by actively attending to the supervisory relationship. Indeed, satisfaction with supervision is linked to perceptions of the supervisory relationship (Bogo and Power 1992; Fortune et al. 1985; Kadushin 1991; Tolson and Kopp 1988).

What steps can a supervisor take to build and maintain positive and productive supervisory relationships? In our view, systematic implementation of the above principles of effective educational supervision. Although consistent use of these principles is important, the supervisory relationship is emotionally laden, dynamic, and complex, and therefore challenging. Furthermore, implementation of these principles must attend to cultural diversity considerations (taken up in chapter 4). Developing and preserving a positive supervisory relationship requires a thorough understanding of its many facets. Because of its centrality to the supervisory process, the supervisory relationship and its various components are reviewed in depth in the next chapter.

4 The Supervisory Relationship

This chapter continues the discussion of features of effective educational supervision, focusing particularly on the relationship between the supervisor and the supervisee. This relationship is, perhaps, the most critical part of the learning experience. An abundance of literature discusses its importance (Bogo 1993: Fortune et al. 1985; Fortune and Abramson 1993; Webb 1988).

The supervisory relationship has a tremendous impact on the development of the supervisee and the effectiveness of supervision. In simple terms, a positive relationship is likely to result in a productive learning experience, and a poor relationship is likely to result in a negative and less productive experience. Therefore, supervisors should do their best to implement strategies to maintain a productive supervisory relationship: a context in which the supervisee is challenged to try out new skills, attitudes, and interpersonal behaviors—essentially, to take chances. The supervisee needs to feel comfortable to be open, ask questions, and risk exposing him- or herself (Gitterman 1989). This can only be accomplished in a trusting, straightforward, and respectful learning environment.

This chapter presents strategies for promoting a positive supervisory relationship. It begins with an overview of the centrality of the supervisor-supervisee relationship, considers it as an interdependent social system, discusses the importance of attending to the affective components of supervision, and promotes open discussion of the supervisory relationship as a way to teach and learn about relationships and to resolve relational difficulties.

The boundary of supervision and therapy is examined, and principles are put forth for preventing boundary transgressions. In addition, the supervisory relationship is presented as a tool for teaching about difference and multiculturalism. The chapter ends with discussion of the separate affective experiences of the supervisee and the supervisor and considers anxiety as a common feature of supervision.

The Supervisor-Supervisee Relationship: An Overview

A positive and trusting supervisory relationship is considered to be at the center of the supervision process (Bogo 1993; Lowy 1983; Manis 1979; Nisivoccia 1990;, Norman 1987; Siporin 1982). A growing body of empirical studies demonstrates that the supervisory relationship has notable impact the supervisee's learning (Bogo 1993), practice orientation (Webb 1988), and satisfaction (Fortune et al. 1985). Indeed, there is evidence that the strength of the relationship is closely related to supervisee perceptions of their practicum experience (Fortune and Abramson 1993). In other words, supervisees who have good relationships are more likely to judge their supervision experiences positively.

The supervisory relationship centers around the instrumental functions of engaging in work and supervision, which include such activities as selecting learning objectives, problem-solving cases, and performing evaluations. Underlying this process is the interpersonal nature of the relationship between the supervisor and the supervisee, including the feelings each brings to the encounter, how they are manifested, and whether or not they are discussed. Considering the instrumental and interpersonal functions of supervision separately is helpful in developing strategies for making the most of the supervisory experience.

Instrumental and Interpersonal Functions

Social work educators have organized the various aspects of the supervisory relationship into two categories: instrumental and interpersonal. These have also been referred to, respectively, as "task" and "expressive" behaviors (Ellison 1994) and "task development" and "emotional support" (Kadushin 1992). "Task behaviors refer to the educational and administrative functions . . . while expressive behaviors reflect the interpersonal and supportive functions" (Ellison 1994:15). Optimally, both are addressed in the relationship (Ellison 1994: Hagen 1989: Kadushin 1992). However, there seems to be some confusion regarding the degree to which supervisors are providing support. While there is some indication that they are actively doing this (Johnston, Rooney, and Reitmeir 1991), there is also evidence that supervisors have a "tendency . . . to neglect the emotive aspects of supervisee learning" (Siddle and Wilson 1984:11), and that the "affective components are less clearly understood" (Norman 1987:374). This is of concern because research suggests that socioemotional factors (e.g., emotional support) have greater influence than task-related aspects (e.g., supervisor practice knowledge and ability to train) of the supervisory relationship on student satisfaction with the supervisor (Baker and Smith 1987). In addition, a positive instructional relationship based on the supervisor's availability and provision of emotional support has been found to advance supervisee learning and increase satisfaction with the practicum (Fortune and Abramson 1993). Unsupportive supervision has been found to be offensive to supervisees (Rosenblatt and Mayer 1975).

While important, the affective components of supervision encompass more than the provision of emotional support. The "relationship" entails the whole "nature of the emotional interaction" between the supervisor and the supervisee (Kadushin 1992:200). This includes who they are as individuals (i.e., personality). Each brings their individual affective states into the relationship, and each experiences emotions related to the other. The instrumental functions of supervision are not carried out by two robots but by human beings who experience feelings. Thus, successful implementation of instrumental activities is largely linked to the state of the interpersonal aspect of the relationship. A supervisee who is irritated by or lacks respect for the supervisor will not be motivated to learn from that person (Kadushin 1992). In turn, the supervisor who is turned off by a student is unlikely to invest what may be needed to create a productive learning environment.

As a result, the affective experiences of supervisee and supervisor can emerge as obstacles to productive supervision. Emotional reactions to clinical work and to supervision itself should be closely monitored and addressed appropriately. Finally, a good supervision model must consider and give direction to both the instrumental and the affective aspects of supervision. TCS provides guidelines to ensure that both are addressed. Although the model centers around target goal attainment and task implementation, it also includes steps dedicated to addressing the interpersonal component of the supervisory relationship.

Because TCS clearly explicates the instrumental functions of the supervisory relationship, problems during implementation of these steps may be due to difficulties in the interpersonal domain. In order to more fully understand the supervisory relationship, it is helpful to separate its interpersonal functions into three parts: the relationship itself, the person of the supervisee, and the person of the supervisor.

The Relationship

The interaction that occurs between the supervisor and supervisee, or the supervisory relationship, can be considered as an entity in itself that needs to be monitored and attended to. This relationship provides the context for learning and quality work. It represents the emotional and interpersonal dynamics that underlie the process of carrying out the instrumental functions of supervision. Supervisory relationships are complex and often emotionally intense experiences. Although they are positive most of the time, conflict is also a common characteristic. .Furthermore, the relationship is a place where issues related to authority are likely to emerge for both the supervisee and the supervisor (Hawthorne 1975; Kadushin 1968). How successes and conflicts emerge and are handled can be a learning experience about helping relationships (e.g., practitioner-client) (Bogo 1993). Indeed, the supervisory relationship can be used as a teaching-learning tool and as a place for self-discovery. Strategies for promoting a positive relationship are presented here, beginning with a discussion of the relationship as an open social system.

The Relationship as a Social System

When considering the interpersonal aspects of the supervisory encounter, it is helpful to view the relationship as a social system (Kadushin 1992). Although it is a subsystem of a larger social system that can include the agency, the client population, funding sources, the school (in internship arrangements), and the community in which it takes place (Kerson 1994), the supervisor-supervisee relationship is at the center of the supervision process. Each person has roles and responsibilities in keeping it trusting and openand in attaining supervisory objectives. Indeed, both must work to ensure the "smooth functioning of the system itself" (Judah 1982:144). The actions of one directly influence the behavior of the other in reciprocal fashion.

Interdependence

The supervisory relationship is interdependent in that the supervisor and supervisee enter into a collaborative process aimed at attaining a particular set of objectives. In order to achieve these objectives, they must work together. Whether the relationship is experienced as positive or negative depends on how both participate. Therefore, both have a responsibility to promote a productive learning environment. In turn, when a negative supervisory relationship emerges, both have a role in its development—recognizing, of course, that a power imbalance is present. However, the expression, "it takes two to tango" applies to supervisory relationships.

The interdependent nature of the supervisory relationship is clear in how it plays out in the moment-by-moment interaction of the encounter. As with any human interaction, supervisory communication does not consist of random behaviors. Rather, it is organized and follows a series of steps, with each person responding to the behavior just exhibited by the other. Each time the supervisee says or does something, the supervisor must choose from a range of potential responses. For example, if a supervisee should roll their eyes as the supervisor makes a suggestion, the supervisor can respond in many ways, including chastising the supervisee, verbally noting the nonverbal behavior, and making an interpretation of the behavior's underlying meaning or ignoring it altogether. Indeed, it is impossible not to respond—both ignoring and silence are responses that convey messages (e.g., "it is acceptable to roll your eyes when I speak").

Just as the supervisor has many options to choose from when responding to particular supervisee behaviors, so does the supervisee when considering how to react to the supervisor's behaviors. For example, if a supervisor gives critical feedback, the supervisee can choose to accept the information, ask questions to clarify feedback, dismiss the feedback, change the subject of the conversation, argue that the supervisor is wrong, remain silent, agree outwardly while internally disagreeing, or attempt to apply it directly to another case. Each participant's behavior is very much related to the context of the supervisory relationship. Therefore, when difficulties emerge in that context, both have a role in their development. Problems and successes between the supervisor and the supervisee do not spontaneously appear but develop and are maintained via interactional sequences. There is a point in the sequence where either can intentionally make efforts to behave in a way that will ameliorate the conflict. For example, in the situation above of the supervisee rolling their eyes when the supervisor speaks, the supervisor can address it directly and inquire about dissatisfaction in the relationship. This is likely be more beneficial in maintaining a productive relationship than ignoring the behavior. Again, just as it takes both parties to make a relationship positive, it takes both to make it negative.

Lack of regard for the interdependent nature of the relationship is likely to result in unidirectional blaming of the other for difficulties that arise. This makes resolution of frustrations troublesome. All relationships are likely to experience conflict, so this is a normal and expected part of supervision. With this in mind, it is helpful to openly discuss and resolve relational conflict, recognizing that both have a role in the difficulty. However, both do not have equal power. Because supervisors are in a position of authority, they have greater responsibility for attending to the interpersonal facet of the supervisory relationship.

Power and Relational Responsibility

As discussed in chapter 3, supervisors are in a position of authority in which they are charged with evaluating the supervisee's performance. Furthermore, they often have the power to impose penalties, if they choose. We share the opinion (Bogo 1993; Martin and Alper 1989; Judah 1982) that this position of power suggests that supervisors have a greater responsibility to take steps toward building positive relationships. Supervisees do not always feel safe to directly address supervision-related problems, fearing negative consequences. Such fears are well founded, as it is not uncommon for supervisors to dismiss their own role in relationship difficulties, placing the blame fully on the supervisee, frequently with negative evaluations such as, "supervisee is unable to effectively use supervision," "supervisee is not open to feedback," or even more serious, "supervisee is oppositional, resistive to learning, and should consider that social work may not be an appropriate profession." While it is true that some supervisees and agency hires are not ready to be social workers, it is strongly recommended that supervisors consider their own role in performance difficulties before making such life-altering determinations.

Remaining aware of and sharing one's own role in conflict is modeling a responsible use of power. Supervisees watch supervisors very carefully (Munson 1993) and emulate their behaviors. How supervisors model the use of power in the supervisory relationship has important implications: how the supervisor interacts with the supervisee may be replicated by the supervisee in work with clients. Indeed, it is important for supervisors to monitor their use of power in the relationship and model open and empowering styles (Dore 1994; Lazzari 1991) rather than punitive or avoidant ones (Hawthorne 1975).

Just as supervisors should avoid assigning complete blame for difficulties on students, supervisees should take care not to dismiss their own role in poor supervision experiences. When unhappy with supervision, supervisees are responsible for taking mature steps to address the problems. A typical negative supervisee behavior that contributes to an ongoing poor supervisory relationship is to complain about supervision to everyone but the supervisor. Supervisees have a responsibility, as adult learners, to address supervision problems openly, directly, and appropriately (i.e., with respect and a genuine wish to improve the situation—not as an excuse to lash out against the supervisor). However, this may not always be safe to do. Staff supervisees must weigh their own survival (i.e., not being dismissed from employment), client care, their learning, and the quality of their work before approaching (or confronting) supervisors. If, after they attempt to discuss relationship problems rationally, difficulties remain, supervisees may need to consider alternate approaches. For example, social work interns can consult with their school faculty liaisons. Staff may find it helpful to brainstorm methods for handling the situation with other staff or hired "outside" consultants.

In our experience, most supervisors are well intentioned. They very much want to do the best for their supervisees, and their frustrations are often related to feeling that relationship difficulties are preventing this. We believe that most supervisors would be open to constructive and direct discussion of their supervisory practice and the nature of their relationship with the supervisee.

In sum, an individual's behavior should not be considered as existing in a vacuum. Although supervisors must take the lead, both participants in the encounter are accountable for creating a productive learning environment. This suggests that supervisees are also responsible for initiating and taking part in learning and supervisory relationship activities. It is easy for either to blame the other for a negative relationship. But to ignore one's own role in the development of such a relationship is faulty and problematic. When difficult supervisee behaviors emerge, good supervisors first examine their own role—i.e., consider that the student may responding reciprocally to their behaviors. Conversely, when things are going well, both should recognize (and identify) their own roles in maintaining a productive relationship. Observing what does and does not work in the supervisory relationship promotes learning about helping relationships.

The Relationship As a Teaching Tool

As discussed in the previous chapter, supervisors are role models who teach such instrumental functions as completing paperwork and developing interventions through modeling, but also teach by example. How the supervisor interacts with clients, staff, and peers teaches the supervisee a great deal about professional (and sometimes unprofessional) behaviors. However, perhaps the greatest lessons are taught by how the supervisor acts with the supervisee. We believe that it is the supervisor's responsibility to model professional, ethical, and productive behaviors within the supervisory relationship, and to openly discuss the dynamics of that relationship itself.

Indeed, the supervisory relationship can be observed and discussed as a way of helping supervisees develop "relationship competence" (Bogo 1993). Social work literature has demonstrated that a practitioner-client alliance is a central condition in effecting positive practice outcomes (Bogo 1993). Therefore, it is critical that supervisees become sophisticated relationship builders. Within the supervisory relationship, they have the opportunity to observe interactions and discuss them openly. By "developing an educational culture where intersubjective and interpersonal data can be processed," supervisees can acquire knowledge and skill at responding productively to relationship difficulties (Bogo 1993:26).

We believe that detailed examination of obstacles, whether they occur in supervisory or clinical relationships, is particularly helpful for developing relational problem-solving skills. It is one thing to be able to articulate such skills as an unemotional outsider to a case, and quite another to be able to apply them when in the middle of a difficult and highly emotional encounter. The supervisory relationship should be a place where, even when in heated disagreement, both parties can share affective experiences openly and directly, and without negative consequences (e.g., poor evaluations).

Although this approach addresses the supervisee's subjective experiences, it differs from therapeutic or "quasi-therapeutic" approaches in that it emphasizes a discovery of alternative interpersonal actions instead of an examination of intrapsychic or family-of-origin "issues." Additionally, supervisors openly share their own subjective perspectives for the purposes of modeling this behavior and actively solving problems. Examining one's own emotional reactions before sharing them helps to develop self-awareness and conscious use of self. It is the supervisor's responsibility to facilitate this exploration of the relationship and to model openness, nondefensiveness, and conscious use of self when working with the supervisee (Gizynski 1978; Kerson 1994; Martin and Alper 1989; Schmidt 1976; Webb 1988). This entails active self-monitoring in order to minimize subjective responses and to increase behaviors that are consciously intentional and in the best interests of the student.

Building the Environment for Self-Examination

Creating an environment in which the supervisee feels secure enough to share subjective experiences is an important part of good supervision. Clinical work, supervision, and education can raise many intense feelings. Becoming a social worker often means challenging old value systems and worldviews as well as having to work with cases that have similarities to one's own life. When supervisees' emotions run high, they risk becoming more focused on their own needs, to reduce their anxiety, than on the best interests of their clients. It is important that the supervisory environment promote both internal reflection and open discussion of subjective reactions. These help to develop self-awareness and conscious use of self, skills that are generally considered to be a "prerequisite of professional social work practice" (Martin and Alper 1989:55). Indeed, an important goal of supervision is for the supervisee to be able to practice with increasing levels of autonomy, which requires increasing levels of self-awareness (Atwood 1986). The supervisor's emotional support is a key ingredient in creating an atmosphere of trust in which supervisees can take risks and expose themselves.

Handling subjective experiences is uncomfortable for many supervisors, who may wish to avoid such topics entirely. However, neglecting these discussions is problematic. Social workers at all levels experience powerful feelings which, if left unmonitored, may negatively affect the client. In addition, neglect prevents learning opportunities related to self-awareness. Furthermore, ignoring the supervisee's internal experiences may cause problems in the supervisory relationship, making the student feel unsupported and unsure how to handle their emotions productively, or if their emotions are "normal."

A concern related to engaging in supervisee self-exploration is maintaining a clear supervision-therapy boundary, that is, preventing supervision from turning into therapy. This is important for maintaining a trusting environment for self-exploration. However, this can be challenging for supervisors who fear "crossing the line." While avoiding discussion of emotions is problematic, discussing personal experiences may feel like a violation of personal boundaries. Indeed, how best to handle subjective experiences is not always clear. The supervision-therapy boundary and guidelines for maintaining the distinction between supervisory and therapeutic inquiry are presented here to assist with this aspect of the supervisory process.

The Boundary of Supervision and Therapy

The literature is replete with statements warning supervisors of the dangers of using therapeutic strategies with supervisees (Hess 1986; Matorin 1979; Munson 1993; Rosenblatt and Mayer 1975; Wilson 1981). When supervision turns into therapy, there are negative consequences for the supervisee (e.g., lack of trust, feeling violated and powerless, sacrificed learning opportunities). Considering the possible explanations why supervision turns into therapy may help prevent this from happening. We posit four reasons here. First, supervision and therapy processes are quite similar (Haley 1976; Kahn 1979; Norman 1987; Reid 1984; Shulman 1994; Storm and Heath 1985), so there are likely to be occasions when the distinction between supervision and therapy become clouded.

Second, many supervisors are promoted from clinical positions. Typically, they were promoted because they were regarded as "expert" clinicians; while they may feel adept operating in the therapeutic domain, they may not yet in their newer role. When supervisors feel unsure about how to assist their supervisees, they may inadvertently change the focus to an area in which they feel more confident—the supervisee's personal material. Supervisors unsure how to proceed, should be careful not to let their own anxiety alter supervision. If the supervisor is operating to reduce their own anxiety, they are not working in the best interest of the supervisee.

Third, some supervisees may prefer the focus of supervision to be on their personal life struggles rather than on their work. Novice social workers, in particular, want to appear competent and fear revealing perceived flaws. Delving into personal issues can be a way to avoid having their work critiqued. A worker's performance cannot be properly evaluated if it has not been discussed. While this may not be the supervisee's intended objective, it can be a effective avoidance strategy, particularly with supervisors who prefer doing therapy to supervision. It is important to remember that most supervisees and supervisors do not do this with ill intentions, but rather as a way to reduce their own anxiety about being judged. Open discussion of this anxiety can minimize violations of the supervision-therapy boundary. Additionally, supervisors should take note of repeated discussions of compelling personal material and consider that this may be a way of avoiding supervision (Kadushin 1968).

Fourth, it is not uncommon for supervisees to actually be experiencing difficult personal issues simultaneous to supervision. This is particularly true for beginning social work students who have moved to a new area to enter school. They may feel isolated and faced with multiple stressors (e.g., learning a new program, homework, finding a place to live), and the supervisor may be their greatest support. Additionally, students commonly experience life stressors (e.g., family loss, divorce, accidents) and want to talk about them. Supervisors should not avoid such discussions. Doing so would be artificial and neglectful, and would convey to the supervisee that their supervisor does not view them as a human being (but solely as a worker).

When supervisees are under personal stress, it is helpful for both to assess the degree to which this may impede their engagement in work and supervision activities. It may be helpful to say something like, "I can see that you feel overwhelmed by (personal event). Would it be more helpful if we put supervision aside for a while so that we can talk about what has happened?" The challenge is to provide support and direction without changing supervision into therapy. Often, supervisees only need to "vent" or share their stress for a brief time before they are ready to move on to supervision. We highly promote the supervisor's provision of emotional support and assistance with simple problem solving. However, we discourage examination of personal history or family dynamics as attempts to intervene. If the supervisee requires this level of intervention, they should be encouraged to talk to a counselor (someone other than the supervisor). At times when the supervisee seems so overwhelmed that they have difficulty functioning, it may be helpful to recommend a brief time away from work.

Because the supervisor is such an important role model, special attention needs to be given to how they handle such interactions. Conveying sincere concern, empathy, and support for the supervisee's struggles is critical. This can be done without entering into discussion of personal history or turning supervision into therapy.

It may be that supervisors are more concerned about transgressing this boundary than are supervisees. In our opinion, that is a good thing. Guidelines to minimize boundary transgressions are offered here.

Strategies for Maintaining a Clear Boundary

Following are general recommendations for maintaining a clear boundary between supervision and therapy. These strategies for supervisors are outlined below and subsequently discussed in depth.

Supervisors should:

- Talk about the boundary and check in when entering personal domain
- Explain supervision
- Be self-reflective
- Avoid discussion of personal issues
- Discuss subjective reactions only as they relate to professional work
- Keep it case-specific
- Avoid immediate transfer of cases due to intense personal reactions
- Focus on the supervisee's behaviors
- Avoid making it personal

Talk About the Boundary and Check in When Entering Personal Domain

Perhaps the most helpful strategy for maintaining a clear distinction between supervision and therapy is for supervisors to engage in discussion about this boundary and share their wish to respect it. They can enlist the supervisee's help in monitoring it to ensure that transgressions are minimized. For example, the supervisor can say, "Please let me know if, at any time, you feel that we are no longer doing supervision but are doing therapy instead." and add that they too will keep an eye on the boundary and speak up if they feel they are in nonsupervision territory. Furthermore, supervisees should be told that they have permission to question their supervisor's inquiries, taking the lead in this regard. Since supervisees have less power in the relationship, they may feel they must respond to all their supervisor's questions. Asking them (giving permission) to challenge questionable exploration is empowering, builds protections into the relationship, and demonstrates a true desire to respect their safety. Such discussions should occur at the start of the supervisory relationship and continue throughout the encounter.

Explain Supervision

Many students enter social work supervision without an understanding of how it differs from supervision in other settings (e.g., retail). They may not correctly assess why they are being asked detailed questions about their thoughts and feelings regarding their work. Indeed, new supervisees may experience such inquiry as intrusive, representative of their supervisor's distrust of their work, or due to an underlying agenda to "therapize" them. Therefore, it is helpful and may be important to educate new supervisees about the nature of social work supervision, explaining that such examination is normal and that its purpose is to improve practice—not to attempt character change or resolution of personal "issues."

Be Self-Reflective

When discussing supervisees' subjective experiences, supervisors must take care to monitor their own internal reactions. Supervisees may convey feelings that are offensive or frightening. In order to minimize impulsive responses and be of best assistance, supervisors must engage in self-evaluation. We recommend that supervisors think carefully about why they are pursuing a particular line of questioning when it pertains to the supervisee's personal experiences. (An in-depth discussion of supervisor self-awareness and conscious use of self is taken up in the next chapter.)

Avoid Discussion of Personal Issues

Another useful approach for maintaining the supervision-therapy boundary is to avoid discussions of the supervisee's personal problems. "The most

important difference between treatment and supervision is one of goal"
(Kahn 1979:520). Remain focused on the function of supervision—i.e.,
supervisee learning and client welfare. Amelioration of personal problems or
"issues" is an objective of therapy. The "key to avoiding this pitfall [doing
therapy with supervisees] is to retain an educational focus" (Matorin
1979:151).

Discuss Subjective Reactions Only As They Relate to Professional Work

When a supervisee's subjective reaction becomes the focus of supervision, it
is important that the supervisor respects the supervision-therapy boundary.
One helpful strategy is to discuss the subjective reaction only as it relates to
the situation that triggered it. In other words, avoid generalizing the reaction
beyond the scope of the immediate case. For example, if Carl, a supervisee,
suggests that he has difficulty working with an elderly man, it is not wise for
the supervisor to try to "discover" the origins of his experience by digging
around in his personal history. It is more helpful to ask about what is taking
place between Carl and his elderly client that is activating his anxious feelings. Focusing on the clinical interaction helps to identify behaviors that
have the supervisee stuck and for which alternative strategies can be generated. Considering alternative strategies is an effective way for the supervisee
to discover ways of working with cases that challenge their feelings, even
with clients who remind the supervisee of people from their own life (i.e.,
countertransference). The following example illustrates how a supervisor
can help a supervisee work with personal reactions without crossing into the
therapy domain.

> Sarah, a hospital social worker, was assigned a case of an overweight,
> elderly man with a history of alcohol abuse. During supervision she
> told her supervisor that she had difficulty with "those types" because
> "they are all manipulative." When asked what she meant by "those
> types" and "manipulative," she shared that her father, now deceased,
> had been an alcoholic. During his last few years of life he was often
> sick, and she had been the family member who cared for him. She felt
> he constantly took advantage of her.
>
> The supervisor first reminded Sarah that her client was not her
> father. Then he asked her to explain what had occurred with the client
> that frustrated her. She said that on the surface, the client agreed to

take on activities but then did nothing to follow through. She reported that he was trying to get her to do things for him, but she refused. The supervisor asked Sarah to describe in detail her interactions with the client regarding setting up activities for him to undertake, how she discovered that he had not performed them, and how she responded. During this moment-by-moment discussion, Sarah discovered that instead of engaging in a mutual problem-solving process, she had taken a directive position and demanded that he carry out activities she thought best for him. She explained that she did this because she "knew" that if she did not push hard, he would resist. Upon reflection, she understood that her approach was probably not the best. Sarah and her supervisor then discussed alternative ways of working with this client that would be more helpful. She decided that she would try to be more empathic and deliberately work to listen to what he would like to do to help his situation.

At the subsequent supervision meeting, Sarah reported that by taking time to listen to the client, she learned that although he was similar to her father in some ways, he was different in many others. She said that once she started to listen, he became more likeable, and she felt that this session went much better than the previous one.

Notice that there were many opportunities for the supervisor to ask the supervisee about her father and her feelings about him, but instead he maintained a focus on the case and her professional behaviors. Although there was no exploration of Sarah's personal relationship with her father and no attempt to address her "issues" with him, Sarah discovered how this relationship could negatively affect her work. However, she learned that it did not have to, and that monitoring her reactions could be useful in separating her feelings about her father from clients that reminded her of him. She also learned that she could effectively work with clients who were "like" people from her personal life. The opposite approach, exploration of her relationship with her father during supervision, would have led to trying to resolve this personal struggle for her, with the hope that this would lead to better work with clients. This would have required two leaps of faith: that relationship issues with her father could be resolved in a supervisory context and that resolution of this relationship would lead to better practice. This approach certainly would have changed the nature of supervision to therapy.

Keep It Case-Specific

As exploration should be related to professional work, discussions of subjective reactions should be kept case-specific, not broadened to a general personal problem. In the above example of Sarah, her strong personal response to the client was discussed in terms of how it affected the specific case. Although her initial presentation generalized her feelings to all people like her father, the supervisor avoided telling her she had "a problem with elderly, overweight men with alcohol problems." Instead, Sarah and her supervisor strategized an alternative approach to the one she had been using to overcome her father-related emotional obstacle. Generalizing her reaction would have suggested that she would be unable to work with clients sharing her father's characteristics until she had resolved these issues, or worse, would have turned those issues into pathologies.

Avoid Immediate Transfer of Cases Due to Intense Personal Reactions

Some social work educators argue that when cases have such personal implications, they should be referred to other practitioners. We feel that this undermines the confidence of the practitioner and prevents opportunities for increasing self-awareness and learning clinical skills. In our experience, it is exceptionally rare that a practitioner is simply unable to work with a client due to personal reactions. Overcoming these reactions and engaging in effective practice, even with difficult clients, is an important clinical skill. The belief that a practitioner must be problem-free to be effective is faulty and unrealistic. All social workers have personal matters that complicate their work, yet they are still able to practice effectively. Furthermore, to attempt to resolve all personal matters is not only impossible but also not the purpose of supervision.

That said, there are occasions when it may be in both the supervisee's and the client's best interest that a case be transferred, for example, if after attempting alternative behaviors, the supervisee is not able to maintain focus on the client. Such instances include times when a practitioner cannot make it through a supervisory meeting without crying, withdrawing, or lashing out. This indicates that the feelings are so strong that the supervisee is having difficulty in other aspects of their life. It may also help to consult a therapist.

Focus on the Supervisee's Behaviors

Another strategy for maintaining the supervisory boundary when subjective reactions are discussed is to focus on how the feelings are manifesting themselves in the supervisee's behaviors. In the example of Sarah, her feelings led her to take a directive stance with the client. By focusing on the way she interacted with the client, Sarah and her supervisor were able to consider alternative behaviors. The supervisee's emotions should not be ignored; instead, the supervisor should respond with empathy and validation, providing emotional support so that alternative behaviors can be discussed. For example, Sarah's supervisor could have said, "Now that you know that your emotional reactions are causing you to be directive with this client, what other behaviors do you think would be more effective?"

Avoid Making It Personal

Discuss the affective response as a specific reaction to a specific event rather than making it a general statement about a personal issue. For example, if a supervisee is having difficulty working with a five-year-old child, the supervisor and supervisee should not generalize this to statements such as, "You have problems with young children." Such conceptualizations are not helpful in developing methods of working with the five-year-old. Additionally, such a generalization may be damaging to the supervisee's confidence and suggest underlying pathology. All workers have "issues." It is not the job of the supervisor to try to correct them. It is, however, the supervisor's role to help the supervisee find effective ways of working with all populations. For example, the supervisee may indeed have difficulty working with all children. However, it is more helpful to consider ways of working with this specific five-year-old and then try to apply them to other cases, rather than attempting to resolve an underlying "problem" with children in general.

Other Boundary Transgressions

In addition to the supervision-therapy transgressions discussed, there are other important boundary considerations in supervisory practice. These include sexual misbehavior, dual relationships, and violations of confidentiality.

It seems a shame to have to include a statement warning against engaging in sexual activity with supervisees. However, because such violations exist, some discussion seems necessary. Supervisors should not use their position of power to act out sexually. Comments about physical appearance, dirty jokes, touching, keeping overly close physical proximity (e.g., seating arrangements), suggestive language or teasing, and requests for "dates" are all inappropriate in the context of supervisory relationships and represent boundary transgressions. Even when there is a genuine attraction between the supervisor and supervisee, engaging in such behavior blurs the professional boundary (the dangers of such dual relationship are discussed below). It also can seriously impede the learning process. For example, a supervisor may not provide negative feedback to a supervisee if he or she feels it may compromise their personal relationship. In addition, as long as the supervisor has evaluative authority over the supervisee, is cannot be safely known whether the supervisee is behaving out of fear of being negatively judged (particularly when grades, promotions, and raises are at stake).

Supervisees are vulnerable to such transgressions because they are in a position of lesser power and do not feel safe to set limits. In situations where supervisees are the perpetrators of sexually inappropriate behavior, they should be immediately confronted and told that such behavior must end. Some supervisees may use sexual behavior as a way to try to undermine the power of the supervisor. Intimidating the supervisor through upsetting actions is a boundary violation. If the supervisor feels threatened or is unable to stop the supervisee's behavior through direct confrontation, they should consult their own administrators (and the school in internship arrangements) to discuss how to handle it.

Maintaining clear boundaries for supervision is severely compromised when dual relationships exist—when the supervisor and supervisee have any type of nonsupervisory relationship outside of the work setting. For example, socializing blurs the supervisory boundary. Should a supervisor have to mediate between the supervisee and another staff member, the friendship and the supervisory relationship are simultaneously challenged. If the supervisor does not side with the supervisee, they risk losing a friendship. Should the supervisor feel compelled to side with the supervisee out of friendship, their role as supervisor is compromised. Additionally, decisions about evaluation, promotions, and raises are all called into question when there is a dual relationship. For this reason, we recommend that supervisors and supervisees maintain only professional relationships and not "be friends" outside of work.

Engaging in business practices together outside of the supervisory context represents another dual relationship. For example, if a supervisor needs their house painted and hires their supervisee for the job, this can be problematic. Will the supervisor feel comfortable negatively evaluating the supervisee if it will mean sacrificing a low-budget paint job? Dating, of course, is another highly problematic dual relationship. We strongly recommend that all dual relationships be avoided.

Although both have a responsibility to keep supervision discussions confidential, this is particularly true for supervisors. Because the student uses supervision as a place to take risks, such as sharing subjective reactions, mistakes, and detailed reports of case work, it is critical that this information not be given to others. If the supervisor tells another staff member about a supervisee's intense emotional reaction to a client and this gets back to the supervisee, the supervisor will no longer be regarded as trustworthy. The supervisory relationship is compromised. If evaluations need to be given to others (e.g., administrators, school officials), the supervisee should be told up front what information will be conveyed. Personal information (e.g., sharing personal issues) does not need to be shared with others. However, problematic behaviors should be relayed, particularly if the supervisee is an intern.

In sum, boundary violations of all types will compromise the supervisee's learning and the supervisory relationship. Supervision will not feel like a safe place to take the risks necessary for professional development. This is particularly true if trust in the relationship is challenged by differences between the supervisor and supervisee in regard to age, race, religion, ethnicity, socioeconomic status, sexual orientation, gender, or geographical background.

Working with Difference

Since all supervisory relationships entail differences between the supervisor and supervisee (e.g., age, race, ethnicity, religion, sexual orientation, socioeconomic status, gender), it is important that these differences are handled in a productive manner. Furthermore, these individual distinctions provide an opportunity to learn about difference and multicultural practice. However, this is contingent upon the presence of a safe environment for self-examination and exploration of the supervisory relationship.

Engaging in open discussion of differences leads to flexibility of thought and can help to develop an understanding that each observation can be interpreted in many ways. Indeed, learning that multiple perspectives exist is important in becoming a nonjudgmental and skilled practitioner. Multicultural practice means understanding and validating multiple ways of knowing the world. More important, the fact that there can be multiple understandings of singular events minimizes the risk of judging perspectives as incorrect, dangerous, or even worse, pathological.

It is important to note the differences between what are considered "hard facts" and the meanings or beliefs that accompany them. For example, there is conclusive scientific evidence that AIDS is the result of a virus. However, there are a variety of different beliefs about how the virus is spread. Some believe that it is spread through curses associated with witchcraft. Still others believe that AIDS was intentionally spread in black populations by the CIA. While this last example may sound incredible to some social workers, it may be experienced as reasonable by others. Certainly, there are many examples throughout American history of "official" institutions perpetrating harm on people of color for "scientific" reasons (e.g., the Tuskegee experiments, in which poor black men with syphilis were intentionally left untreated for research purposes). As another example, there may be scientific evidence that shows that law enforcement reduces crime, but law enforcement may not be equally beneficial for all members of society. Hence, a variety of perspectives about law enforcement exist. In supervisory practice, it is best to remain open to multiple perspectives without assuming that only one is correct.

This sounds simpler than it is. Accepting that there are multiple visions of phenomena means questioning preconceptions and personal worldviews, often tied to religion and culture. For example, a supervisor may believe that the police provide community protection, while the supervisee may view police as abusive and contributing to community unrest. Whose view is correct? Indeed, both may be right. Coming to terms with this difference through open conversation about the role of the police, how they are experienced differently across communities, and for whom they are and are not helpful can help both the supervisor and the supervisee to learn about difference. Indeed, the practitioner who recognizes that there are many different views of the police is more likely to help their clients make appropriate choices. If not aware that multiple perspectives exist, the practitioner will likely assume that contacting the police will always be helpful. The imposition of this (largely white, middle-class) view can impinge on the practitioner-client relationship and even put the client in danger. (For an excellent example of when contacting the police is not a viable option, and perhaps even dangerous, for a rape victim, see Fine 1992.)

We recommend that supervisors talk about difference and multicultural thought early in the supervisory encounter. They must model openness to varied positions put forth by the supervisee and talk about each perspective as "one of many views." We do not mean this as a way to dismiss people's opinions. Much the opposite: we recommend that supervisors validate differing perspectives and seek to understand how they are tied to differing backgrounds. In short, supervisors should be careful about putting forth their understanding as the only correct view. If they model this, supervisees are likely to resist sharing their perspectives and to learn to behave similarly with clients. This is of particular concern when the supervisee is a member of an oppressed group, who may be quite familiar with having their views disregarded as invalid or wrong.

Indeed, difference should be talked about as an opportunity to learn new ways of thinking and to grow professionally, rather than as a threat. New social workers often enter the field with fairly rigid belief systems—e.g., abortion is bad, drinking a case of beer each night is normal, spanking is good for children, compassion is all that is needed to help people, men cannot handle talking about emotion, women are overemotional. A challenging but exciting role of the supervisor is to help supervisees discover that their views may not be correct or incorrect, but represent one set of beliefs. However, it is important that the discussion does not stop with an understanding that multiple perspectives exist but acknowledges that they exist in a world in which some are considered to be more valid than others, depending on who holds them. The mainstream cultural model in the United States is overwhelmingly white, upper middle-class, and male; perspectives that agree with it are considered to be valid and important. Positions that differ from, and thus challenge, mainstream thought are often dismissed or ignored. Thus people from groups outside of the mainstream have unfortunate and long histories of experiencing oppression and being silenced. It is not enough to teach that blacks are different from whites or that Protestants differ from Muslims; it must be clear that their differences are ranked in a hierarchical sense.

For the purposes of this discussion, multiculturalism refers to the notion that there are multiple ways to explain the world. This said, relevant perspectives are not always helpful. For example, clients may have belief systems that are valid but that are also perpetuating their struggles. Multicultural practice means seeing all perspectives as rational and then exploring the degree to which they are helpful or hindering. Furthermore, problems faced by people from oppressed groups may be complicated by feelings of loyalty to cultural practices that may be hindering (this is true for white, upper middle-class males as well!). It is a real skill to enable discussion of difference and hierarchy while helping a person overcome struggles related to cultural heritage—particularly when it conflicts with mainstream thought.

Consequently, it is important that supervisors model multicultural practice by engaging in multicultural supervision. Supervisors and supervisees bring their personal histories and attributes to the supervisory relationship. Often, they differ on characteristics such as age, ethnicity, race, religion and religiosity, sexual orientation, socioeconomic and geographical backgrounds, language, and of course, gender. In fact, all supervisory relationships can be considered cross-cultural (Kaiser 1997). Such differences may be a source for learning but also may cause misunderstandings. Kaiser (1997) promotes "shared meaning" as a goal to be worked toward in the supervisory relationship. The more dramatic the difference in background, the more difficult this goal will be to achieve.

Reaching shared meaning suggests that the supervisor and supervisee have done their work in remaining open to each other's interpretation of events. It does not mean that they must adopt the same perspective, or even agree. However, supervisors should be careful not to immediately place their own view above the supervisee's. This is parallel to practitioners instantly putting their own perspectives above the client's. Indeed, achieving shared meaning is an opportunity for supervisors to learn more about practice and develop an understanding of multiple perspectives.

Nevertheless, it is critical to remember that a large body of empirical research is available to guide clinical decisions. Once open discussion of multiple perspectives occurs, supervisees may be more ready to consider scientific evidence. It is important to evaluate the degree to which phenomena have been verified through multiple studies across multiple populations. Scientific knowledge is at best tentative, but through a convergence of findings from repeated studies, it often presents the most credible information attainable (see Kirk and Reid 2002 for more in-depth discussion of evaluating knowledge). To return to our AIDS example, since we know that HIV can be transmitted through sharing infected needles, we would want to help an intravenous drug user who believed that AIDS was the result of bad karma to develop whatever perspective about AIDS might be necessary to convince them to use clean needles. In sum, we recommend first, maintaining an open stance regarding multiple perspectives, and second, mutually evaluating available empirically based knowledge for its application to individual cases.

The Persons of the Supervisee and the Supervisor

The first part of this chapter focused on the nature of the relationship between the supervisee and the supervisor. The rest will discuss the affective domain of the individual players, each of whom brings unique characteristics—and anxieties—to the encounter. We will begin by discussing the affective considerations for the supervisee, including anxiety, its role in supervisory process, how it is revealed, and how to address it. Next, we will discuss the person of the supervisor.

The Supervisee

The primary responsibilities of the supervisee are to be open and take risks, to actively participate, and to act ethically and professionally (Munson 1993). Successfully carrying out these responsibilities is contingent upon the supervisee's individual characteristics, their level of anxiety about their performance and safety, and the supervisor's ability to both monitor and support them.

Supervisees bring unique "selves" to the supervisory process. They arrive with individual and varied strengths and weaknesses. In addition, they vary in skill level, motivation, prior experience, and sociability. They also each arrive with some anxiety about what is to take place in supervision. They may wonder:

"What will be expected of me?"
"Will my supervisor be a nice person?"
"Will my supervisor want to teach me?"
"How will I be evaluated?"
"Is my supervisor going to think I am incompetent?"
"Will my years of experience be recognized?"
"Is my supervisor a stickler for paperwork?"

Thus, it is important that their affective experiences be acknowledged. Addressing anxiety can help the supervisee be more attentive when undertaking instrumental functions. When emotions are high, as at the beginning of the supervisory encounter, it is difficult to absorb new information needed to carry out one's job. Intense subjective responses occur throughout the supervision experience. Because it is a common feature of the process, supervisee anxiety is discussed in depth here.

Supervisee Anxiety

Supervisee anxiety is not only common but also recognized as natural and anticipated (Judah 1982; Wilson 1981). Regardless of how it is experienced, when the level of emotional response becomes high enough, it begins to interfere with productive supervision. High anxiety may prevent the supervisee from being a willing or cooperative participant, and even from being able to attend to supervision at all.

The following metaphor illustrates this point nicely. Picture anxiety as water filling up the human body. Once the water (i.e., anxiety) rises above a person's ears, it becomes difficult for this person to "hear." Similarly, supervisee anxiety can easily become an obstacle to implementing TCS procedures in performing the instrumental functions of supervision. Therefore, it is important for supervisors to address and work to reduce high supervisee anxiety.

Supervisee anxiety does not always interfere with supervisory activities. Most people walk around with many concerns that do not impede productivity. However, it can still be helpful to inquire about the supervisee's affective experiences. This demonstrates support and caring for the supervisee as a person. Furthermore, it is not uncommon for underlying or "hidden" anxiety to "seep out" into supervision and sometimes distract from the purpose of the encounter. When the anxiety begins to distract the supervisee or supervisor, it should be addressed. In short, supportive inquiry followed by empathic discussion of anxiety can go a long way to reduce it.

Sources of Supervisee Anxiety

Supervisors who are aware of possible reasons for supervisee anxiety are more able to tune in to the student's unvoiced affective experiences. Supervisee anxiety can be related to many different sources including school (in internship arrangements), work demands, performance expectations, personal circumstances, client welfare, agency politics, and the diversity of ideas and people. However, it is often related to engaging in supervision itself—becoming a supervisee and the relationship with the supervisor are two notable sources.

Anxiety is commonly associated with starting a new endeavor, such as entering social work school or beginning a new job. The start of supervision causes anxiety because it represents many unknowns. New social workers are challenged to incorporate new knowledge, adopt and integrate new value systems, employ new skills, open themselves up for critical review, work with a variety of people and ideas, and repeatedly encounter novel circumstances. Furthermore, supervision may mean entering situations in which they feel they have little competence and are unsure of how to operate. This may be particularly distressing for those entering social work as a career change from a position in which they were competent and the one in charge.

Taking part in supervision is in itself a source of anxiety. It requires supervisees to make themselves vulnerable to scrutiny and critical feedback and to defer to the authority of their supervisor. In addition, new social workers often enter into the supervisory relationship without an understanding of what it entails. As stated earlier, they may have a business-sense understanding of the word "supervision." This can be a source of confusion and resentment about a supervisor's behaviors.

Unfortunately, staff orientations rarely explain the supervisory process in depth. Similarly, schools of social work do not adequately prepare students to utilize supervision appropriately (Martin and Alper 1989). Not knowing what to expect from the conferences and relationship is likely to increase supervisee anxiety. It is important that supervisors take time to discuss the supervisory process. Furthermore, models should integrate orientation about supervision (e.g., its history, function, and process) into operations. TCS was designed to include such steps.

Other common worries for supervisees include formal evaluations, applying interventions "correctly," and confronting difficult clients. Learning new material, integrating new value systems, and working with diverse people and ideas are all stress-producing. Finally, the development of self-awareness is associated with significant supervisee anxiety (Kadushin 1991; Webb 1988). Self-reflection often means confronting preconceived notions of one's competence, knowledge, and lack of prejudices. Supervisors should also recognize that non-work related issues may enter into the supervision setting and impede successful learning and supervision.

Identifying Supervisee Anxiety

Although some supervisees freely talk about their anxiety, many do not for a variety of reasons, including a fear that revealing anxiety will result in negative appraisals by the supervisor, not realizing that discussing their emotional experiences is acceptable in supervision, believing that the supervisor's agenda takes precedence, and assuming that the instrumental functions of supervision leave no room for the affective components. Hence, it is not uncommon for supervisees to experience anxiety but feel uneasy about sharing it. Supervisee anxiety is not always easily identified, despite often being present.

To promote sharing of supervisee anxiety, it is helpful to normalize anxiety as a common experience and offer an environment in which discussion of affective responses is acceptable. This is particularly true when supervisors suspect students are experiencing stress but are not openly sharing concerns. For example, some may not verbally express their worries but may send cues (i.e., nonverbal behaviors) that there is something on their mind. When supervisees are hesitant to express their worries, supervisors should attempt to elicit them in a supportive manner.

However, some supervisees may not show any overt signs of stress and yet be experiencing a great deal of it. Some show their underlying anxiety in less than acceptable manners (e.g., bad behavior). Supervisors should consider that when supervisees are acting inappropriately, they may be experiencing high anxiety.

Difficult Supervisees: Is Anxiety Related?

In cases where supervisees deny anxiety but act rebelliously or inappropriately (e.g., not showing up on time for supervision, not implementing interventions discussed in supervision, having difficulty carrying out simple operations such as paperwork), supervisors should consider that anxiety may be the underlying cause of the behavior. Addressing the student in a supportive manner can help them change poor behavior. Indeed, many supervisors' first instinct would be to discipline the supervisee. We recommend exploration of anxiety as a first step. Subsequent to these efforts, discipline is a legitimate option.

Kadushin (1968) and Hawthorne (1975) show how defensive reactions to anxiety related to authority can result in "game playing" on the parts of both the supervisee and the supervisor. The initial "payoff" of engaging in games of defensiveness is lowered stress. However, learning is seriously impeded and underlying resentments are likely to grow. On the surface, anxiety may not appear to be involved, but it is likely the source of game playing. The relationship is one of unbalanced power in which the supervisor is in authority. Both supervisors and supervisees are often uncomfortable in their positions related to authority. Supervisors are often surprised by the intensity with which their students experience the differences in power between them (Kadushin 1974), and many supervisors do not like being associated with authority (Hawthorne 1975). It is often helpful to openly discuss the phenomenon in the supervisory relationship, as part of the effort to develop a safe and trusting relationship in which inquiry into affective reactions is acceptable.

The Revealing of Anxiety Continuum

Supervisee anxiety is revealed in many different ways that falls along a continuum from indirect to direct. Some students are quite open about their stress, as in the example of Melody, who at the very start of the supervision meeting stated, "I can't think about cases when I have so many assignments due for school." Other supervisees are less forward about their anxiety, either keeping it hidden or revealing it through atypical behaviors (Kahn 1979). Indeed, when supervisees are acting out of character, this may be an indication that they are experiencing anxiety but not openly sharing it. The following example illustrates a supervisor recognizing and addressing atypical behavior as a reflection of underlying anxiety.

> Scott, a supervisee who usually actively participated in supervision, was withdrawn and agitated during the meeting. When the supervisor inquired about an interaction with a client, he responded by saying, "Do I have to talk about this?" The supervisor explored Scott's reluctance to discuss the case. At first, he said that he "just didn't feel like it," but through facilitative confrontation (Shulman 1993), which included pointing out that his behavior was atypical, Scott shared that he wanted "to get supervision over with as soon as possible so [I] can go home and finish writing this stupid paper [for school]." He added that the paper had him "stressed out" and that he was unable to concentrate on much else. The supervisor asked Scott if he would like to reschedule for later in the week. Scott was highly appreciative and did reschedule.

The supervisor could have responded to Scott's reluctance to talk about the case by becoming demanding and even punitive. However, recognizing that this was not typical behavior for Scott enabled the supervisor to consider that he might be reacting to stress, and furthermore, to support Scott by rescheduling their meeting—promoting a positive supervisory relationship. Had the supervisor taken a demanding position, forcing the meeting to continue, it is unlikely that Scott would have been able to actively or productively participate—and probable that their relationship would have been harmed.

Regardless of whether anxiety is revealed openly, subtly, or with no overt signs, supervisors should actively tune in to their supervisees' affective states. Anxiety can be a real obstacle to a productive supervision meeting. When intense feelings and intrusive thoughts preoccupy supervisees, it is difficult for them to fully participate; they may just "go through the motions" of supervision, while consumed with other issues. Attending to supervisee anxiety helps maximize the benefits of supervision encounters, reduce supervisee-supervisor power struggles, and promote positive feelings about work, clients, and the supervisory relationship.

The Supervisor

Supervisors have many responsibilities that include teaching practice, overseeing cases, making administrative decisions, and being supportive. In the role of educator, the supervisor must remain flexible to accommodate diverse ways of knowing, learning styles, and pacing while making knowledge accessible. In addition, they are responsible for modeling openness related to affective responses, self-reflection, and ethical behavior. This means being able to take a nondefensive and nonauthoritarian position when confronted by difficult or challenging supervisee behaviors.

Indeed, supervisors feel a tremendous amount of responsibility for their supervisees, their supervisees' caseload, and their own work. They want to be good teachers, administrators, and supports. However, over 60 percent of supervisors report having had no academic training for this role (Munson 1993). In addition, most do not receive supervision for their supervisory work. Because there are rarely support mechanisms in place for supervisors, their anxiety is very seldom addressed. However, it is a real concern. The overwhelming number of supervisor roles may be responsible for burnout

(Shapiro 1989) and the high turnover rate of social work practicum supervisors, estimated to be around 50 percent each year (Rosenfeld 1989; Hagen 1989). Furthermore, supervisor anxiety can be another obstacle to successful supervision.

Supervisor Anxiety

Stress in the supervisor is also a common and expected feature of supervision. As stated above, it can impede effectiveness, particularly when supervisors begin behaving in ways to reduce their own anxiety to meet their own needs, rather than acting in the best interests of their supervisees and their supervisees' clients. Because the supervisor is in a position of authority, they are at risk of exploiting that position when they become overwhelmed. For example, rather than remaining open to the idea that atypical supervisee behaviors may be related to work stress, the supervisor may instead become intolerant of any poor behavior, using threats to bring the student in line.

The supervisor is a powerful role model who conveys much about the professional helping behaviors that supervisees are likely to emulate. Therefore, it is important that supervisors obtain support when feeling overwhelmed. It is also important to be continually self-reflective and employ conscious use of self. Because of the centrality of the person of the supervisor in effective supervision, an entire chapter has been dedicated to the supervisor's conscious use of self and methods for ensuring that behavior is in the best interest of the supervisee (see chapter 5).

Conclusion

Luckily, the establishment of a positive supervisory relationship is not solely based on the "fit" between supervisor and supervisee personalities. Indeed, a great deal can be done to develop a productive alliance. In our view, systematic implementation of the principles associated with effective instruction (discussed in depth in the previous chapter) will likely produce a positive relationship. These features provide supervisors and supervisees with process objectives to work toward, but attending to the supervisory relationship itself is also important. This means engaging in ongoing and open discussion about the experience.

Attending to the supervisory relationship is highly beneficial for teaching about helping relationships in general. Since the supervisory and practitioner-client relationships can be considered parallel processes (Kahn 1979; Shulman 1993) and even isomorphic (Storm and Heath 1985), such discussion provides opportunities for supervisees and supervisors to learn first hand about relational process and handling differences (Bogo 1993). How relational difficulties are handled in supervision demonstrates how to deal with relational difficulties in clinical work. Poor handling of supervisory conflict (e.g., taking a rigidly authoritative position, ignoring behaviors, engaging in unilateral blame) models problematic relational behavior. In addition, such behaviors impede supervisee learning and lower the quality of the supervisory relationship.

Conversely, open discussion of tension between the supervisor and the supervisee, in which mutual work to resolve the conflict can take place, demonstrates a effective method for handling relational difficulties with clients and allows the supervisor to model a positive use of power. Because both supervisory and clinical relationships are hierarchical, how supervisors handle this arguably "teaches" supervisees about use of power in clinical relationships. Furthermore, open discussion of supervisory conflict shows students that their supervisor is invested in their learning and considers their perspective of the conflict as valid. This is likely to result in more trusting supervisory relationships than no discussion would. Finally, because of the supervisory relationship's centrality to productive supervision, TCS includes steps to attend to the relationship and the supervisee's affective responses. We also recommend that supervisors attend to their own emotional reactions and work toward conscious use of self.

5 The Person of the Supervisor

This chapter takes an in-depth look at a significant part of supervision that has largely been overlooked. As discussed in chapter 4, the supervisor's experience is an important aspect of the encounter. How supervisors handle themselves has a major impact on the quality of learning for supervisees. Because supervision typically involves intense emotions, the supervisor's ability to monitor and utilize their personal reactions is in the best interest of the supervisee's learning.

This chapter first looks at the supervisor's influential role and reviews positive supervisor attributes. A brief overview of the concept of use of self is given; then the multiple sources of supervisor anxiety are presented to demonstrate the many challenging tasks and issues that face supervisors and cause stress. The necessity of self-awareness, methods for achieving insight, and supervisors' conscious use of self are considered. The chapter ends with a brief discussion of strategies for decreasing supervisor anxiety.

The Supervisor's Influential Role

As stated in the previous chapter, a growing body of empirical studies demonstrate that the supervisor-supervisee relationship has notable influence on supervisee learning (Bogo 1993) and practice patterns (Tolson and Kopp 1988). While both have responsibility in creating a positive and open relationship, the supervisor is in authority and can take the lead (Bogo

1993). Therefore, a productive alliance is largely based on their behaviors and attributes. Educators cite the supervisor as the central component influencing supervisee learning (Bogo and Power 1992; Kadushin 1991; Tolson and Kopp 1988). Moreover, the supervisor's skills and abilities have been found to affect supervisee satisfaction (Fortune et al. 1985) and the success of internship experiences (Abramson and Fortune 1990).

Supervisors are role models (Munson 1993; Shulman 1993), and perceive this function to be the most important in supervision (Freeman and Hansen 1995). The manner in which the supervisor interacts with the supervisee provides cues about professional social work behaviors. By watching the supervisor's "professional behaviors and attitudes . . . supervisees learn experientially about relationship theory and skill" (Bogo 1993:32); they then utilize this knowledge in their client relationships. They learn contracting (Fox and Zischka 1989), giving feedback (Freeman 1985), tuning in, using empathy and confrontation, and dealing with authority (Beless 1993), as well as the profession's ethical stances concerning self-determination (Koerin, Harrigan, and Reeves 1990), "rights, justice and human dignity" (Kerson 1994:14), by observing their supervisors in action. Similarly, supervisees learn professional behaviors through role plays and demonstrations of how to use graphic materials such as genograms and ecomaps.

Supervisors are responsible for facilitating exploration of the supervisory relationship, modeling openness, nondefensiveness, and conscious use of self (Webb 1988). Of particular importance is the ability to model sensitive handling of hierarchical issues inherent in a relationship in which one is the "expert" and the other is seeking professional expertise, whether client-practitioner or supervisee-supervisor. To model this behavior, the supervisor must possess the attribute of self-awareness and employ conscious use of self with the supervisee (Gizynski 1978; Kerson 1994; Martin and Alper 1989; Schmidt 1976; Webb 1988). This entails active self-monitoring in order to minimize subjective responses and increase behaviors that are deliberate and in the best interest of supervisees. When supervisors are self-reflective, they are better able to model desirable attributes.

Positive Supervisor Attributes

Ellison (1994) constructed, from current research, twelve supervisor attributes that are "associated with quality supervision: (a) available for supervision, (b) desire to teach, (c) responsive to supervisee's feelings, (d) provide feedback, (e) serve as a role model, (f) structure the learning experience, (g) prepare supervisees for autonomous practice, (h) be supportive, (i) teach and communicate theoretical and practical knowledge, (j) help supervisee with self-awareness, (k) be fair and objective, (l) use androgenic teaching methods" (13). These combined qualities and behaviors provide an "ideal type" (Bogo 1993) for supervisors.

Each supervisor acquires strategies for performing these functions. However, because supervision generally entails two individuals coming together at a certain point in time, within a particular context, no two supervisory relationships are the same. This challenges the supervisor to closely consider which strategies should be used, when, and how in relation to a particular student. It has been noted that as a supervisee develops, the supervisor changes his or her behaviors in reciprocal fashion (Bogo 1983; Freeman and Hansen 1995; Walther and Mason 1994). Indeed, supervisors change how they behave (or use themselves) with different supervisees and according to individual skill development.

In addition to professional skills and knowledge regarding practice, learning, and teaching, the supervisor brings their personality, history, physical appearance, and emotional world to the supervisory relationship. Thus, in order for a supervisor to actualize Ellison's (1994) attributes, they must consider their "self" within the relationship—in other words, must understand the person of the supervisor in order to successfully create and maintain a productive supervisory relationship. As in clinical social work, self-awareness and conscious use of self are important skills in supervision (Kerson 1994; Wilson 1981).

Use of Self

The concept of use of self in supervision has been borrowed from psychotherapy literature. The idea that the person of a clinician is a feature that can be observed and used in a particular way is common to models of clinical practice. Psychoanalytic therapy was the first to train analysts in this regard (Aponte and Winter 1987). Classic psychoanalysis requires that therapists monitor and control their subjective reactions in order to be a "blank screen" and maximize fantasy and transferential expressions in the client (Payne 1991). The practitioner's subjective reactions, called countertransference, are believed to originate in the clinician's "unconscious" and are "related to the analyst's unresolved, neurotic 'complexes'" (Aponte and Winter 1987:91). It is believed that countertransference, if unmonitored, can influence the way a clinician behaves with a client, potentially hindering treatment (Strean 1986). When countertransference is occurring and out of the clinician's awareness or control, they are responding more to their own needs than the client's.

Family therapy expanded upon the notion of intentionally employing the therapist's personhood for clinical purposes, and refers to this activity as "use of self" (Minuchin and Fishman 1981). The "self" consists of all facets of the person of the clinician, including feelings, thoughts, and ways of behaving as well as "fixed attributes such as age, sex and physical characteristics" (Webb 1988:38). While practitioners do not have control over them, fixed traits nevertheless have an impact on the therapeutic relationship. They can be "used" in the ways clinicians emphasize particular aspects of self when working with certain clients and deemphasize those same aspects with others. Practitioners change body posture, how concepts are couched, manner of speech, type of language, pacing, how they dress, what they tune in to, what they call attention to about themselves, facial expressions, and timing of humor depending on the client and the particular moment in treatment. In addition, the way in which clinicians use confrontation, show support, and share personal information varies from client to client, and often changes from session to session with the same client.

Structural family therapist Salvador Minuchin compares the therapist's use of self in building therapeutic alliances with families to Woody Allen's character in the movie *Zelig* (Minuchin and Nichols 1993). This character is much like a human chameleon who physically changes appearance in order to fit into his current surroundings. With each family, the structural family therapist adopts their unique style and becomes, essentially, "one of them."

Other therapy models also call upon clinicians to use themselves to achieve therapeutic ends. For example, experiential models of family therapy posit the therapist's personality as a "central feature of the dynamics of therapy" and promote its use in order to provide the "experience of authenticity for the family" (Rhodes 1986:447). The neurolinguistic programming model calls for therapists to intentionally "mirror" client behaviors, such as pacing of interactions and nonverbal behaviors, in order to order to establish rapport (MacLean 1986). Use of self "stances" have also been put forth by constructivist theorists (Real 1990).

The process of using the self has been compared to "the kind of control an actor has of a performance" (Kerson 1994:15), with the therapist deliberately using his or her person as a tool in the therapeutic process (Satir 1987). Some have argued that it is the most important tool in the process (Lambert 1992). Research has demonstrated that a central feature of therapeutic success is the working relationship between the client and the practitioner (Frank and Frank 1991; Marziali and Alexander 1991).

It is likely that the supervisory relationship has equal importance in educational success. Similar to the clinician, the supervisor is able to employ use of self with supervisees. Like the family therapist, the supervisor alters their posture, pacing, use of humor, self-disclosure, focus of learning, way of offering support, method of providing feedback, and confrontation, depending upon the supervisee and the moment in supervision. Like clinicians, supervisors also use their personhood as a tool, employing use of self for creating and maintaining productive supervisory relationships. However, doing this calls for attention to the self, intrapsychic operations, and the impact of their behavior, because the "entity of the self . . . is elusive" and "we are not always aware when it operates" (Baldwin 1987:7).

It is vital that supervisors primarily function in response to supervisee needs rather than their own. A potential source of obstruction in clinical practice is anxiety in the therapist. In the same way, anxiety in the supervisor, especially if not properly monitored and used, can be a major threat to the supervisee's growth and education (Gizynski 1978). This is of particular importance because there are many potential sources of anxiety for the supervisor.

Sources of Supervisor Anxiety

Although supervisor anxiety has been recognized as a common feature of the supervisory process (Munson 1993; Wilson 1981), the issue has received minimal attention in social work literature. This is disconcerting, considering the notable impact the supervisor has on the supervisee's experience. Anxiety can result in a narrowed range of responses that are more related to the supervisor's needs than the supervisee's. Not surprisingly, there is evidence that supervisor stress and effectiveness are associated (Shulman 1993).

Unfortunately, multiple aspects of the supervisory encounter can cause supervisor anxiety. Organized here into six categories, these include multiple roles and educational tasks, transition from worker to supervisor, the supervisee, supervisor authority, context, and self-awareness. Most of the categories are divided into subcategories for a more refined explication.

Multiple Roles and Educational Tasks

A primary source of anxiety is the overwhelming number of roles and educational tasks supervisors face. In social work practice there is an abundance of material that a supervisee needs in order to provide solid services to client populations. Although much of the supervisee's knowledge may be acquired in the classroom, it is the supervisor who is charged with the primary responsibility for helping the supervisee develop their practice skills. Hence, supervisors "experience pressure about the totality of what needs to be taught" (Matorin 1979:153).

There are many other teaching considerations requiring supervisors to engage in multiple tasks, including creating a positive learning climate (Manis 1979), modeling interpersonal and professional behaviors (Shulman 1993), providing structure (Fortune and Abramson 1993; Fox and Zischka 1989; Kerson 1994), giving constructive feedback (Fox and Zischka 1989; Freeman 1985), selecting appropriate learning tasks and assignments (Dea, Grist, and Myli 1982; Gitterman 1989; Nisivoccia 1990), educating, socializing (Webb 1988), gatekeeping (Moore and Urwin 1991), providing emotional support (Ellison 1994; Matorin 1979), linking practicum experiences to classroom/textbook knowledge in internship arrangements (Sheafor and Jenkins 1982; Vayda and Bogo 1991), integrating research (Raskin 1989b), and attending to issues of cultural diversity (Becherman and Burrell 1994). Additionally, these must be done while making administrative decisions in accordance with agency, school, and other contextual constraints (Kerson 1994), such as the recent impact of managed care (Munson 1996). The supervisor must integrate and organize these multiple duties, which can be a highly stressful endeavor.

Besides performing these tasks, the supervisor often simultaneously functions in other roles. For example, internship supervisors are typically agency employees who have work-related obligations and responsibilities to clients. It is a complex challenge to balance the needs of the agency, the school, the supervisee, and the client. The supervisor may be unsure of how to prioritize responsibilities and decide which task needs to be done at what time. In fact, the "most commonly mentioned problem" of supervisors is the role strain on the practitioner who is accountable for both work-related and educational functions (Fellin 1982:105). It has been suggested that the overwhelming number of roles is responsible for supervisor burnout (Shapiro 1989) and for the high turnover rate of practicum supervisors, estimated to be around 50 percent each year (Bogo and Power 1992; Hagen 1989; Rosenfeld 1989).

Transition from Worker to Supervisor

Other sources of anxiety come into play when newly adopting the supervisory position. The acquisition of a new role, even when anticipated, "involves adaptation and stress" (Koerin, Harrigan, and Reeves 1990:200). It entails a multitude of changes including new tasks, routines, identity, and relationships. Anxiety accompanies any change in varying degrees, and is an inevitable feature of role transition.

In supervision, the transition does not usually entail exchanging one work-related responsibility for another but rather adding the role of supervisor to work-related duties. It is not uncommon for social workers in direct practice to be given supervision responsibilities without a decrease in their overall job responsibilities (Shulman 1993). This is particularly true for practicum supervisors. In this day of shrinking resources for social work practice, workers may already feel they are being stretched to meet agency needs. Being asked to "take a supervisee" may be flattering but also stressful.

Competence

New supervisors often feel insecure about their ability to perform the job. A common feeling that arises during the transition to supervisor is fear that one lacks the skills required of an educator (Wilson 1981). Actually, this is not an uncommon anxiety for seasoned supervisors as well. Many social work practitioners move into supervisory positions, frequently without the benefit of formal education to guide supervisory practice (Akin and Weil 1981). In fact, supervisors cite recalling their own experiences as a supervisee as the major source of their abilities (Strom 1991). Furthermore, there has been a lack of available, well-articulated supervisory models to guide practice. Operating without structured guiding principles contributes to supervisors not knowing "what to do"—a significant source of anxiety.

Although accomplished clinicians are likely to be selected for supervision duties, having solid practice skills does not mean possessing teaching abilities. "Unfortunately, in our society, teaching methods are taken for granted. If someone has substantive or practice competence, the assumption is that one knows how to teach it" (Gitterman 1989:86). While supervisors have substantial experience dealing with interpersonal behaviors, they often are not as skilled in the teaching dimensions of supervision (Ellison 1994; Manis 1979) and may be unsure whether their interpersonal helping behaviors are appropriate when educating social work supervisees. Lacking a base of teaching knowledge from which to operate may cause a supervisor to feel uncertain about how to proceed, challenging his or her sense of competence. Practitioners who take on the role of educator often experience "pervasive self-doubt about what he or she has to offer a supervisee" (Matorin 1979:150).

In addition, feeling responsible for another's education, which represents an investment of money (in internship arrangements), time, emotions, and hopes for the future, can be daunting. Supervisors frequently fear failing to meet students' needs (Kadushin 1992; Wilson 1981), especially when working with experienced or exceptionally bright supervisees (Bogo and Vayda 1998). Supervisors may not have kept recent with research and theory (Selig 1982) or may have to partake in unfamiliar activities, such as assisting a supervisee engaging in group work. Wanting to be perceived as competent, supervisors may fear giving up the "more knowing stance" (Wijnberg and Schwartz 1977:109) due to anxiety. Knowing more than the student does about all areas of social work practice is not a necessary, or even reasonable, prerequisite for performing supervision. Anxiety related to wanting to feel competent may be what causes new supervisors to retreat from practicum duties to the safe harbor of direct practice.

The Supervisee

Multiple sources of supervisor anxiety emerge from work with the supervisee. Because there are a large number, they are organized here by subcategories. These include supervisor stress related to supervisee anxiety, supervisor expectations of supervisee performance, the process of selecting learning assignments, the role of the supervisor's personal issues, and issues related to cultural diversity.

Supervisee Anxiety

Supervisors need to be supportive when encountering supervisee anxiety. However, the stress that such anxiety can cause may interfere with their ability to provide support. As stated in the previous chapter, supervisee anxiety is recognized as a natural and expected component of supervision (Bruck 1963; Judah 1982; Wilson 1981). It results from many factors, including the transition from work to school and adopting the role of supervisee, the integration of personal and professional selves, and the process of socialization into a new profession (Webb 1988). Furthermore, learning new knowledge, adopting and integrating a new value system, employing new skills, working with a variety of people, and repeatedly encountering new circumstances all are stress-producing experiences.

Involvement with supervision is in itself anxiety producing for supervisees. They have entered an environment in which they must make themselves vulnerable to scrutiny and critical feedback. In addition, they must learn to negotiate the personality and teaching style of the supervisor, as well as issues of dependence and autonomy (Kerson 1994), professional competence (Bruck 1963), and authority (Kerson 1994; Munson 1993). Supervisee problems with authority can be a major obstacle to learning, especially if they have had previous negative experiences that are unresolved (Pettes 1979). Supervisees are often fearful about directly confronting their supervisors when unhappy about aspects of their supervision (Rosenblatt and Mayer 1975). A potential result is negative behaviors that trigger anxiety in the supervisor and in turn may exacerbate the undesirable behavior that is causing the supervisee's original discomfort. Often new staff are unaware of what social work supervision entails, and schools do not adequately prepare practicum interns to utilize supervision appropriately (Martin and Alper 1989). Not knowing what to expect from the supervisory conference and relationship is likely to increase supervisee anxiety. Significant anxiety can be aroused by the process of developing self-awareness (Bruck 1963; Kadushin 1991; Webb 1988). The supervisor is the person most central to assist with this (May and Kilpatrick 1989).

Supervisee anxiety can trigger stress in the supervisor, especially if they do not feel equipped to handle it. Research identifies "good, supportive supervisors as the main source of help in dealing with stress" (Munson 1993:233). However, feeling anxious about how to respond can result in supervisor behaviors that intensify rather than reduce stress. A few models exist to assist supervisors with students' anxiety. Grossman, Levine-Jordano, and Shearer (1990) present an "educational framework" for working with supervisees' emotional reactions to clients. Wilson (1981) offers techniques for reducing supervisee anxiety in her supervision manual. Catalano (1985) specifically identifies and offers an approach for dealing with "clinical panic" in the supervisee. This emotional state is generally triggered by a client in crisis, which generates a crisis reaction. Finally, Munson (1993) provides an in-depth look at stress in supervision and gives strategies for dealing with it.

Expectations

Clarity of expectations for the supervisee and supervisor is an important feature of quality supervision (Curiel and Rosenthal 1987; Fortune et al. 1985) helpful in reducing stress for both. Lack of definition in this area has been identified as a factor in supervisor burnout (Shapiro 1989).

Supervisors' past experiences with providing or receiving supervision are usually their primary source for expectations about the process, which may differ from supervisee expectations. Differing ideas about performance can negatively affect the quality of the supervisory relationship (Munson 1993; Triezenberg 1984). For example, supervisees view autonomous practice as a more important aspect of the practicum than their supervisors (Rotholz and Werk 1984). This discrepancy is likely to result in conflict when the supervisee is pushing for independence while the supervisor retains control.

How much to expect from the supervisee in terms of practice knowledge, amount of work, analytical capacity, motivation to learn, and deadlines are common sources of stress for supervisors. Often, these performance levels are subjective feelings about what a supervisee should be able to do, not objective measures. Because expectations are usually not clearly outlined at the start of the encounter, supervisors are likely to use personal judgments, thus evaluating the intern in terms of highly individualized and subjective criteria rather than more objective measures.

Many supervisors, especially those just beginning, have high criteria for supervisees. For example, it is not uncommon for a new intern to be expected to "act like a professional," even though they may not yet know what this means. This performance expectation can result in the supervisor negatively perceiving and responding to the supervisee's emotional experience. While most supervisors are adept at attending to clients' emotional needs when providing direct service, there is evidence that they do not do this as readily with supervisees (Munson 1996; Siddle and Wilson 1984). This is of some concern because supervisees experience high levels of anxiety, especially in the beginning (Nisivoccia 1990), and need to feel emotionally supported.

Supervisors and supervisees possess different views about what supervisor behaviors constitute sound practice (Rotholz and Werk 1984). For example, they often hold different notions about the most effective educational methods. As discussed in chapter 3, there are a range of supervisee learning styles (Berengarten 1957; Rogers and MacDonald 1992). Educators emphasize the importance of supervisors adjusting their teaching styles to accommodate the supervisee: "Learning is more effective when teaching is consonant with the supervisee's style" (Webb 1988:37). This is complicated as supervisees mature; the supervisory relationship often becomes more collaborative and less directive (Kadushin 1992), challenging supervisors to alter their teaching style. This may take them into unfamiliar territory and raise anxiety, which in turn may cause them to "fall back" to their most comfortable method of teaching. For the supervisee whose learning style is different, anxiety will likely increase and learning will be impeded.

Finally, conflict may result from different beliefs about "how to help" clients. For example, a supervisor may promote the use of psychodynamic theories and methods while the supervisee favors a family systems approach. This clash of perspectives can be a source of anxiety.

Selecting Learning Assignments

In one study, 85 percent of supervisors surveyed experienced role strain in the process of developing supervisee assignments, which was attributed to the natural tension that exists among organizational needs, client service needs, and supervisee learning needs (Gitterman 1989). Deciding "'what' to teach and 'when' to teach it" means assessing the supervisee's abilities and style in relation to a particular client's need and style (Gitterman 1989:83). This is not always a clear-cut and easy task, especially for new supervisors. "Beginning supervisors expend considerable energy selecting case experiences for their supervisees" (Matorin 1979:153).

The selection of learning assignments raises questions about the degree to which supervisees should be protected from or exposed to complex cases (Bogo and Vayda 1998). Multiproblem cases raise anxiety for supervisors, who fear that supervisees will be overwhelmed and unable to provide quality service, posing a threat to their growth and the client's care. As a result, supervisors may become overprotective. Younger and less experienced supervisees may trigger greater anxiety in supervisors, suggested by one study's finding that supervisors are more protective with undergraduate than graduate interns (Curiel and Rosenthal 1987). Particularly in internship arrangements, a danger is that supervisees will not be given an opportunity to develop skills to autonomously operate in the "real world" (i.e., after graduation)—where they will be freely exposed to complex cases. While it is important to include supervisees in the process of selecting their learning goals and tasks (Fortune and Abramson 1993), anxiety in the supervisor may be an obstacle to achieving this.

Personal Issues

Supervisors are first and foremost human beings. They bring to the supervisory relationship a personal and professional history that influences their own perceptions, feelings, and behaviors regarding interpersonal relationships (including supervision). The supervisor's family of origin is a factor in the supervisory relationship but has been given insufficient attention (Munson 1996). Furthermore, supervisors have lives outside of work that are often filled with multiple stressors.

It is not uncommon for the supervisory experience itself to trigger anxieties that stem from within the person of supervisor. For example, a supervisor with the "need to be liked" (Wilson 1981) may not give appropriate feedback and may avoid confronting the supervisee about practice behaviors. Others who "need to be needed" (Kadushin 1992; Wilson 1981) may fear and therefore sabotage supervisee autonomy. Furthermore, some "need to be respected" and misinterpret this to mean that subordinates must fear them. Supervisors who make this error will treat supervisees in a punitive fashion, raise their anxiety, stunt their learning, and create an unsafe and unpleasant learning environment.

An additional source of supervisor anxiety is personal concern over reputation. It is not uncommon for supervisors to worry about what is being said about them by supervisees, agency personnel, and the school. There is also a worry that if the supervisee is making errors, it reflects poorly on them.

Some supervisors' anxiety is related to a need to preserve their personal beliefs. This may result in a mistaken perception that supervisees should view the world in accordance with the supervisor's understanding of what social workers should think. Students need to be able to process perceptions about people of difference and attempt to reconcile professional values with their own. Supervisors who react negatively to judgmental statements may cause them to withhold their perceptions, resulting in a restricted learning experience. Furthermore, supervisors who react this way are, ironically, being judgmental.

Finally, as stated earlier, supervisors may feel ill equipped to help supervisees learn. Worried about appearing proficient, they may intentionally keep supervisory discussions away from the supervisee's clinical work. Additionally, they may steer supervision in the direction of "social" conversations, or talk about their own personal issues. Of even greater concern is that this anxiety will cause the supervisor to focus on the personality of the supervisee rather than on their learning and performance—a safer endeavor for most clinician-turned-supervisors, but one that supervisees have found objectionable (Rosenblatt and Mayer 1975).

Encountering Diversity

Interacting with people who are different in terms of age, culture, gender, sexual orientation, and socioeconomic status can be anxiety producing. In fact, practicum supervisors have "requested seminars . . . that deal with ethnic/cultural/racial/gender/experiences/differences" (Holtzman 1994:147), to assist them in working with supervisees who are different from themselves. Unfortunately, there is a paucity of literature that examines the influence of diversity on the supervisor-supervisee relationship. Hence, little is available to guide supervisors and supervisees in handling difference in their relationship. (See Kadushin 1992; Kaiser 1997; and Sweitzer and King 1999 for some help in this area.)

Supervisor Authority

The fourth category of anxiety, authority, has also been subdivided due to the large number of sources. This is an area with which supervisors often struggle (Wilson 1981; Kerson 1994). Because the supervisor is generally accountable to the agency, its clients, and the school (in internships), and ultimately is responsible for producing a formal evaluation of the supervisee's performance, they have formal authority over the supervisee. Supervisors may experience anxiety regarding authority, based on previous personal and professional experiences. In addition, they may have never been in such a situation. They may "play games" of defensiveness, abdication, and power in response to the anxiety triggered by being in a position of authority (Hawthorne 1975).

The supervisory relationship is hierarchical (Jacobs 1991; Hamilton and Else 1983), with the supervisor having greater power (Jacobs 1991; Johnston, Rooney, and Reitmeir 1991). However, the current emphasis in the literature is on the creation and maintenance of a more egalitarian relationship (Knowles 1970; Lazzari 1991). Supervisors are faced with an inherent conflict between the reality of their hierarchical position and the egalitarian emphasis. Furthermore, there are no mechanisms readily available to reconcile this conflict, which can contribute to supervisor discomfort with authority.

Supervisors may also struggle with their own feelings related to accountability. Being responsible for the supervisee's education, they may experience anxiety when confronted with a failing, negative, or acting out student. They may worry that others are condemning them for inappropriate supervisee behaviors. In addition, supervisors may blame themselves (Wilson 1981), despite the fact that they cannot truly control supervisee actions. Supervisors may exhibit unhelpful responses ranging from attempting to be overcontrolling to distancing themselves by dismissing the behavior as rooted in the supervisee's pathological personality.

Feelings related to authority and accountability can influence the degree to which a supervisor allows supervisee autonomy regarding practice and learning. A central goal of educational supervision is autonomous practice (Rotholz and Werk 1984). Functioning independently entails a reflective process of self-evaluation and self-directed learning. Hence, a major objective in supervision is to provide activities that "help supervisees help themselves learn" (Blake and Peterman 1985:24). The supervisor who is uncomfortable with supervisee-directed learning and autonomous practice may restrict independent activities, thus sabotaging the student's ability to become self-reliant.

Finally, the evaluation of supervisee progress raises anxiety for supervisors (Pettes 1979; Wilson 1981). It is a complex process that inevitably entails subjective responses to supervisee performance. Supervisors may be anxious and lack confidence about their judgments. In addition, they may have difficulty separating feelings about the quality of the supervisory relationship from perceptions of the supervisee's abilities (Kadushin 1992). They may feel uncomfortable giving critical feedback, due to the common errors made during evaluation presented by Kadushin (1992). Supervisors who experience the evaluation process as overly stressful are at risk of making supervisee appraisals that originate more from their own needs than the supervisee's.

Power Struggles

Supervisors and supervisees occasionally have disagreements, even in positive relationships, due to conflicting needs, agendas, expectations, and ideas about how best to treat a case, and miscommunication. Open disagreements are an expected part of the supervisory relationship, and in fact may assist in promoting growth and learning. However, when disagreements are not openly discussed and resolved, they may emerge in other, often seemingly unrelated, interactions. A common way that conflict is played out is in supervisee challenges to recognized rules regarding the supervisory meeting. For example, a supervisee who is upset about a disagreement with the supervisor about a particular issue does not discuss it but instead comes late to meetings, sends nonverbal messages that convey lack of respect or disagreement with the supervisor, does not follow through on the supervisor's requests (e.g., to complete paperwork in a timely fashion), dismisses the supervisor's suggestions or feedback, or does not utilize supervisory discussions in practice. The disagreement becomes a power struggle when both are more interested in "winning" (having things go their own way) than in resolving it. Typically, this means that the pair are not openly trying to examine why the power struggle exists, to identify the underlying issues that are at the crux of the relational conflict.

Whether the power struggle is overt or covert, it raises anxiety in the supervisor, who must do something about it. Anxiety may cause supervisors to respond by utilizing authority autocratically. This intensifies the battle and demonstrates to the supervisee, "I have more power than you." Another common reaction is to avoid addressing the power struggle. Neither response helps the supervisee to learn how to negotiate and resolve power struggles, an important skill in social work practice. Both prevent supervisors from receiving feedback about their behaviors that may be contributing to the supervisee's dissatisfaction. In other words, by retreating to a position of either authority or abdication, the supervisor lets him- or herself "off the hook" and does not learn to become a better supervisor. Furthermore, an opportunity for both supervisor and supervisee to experientially learn how to effectively address power struggles is lost. By dealing with the conflict through avoidance or power play, supervisors are in danger of teaching supervisees to model these ineffective methods and use them with clients.

Overcoming Power Struggles

The first step toward productive resolution of a supervisor-supervisee power struggle is to identify it as such. This is more difficult than it may sound. Often when a power struggle is occurring, it appears to the supervisor that the supervisee is simply behaving badly. However, the supervisor should consider that the supervisee may be "acting out" resentment from a past, seemingly unconnected incident. If so, the pair are fighting with each other over unrelated issues rather than addressing the true problem. Therefore, even if the supervisor is successful in stopping the problem behavior, the resentment and relational obstacle remain present—if not stronger.

When faced with a power struggle, supervisors have three choices: 1) use their position of authority to override the supervisee and "win"; 2) let go of the power struggle and let the supervisee win; or 3) share the perception that they have entered into a power struggle and convey a wish to resolve it openly through exploration of its development. The first option, using authority to stop the supervisee's behavior, risks teaching the supervisee to use an authoritarian stance when faced with their own struggles in positions of authority (e.g., the clinical relationship). In our view, this is problematic. The second option, letting the power struggle go, is also problematic. Although it takes two to maintain a power struggle, abdicating demonstrates that poor behavior is acceptable and does not teach how to resolve relational difficulties.

We favor the third option, active and open exploration of the power struggle's emergence. Both the supervisor and the supervisee must take a nondefensive stance and acknowledge their role in the conflict's development. It is common for supervisees (or supervisors) to share resentments or disappointments when this approach is taken. Open discussion typically resolves them, brings the pair closer, and effectively teaches the supervisee how to handle power struggles when they emerge in clinical relationships.

Boundary of Supervision and Therapy

The supervisor's position of authority brings with it the power to direct areas of exploration for learning. One important area is developing self-awareness.

Supervisees are encouraged to explore the "self" for personal and professional growth. However, supervisors are often wary about discussing a student's personality or personal issues due to fear of "therapizing" or "caseworking" them (Webb 1988). In addition, supervisees have found approaches that aim to uncover and address their personal issues for personal and professional growth to be "objectionable" (Rosenblatt and Mayer 1975).

However, supervisors also recognize the importance of coaching supervisees to work productively when personal issues emerge as obstacles. It is important to talk about supervisee personal matters when they interfere with the ability to practice (Norman 1987). The boundary between supervision and therapy can at times be tenuous, and negotiating it can seem difficult. And the fact that the interactional processes of supervision and therapy are similar (Kahn 1979; Norman 1987; Reid 1984; Rich 1993; Shulman 1993; Storm and Heath 1985) can challenge the supervisor's ability to maintain a distinction between the two (see chapter 4 for further discussion and guidelines). Working with this boundary is a source of supervisor anxiety.

Context

Supervision occurs within an environment that influences learning, practice, and the supervisory relationship through such factors as the agency, the school, the geographical location, the law, funding sources, and accreditation bodies (Kerson 1994). The supervisor operates within a system that must accommodate these interdependent components, and therefore is required to perform many systemic role functions, in addition to the many complex responsibilities of a educator and clinical consultant.

Although they must balance administrative, educational, and supportive tasks, educational supervisors are supposed to give clear priority to the teaching function of supervision (Kadushin 1991). However, heavy work-related responsibilities often pull them away from educational activities. It is important that the agency and the school provide support for the supervisor (Gordon 1982; Wilson 1981) in order to maintain an educational focus. Agency support for educational activities (e.g., reduction in caseload) is a factor in supervisor satisfaction (Rosenfeld 1989). When a supervisor "does not feel he has such sanction, he will not have the self-confidence to take decisive action" (Wilson 1981:30). It is likely that without such support, supervisors will give teaching a lower priority than competing needs. One study found that 29 percent of internship supervisors surveyed reported that they felt a "lack of support" from the school of social work (Strom 1991).

Low agency morale and excessive clinical challenge are additional contextual factors that "put a strain on the supervisory relationship" (Homonoff et al. 1995:335). Negotiating multiple role expectations, particularly in relation to contextual issues, can be a highly stressful process and "may contribute to higher turnover rates and burn-out of supervisors" (Raskin 1989a:185).

Time

Related to contextual stressors is the problem of diminishing agency resources for educational supervision (Schneck 1995; Skolnik 1985). Supervisors are increasingly pressured to take on additional responsibilities (cases) on top of an already overwhelming workload. This often leaves little time for supervision. When they are unable to invest in their supervisees due to time limitations, the supervisory relationship and the overall quality of the encounter suffer.

Research has demonstrated that supervisors do not have adequate time to supervise (Galm 1972; Kadushin 1992; Shulman 1993), and that this is a major point of dissatisfaction with the role (Kadushin 1974; Rotholz and Werk 1984; Strom 1991). Supervisees also complain about their supervisors' lack of time and report that it is a recurrent cause of unstructured scheduling of supervisory meetings (Curiel and Rosenthal 1987). Availability of the supervisor is a factor in intern satisfaction (Fortune and Abramson 1993); and supervisors are likely to experience guilt and anxiety related to allocation of limited time for supervision.

Triangulation with Other Staff

A potential source of supervisor anxiety is having to deal with co-workers. It is not unusual for supervisees to develop relationships with other staff and at times seek guidance from them. While this is often a positive element in supervisee learning, it can also be problematic. When tension arises in the supervisory relationship, a third person may be brought in by either participant for support or to build an alliance—forming a triangle of two against one. Although triangulation (Kerr and Bowen 1988) may function to relieve the immediate stress in a two-person system, the underlying conflict remains unresolved.

Both the supervisor and the supervisee can engage in this type of behavior. Some common examples include a supervisee seeking out another staff person for support and education instead of going to the supervisor, a supervisor conferring with a colleague or another supervisee about an intern's "limited abilities," a supervisee and a staff member uniting by sharing views on the supervisor's ineffectiveness as a clinician and/or educator, and a supervisor or a supervisee privately complaining about the other to colleagues. Other examples include staff members attempting to "move in" on the supervisee because of problems in their own relationship with the supervisor. They may seek to influence the supervisee to take on views that contradict the supervisor's and undermine their authority.

Regardless of the arrangement, the purpose of triangulating is to solicit support from an outside person against the other in the supervisory relationship. Triangles (a type of power struggle) are not neutral and involve two-against-one coalitions. Rather than addressing problems directly and openly, they extend the conflict to include third and often fourth parties. The underlying issue is not addressed or resolved. Supervisees in placements that utilize multiple settings and/or secondary supervisors are at particular risk of triangulation (Marshack and Glassman 1991). Triangulation can be a source of anxiety for the supervisor, particularly if he or she is the odd person out.

Secondary Status

An additional contextual source of supervisor anxiety specifically concerns internship supervision: how the practice of field instruction is viewed by the academy. Practicum education does not receive the same recognition as other parts of the social work curriculum. In fact, its secondary status in regard to educational functions and research is well documented (Holtzman 1994; Raskin 1989; Shatz 1989; Sheafor and Jenkins 1982; Skolnik 1985). Many schools of social work place a high value on research and view those who conduct scientific investigation as more important than those who only teach. Few field instructors conduct scientific studies.

This secondary status can be a source of anxiety for intern supervisors. It may serve to diminish their position as expert and teacher in the eyes of the school and the supervisee, and perhaps most critically, in their own view. Being perceived as below school faculty, who have greater status, can make supervisors feel defensive about their teaching and practice abilities. To be effective, it is important for them to feel validated as experts by the profession.

Self-Awareness

As can be seen from the multiple sources presented, supervisors often experience anxiety about the supervisory encounter, which "leads to much self-examination and produces new areas of self-awareness as supervisors agonize over these various concerns" (Wilson 1981:29). The process of developing and experiencing self-awareness is in itself highly stressful. It is often the most difficult aspect for supervisees in the process of becoming a social worker (Schmidt 1976). It is likely that it is difficult for supervisors as well. Many do not consider the possibility of having to employ their self-awareness skills when working with supervisees. When they are surprised by their own reactions, it is often distressing. Moreover, acknowledging that their behaviors may be more related to their own issues than something the supervisee did can be difficult. Self-awareness activities challenge supervisors to uncover causes of intense reactions and sometimes admit to flaws in their work. Although it is a source of anxiety, engaging in these activities during supervision is important for supervisors.

Educational supervision is a complicated and often difficult endeavor. It calls for attention to a wide variety of interpersonal considerations and environmental demands and thus contains many potential sources of supervisor anxiety. Being aware that these multiple stressors exist and are an expected part of the job can normalize supervisors' experiences and help them to both identify and handle stress. When unaware of their anxiety, they are likely to act defensively and in ways to reduce their own stress at the expense of supervisee learning. Therefore, it is critical that supervisors routinely monitor their feelings and behaviors in order to assure quality supervision.

The Necessity of Self-Awareness

Anxiety in the supervisor is a normal experience and should be viewed as such. "In fact, there is cause for concern when a supervisor is so self-confident that he fails to experience these feelings from time to time" (Wilson 1981:27). Anxiety can be seen as positive because it motivates the teaching-learning process and activates growth in the supervisor. Nevertheless, if it remains out of the supervisor's conscious awareness, anxiety can be dangerous to the relationship and to the supervisee's success. It is important that supervisors seek to identify "hidden" anxieties through steady self-reflection. "Such self-examination can free energy to refocus on educational issues" (Matorin 1979:152). Anxiety can prompt supervisors to react to their own stress-related needs rather than making thoughtful choices about their behaviors. Monitoring it allows them to intentionally alter their behavior to promote and maximize supervisee learning experiences and minimize potentially damaging supervisor conduct. This deliberate manipulation of behavior is referred to as "supervisor conscious use of self."

Additionally, supervisor self-awareness is important for supervisee self-awareness. If supervisors are "critically reflective" about their practice, they can "demonstrate and describe this process to supervisees" (Rogers and MacDonald 1992:167). Supervisors are central in helping supervisees to develop self-awareness skills, especially as role models.

Self-examination of anxiety involves consideration of its affective, cognitive, and behavioral implications. The anxiety may produce strong feelings (anger, frustration), alter thinking (create difficulty concentrating, daydreaming, distorted beliefs about supervisee intentions), and cause supervisors to act inflexibly (taking an authoritarian stance, withdrawing, not complimenting the supervisee). Self-examination should seek to ascertain the consequences of anxiety in each of these domains and to identify the source of the stress in order to reduce it.

In our view, it is most important to focus on how the anxiety is manifest in the behavioral domain, because supervisees directly experience only the supervisor's behaviors. While a supervisor may have negative feelings or thoughts about a supervisee, it is their behaviors that can ultimately be detrimental to the relationship and supervisee learning. Indeed, supervisors can think poorly of supervisees but act productively with them.

Awareness of one's actions enables active modification of them. Behaviors can be identified with relative ease through retrospective processing, such as review of process recordings or analysis of videotapes. Understanding how one responds in a particular situation allows consideration of alternative behaviors that can be tried out in future interactions. For example, a supervisor learned, by listening to a tape of a supervision meeting, that he was being highly directive with a particular supervisee. This supervisor usually did not behave this way but was anxious about this student's ability to perform competently. He recognized that if he continued to be directive, the supervisee would not improve and his confidence in her would remain low. Although he was still anxious about her practice, the supervisor was able to modify his behavior to involve greater supervisee input during case planning discussions.

There are times, however, when supervisors experience difficulty in trying out alternative behaviors. This occurs when anxiety is particularly overwhelming, resulting in an emotional "block." In such cases, it is important
to have mechanisms for identifying and addressing the source of anxiety so
that it no longer restricts the selection of behaviors.

Methods for Aiding Supervisor Self-Awareness

Few guidelines have been developed to assist supervisors in monitoring
subjective responses and increasing self-awareness. Wilson (1981) provides
perhaps the only set of activities specifically designed for supervisor anxiety:
eight exercises aimed at building supervisor self-awareness. These highly
beneficial procedures address two considerations related to use of self:
intrapsychic reactions and potential behaviors. By using these activities,
supervisors can enhance insight into their thoughts and feelings about the
supervisory encounter and learn to anticipate personal reactions that may
not be ideal.

While insight into *potential* conduct is helpful, it is also important for
supervisors to identify their *actual* responses to real supervisee behaviors.
Additional approaches to enhance the supervisor's understanding of self in
the supervisory relationship are put forth here. These methods fall into three
categories: retrospective processing, accessing supervisee perceptions of
supervisor behaviors, and education.

Retrospective Processing

Retrospective analysis of the supervisory meeting is a helpful method for
reviewing feelings, thoughts, and behaviors in order to improve supervision
practices. "Supervisors can use this ability [critical reflection] to help them
make decisions regarding their supervisees such as: when to ignore or confront certain behaviors, assessing a supervisee's readiness for specific assignments, choosing appropriate strategies for supervisee learning, and other
decisions requiring a balance between individualizing the supervisee and
meeting the requirements of the setting and the school" (Rogers and Mac-
Donald 1992:175).

There are a number of different retrospective analysis approaches. In general, these include independent mental review of meetings, review of

practicum encounters with a consultant (e.g., peer, supervisor), process recordings, and audio and video techniques. Each approach has its benefits and limitations, but all are useful for considering the strengths and weaknesses of one's own performance.

Independent mental review is the most readily available and probably the most commonly used method of retrospective analysis. It is not constrained by time or space. It is, however, limited by the supervisor's ability to objectively and fairly review their own performance. In particular, the content being examined is determined by the supervisor's memory and perception of events. They may review only interactions they view were important and miss behaviors that have had major impact on the supervisory process.

Mutual review involves critiquing recent supervisory conferences with an outside, objective person (e.g., peer, consultant, supervisor) or group. While this process is subject to some of the same initial constraints as independent review (i.e., sharing only what the supervisor views as important), discussing supervisory encounters with another person has some additional benefits. Important material that the supervisor may have bypassed can be addressed with the guidance of the "outside" reviewer, interactions can be examined with a greater degree of objectivity, and a wider range of alternatives to undesirable behaviors can be considered. Furthermore, supervisors can receive validation and support for their work—important factors in their satisfaction and reduction of stress.

Both independent and mutual mental review are helpful for identifying supervisors' general thoughts and feelings about interactions, but they are of limited use for reviewing specific and transient behaviors. Understanding one's behaviors is a critical part of handling anxiety in a professional manner. Thoughts and feelings in and of themselves are not usually problematic, but they do influence behavior—and, as stated earlier, the supervisor's behavior is what the supervisee experiences and what has the greatest impact on the relationship. For example, a supervisor who is aware of negative feelings toward a supervisee may still be able to maintain a professional stance and work in the supervisee's best interest. However, there is always the chance that these feelings will "seep out" in subtle behaviors (e.g., facial expression, patterns of sighing, frequently interrupting the supervisee) and become known to the student. Furthermore, the supervisor may be keenly aware of their feelings and thoughts but not of their actions. The presentation of self that he or she believes is being put forth may be very different from what the supervisee actually experiences. It is therefore vital for supervisors to have mechanisms available for identifying and reviewing interpersonal behaviors.

The process recording (a written verbatim account of interactions, usually with added notations) is the tool most frequently used by supervisees for reviewing their practice and enhancing self-awareness. It has also been promoted for educating supervisors and for considering supervisor use of self (Glassman 1995). Supervisor process recordings are useful for identifying sequences of interactions. By reconstructing what occurred in a meeting, supervisors are able to observe their behaviors in relation to the supervisee's statements, which enables them to identify, sometimes with the aid of a consultant (e.g., supervisor, peer), occasions when they responded to a supervisee's behavior in a manner that was less than productive (e.g., changed the conversation unexpectedly, used sarcasm), possibly due to anxiety. Upon identifying such behaviors, they can consider alternative responses. If necessary (i.e., when faced with an emotional block), they can explore the intrapsychic dimensions of the behaviors.

While process recording is useful, it is subject to recall distortions and is limited to documenting the content of interactions. What is not usually captured is *how* statements were conveyed (e.g., tone, pacing, nonverbal cues), unless detailed notes record these facets of the communication. However, such notes are subject to the same distortions.

Audio and video recordings of supervisory sessions are less vulnerable to distortions from recall and provide more accurate accounts of interactions. They offer potential as mechanisms for gaining more discrete understanding of supervisor behaviors. Both media have advantages and disadvantages. Audiotaping is relatively easy—equipment is readily available and simple to operate. Videotaping captures a great deal more than audio (e.g., nonverbal details), but the equipment is more expensive and difficult to operate. Star (1979) examined the use of videotape as a vehicle for self-image confrontation for supervisees and found that it had a significant influence on perceptual change of self. It is likely that this approach would be similarly helpful for supervisors. Tape recording should be used with caution because if the process is too intrusive, it can create additional anxieties for the person under review (Munson 1993).

A potential problem in using video and audio to record and observe one's own behavior is that perceptions of interactions can be influenced by feelings related to the context in which the interactions originally took place. In other words, if a supervisor believes a supervisee to be acting in a manipulative manner during the actual supervisory meeting, it is likely that he or she will continue to perceive the supervisee in this way when reviewing the tape recording. Supervisors may see their behaviors as appropriate and even productive if their perceptions are not challenged. It is helpful to have an "outside" person guide the critique and question them about their behaviors and subjective reactions.

An approach that incorporates reviewing taped meetings with a "recall consultant" (outside person) is interpersonal process recall (IPR) (Kagan and Kagan 1990). IPR has been primarily used as a training model for counseling supervisees and as a research methodology (Elliot 1984). It has also been used successfully to train beginning and experienced therapists, paraprofessionals, and medical school supervisees (Bernard 1989). The IPR process involves tape recording an interaction (e.g., supervision) and, soon after, critiquing it with the consultant. During the review, the tape is stopped at various points of interest and the participant (in this case, the supervisor) is asked to recall the perceptions they were experiencing when the moment was recorded. This process can aid the supervisor's self-awareness by motivating them to question behaviors and to link them to related thoughts and feelings.

Bernard (1989) demonstrated IPR as a useful tool for training supervisors. She reports that among several supervision models used in laboratory training of clinical supervisors, IPR "addresses relationship variables most directly" (106). Additionally, this method was helpful in identifying supervisor behaviors that were likely contributing factors in relationship difficulties with supervisees. An interesting, incidental discovery was the common observation among the supervisors that they failed to demonstrate empathy with the supervisee and appeared like a "cold fish" (108).

IPR has yet to be used in social work to assist supervisor self-awareness. However, one study that used it to look at supervisory process suggested that the experience provided supervisors with new insights about their behaviors (Caspi 1997). IPR has potential value as a method for supervisor self-discovery.

Accessing Supervisee Perceptions

Supervisees' perceptions of which supervisor behaviors are helpful or hindering are an important resource for supervisors seeking to enhance their self-awareness. There are various methods available for accessing these perceptions, including asking the supervisee directly for feedback, using an out-side person to relay the information, IPR, and standardized instruments and hand-tailored questionnaires.

The most direct way for supervisors to learn about their supervisees' per-ceptions of their behaviors is to ask for this type of feedback. Unless an open and trusting relationship has been developed, receiving unfiltered percep-tions is unlikely. A supervisee may not feel safe enough to openly disclose negative perceptions directly to the supervisor. This is particularly true if the aim of the questioning is to gain information about behaviors related to anx-iety—an area in which the supervisor is likely to be defensive. Also, the supervisor may not be open to criticism from a supervisee with whom there is conflict.

This problem can be minimized by providing a less threatening environ-ment for students to voice their perceptions. One method of doing so is to use an outside person to collect and relay the information to the supervisor. By promising not to reveal the supervisee's responses to the supervisor until after formal evaluations (particularly at the end of the supervisory encounter) have been submitted is an additional strategy. A disadvantage of interviewing supervisees (whether the supervisor or an outside person does it) is that the responses will likely furnish global perceptions of the supervi-sor rather than feedback about specific behaviors. Additionally, supervisee recall distortions may complicate attempts to gain distinct information.

IPR enables access to specific information about discrete supervisor actions. The recall consultant can review the taped meetings with super-visees to gain insight into which particular behaviors were helpful or hinder-ing. This type of feedback can be used to enhance supervisor self-awareness. It is possible for the supervisor to view their own behavior as not helpful while the supervisee sees the same action as positive. Of course, the reverse may also occur. IPR can be especially effective for securing feedback about moments when the supervisor felt anxious by identifying these times before reviewing them on tape with the supervisee.

An additional strategy that has been largely unexplored in social work is the use of instruments (e.g., inventories) for collecting supervisee percep-tions of supervisor behaviors. Munson offers the only form for this purpose specifically designed for social work. Vonk and Thyer (1996) discuss five instruments that can be used to evaluate the quality of supervision. How-ever, these were developed by and for disciplines other than social work, and none has been specifically constructed to examine social work supervision.

Nevertheless, Vonk and Thyer argue that these forms have value for social workers and would promote "more intentional and systematic development of individual supervisors" (1994:15). Although their focus is evaluation, the information they provide can be used to enhance supervisor self-awareness. Supervisors can ask supervisees to complete the inventories and use the responses to refine their practice.

Supervisors can also use the inventories as tools for self-evaluation. A major drawback of many instruments is that they tend to capture global responses rather than specific behaviors. For example, a supervisee may evaluate their supervisor as "supportive," but their response does not identify which specific behaviors conveyed this. A potential way to address this problem is to ask for narrative responses to accompany outcome-based feedback. In this example, a follow-up inquiry could be included, such as "What particular supervisor behaviors did you find to be supportive? Please give examples," or, "Please identify instances in which you found your supervisor to be supportive." Modifying existing inventories to capture such unique information is one way of creating a "tailor made" instrument (Galassi and Trent 1987), an approach that has been used to collect data for which no acceptable standardized form exists.

Education

Beyond the experiential learning that takes place on the job, building one's knowledge base about supervision techniques, common themes, and issues helps to enhance self-awareness and reduce anxiety. The process of learning promotes self-reflection. As supervisors integrate new knowledge, it is likely that they will undergo a self-examination process, that is, relate to the information by reflecting upon how they handled similar situations with their supervisees and considering ways to use the information. Furthermore, a solid knowledge base grounded in the literature is essential for formulating a conceptual framework to guide supervision practice. In other words, the knowledge base serves as a "conceptual map" that informs the direction of the teaching-learning encounter. This helps minimize haphazard supervisory experiences and reduce supervisor anxiety.

Supervisors generally educate themselves through readings and by attending seminars, training, and courses. Reading is a common and helpful way to increase awareness of themes and issues in educational supervision. Although limited, case vignettes can be located that illustrate behaviors that supervisors can use in particular circumstances (for example, see Shulman 1993, 1994). This allows them to consider and compare their own manner of dealing with similar situations. Additionally, seminars in supervision (Abramson and Fortune 1990), supervisor training (Bogo and Power 1994; Rogers and McDonald 1992), conferences, and supervision courses in schools of social work help to increase knowledge about common issues. Furthermore, they are often good places to process one's own actions related to particular concerns.

Decreasing Supervisor Anxiety

Once supervisor anxiety has been identified, it can be reduced so that it is no longer disruptive. Occasionally, supervisor stress is so high that it interferes with the ability to accurately examine behaviors, or even to employ self-awareness skills at all. When stress is high, defensiveness is also likely to be high. Therefore, it is sometimes necessary to reduce anxiety prior to engaging in self-awareness activities. This can be accomplished in a variety of ways.

Processing the anxiety through ventilation and consultation with peers can help to decrease it (Wilson 1981). Support from peers is also beneficial. Supervision seminars can serve as "a supportive arena for learning at a critical point of role transition and self-doubt" (Abramson and Fortune 1990:185). One study found that "access to ongoing emotional support was associated with being an effective supervisor" (Shulman 1993:64). The discovery that others share similar instructional issues, feelings, situations, and anxiety is helpful when assuming a new role (Bogo and Power 1994). Supervisors may also find support from groups formed to process and decrease anxiety and to nurture each other professionally.

Workshops and seminars can also help reduce stress and contribute to growth. "Ongoing continuing professional development via special seminars/workshops are so important as an antidote to 'burnout' and stress" (Holtzman 1994:146). Using anxiety to increase professional knowledge through readings and educational workshops is a healthy and mature response to stress.

Anxiety is often due to lack of clear or mutual understanding of the rules of supervision. Clarification of roles and a clear agreement on the structure of the supervisory meetings (Freeman 1993), in addition to well-articulated learning objectives and evaluation processes, are important vehicles for reducing anxiety. These can be clearly stated in the form of contracts, "a dynamic tool which reduces anxiety" in supervision (Fox 1983:38).

Finally, anxiety can be caused by a lack of direction in supervision. It is not unusual for supervisors to feel lost about how to proceed. Having a model to refer to for guidance in the supervision encounter can helpful to reduce this anxiety. Because the approach presented in this book, the task-centered model for educational supervision (TCS), provides discrete steps for proceeding in supervision, its use will likely be helpful—particularly in regard to figuring out "what to do next."

Conclusion

This chapter examined the person of the supervisor as a major facet of the supervisory experience, particularly, the centrality of the supervisor in supervisee success. Because supervisors are role models who demonstrate professional behaviors, they must possess self-awareness in order to attend to their anxiety.

An overview of the concept of use of self was followed by a discussion of how it relates to the supervisory relationship. "Of all the dimensions of supervision and clinical social work, use of self is among the most artful" (Kerson 1994:15). It requires a high degree of self-awareness. When supervisors are aware of their behaviors and acknowledge when they are related to anxiety, they will be better able to select from a range of alternatives instead of simply reacting. This conscious process of identifying behaviors, thoughts, and/or feelings related to anxiety, then deliberately deciding how to behave in a way that will maximize the supervisee's experience represents supervisor conscious use of self.

The ability of the supervisor to intentionally use particular behaviors is central in establishing a productive learning environment for the supervisee. Supervisors must "consciously sustain and stimulate a climate of trust, respect, interest and support" (Fox 1983:43). They must attempt to be non-judgmental, which is important in reducing supervisee anxiety (Schmidt 1976). The process of suspending judgment often challenges supervisors to control their emotions (Atwood 1986) and withhold automatic subjective reactions. This requires self-awareness,which "on the part of supervisors . . . is clearly a prerequisite to 'conscious use of self' in supervision" (Martin and Alper 1989:54).

The literature suggests that "the dearth of talented supervisors is often of concern to educators" (Kaplan 1988:141). Considering the many potential sources of supervisor anxiety, this is perhaps not so surprising. We hope that the conceptual categories of anxiety assembled here will help supervisors understand and manage their behaviors productively. They can look to the categories and self-reflect to discover the potential sources of their anxiety, as well as consider how these sources may be influencing their use of self. Those responsible for supervising, training, and providing feedback to supervisors may also find the categories useful in locating the source of, normalizing, and processing supervisor anxiety. Once the source is identified and brought to awareness, the supervisor can monitor the issue and employ conscious use of self that is in the best interest of the supervisee.

Finally, it is important to note that not all potentially negative supervisor behaviors are related to the experience of anxiety. For example, supervisors who overidentify with or are exceedingly fond of their supervisees may not feel anxiety but still engage in behaviors that are not in the student's best interest.

The task-centered model for educational supervision, presented in the following chapters, often emphasizes the role of the supervisor and the supervisory relationship. The model's clear structure and guidelines should do much to reduce supervisor anxiety.

6   Preparing for Supervision Beginnings and Endings

The previous chapters have given an overview of the various facets of the educational supervision encounter. This chapter is concerned with the beginning and ending of supervision. The first part presents steps supervisors should consider in preparing for the initial meeting. Instrumental and affective considerations for making new supervisees feel welcome and less anxious about their experience are discussed.

The second part presents issues related to endings. Though it may seem strange to introduce this topic in the middle of this book rather than in the final chapter, we believe it is important to plan for the end of supervision right from the start, for two reasons. First, many endings occur suddenly. Being cognizant of ending issues can help supervisors feel more prepared to handle them. Second, endings are facilitated by reviewing supervisee progress. Therefore, it is important to consider methods for monitoring progress from the beginning. We offer areas for forethought to facilitate the ending process.

Preparing for the Start of Supervision

Prior to meeting for the first time, supervisors should carefully consider the needs of the new supervisee. They should go out of their way to be welcoming and provide the best setting for successful work and supervision. Indeed, there is evidence that initial impressions of supervision are related to satisfaction at the end of the encounter (Fortune 2000), and satisfaction and positive perceptions are important conditions for learning (Kissman and Tran 1990). Some of the areas that should be considered prior to the supervisee's arrival are orientation, resources and support, and anticipation of affective responses.

Orientation

New staff and interns need to be oriented to the agency. This typically is done through activities such as touring the facility, meeting staff, and discussing policy and procedures (e.g., completion of paperwork, how cases are assigned). While some larger institutions (hospitals) have formal orientation programs, many small agencies do not. Furthermore, large institution orientations usually provide general knowledge (e.g., what to do in case of fire, how to report a problem with a paycheck) rather than information for performing specific job activities. Therefore, it is important that supervisors consider how they will orient the new supervisee.

It is equally important to prepare staff for the new employee or intern. Supervisors should take time to alert the staff to the new person's impending arrival and familiarize them with the worker's role and responsibilities. When staff are prepared they are welcoming. When not prepared, they are more likely to react with irritation (usually at the agency administrators, sometimes at the new worker), which results in an uncomfortable first experience of the agency. Notifying staff is particularly important when internship arrangements are made solely between one agency social worker and the university. In this situation, it is also important to secure permission and support from administration prior to accepting an intern. Although it is uncommon, arrangements are sometimes made without the notification of staff and administration; this typically results in a problematic experience for the intern.

Provision of Resources and Support

Prior to starting supervision, it is important to ensure that sufficient resources exist, including office space, access to phones and computers, and secretarial assistance, and some collegial support will be offered. Even small demonstrations of support can go a long way. For example, one intern commented that the agency had added her name to the door of a shared office space. She said that this gesture made her feel welcome and that she belonged at the agency. At a previous agency there been no public acknowledgment of her arrival or space; this had left her feeling inconsequential and had decreased her motivation to participate.

Another important resource to consider, particularly in internship arrangements, is the provision of multiple opportunities for learning. Supervisees appreciate diverse learning assignments (Fortune and Abramson 1993; Fortune et al. 1985; Raskin 1982). Perhaps the most important are those that involve face-to-face work with clients. Supervisors must consider whether they will have enough clients to refer to their interns. Agencies are increasingly having difficulty getting reimbursed by third-party sources for work performed by interns. This has limited both the number and range of opportunities available. If funding issues are considered prior to taking on an intern, agencies are better able to provide a range of learning opportunities.

Another consequential resource to consider is the supervisor's time. Again, careful advance planning to ensure adequate time and space for supervision is important. Many supervisors are frustrated by busy schedules and lack of time for supervision (Kadushin 1974; Rotholz and Werk 1984; Shulman 1993; Strom 1991).

Similarly, it is important that supervisors maintain consistency. This demonstrates a commitment to the supervisory relationship. Supervision should be regularly scheduled and without frequent interruptions. For example, we recommend that supervisors not answer the phone during meetings and post a sign on the door indicating they should not be disturbed. That said, we recognize that this is not possible in settings that require the supervisor to be "on call" (e.g., in case of emergencies). In such situations, supervisors should carefully consider how to arrange meetings with the least interruptions. For example, one busy supervisor asked if the supervisee was willing to meet for regular supervision in the supervisor's office before the start of the formal work day. This proved effective because few staff members knew that the supervisor was in the building at that time.

When supervisors are not available for regularly scheduled, uninterrupted meetings, supervisees often feel unsupported, and their work can reflect this. Supervisors should take care to provide supervisees with the resources necessary to do their jobs well. This conveys that they matter and are supported, and that their learning is primary.

Anticipating Affective Responses

As discussed in chapters 4 and 5, it is common for both supervisors and supervisees to have anxiety about supervision. Therefore, it is highly beneficial for supervisors to prepare themselves emotionally. Shulman (1993) recommends that they use the skill of "tuning in" prior to the start of supervision in order to "sensitize oneself to the concerns, feelings, and issues that may be present in a relationship but that are not easily communicated" (36). This involves anticipating what both the supervisor and the supervisee might experience. Supervisors should first tune in to their own feelings about the impending encounter. Then they can more effectively remain open to the supervisee's emotions. Second, supervisors should try to anticipate supervisee concerns so they can more accurately provide support and information in the supervisee's interest. We recommend this type of anticipatory work for developing a positive supervisory relationship.

Evaluations and Poor Supervisee Performance

It is helpful to begin thinking about the formal evaluation process even prior to the first meeting with a new supervisee. Supervisors should carefully consider the criteria they will use to judge performance. This increases the likelihood of selecting learning assignments that are in line with evaluation criteria—important for keeping supervision focused and evaluations fair. As stated earlier, performance competencies are often outlined in formal evaluation forms and job descriptions. Additionally, supervisors should make these criteria known to supervisees early in the encounter. It is unfair for students to be in the dark about how they will be evaluated. It is also important for them to know performance expectations so that they can have input into the direction of their learning. We recommend that selection of learning goals be a mutual process, and this is reflected in TCS procedures.

Performing Formal Evaluations

Formal evaluations often provoke high anxiety for both the supervisee and the supervisor. The hierarchy of the supervisory relationship becomes most overt, raising issues related to authority for both. However, if learning objectives reflect formal evaluation criteria and the principles of giving good feedback (outlined in chapter 3) have been followed, performing formal evaluations should be fairly straightforward, with no surprises. Both will already be familiar with performance competencies because they have been reviewing and using them as learning objectives throughout supervision. In addition, if ongoing, specific, and timely feedback has been provided, both should know which competencies have and have not been worked on, which have been performed well, and which need to be improved.

We recommend that in formal evaluations, each independently completes the evaluation form and then the pair meet to compare judgments. Agreement on discrete areas of performance can be quickly reviewed, allowing time for in-depth discussions of discrepancies. Another advantage of independent scoring followed by mutual review is that it promotes supervisee self-assessment, an important skill and requirement for autonomous practice. In addition, we have found that supervisees often rate themselves lower than their supervisor does. This prevents the supervisor appearing overly critical, and even makes their evaluation seem bolstering. Nevertheless, some supervisees will give themselves glowing assessments, avoiding any negative critique. This is more likely to occur if quality feedback principles (ongoing, timely, specific) have not been employed. Indeed, such a discrepancy gives the supervisor and supervisee much to explore in regard to their supervisory process and relationship.

Finally, we recommend that supervisors be aware of common errors in making evaluations (Kadushin 1992:365–368), and take care to avoid them: 1) the "halo effect," in which the supervisor's global judgment about the supervisee's overall performance biases assessment of discrete activities; 2) "leniency bias," in which the supervisor fears giving negative assessments in positively skewed evaluations; 3) "central tendency error," in which the supervisor gives an "average" score when not sure of the supervisee's actual performance; 4) "recency errors" and "errors of overweighting," in which recent, usually dramatic, events outweigh "typical" performance throughout the evaluation period; 5) "contrast errors," comparing the supervisee's performance to other workers or the supervisor's own standard, rather than to objective criteria; and 6) "negativity effect," the tendency to focus more on the negative than the positive aspects of the worker's performance. Equal time should be given to both. Errors in evaluation are more likely to occur if the supervisor has a personal bias against or in favor of the supervisee. However, these types of errors are usually unintentional and can be minimized through active self-reflection and supervisor self-awareness of their affective reactions to the supervisee.

Poor Supervisee Performance and Gatekeeping

Unfortunately, not all who enter social work jobs or internships are fit for the profession (Thomlison et al. 1996). It is often the supervisor who has to make this determination (Moore and Urwin 1991). Typically, this is done at formal evaluations where the supervisee is told that they have not performed to expectations and will receive a failing grade (for internship), are fired, or are on "job probation." This type of action is difficult for many supervisors, who often doubt their own assessments of the supervisee's performance (Hartman and Wills 1991). Because much of supervision occurs in the private one-on-one setting, supervisors are typically the only ones able to effectively judge performance. It is easy to see why many supervisors feel insecure about making such a consequential determination. Fortunately, there are steps they can take to minimize the difficulty of reporting poor performance or terminating workers.

First, by putting the principles of quality educational supervision into practice, supervisors are able to open conversation about performance, feedback, and defensiveness early in the relationship. In particular, by providing ongoing, immediate, and specific feedback about performance, they can identify poor implementation of skills early—allowing the supervisee to take corrective action. Indeed, poor evaluations are complicated by lack of ongoing feedback throughout the encounter to inform the supervisee about what areas need work.

Second, supervisors should document supervisee performance, particularly if it is well below standard. Using TCS, supervisors and supervisees actively evaluate performance on discrete activities throughout the encounter, so poor performance is identified early. Because TCS utilizes contracts and rating forms, documentation about how well specific activities are carried out is available. In addition, supervisors should keep records of events that have been handled poorly by the supervisee, particularly those in which client welfare is at stake.

Third, when supervisors question their ability to be objective about a worker's performance, it is helpful to consult with colleagues. Personality conflicts occasionally arise between supervisors and supervisees, resulting in feelings of dislike and resentment and a dynamic of power struggle. For example, a supervisor, Ruby, was particularly angry at Bill, an intern, because he ignored her suggestions. Ruby felt that Bill was defiant and was considering failing him. She first consulted with a colleague, who put forth alternative considerations for why he acted that way. Rather than viewing Bill as defiant, the colleague suggested that he might be frightened or feel he did not have enough independence. This led Ruby to raise and openly discuss the issue with Bill, rather than make a unilateral determination. In this discussion, Bill shared that he often felt that his own ideas were dismissed, which made him resentful. The result of exploring the issue openly was that Ruby and Bill felt better about their relationship and became more open to each other's suggestions.

Finally, most agencies have formal grievance policies that serve to protect both supervisors and supervisees. By allowing for due process, "outsiders" can evaluate whether the negative assessment is warranted and supported. Supervisors should familiarize themselves with agency policy in this regard.

In sum, supervisors should give careful consideration to available supports, process, content, and structure prior to the first meeting. This will promote quality educational supervision, enabling the focus to remain on the supervisee's learning. In addition, such preparation will allow for optimal supervisory performance, which should result in maximized client services. Indeed, if worker supervision is not at its best, it is likely to result in less than optimum worker performance with clients.

Ending Supervision

The ending phase of supervision, often called "termination," refers to a process that begins weeks (approximately four to six, when possible) before the last meeting. The ending phase is a unique part of the supervisory process. While the start of supervision is concerned with developing relationships and opening up areas for exploration and the middle focuses on maintenance and problem solving, the ending phase is about stopping relationships and bringing work to a close. It entails careful and systematic preparation for ending the supervisory and clinical relationships. This involves reviewing what work needs to be completed and making decisions about instrumental functions (e.g., case dispositions, completion of paperwork) as well as affective considerations (e.g., handling emotional reactions). To accomplish these tasks, time needs to be set aside specifically for them.

Supervision can end in a variety of ways. Some allow for more time for properly addressing endings concerns than others. Either the supervisor or the supervisee can initiate the ending by taking another job, moving to a new location, or accepting a promotion. Furthermore, jobs can be lost due to funding cuts or poor performance. These types of endings are often unexpected and therefore require rapid attention to ending concerns. In contrast, endings related to the completion of a school program (as in internship arrangements) are predictable and thus allow for greater preparation.

Regardless of the available time, important decisions need to be made. For example, it is necessary to consider the disposition of cases (which can be ended, which need to be transferred to another clinician for ongoing treatment), complete paperwork, make staff aware of the ending and planned transitions, carry out the final formal evaluation, and tie up any loose ends.

Supervisees appreciate receiving an overview of these activities. As one put it, open discussion of what needs to be accomplished is important in "setting the stage" for the ending process. Education about this phase helps make ending work explicit. Such education should build upon the supervisee's knowledge, content learned in the classroom (in internship arrangements), and their own past experiences with "endings." While many of the activities discussed appear straightforward, supervisors should remember that endings often provoke strong feelings, so it is important to attend to affective reactions related to the person's departure while ending assignments are being carried out. The following section reviews supervision ending activities and considers their related affective components.

Ending Activities

Activities discussed here include attending to time left to accomplish work, completing paperwork, reviewing cases, carrying out final evaluations, engaging in a retrospective of the supervisory encounter, changing educational focus to reflect endings, identifying postsupervision objectives, and participating in ending rituals. This section concludes with preparation for affective reactions related to ending. Although either the supervisor or the supervisee can initiate the ending of their work together, because it is more common for workers and interns to leave, the following is written with that scenario in mind. (For a more in-depth discussion of ending and transition considerations when the supervisor leaves or is promoted, see Shulman 1993.)

Attending to Time

As the supervisory relationship nears its end, the supervisor should begin reminding the supervisee of how many more weeks remain. This will facilitate ongoing discussion of the number of sessions left for work with cases and for supervision meetings. Focusing on the end keeps attention on completing what needs to be done in an organized and timely manner. Engaging in proper "good-byes" and finishing paperwork requires time.

It is also helpful to raise this time limitation at each remaining supervision meeting because discussion and work around endings in supervision is often avoided (Shulman 1993). The experience of stopping a relationship represents a loss. Therefore, affective reactions may be present, particularly if the encounter has been highly productive. Confronting the reality of the ending may be difficult.

Completing Paperwork

It is not uncommon, in this time of abundant forms, for workers to fall behind in completing necessary paperwork. Therefore, it can be beneficial to discuss what needs to be done prior to ending. Indeed, it may be necessary to schedule time to ensure its completion. Supervisors should inquire about whether paperwork is up to date, remind supervisees of the impending deadline, and offer whatever supports (e.g., stopping referral of new cases) are necessary in order for the intern to complete it. Supervisors should consider that emotional reactions to ending may be in play when supervisees are having difficulty completing paperwork. These reactions may be excitement over starting their next adventure, a feeling of greater autonomy from work responsibilities, or difficulty coming to terms with the ending.

Reviewing Cases

As the supervisee prepares to leave the agency, a review of the status of each case should take place. This is important for case disposition and for anticipating which clients may have difficulty with the ending. As each case is reviewed, careful consideration should be given to whether or not treatment should continue. It may be decided that the client is ready to end. Making this type of determination requires adequate time to explore the client's perception of their readiness to finish and to allow them to prepare emotionally. When such time is not available, this determination is difficult to make. If the supervisor, supervisee, and client feel that treatment should continue, transfer decisions need to be made. It is helpful to include the supervisee in this discussion, since they likely know the case well and have a sense about which colleagues may be well suited for the client. Often, supervisors will choose to take on their supervisees' cases, since they are most familiar with them.

Additionally, the supervisee's cases should be reviewed in order to try to anticipate which clients may have strong negative reactions to ending (e.g., feelings of abandonment, anger, avoiding meetings). This process is helpful in minimizing surprises and difficult encounters, and it keeps the supervisee client-focused. This is particularly important for those who are leaving their current position and so are initiating the end of treatment. For example, supervisees who are about to complete the internship are likely to be focused on their future jobs or summer vacation plans. It is not uncommon for them to be less invested in their cases, since they may have "one foot out the door." Engaging supervisees in active discussion of their clients' experience of ending can help maintain a focus on their clinical work. Furthermore, we recommend that supervisors inform them of the risk of losing focus on clients in favor of their personal interests and explore whether or not they are experiencing this "pull." Indeed, supervisors may suggest that while supervisees may be moving on to bigger and better things, their clients are remaining in their current situations and may feel left behind.

Marisol, a student intern, felt that ending with a client would go smoothly because *she* was not feeling any intense emotions about it. When the supervisor asked about her current experience, she shared that she was excited about finishing the practicum and having the first year "under her belt," and looking forward to her summer vacation. In response, her supervisor told her that it was common for workers moving on to other experiences to become focused on these opportunities. He joined in her excitement, but reminded her that the clients still needed her full attention. He then gave a brief explanation about common client reactions to endings. This led to a conversation about how although Marisol did not feel sad about ending, her client might, and might want to talk about it. Furthermore, the client might be experiencing feelings about being "left" in his current situation. This caught Marisol by surprise, because "termination" had been discussed in class and she felt she should have been more aware of what was taking place. The conversation helped her regain her focus.

Marisol later shared that this encounter with her supervisor was extremely helpful in her work with this and other clients. She was better able to tune in to her clients' emotional experiences and address the endings directly and professionally. She added that she found this supervisory session to be one of the most rewarding. Had the supervisor not discussed common client reactions to ending, she would probably not have talked about it with the client. Also, Marisol felt that the supervisor effectively called attention to the fact that she was more focused on her own excitement than on her clients by presenting information on common supervisee and client reactions to ending.

Final Evaluations

The final evaluation of supervisee performance is an important last step in the supervisory relationship. It is a formal activity that brings a sense of completion to the encounter. We encourage an emphasis on strengths and accomplishments rather than on poor aspects of the supervisee's work. However, review of areas to be improved can be helpful in mutually formulating objectives for postsupervision work. If providing negative feedback for this purpose, do that first and end with positive feedback. It is much nicer to end on this note—even when the relationship has been poor.

The final evaluation should include an opportunity for supervisees to provide feedback on their supervision experiences and the agency. This can be done through direct conversation, a written letter, or available supervision evaluation instruments (Munson 1993; Vonk and Thyer 1996). While some supervisees may feel unsafe sharing the negative aspects of their supervisor's work, most (in our experience) will provide helpful feedback. Indeed, most supervisors want to be good at what they do and find it helpful (albeit sometimes painful) to hear what they could improve. It is important that the supervisor convey and maintain an open stance and not retreat to a defensive position of authority. Students who do not feel safe to openly critique their supervisors should be provided with the option of giving feedback after their own final evaluation has been completed.

This mutual and bidirectional evaluation process should represent a move toward a more egalitarian relationship. Indeed, after the conclusion of their formal work together, supervisors and supervisees are unlikely to remain in their current hierarchical positions. This is particularly true of graduating interns who are soon to become colleagues. Indeed, we know of a supervisor who ends the final evaluation with interns by exclaiming, "Congratulations! I am sad that you are no longer my intern, but I am glad to now be able to call you my colleague." We support this type of ending statement, which suggests the conclusion of one relationship and the beginning of another, but only when the feelings are genuine and match the nature of the supervisory relationship. If the relationship has been strained and difficult, such a declaration will be experienced as "fake" and not help to bring closure. Particularly in poor relationships, the final evaluation is an opportunity for learning. Both can explore why the relationship did not go well and consider ways it could have been improved (Shulman 1993). An honest discussion is likely to help both the supervisor and the supervisee consider their behaviors, and perhaps gain information that will improve future professional relationships. This approach will also feel like a healthy and truthful conclusion.

Retrospective of the Supervision Encounter

A particularly productive ending activity is the supervision retrospective. This entails reviewing the entire relationship from start to finish. Supervisees appreciate observing how much they have advanced since the first meeting. Returning to the beginning and reviewing accomplishments, important developmental moments, and overall growth provides a complete picture of supervisee progress and makes ending less difficult. Indeed, observing progress and successes through a retrospective review increases supervisees' confidence about working autonomously.

The use of written, weekly, education-focused contracts throughout supervision aids the process. By reviewing these, supervisees can tangibly and clearly see what they have accomplished and how far they have progressed. Indeed, it is common for them to look back at their first set of contracts and be amused by the relative simplicity compared to their current level of practice. Additionally, this complete set of contracts can be considered a portfolio of the supervisee's work. Ongoing, written contracts that articulate clear educational and practice objectives are a central part of TCS.

Changing Focus of Objectives to Reflect Endings

During the ending phase, the supervisor should avoid trying to "get it all in" out of concern that they have not provided the supervisee with enough education. The end of supervision and clinical work does not mean the end of learning. Indeed, this part of supervision and practice is ripe with learning opportunities. The focus shifts from improving skills related to helping clients progress to managing endings. Learning and practice objectives reflects this new aim.

Postsupervision Objectives

Although the focus of learning changes to emphasize endings, supervision should also identify educational objectives for postsupervision practice. In conjunction with completing the final evaluation, areas for ongoing work should be highlighted. Supervisees should leave the supervisory experience with a clear sense of their target goals for accomplishment in their subsequent work. Indeed, planning for endings should include preparation for new beginnings.

Ending Rituals

In addition to the formal ending activities (final evaluation, exit interview), supervisors and supervisees often engage in informal closing rituals. These include going out to lunch, having a "good-bye" party, exchanging small gifts, presenting a "going away" card signed by staff (often with a note of appreciation), and sharing written letters of acknowledgment and thanks. Such activities help bring closure to work relationships. In addition, they are usually appreciated by the departing person because they offer a (typically) rare opportunity for them to learn of their value and contributions. Indeed, the accolades that accompany these types of ending rituals are infrequent during day-to-day work. However, these informal rituals should not replace frank discussion of endings (Shulman 1993). Instead, affective considerations should be actively attended to—particularly if there are cues that strong emotional reactions are present and impeding either supervisory or clinical work.

Affective Reactions of Supervisees and Supervisors

In our experience, the end of the supervisor-supervisee relationship is usually positive, a time when praise is shared and gratitude conveyed. Nevertheless, supervisees and supervisors commonly experience challenging feelings during this phase. It is not unusual for supervisees to feel guilt, sadness, or relief about ending work with clients. In addition, ending supervision can bring on affective reactions for both.

Supervisees

Because supervisees will likely have strong feelings related to endings with clients, it is helpful to educate them about this reaction in order to normalize it. Asking supervisees to think of clients who may trigger strong reactions can help them to prepare for potentially difficult encounters. As stated earlier, supervisees often feel sad or guilty about ending relationships, particularly when they believe that they represent a client's only advocate. A supportive supervisory environment enables them to express these reactions rather than lose the opportunity to learn how to handle them and risk engaging in actions to reduce their own anxiety. For example, supervisees may make promises they may not be able to keep—e.g., that they will remain in contact with the client. Indeed, lack of open discussion about affective reactions is likely to interfere with both practice and learning.It is important to encourage supervisee self-awareness and to provide support during this process.

Supervisees may also have strong feelings about the end of the supervisory relationship. It is not uncommon for staff and interns to be quite fond of a supervisor. They may have learned a great deal and invested much in this person's knowledge. In addition, they may have anxiety about their ability to work independently. Honest expressions related to this separation are helpful, allowing for clarification of the relational transition and opportunities for supervisors to convey (e.g., through review of the supervisee's work) their opinion of the supervisee's competence. Furthermore, discussing affective reactions can help experientially teach supervisees about endings. Indeed, feelings about ending with their supervisor may mirror their clients' feelings about ending with the supervisee. As discussed below, this parallel process offers a unique opportunity for learning.

Supervisors

Supervisors also experience feelings about ending the supervisory relationship. They have often invested a great deal of time and energy in the encounter. It is not unusual for them to have "parental" feelings toward their supervisees.

We recommend that supervisors engage in active self-awareness in order to minimize subjective reactions that may impede their ability to effectively teach about endings. Because supervisees carefully observe their behaviors, it is important that supervisors are able to appropriately demonstrate the ending process.

Teaching About Endings Through Parallel Process

The supervisory and worker-client relationships both involve negotiating affective concerns related to ending. This parallel process provides a unique learning opportunity (Kahn 1979; Shulman 1993; Wall 1994). By carefully observing experiences related to the conclusion of the supervisory relationship, supervisees learn about the ending process with clients. Supervisors can teach about endings through direct demonstration and modeling—e.g., how they handle affective reactions, the process of reminding that the end is drawing near, how to raise issues related to ending (Shulman 1993). Indeed, one supervisee stated that she learned how to prepare for endings with clients by observing how her supervisor prepared for endings with her (in the supervisory relationship). As stated earlier, educators have identified that by observing supervisors in action, supervisees learn important social work skills (Beless 1993; Bogo 1993; Freeman 1985; Fox and Zischka 1989; Kerson 1994; Koerin, Harrigan, and Reeves 1990).

Conclusion

It is helpful for supervisors to plan carefully for the first encounter with forethought about both instrumental and affective components of the super-

visory process. We believe such preparation should also include consideration of the ending of supervision. Planning for final episodes from the start
enables better handling of sudden endings and allows the supervisor and
supervisee to set long-term goals and actively attend to mechanisms for monitoring progress toward them. Finally, knowing that the relationship will end
and that the supervisee may someday work autonomously can help reduce
their dependency on the supervisor.

After supervisors have taken steps to prepare for beginnings and endings,
they are ready to have the first supervision meeting with the supervisee and
begin utilizing TCS. The following chapters introduce and present the steps
of TCS, which guides the sequence of the supervisory encounter.

7 The Development and Basic Principles of TCS

This chapter provides an overview of the development of the Task-Centered Model for Educational Supervision (TCS). Chapter 1 formally introduced TCS and its activities; subsequent chapters will discuss its steps and functions in great detail. Here we continue the introduction to the model by reviewing the various considerations that went into building it. The purpose is to provide greater understanding of TCS through explication of its origins. The chapter concludes with an overview of its basic principles.

Building TCS

Three areas provided the foundation for the model: the task-centered model for social work practice, which was identified as a promising approach for supervision; principles of quality educational supervision (discussed in depth in chapter 3); and the dimensions of the supervisory encounter, including structural arrangements, educational content, emergent issues, and supervisory process. Attention to these dimensions resulted in our decision to develop TCS as a process model rather than one that prescribes structure or content.

However, a personal supervisory experience provided the impetus for formal development of TCS. Although he had both classroom and clinical experience, the first time the lead author was responsible for providing educational supervision, he felt ill equipped. He began seeking a model to help guide his supervisory work. First, he asked colleagues about their supervisory approaches and received two responses. One group said that they drew upon their own experiences as supervisees, attempting to do (or not do) what their supervisors did with them. The second group said that they worked extemporaneously, "winging it" and learning through trial and error. Neither was satisfying to the lead author, who continued to search for a structured model in the literature. A wide variety of supervision approaches existed, but none provided a clear, step-by-step process for attaining learning objectives. Unfortunately, helping interns reach learning goals and satisfy the requirements of their graduate education is precisely what he was being asked to do. Therefore, he decided to develop his own process model for social work field instruction.

TCS was formally developed as part of the first author's doctoral dissertation, with the guidance of the second author, who was the dissertation chair (Caspi and Reid 1998). TCS was constructed using developmental design and research methods (Rothman and Thomas 1994), which involved designing, pilot testing, collecting data about the model's performance, and using this information to make informed revisions. The outcome is a tested, refined, and ready-to-use model.

During the design stage, a thorough review of the literature clarified the considerations that provided the basis for its development: the task-centered practice model, principles of quality supervision, and the dimensions of the supervisory encounter.

The Task-Centered Model

A primary foundation for TCS was the literature and research on the task-centered model of social work practice (Reid 1997; Tolson, Reid, and Garvin 1994). Since its evolution in the mid-1970s as a model for casework (Reid and Epstein 1972), task-centered practice has been developed as a major approach in clinical social work (Hepworth and Larsen 1990; Kanter 1983; Reid 1997). A primary reason for the popularity of the model is that it provides practitioners with clear and specific guidelines, which are often missing in more traditional practice approaches (Kanter 1983).

Task-centered practice has a history of continuous development through direct practice and research in which adaptations have been developed for most social work settings (Reid 1992). Furthermore, the model has been "extensively validated in research in a variety of settings" (Payne 1991:109), and for a substantial assortment of presenting problems (Reid 1997). The results demonstrate that "task-centered methods appear to work in a broad range of situations and are generally well-received by clients" (Reid 1986:285). Task-centered strategies have also been used to help guide both educational supervision (Basso 1987; Kaplan 1991; Larsen 1980; Larsen and Hepworth 1982) and agency management of staff (Parihar 1984). Additionally, evidence supports use of these strategies for supervision (Larsen and Hepworth 1982; Stuyvesant 1980).

The use of task-centered practice procedures and principles for supervision makes sense. Among the model's basic characteristics and principles (Reid 1992:3) is the provision of structure, in particular, a well-defined series of activities that result in the formulation of specific tasks, which are then undertaken by both the client and the practitioner to solve target problems. The approach is easily adapted for social work educational supervision, where tasks are developed and carried out by the supervisee and the supervisor in order achieve practice and educational goals. Well-defined and agreed-upon tasks give direction, outline clear expectations, and provide measures for accountability. Hence, they reduce anxiety for both supervisor and supervisee by clarifying roles and providing coherent and lucid strategies for reaching objectives.

In sum, the identification of the need for a process model (discussed in the first chapter) and the availability, applicability, and evident effectiveness of the task-centered practice model suggested the use of task-centered technologies for supervision. Therefore, the task-centered practice model's structure and principles were adapted for this purpose. In particular, the model's systematic procedures for problem solving were modified to provide the framework for supervision goal attainment.

Principles of Quality Supervision

A second consideration in building TCS was the features associated with quality educational supervision. The literature on supervision is both vast and disconnected. It includes many "expert" suggestions and a body of empirically supported recommendations to guide a broad spectrum of supervisory considerations. However, throughout the literature run a fairly common set of principles for quality educational supervision. These have been organized and presented in depth in chapter 3.

The challenge for supervisors is putting the large number of principles associated with good supervision into practice. Indeed, this is a difficult and often overwhelming task. It was important that TCS be designed not only to accomplish but also to provide steps for actively and systematically employing these principles. As will be demonstrated throughout the presentation of the model in the following chapters, TCS does provide a well-organized process for actualizing them. Various considerations associated with quality supervision are discussed at the point they are likely to emerge when utilizing TCS.

Dimensions of the Supervisory Encounter

As discussed in the first chapter, supervision can be conceptualized in terms of three dimensions: structure, process, and content. When developing TCS, decisions needed to be made about which of these the model would address. It was determined that TCS should provide a process for conducting educational supervision usable within almost any structural arrangement for acquiring a broad spectrum of learning and practice content.

Multiple structural models exist for conducting supervision, including traditional one-to-one, group, peer, secondary (Marshack and Glassman 1991), interpersonal process recall (Elliot 1986), and field units (Lammert and Hagen 1975; Norberg and Schneck 1991; Pilcher and Shamley 1986). Furthermore, we can expect that structures will continue to appear and evolve, often in reaction to shrinking resources for social work practicum education. It was important that TCS process be flexible in order to adapt to new and changing structures.

Models that outline learning content exist (Collins and Bogo 1986; Fortune 1994; Larsen 1980; Pilcher 1982), and typically offer a "core" set of competencies that represent the central material to be mastered. However, it is difficult to spell out the full range of learning competencies, since so much of what is learned in supervision is emergent—e.g., knowledge or skills acquired in order to ameliorate specific cases. In addition, the importance of content can differ according to geography or practice population. Different knowledge and skills are required to work with urban and rural groups. Agencies focused on particular populations (e.g., mentally ill, substance abusers, families in crisis) each require a unique set of skills. Furthermore, clinical settings often differ in their practice orientations, requiring staff and interns to become proficient in the favored approach. Finally, people enter supervision with learning interests of their own. Indeed, inquiring about and incorporating the learner's objectives is an important part of quality supervision.

Because learning content varies widely, it was necessary to formulate the TCS process to address a broad spectrum of competencies. TCS directs supervisors and supervisees to collaborate in selecting learning content for immediate work at each supervision meeting. Making this selection part of the supervisory encounter enables incorporation of content from multiple sources. However, this need not be a haphazard process. We recommend that core content models, job descriptions, and formal evaluation forms be used to focus the selection of competencies—ensuring that what is required is addressed while enablingidiosyncratic or emergent material to be incorporated.

Existing approaches that guide process are typically formulated to address specific concerns of supervision (see chapter 2 for an in-depth consideration of approaches). In our search, no comprehensive model was available that provided discrete guidelines for systematic attainment of learning and practice objectives. Thus, it was important to develop TCS to be educationally focused, and provide steps for achieving objectives and putting the principles of quality educational supervision into practice.

Basic Principles of TCS

TCS's basic characteristics and principles were formulated to provide a theoretical and literature-based framework for the procedures. The eight basic characteristics and principles of the task-centered approach (Reid 1992:3) are consistent with the values posited by supervision educators. In addition, they address major concerns about various dimensions of the supervision process identified in the literature: andragogy, feminist pedagogy, supervisee autonomy, feedback and evaluation, structure, contextual factors, furthering the base of empirical supervision research, selecting learning assignments, and reconciling supervisee and professional goals. The principles of the task-centered practice model have been modified to reflect its application to supervision, and are described below. (Note: All quotes are [Reid 1992:3] unless otherwise noted.)

Empirical Orientation

The relative lack of empirical research on educational supervision has been noted in the literature (Ellison 1994; Raskin 1989; Shatz 1989; Sheafor and Jenkins 1982). However, many statements of what constitutes quality supervision are put forth by educators. Task-centered practice gives preference to "methods and theories tested and supported by empirical research." The model favors available empirically supported techniques but also looks to concepts and strategies thought to provide good supervision.

Issues of accountability and quality supervision are of concern to the profession (Kilpatrick et al. 1994). Much of what occurs in supervision goes on behind closed doors, leaving all involved unsure whether the supervisee is receiving quality education. By participating in task-centered supervision, the supervisee actively formulates tasks to achieve practice and learning goals. Both tasks and goals are outlined in contract form, which enables weekly monitoring of the supervisee's activities and progress and evaluation of the success of task implementation. In this way, "outcome data are systematically collected." Furthermore, the empirical orientation emphasizes "a sustained program of developmental research . . . to improve the model." The task-centered model for supervision has been constructed, and will continue to be refined, through processes of developmental study.

Integrative Stance

Task-centered practice "draws selectively on empirically based theories and methods from compatible approaches." A handful of supervision approaches have been put forth for specific purposes (e.g., dealing with supervisee anxiety, integrating classroom and field work, teaching group work). When a supervisor and supervisee are challenged by an issue that a "specific purpose" model addresses, they can look to the model for strategies and theories to employ within the procedural context of task-centered supervision. Furthermore, a task-centered supervision approach can be readily integrated with learning objectives outlined in a model that puts forth a core set of knowledge and skills for professional practice.

Focus on Supervisee-Acknowledged Goals

"Educational needs are not considered problems in learning" (Lemberger and Marshack 1991:189). Therefore, this principle is modified for supervision by changing the focus from problems to "supervisee-acknowledged objectives." This is consistent with andragogical thinking, which promotes supervisee-directed learning (Knowles 1972). Although many learning and practice objectives are outlined by the various components of field education (e.g., school, agency, supervisor, client, context), the focus is on specific goals that the supervisee explicitly acknowledges as important to them. Objectives may need to be explained and understood before they have relevance for the supervisee.

Systems and Contexts

Field learning occurs within a context of multiple systems. Environmental factors have substantial influence on what needs to be learned at what point in time, and how learning tasks will be implemented. The influence of contextual factors on field experience has been noted in the literature (Kerson 1994). Multiple systems provide supervisees the opportunity to develop learning assignments for various levels of practice.

Planned Brevity

Practicum instruction is inherently short-term. Unlike clinical supervision of staff, which can occur throughout the tenure of one's employment, the internship experience is limited (usually around eight months for concurrent placements). However, we encourage conceptualizing staff supervision in terms of time-limited principles. For example, the supervisor and supervisee should agree to attain specific objectives within a clearly articulated time frame. Having a short-term structure "tends to mobilize efforts" and "force a focus on attainable goals" (Reid 1992:5), and thus helps prepare the supervisee for autonomous practice (Kadushin 1992).

Collaborative Relationship

Task-centered practice emphasizes a "caring but collaborative effort." This is syntonic with andragogical principles and supervision literature, which both highlight the importance of a collaborative relationship. In fact, the supervisor-supervisee relationship is considered by many educators to be at the center of the supervisory experience (Bogo 1993; Lowy 1983; Manis

1979; Nisivoccia 1990; Norman 1987; Siporin 1982). It is where the student is challenged to try out new skills, attitudes, and interpersonal behaviors — essentially, to take chances. To do so in a productive manner, the supervisee needs to feel comfortable enough to be open, ask questions, and risk self-exposure (Gitterman 1989). This can only be accomplished in a safe and straightforward learning environment (Manis 1979) where there is trust between the student and instructor as well as "warmth, acceptance, genuineness, and interest" (Bogo 1993:34). There are no "hidden agendas" in task-centered practice. Educational assessments and supervision procedures will be shared openly.

Bogo (1993) cites a growing body of empirical studies that demonstrate that the relationship between supervisee and supervisor has notable impact on learning. It is within the supervisory relationship that many of the major dimensions of the field experience occur: the balance of supervisee autonomy and dependence (Kerson 1994; Matorin 1979), supervisor authority (Hawthorne 1975; Wilson 1981), supervisee anxiety (Bruck 1963; Kaplan 1991; Munson 1984; Wilson 1981), supervisor anxiety (Matorin 1979; Wilson 1981) and conscious use of self (Kerson 1994), and parallel process (Kahn 1979; Shulman 1993). Also, the relationship can be observed and discussed by the supervisor and the supervisee as a way of helping the student develop "relationship competence" (Bogo 1993). The supervisee learns collaborative behaviors that can be used in practice with clients by experiencing them within the supervisory relationship. Hence, the supervisor is recognized as a role model, an important function (Kerson 1994; Matorin 1979).

Furthermore, client self-determination, "a fundamental social work value" (Chambers and Spano 1982:229), can be modeled by supervisors who are sensitive to supervisees' self-identified learning needs (Koerin et al. 1990). The ability to direct the course of their learning allows for experiential insight regarding issues of self-determination, is consistent with social work values, and is in line with adult learning principles.

Structure

As previously stated, practicum instruction "typically is varied, uneven, and unsystematic" (Larsen and Hepworth 1982:50). The task-centered model is "structured into well-defined sequences of activities" that inform the processes or steps toward achieving objectives. "There needs to be a defined structure that will enable the supervisee to work on [the] resolution" of agreed-upon learning goals (Wijnberg and Schwartz 1977:112). In addition, the task-centered model provides organization at various levels—guidelines to direct what occurs within and between sessions as well as over the entire course of the practicum; mechanisms to link content from meeting to meeting. The only other approach identified in the literature that provides such structure is one that also uses task-centered strategies (Larsen 1980).

Supervisees experience high anxiety about the field practicum, both before (Rompf et al. 1993) and during field work. "Supervisors can reduce supervisee anxiety by providing structure" (Freeman 1993) and can reduce their own anxiety by creating a map to guide the teaching-learning encounter.

The provision of ongoing and accurate feedback is recognized as a central feature of a positive field experience (Freeman 1985; Hartman 1990). Task-centered procedures allow for ongoing feedback on progress through systematic reviews of task implementation. This offers the supervisee a way to evaluate their own practice and learning. It also enables the supervisor and supervisee to collaboratively engage in the evaluation process by reviewing learning objectives and task implementation. This makes the evaluation (and ultimately the grading) process less vulnerable to purely subjective assessments of progress and activity. A helpful component of the feedback process is the use of contracts to provide clear direction and offer "a concrete and objective means for measuring and documenting progress and performance in relation to goals developed by supervisee and supervisors" (Fox and Zischka 1989:103).

Goal-Achieving Actions (Tasks)

Learning through doing is a long-standing and important tradition in social work, and is emphasized in the field education literature (Council on Social Work Education 1975, George 1982). Task-centered practice reflects this by stating that change is brought about by taking action—"doing." The field practicum provides the setting for experiential learning: supervisees develop their knowledge and skills by selecting and implementing goal-achieving tasks. The primary function of the supervisory meeting is to "lay the groundwork for such actions."

An "ultimate goal in the use of tasks is empowerment of the client—to enable clients to design and carry out their own problem-solving actions"

(Reid 1992:38). This is consistent with feminist pedagogy, which emphasizes empowerment (Dore 1994). In the task-centered supervision setting, students are empowered by developing and integrating skills for goal achievement and problem solving. This strengthens their ability to engage in autonomous practice, an ultimate goal of the practicum. It has been suggested that when supervisees realize the utility of problem solving, they develop positive attitudes toward learning and teaching (Lowy 1983).

8 The Social and Direct Teaching Functions of TCS

As discussed in chapter 1, the TCS model entails a series of steps that are carried out by the supervisor and supervisee. This chapter presents the social and direct teaching functions of TCS. These are typically used prior to the task planning and implementation sequence, which is outlined in subsequent chapters. Illustrative vignettes are provided in order to show the model "in action."

The process of TCS involves a collection of sequenced stages that can be organized within three phases: beginning, middle, and ending. Each phase entails similar stages but emphasizes different facets of relationship and skill development. The beginning phase is primarily concerned with building productive relationships (supervisory and clinical), the middle phase with maintaining them, and the final phase with endings. As supervisee skill increases, the process and content of supervision changes. These variations are discussed throughout the presentation of TCS.

The beginning phase is rather brief in duration and ends when the first contract is completed. This may take place during the first supervisory conference or over the course of a few meetings. In general, this phase consists of orienting supervisees to the agency, clarifying roles and performance expectations, building supervisory relationships, and collaboratively setting broad objectives for supervision. The first sets of TCS target goals and tasks are derived from these activities. For example, for the goal of orienting the supervisee to the agency, the first set of tasks might include reading the agency policy manual and arranging meetings with staff.

The social and educational stages continue throughout the supervision encounter. However, the explaining supervision and TCS stage is typically employed only during the beginning phase. The stages that provide the sequence and structure of the supervisory conference at the start of TCS, until the completion of the first contract, are listed below. The stages presented in this chapter are in bold. In-depth descriptions of these steps (highlighted in bold), which represent the social and direct teaching functions, follow.

Outline of TCS Prior to Completion of the First Contract

Social stage
Explaining supervision and TCS
Educational stage
Target goals stage
    Identifying, prioritizing, and selecting tasks
    Anticipating and negotiating potential obstacles
Contracting

Social Stage

The social stage marks the first step of the supervision meeting and is a feature of each phase. The duration is usually brief (e.g., about five minutes of a one-hour meeting, longer depending upon need), and generally consists of welcoming sequences and "small talk" to help make the transition from outside interests to supervision activities. During this stage, the supervisor is particularly concerned with attending to supervisee anxiety. As noted earlier, such anxiety is a common experience in the social work practicum (Judah 1982; Munson 1984; Wilson 1981) and a feature of staff supervision (Kadushin 1992). Therefore, it is important that the supervisor offer an opportunity to process feelings of anxiety to reduce the stress level before "getting down to business" (e.g., discussing cases, setting up goals).

Supervisee anxiety in the beginning phase is generally related to starting work in a new setting and dealing with many unknowns. Concerns often include questions about agency procedures and rules, the supervisor's expectations, work load, and apprehensions about clinical work (e.g., safety when doing home visits, handling actively psychotic clients). While addressing such concerns, the supervisor makes use of social work engagement skills (validating supervisee fears, empathy, normalizing) to develop a safe and trusting relationship. This may include a brief review of how the supervisee is coping with many changes related to new beginnings, such as starting a new job, field placement, or school, or living in a new location. Although the duration of this stage is usually brief, the emotional support that characterizes it continues throughout the supervision meeting.

Provision of support and attention to supervisee anxiety should not be confused with therapy. Anxiety is a normal and expected feature of the supervisory process, and the objective of addressing it is to help the supervisee focus on the work at hand, not to "fix" the supervisee's personality. Talking about anxiety so that it can be normalized and validated greatly reduces it, allowing the student to attend to supervision. However, occasionally the anxiety can be so overwhelming that simply talking about it does not lower its intensity. At such times, the supervisor and supervisee should work together to identify strategies by which the supervisee can continue performing despite the anxiety. (For a more in-depth discussion of addressing supervisee anxiety and the boundary between supervision and therapy, see chapter 4.)

It can be educational for supervisees to observe how their supervisors attend to student anxiety. Through such observation and direct experience, supervisees learn behaviors they can use in their clinical work. They can also learn much by talking about those skills, examining how they are implemented in the supervisory relationship, and considering their relevance for clinical work.

As discussed earlier, good supervision should integrate both affective experiences and instrumental components (Kadushin 1992). Affective aspects include emotional responses to clinical and supervisory experiences, while instrumental components are the concrete or physical activities that need to be undertaken in order to reach supervision goals, such as case planning and selection of educational objectives. Although it is necessary to engage in certain tasks during supervision, it is also important that supervisees feel emotionally supported by their supervisors. Because the TCS process largely involves goal-attainment procedures, these instrumental functions could dominate the supervisory relationship. Additionally, because many social work settings are busy and chaotic, supervisors may feel overwhelmed, constrained by time, and thus pressured to do supervision quickly. In such cases, the tendency to skip the social stage and neglect affective concerns in favor of reviewing cases runs high. This stage was deliberately included to ensure that time is allocated for attention to the supervisee's affective experiences. We strongly recommend that supervisors not bypass the social stage in an effort to save time. Indeed, there are dangers to doing this.

Dangers of Bypassing the Social Stage

The social stage should be considered as important as any other part of supervision. Skipping it may have a negative impact on the supervisor-supervisee relationship. Supervisors who immediately jump into instrumental activities run the risk of conveying greater interest in supervisee activities than in supervisees themselves. Taking a few minutes at the beginning of the meeting to "tune in" (Shulman 1993) and acknowledge the supervisee's emotional state may minimize the development of negative feelings about the supervisor. Negative feelings often result in power struggles and compromised learning.

The social stage is an opportunity to discuss feelings about supervision and the supervisory relationship. Because that relationship can, at times, be emotionally intense, processing its dynamics is critical. Conversely, bypassing this stage and avoiding discussions of intense feelings can be problematic. Negative feelings are likely to increase and interfere with active and positive participation. Furthermore, neglecting to acknowledge relationship dynamics while continuing with supervision activities demonstrates that addressing such things is not acceptable, setting a poor example for supervisees about how to handle such issues with clients. Throughout their time together, supervisors should regularly check in with supervisees about the status of their relationship. Inquiry about the provision of emotional support is particularly important. This requires supervisors to be open to critical feedback about their own performance. Exploration of supervisory relationship problems may be facilitated by normalizing their potential to occur. The social stage is also highly beneficial for minimizing obstacles to implementing TCS. When a supervisee's anxiety about an issue is not directly related to TCS procedures (e.g., intense feelings about a client, a personal issue, or the supervisor), it impedes the process and productivity of supervision. Indeed, a supervisee experiencing strong emotional reactions will likely have difficulty attending to supervision activities. In reciprocal fashion, the supervisor will recognize that the feelings are present (e.g., through nonverbal behaviors), and will likely be distracted. In sum, attending to emotional experiences reduces negative or unproductive supervisory encounters.

The following vignettes illustrate proper uses of the social stage. The supervisor takes time to acknowledge the supervisee's affective reactions, thus reducing their anxiety. The result is progress toward a positive supervisory relationship. Furthermore, the supervisor models relationship-building skills, demonstrates value of the person of the supervisee, and conveys that anxiety is legitimate and safe to express—the foundation of an open and trusting relationship. Learning is about taking risks. Therefore, it is important for supervisors to develop an environment where supervisees feel safe to engage in and openly discuss new experiences.

Social Stage Vignette #1

The following exchange illustrates the social stage in action. The social work field instructor uses and models engagement techniques (e.g., conveying warmth, empathy, validation, normalization) to build a safe environment for the intern. In addition, the supervisor uses nonverbal engagement techniques such as matching the intern's intensity, pacing, and tone. The time spent on the social stage is brief but important. Notice how the supervisor uses the intern's responses to naturally segue to the next stage in TCS.

> SUPERVISOR: Welcome to the agency. It's nice to finally meet you in person.
> INTERN: Yes, it's nice to meet you.
> SUPERVISOR: Have you had an opportunity to tour the building?
> INTERN: Yes, the secretaries showed me around before our meeting.
> SUPERVISOR: Did you get to meet Sam, the other student intern?
> INTERN: No, not yet. Will we be sharing the same office? (nervously)
> SUPERVISOR: Yes. We are a little short on space, but the office should be large enough for the two of you. If not, or there are any problems, let me know and we can try to figure something out.

Here the supervisor is demonstrating openness and support specifically related to the intern's concern about her co-worker. Notice the use of language that emphasizes "we" rather than "I," suggesting a collaborative endeavor rather than a relationship in which the intern must rely on the instructor to take care of problems encountered at the agency. When the supervisor takes sole responsibility for supervisee problems, it demonstrates "I (the supervisor) have the power," potentially creating both dependence and resentment. Notice also that the supervisor takes note of the thinly veiled anxiety underlying the intern's question about sharing the same office but chooses not to address it at this point. The instructor does, however, make a mental note of it in case it comes up again.

> INTERN: Thanks. I think the space will work out fine. I have never had an office before, so half an office is better than none! (Both laugh.) I just hope that Sam is a decent person.

This time the intern is more direct about her anxiety, and the supervisor responds by reflecting back her concern, demonstrating the skills of tuning in and acknowledging the supervisee's affective experience.

> SUPERVISOR: You're worried about Sam?
> INTERN: Well, in my old job as a customer service representative, I had to work with this guy, Fred (she makes a face indicating disgust at the mention of his name), who was very annoying. He was always talking at me. Even when I was on the phone with a customer, he would be there yapping away!
> SUPERVISOR: How irritating.
> INTERN: It was!
> SUPERVISOR: Did you try anything to make the situation better?

Notice that in the above response the supervisor uses an empathic response ("irritating") but moves the discussion to the intern's behaviors. The intern obviously still feels quite emotional about her last work experience, and this needed to be "heard" and validated by the supervisor. Additionally, learning how the intern handled past interactions with co-workers will shed light on how she is likely to relate in her present situation. It will also reveal whether or not and how she used her supervisor at the time. Field instructors should take the time to learn about and validate the intern's experience in a non-judgmental way, for undiscussed and unresolved past work and supervisor experiences can negatively affect the supervisory relationship.

> INTERN: Well, at first I was afraid to hurt his feelings by telling him that he talked too much or telling him to shut up. But after a while I

went to my supervisor, and she just told me, "That's the way he is" and "Just ignore him."
SUPERVISOR: That doesn't sound very satisfying.

Although the field instructor notes that the intern did not confront her co-worker directly but instead decided to discuss it first with her supervisor—seemingly with the hope that the supervisor would take care of it—the instructor chooses to validate the student's affective experience, as this is the early relationship-building stage of their supervision encounter.

INTERN: It wasn't. It sort of made me mad.
SUPERVISOR: I guess that you did not have the greatest experience with this supervisor?
INTERN: Well, aside from that, she wasn't terrible . . . I suppose.
SUPERVISOR: Well, let's talk about supervision and supervisors for a moment. We are going to be meeting for supervision each week, so I am interested to learn about your other supervision experiences and your thoughts about ours. How much . . . what do you know about social work field instruction?

Social Stage Vignette #2

The second vignette also shows the social stage in action, with a different intern. Noticethat again, the stage itself is rather brief, but in this situation the supervisor chooses to move directly to the educational stage (the third stage of TCS), adjusting the sequence based on the student's area of greatest anxiety. Notice how he uses the concept of "starting where the student is" to both transition to the educational stage and make the decision to postpone discussion of supervision (the explaining supervision stage) until the anxiety has been addressed. To begin, the supervisor asks about a likely source of anxiety for supervisees who have recently moved to a new location.

SUPERVISOR: I saw on your field application that you are originally from (out of state)?

Based on prior experiences with interns from out of state, the supervisor assumes that the intern is likely experiencing high stress from multiple transitions and begins inquiry in this area to demonstrate support and to validate the intern's affective experience. Furthermore, the instructor modeling relationship-building skills, in particular, the skill of "tuning in" (Shulman 1993).

INTERN: Yes.
SUPERVISOR: Wow . . . so you have had a lot of transitions in your life lately. Moving, starting school, beginning the field placement.
INTERN: Yes. It can feel overwhelming at times!
SUPERVISOR: I bet. How has it been, making all of those changes at once?
INTERN: Okay. Sometimes it's hard because I don't really know anyone. But the classes seem like they will be interesting.
SUPERVISOR: Yes, transitions can be difficult. I have observed past student interns, who have also been from out of town, come to this area not knowing anyone and end up quite close to many people in the program. It is likely the same will happen with you.

The supervisor ignores the intern's second sentence, choosing to continue discussing the potential area of anxiety with the aim of validating the intern's experience. At the same time, the instructor avoids further exploration of the anxiety (which might be experienced as "therapizing"). Next, he normalizes the experience and offers a positive view of it by relaying stories of prior interns.

INTERN: One-to-one I am fine, but in large groups . . . I don't do well in large groups!
SUPERVISOR: So, you are experiencing some stress about all the changes you have had to make. How are you feeling about this field placement? Is this something you are looking forward to, or does it add to the stress?

The supervisor makes note of the large groups comment (knowing that the intern will be facilitating large groups in the near future) and moves to focus on one of the intern's many stressors related to transitions—the field placement. The instructor is attempting to transition to the explaining supervision stage here. Notice that when he learns of the student's anxiety about clients, he abandons implementing that effort, moves to the educational stage, and then returns to complete the explaining supervision stage.

INTERN: Well, it adds to the stress, but I am looking forward to getting started. I decided to get my M.S.W. because I want to work with

people, and it sounds like I will get some good experience working with people at this agency.
SUPERVISOR: Yes, I think so. For right now, however, what can we do to help this experience be less stressful? Is there anything that we— you and I—can do to make this transition less overwhelming?
INTERN: Well, I think I would feel better if I knew a little more about what I will be doing around here. How many clients will I have? Is there anything I can read to help me understand more about how to help them? Will I have to go to their homes?
SUPERVISOR: It sounds like you have a lot of questions. It also seems as though you are most interested in learning about the client population you will be working with. Is that right?

Although the intern conveys anxiety about a few areas, the supervisor hears that working with clients is creating the most stress. Notice that the instructor checks this out with the intern before moving on. This demonstrates and models the skill of clarification.

INTERN: Yes, I think that is the part I am the most freaked out about!
SUPERVISOR: Okay, let's talk about that a little. Afterward, I would like to also talk about what we will be doing here in supervision.

Here the supervisor makes the transition to the educational stage but indicates that when done, they will return to explaining supervision.

Beginning the supervision process by attending to supervisee anxiety is akin to the clinical skill of "starting where the client is." This technique can be modified to "starting where the supervisee is" (Matorin 1979:151). Using this approach, the supervisor temporarily puts aside their own agenda and takes their lead from the supervisee. The objective is to help them focus on supervision. If the supervisee has a pressing issue but is forced to put it on hold until the supervisor's agenda is realized, they will likely have difficulty attending to supervisionr. Taking a few minutes to allow supervisees to express needs (i.e., their agendas), can help clear the way for a focused and productive supervisory session, as well as reduce power struggles.

Starting Where the Supervisee Is: Preventing Power Struggles

As stated in great detail in chapters 4 and 5, anxiety is a common feature of both field practica and employment settings. Supervisees typically come to supervision meetings with much on their minds. This stress can be overwhelming and leave them little energy or motivation to partake in supervision activities. Simultaneously, supervisors often have much they feel they need to address. Balancing both sets of needs can be challenging, and if not done properly may result in a power struggle. Indeed, whose agenda will initially take priority must be negotiated. This can be done verbally, by laying it out on the table and coming to an agreement on how to proceed, or through gamesmanship of power. Thus, it is important to take a few minutes to tune in to and acknowledge each person's pressing issues at the start of each supervision meeting. Because they hold greater power, supervisors should take the lead.

Power struggles in supervision can be thought of as competing agendas — the supervisor's and the supervisee's. When the supervisor makes their agenda the priority, it is common for the supervisee to go along with it, respecting the hierarchy of the relationship. However, this practice runs the risk of the supervisee pretending to be participating (e.g., maintaining eye contact, nodding head) but secretly remaining preoccupied with their own agenda. This outcome is typically a result of the supervisor failing to acknowledge the supervisee's needs and the supervisee, in turn, resisting the supervisor's direction and possibly developing resentment. Starting where the supervisee is helps prevent power struggles and resentment—two processes that can interfere with supervisee learning.

When supervisors have pressing issues and are unable to start where the student is, they should share their need to put their agenda first. This can be done while assuring supervisees that their needs will also be discussed. There are times when supervisors do need to give a higher priority to their agenda, such as when a client's welfare is at risk. However, such crises are generally emotionally laden and therefore, the student's affective experience should be addressed once the crisis is under control.

If a power struggle has developed, we recommend putting instrumental functions aside and discussing this relationship dynamic. Exploring the origin and process of its development is useful in resolving the conflict, improving the supervisory relationship in general, and teaching about relationship dynamics—knowledge that can be carried over to clinical practice. The benefit of taking a few minutes to acknowledge the person of the supervisee prior to jumping into case discussion or other instrumental tasks is further illustrated in the following vignettes. The first demonstrates the power struggle and resentment that can arise when the supervisor, Kathy, does not tune in to the supervisee's (Bill's) anxiety. The second scenario presents the same situation, but a different supervisor response: Kathy attends to Bill's anxiety, resulting in a better supervision encounter and laying the groundwork for a more positive relationship.

Scenario #1: Supervisor Ignores Student's Anxiety

KATHY: Welcome, Bill. I hope you're ready to get started. I scheduled an appointment for you with a new client at noon.

BILL: That's two hours from now! I just got here!

KATHY: Let me get you up to speed with how to fill out the intake paperwork.

BILL: Who are these people I have to meet?

KATHY: Oh, I think it is a woman and her son who is causing her problems. Anyway, this is our cover sheet. Make sure the client reads this and signs it here . . .

BILL: (interrupting) What is her son doing? Is he learning disabled? I am not sure I will know what to do with them.

KATHY: Don't worry so much. You'll be fine. This is the release form, it's the pink one, and this blue one is the confidentiality form . . . and don't forget to have them fill out the insurance form — that's the green one. Later, I will show you where the progress notes are. Now, let me introduce you to our day care program coordinator.

BILL: I don't think I am ready to see a client yet. I don't know what to do.

KATHY: (becoming angry) Come on, Bill! All you have to do is talk to them and fill out the paperwork!

Because Bill is so anxious about having to conduct his first clinical interview with real people, he is unable to hear the directions Kathy is trying to give him. Just prior to the client meeting, he realizes that there are forms he must fill out but cannot remember which he was supposed to bring for the intake. And he is not sure how to fill them out, which raises his anxiety even further. During the client meeting, he is so anxious about the forms that he has difficulty paying attention to the client. Furthermore, he feels angry about Kathy's insensitivity and lack of support. He is beginning to develop feelings of resentment and lack of trust.

Scenario #2: Supervisor Addresses Student's Anxiety

KATHY: Welcome, Bill. I hope you're ready to get started. I scheduled an appointment for you with a new client at noon.

BILL: That's two hours from now! I just got here!

KATHY: I guess you were expecting more time to prepare before you got started?

BILL: Yes. I have never done this before!

KATHY: Okay. Well, it is too late to reschedule the appointment, but we can talk about it to help you feel more ready.

BILL: Yes, I would like that.

KATHY: What do you think would be helpful for you?

BILL: I am not sure. I have never done this before, so I feel like I don't know anything.

KATHY: Yes, I can see how you might feel overwhelmed. When starting work with a client, there are really two things that need to be done. First, it is important to build a working relationship. This requires good listening skills, and clarifying that you understand how they see things. The second is completing the intake forms. Before I show you the forms—which are pretty straightforward—how do you feel about your relationship-building skills?

BILL: You mean all I have to do is listen and ask about how they see the problem?

KATHY: Basically. If things get slow, you may have to be creative about generating conversation, but for the most part just listening and understanding the client is an important skill and is a good starting point for you. How do you feel about that?

BILL: I think I can do that. We have been practicing engagement skills in role plays in my classes at school. What is the client's problem?

Kathy gives a brief overview of the case.

KATHY: Great! Are you ready for me to show you how to fill out the paperwork? The questions on the intake forms are also helpful for giving direction to the first meeting.

BILL: Yes.

As can be seen, attending to the supervisee's affective responses helps to prevent the kind of resentment and power struggle in the first scenario. In addition, by starting where the supervisee is (i.e., acknowledging his agenda), Kathy creates an environment that enables Bill to attend to supervision and hear her lesson. It is interesting to note that the supervisor gets her agenda met better in the second scenario than the first, by temporarily setting her own needs aside and focusing on the student's.

Although the social stage is brief, attention to the affective experience of the student and provision of emotional support should be ongoing. Revisiting or addressing affective responses mid-supervision session is recommended. There may be occasions when supervisees raise issues that warrant more attention than the social stage's prescribed time frame. The model's guidelines should not be followed in rigid fashion; they allow for deviations when such circumstances present themselves. This serves to reduce power struggles and to minimize obstacles to implementation of TCS.

However, the supervisor should also consider that repeated discussions of supervisee anxiety or resistance to proceeding with the model may reflect discomfort with scrutiny of their work with clients. In other words, some supervisees may prefer to discuss personal issues rather than reveal detailsand receive critical feedback about their clinical work (Kadushin 1968; Munson 1993). In addition, some supervisors who are anxious about their own abilities in clinical supervision may prefer to engage in social talk or to work with the supervisee's affective state as ways to avoid proceeding (Hawthorne 1975). Discussion of anxiety may be more comfortable for supervisors who are also clinicians. They should be careful not to turn the social stage into therapy. It is meant to be brief and enable the smooth and productive implementation of the instrumental activities of supervision.

Explaining Supervision and TCS

Explaining supervision comprises the second step in the beginning phase, during which supervisor and supervisee review the purpose and structure of supervision. This stage has three aims: to educate students about the supervision process in general and describe how it is typically conducted at the agency; to review TCS procedures; and to work out a structural arrangement (work schedule and frequency, duration, and location of meetings). During the discussion of the supervision process, particular attention is given to exploring, identifying, and clarifying expectations. The supervisor inquires about the supervisee's understanding of social work supervision, seeks to fill gaps in knowledge, clarifies differences in perception, and works toward a mutual understanding of expectations.

Education About Supervision

Many students and staff, particularly new ones, do not know what social work supervision entails. Although most have had experiences with "supervisors" in other work settings, they commonly have had little exposure to the structure and purpose of social work supervision. There is also evidence that schools of social work do not adequately prepare students to utilize supervision appropriately (Martin and Alper 1989). Hence, interns and new staff frequently enter supervision with little understanding of its function. Supervisors frequently observe high anxiety related to not knowing what will occur. Such stress can be greatly reduced through education and discussion of process.

Educating about the structure and purpose of supervision serves three main purposes. First, it ensures that learners understand supervision so they can make sound choices about their education. Second, it clarifies supervisor and supervisee expectations and roles, and the purpose of the encounter. Clarity of expectations is recognized as critical for a productive supervisory experience (Fox and Zischka 1989; Munson 1993). Third, as there is often little discussion between supervisors and supervisees about the supervision process, particularly the supervisory relationship (Shulman 1993), talking about that relationship, expectations, roles, and the purpose of supervision is helpful for reducing supervisee anxiety (Munson 1993) and for negotiating problems that may arise during the encounter (Shulman 1993). By bringing up such topics in the beginning phase, the supervisor demonstrates that these issues are open for discussion.

However, explaining supervision may not be as easy as it sounds. During this step of the model, supervisors should, essentially, be prepared to answer the question, "What is social work supervision?" This may not be easy for many field instructors who are themselves unclear about the answer (Shulman 1993). Not only is the supervision process complex, but the term "supervision" itself has many different meanings within social work. Additionally, in different settings, the supervisory function and process differ. What is helpful at this stage is a general overview of the process rather than an in-depth discussion of social work supervision. Bombarding the student or staff member with lengthy descriptions will likely be overwhelming, confusing, and unhelpful.

Moreover, it should not be assumed that interns and staff have no knowledge at all about supervision. Levels of experience vary. Therefore, supervisors should first ask what the worker (or student) knows about social work supervision. Such inquiry can be helpful in learning about their expectations. The subsequent discussion should focus on achieving clarity about expectations, roles, and the purpose of the encounter.

Indeed, many problems can be prevented through such clarification at the start of the supervisory process. Conflict can occur if time has not been taken to come to a mutual understanding of expectations and supervisors and supervisees participate while holding differing definitions of the process. Because new supervisees frequently enter into social work settings carrying an administrative (e.g., business or retail) definition of supervision, they are likely to relate to their supervisors accordingly. This can become problematic when the instructor, operating from a different definition, behaves in ways that appear confusing and even objectionable. For example, typical social work supervisor behaviors, such as detailed inquiry about supervisee work and about affective reactions, may be perceived as intrusive, judgmental, and untrusting.

This situation is illustrated in the following vignette in which Evelyn, the supervisor, is asking Harry specific questions about his actions with a case.

> HARRY: Well, everything's going great with Mrs. Smith. We met once this week and she seems to be doing well.
> EVELYN: That's great! So, tell me what happened when you met her.
> HARRY: When she came in we started with the intake forms—I filled them all out the way you showed me. And then she told me about what was bothering her—that her mother was dying and that she was the only one of her siblings taking any responsibility. And then we came up with a plan that she thought would be helpful.
> EVELYN: Sounds like it went well. Tell me about the plan.
> HARRY: (getting annoyed) Oh, we developed some long-term and short-term goals and wrote them out. It's in her chart if you want to see it.
> EVELYN: (becoming frustrated) So what were your short-term goals?
> HARRY: I told you, they are written in the chart. The client seemed happy with them.

At this point Harry is becoming increasingly annoyed and defensive. He feels that Evelyn is doubting his word that things went well. He assumes that she is asking questions because she does not believe him, and that it actually went as well as he suggested. In turn, Evelyn has become frustrated with

Harry. From her view, he has only given her vague answers and does not seem willing to offer specifics about his interaction with the client. She feels that he is being defensive and possibly hiding something from her. This conflict can be understood in terms of differing definitions, and thus expectations, of the supervision process. Harry is operating from prior experiences with retail managers, in which detailed inquiry into his performance meant that his supervisor was upset with him. Conversely, Evelyn is operating from a definition of social work supervision, in which detailed inquiry is a common technique aimed at enhancing learning. Discussion of their behaviors in the context of clashing definitions can be helpful in resolving the immediate conflict and preventing future negative encounters of this type. Education about social work supervision can put such inquiry into context, helping the supervisee understand that its aim is to facilitate learning, not question competence.

In sum, the objective of this step of the educational stage is for the supervisor and supervisee to come to a mutual understanding about the function and process of supervision. This should include agreement on reports on clinical decisions, rules for self-disclosure, and the operational definition of educational supervision. The following section is provided to assist with this discussion.

What Is the Purpose of Supervision?

Even for social workers who have experienced supervision, its purpose may remain unclear. This is particularly true for supervisors who have experienced less-than-favorable supervision themselves. Additionally, supervision can serve multiple or different purposes in different settings, including overseeing and monitoring worker performance, providing support, and education. Beginning a supervisory relationship without discussing its function and process can be problematic. Indeed, understanding the complexity of the encounter and its multiple purposes is critical for supervisee participation. The following is included to assist field instructors and staff supervisors in explaining supervision.

> Supervision has a long history in social work. The basic structures existed prior to the development of formal schools of social work (George 1982). It is a long-standing tradition that supervisors meet regularly with practitioners to discuss their work. The purposes of these

meetings have been conceptualized as falling into three categories: administrative review of the practitioner's work; provision of emotional support; and education (Kadushin 1992). Which category is emphasized depends on the context in which the supervision occurs.

Supervisors should briefly describe the three categories of supervisory functions and reach agreement with supervisees on which will be primary. This is important not only for clarity of expectations but also because the process and structure will differ according to the central function. Because this book and TCS are about educational supervision, discussion of this function and its related considerations follow.

In educational supervision, such as practicum instruction, the supervisee's learning takes priority. The administrative and supportive functions remain present but are secondary. Its objective is to enhance supervisee professional development through a teaching-learning process with the goal of improved job performance. Educational supervision may also be selected to address continuing education requirements for licensing.

In any case, supervision in the workplace is not always understood to be educational, and its definition should be discussed. The same is true in field practica. While it may seem that all interns will presume the primary function to be educational, this assumption is problematic. As discussed earlier, interns may have never experienced "educational" supervision and believe that their agency supervisor's primary role is management.

It is important that supervisors explain educational supervision's unique processes, including detailed inquiry into the supervisee's performance, affective reactions, belief systems, and understanding of theory. Supervisees should be told that their work will be closely examined for the purpose of learning, not because the supervisor does not trust or thinks poorly of them. Such close examination is often intimidating and without explanation of its purpose, may be experienced as offensive.

Supervisors should also point out that education entails not only developing social work skills and knowledge but also integrationg social work attitudes and values. Sometimes personal belief systems conflict with the profession's values and create supervisee discomfort, which may affect practice in a less than productive way. Supervisees should be told that learning about one's "self" is critical for making professional rather than personal judgments. Therefore, supervisor inquiry into the supervisee's "self" may occur and will be discussed as it interacts with clinical practice.

Accordingly, the issue of the supervision-therapy boundary should be discussed. The supervisory pair should understand that the purpose of exploration into the supervisee's self is neither therapeutic nor designed to promote personality change. Instead, the function is to promote supervisee insights into how their affective reactions and professional behaviors are linked, so they may become a more effective helper. The supervisor and student should contract to work together to identify whether or not the therapy-supervision boundary has been crossed and to allow the supervisee to stop the exploration without negative consequences, if it should become too difficult.

Finally, the ongoing goal of educational supervision is professional development and improved job performance. In practicum settings, the long-term objective is to prepare students for postgraduate work, which largely entails autonomous practice. Nevertheless, it should be remembered that supervision must also protect and provide services *in the best interests of clients*. In many settings, this is complicated by an administrative mandate that supervisors work in the best interest of the agency. Such mandates, typically rigid in nature, often clash with both client interests and supervisee learning. Therefore, the purpose of supervision must be clarified and understood within its present context.

In sum, supervisors should contextualize and explain social work supervision in general and educational supervision in particular. Additionally, they should elucidate the unique dynamics of the social work supervisory relationship so that mutually agreeable arrangements can be developed for addressing them. Clarity of expectations is critical for a positive supervisory experience.

Explaining TCS

Supervisees generally appreciate knowing the sequence of events that will occur within and between meetings. Supervisory encounters that are haphazardly or inconsistently structured often result in supervisee confusion and anxiety. Because TCS provides a clear, step-by-step process, reviewing the model's guidelines can greatly reduce such stress. As one intern who had been supervised using TCS put it, "I liked knowing what to expect . . . [and] what was expected of me." It is recommended that supervisees be given their own copy of the TCS guidelines (see the appendix) for personal review and reference, and to promote participation in their own learning process. Discussion of the TCS process includes an explanation about how to fill out the model's forms.

Once the model has been explicated, the supervisor should explore the supervisee's wish to use it. We caution against imposing any supervisory model. Although our experience has been that supervisees greatly appreciate having a well-defined process to follow, some may not, reflecting a particular learning style preference. Reluctance to use the TCS model should be explored so that the supervisor has a clear understanding of the student's learning preferences and can discover which parts of the proposed process are unsatisfactory. This can help the supervisor know how to proceed in a way that is mutually acceptable. This may include parts of the TCS process while sidestepping others. As stated earlier, most supervisees are excited about TCS, and those who have voiced hesitation have been willing to temporarily "give it a shot." After initial trials, almost all have elected to continue using the model, and have been active and enthusiastic participants in the process.

Supervisee Reluctance to Use TCS

Although flexibility on the supervisor's behalf is strongly encouraged, supervisee rigidity and reluctance to try out the TCS model should be explored. Such behavior may be an indication of the supervisee's personal feelings about authority, their own competence, or worker autonomy. Furthermore, wholesale refusal of the offer to use TCS suggests future challenges to the supervisor in other areas of the relationship. Supervisors should handle such early refusals cautiously, and in the spirit of understanding the supervisee's position. Avoidance or unquestioning acquiescence on the supervisor's part is likely to result in an ongoing power struggle or power imbalance. In either case, the primary focus on education is lost to an underlying process of game-playing (Hawthorne 1975; Kadushin 1968).

Supervisees may have legitimate reasons for their reaction to TCS. Time taken to understand, rather than judge, their unwillingness to participate usually results in increased openness and trust in the supervisor. Additionally, experiencing, identifying, and resolving relationship obstacles first hand can be a powerful way for supervisees to learn about handling difficult professional relationships (e.g., with clients).

Determining Structural Arrangements

Although TCS outlines steps to be carried out within and between supervisory meetings, it does not offer a structure in which the process should be implemented. In other words, it does not prescribe the frequency, duration, or location of meetings. Often these structural arrangements are worked out prior to the implementation of TCS, but they are included in the beginning phase to ensure that they are not overlooked. Consistency and clarity about such arrangements are important and should be taken seriously by both supervisors and supervisees. Moreover, considerations regarding potential interruptions to the supervision process—taking phone calls, responding to beepers, or allowing others to enter the room during supervision—should be discussed as well. We strongly recommend that supervision be arranged so that there is the least likelihood of interruptions.

Structural arrangements are often dictated by outside considerations, such as accrediting or licensing institutions. For example, the Council of Social Work Education sets the mimimum requirements for student field work supervision that schools of social work must follow. The most common arrangement, the "traditional method," entails the supervisor and supervisee meeting one-on-one, for one hour each week, for the duration of the practicum. Alternative arrangements exist (see chapter 2), including the use of multiple field teachers as in task or secondary supervision (Marshack and Glassman 1991), multiple students as in group supervision (Kaplan 1988), and multiple field settings (Henry 1975). (Using TCS within traditional, secondary, group, peer, and consultation structures is discussed in chapter 12.) Because resources for field education are diminishing, new and inventive arrangements are likely to emerge in the coming years. TCS was developed to offer a process that can be implemented within multiple contexts with only minor alterations.

In work settings, supervision often reflects minimum state licensing or certification requirements. The frequency and number of hours of supervision meetings vary from state to state. Furthermore, there are a wide variety of structural arrangements available for satisfying supervision dictates, so the details must be discussed, made explicit, and agreed upon. Even if supervision is not required, these arrangements need to be resolved by the participants.

Working Out the Structure of the Supervision Meetings

It is important that the supervisor take agreed-upon structural arrangements seriously. The meeting is at the center of the supervision process. It is a time when the student can expect the supervisor's undivided and uninterrupted attention. Therefore, the meeting should become a standard part of the supervisor's and the supervisee's schedules. It should occur at a convenient time for both, and every effort should be made to make it a priority.

Supervisors convey a great deal through their behaviors about how seriously they take supervisee learning. Supervisors who miss or frequently postpone meetings, or take phone calls during them, are sending a clear message that the learning experience is less important than other matters. They should make every effort to communicate that the meeting is the supervisee's time and that the focus is the supervisee's learning, concerns, and work.

While it is unrealistic in many social work settings to completely prevent missed or interrupted meetings, supervisors and supervisees can take action to prevent disruptions. This is particularly recommended in chaotic work environments. Unfortunately, when crises abound, educational supervision is often moved to the back burner. The supervisor should carefully consider the potential for such interference and work with the supervisee to develop an arrangement where supervision can be the priority. This requires some flexibility and creativity. For example, Jordan noticed that during meetings in his supervisor's office, there were frequent interruptions. One day they had to meet in the agency library because his supervisor's office was being painted. There were almost no interruptions. There was no phone in the library, and staff did not know where the supervisor was. Jordan pointed this out and requested that they continue to meet in the library. The supervisor agreed. Other arrangements may include scheduling supervision at a time of the day when disruptions are least likely (e.g., early morning before staff arrives). While staff supervisors are typically required to provide clinical supervision as part of their job responsibilities, intern instructors are usually volunteers. They do not often get work release for accepting interns, which means increased responsibilities for already busy workers. Although interns can assist with cases, they rarely reduce field instructor workloads. It is important that agency workers seriously consider, prior to becoming field instructors, whether or not they can truly handle the added responsibilities.

TCS only provides a discrete stage for discussing the nature of supervision at the start of the encounter. However, continued conversation about its purpose and process is recommended as needed. Such dialogue is helpful for maintaining clarity of expectations and a productive supervisory relationship.

Educational Stage

The educational stage is an important part of each phase, and comprises the third step of the beginning phase. Its purpose is to set aside time to engage in didactic instruction. This involves the supervisor's providing information to the supervisee in the form of two-to-five-minute "mini-lessons." The following scenario illustrates the process.

> While listening to a tape recording of Peter's session, Leslie, Peter's supervisor, noticed that he did not employ empathic responses to client statements that seemed to be laden with intense emotions. Leslie conveyed this observation to Peter and asked if he understood the concept of empathy. Peter thought that he did, but added that it would be helpful if Leslie could explain it to him. Leslie then gave a brief overview of the concept, including examples from her own practice. Peter listened intently and then relayed the definition back to Leslie in order to clarify his understanding. With a clearer grasp of the concept, they were then able to set up a learning assignment for Peter to implement empathy in his work with clients.

Didactic instruction can relate to either emergent or anticipated needs of the supervisee. Areas for teaching should be collaboratively identified. Supervisor-delivered lessons should be both relevant for and desired by the supervisee. The amount of time spent on direct teaching varies according to supervisee needs. Flexibility in content and duration is important.

The Changing Need for Didactic Instruction

Starting a new position generally entails the need for much information. Therefore, in the beginning phase it is usually necessary to spend more time giving didactic instruction to the new intern or worker than the mini-lessons described above. As the supervisee becomes more knowledgeable about the agency, didactic instruction should decrease. Furthermore, as students progress, the supervisor's teaching stance generally moves from directive to supervisee-centered. For example, in the beginning phase, supervisors typically take the lead, orienting supervisees to the agency and providing information that they may not even know is needed. As students master this information, they are more able to actively participate in the direction of their learning and request specific information in the form of didactic instruction. The goal of this stage is to provide details so that supervisees can better do their job, not to deliver broad-based knowledge. In other words, the information should be purposeful, useful, and targeted.

Although teaching moments can occur at any point in the supervisory meeting, time specifically set aside for didactic instruction is important (Caspi and Reid 1998). When asked, supervisees report appreciating moments of education and indicate that such instruction is an important part of satisfactory supervision (Baker and Smith 1987; Caspi 1997; Fortune and Abramson 1993; Fortune, McCarthy, and Abramson in press; Knight 1996). It is not uncommon for supervisees to receive no didactic instruction, which is a disappointment to many. In fact, field students identify teaching as one of their supervisor's primary functions (Ellison 1994). As one put it, "teaching is what field supervisors are *supposed* to be doing." While interns expect to learn from instructors, staff often desire ongoing education as a part of their work experience. Furthering one's knowledge aids motivation for work, keeps the job "fresh," and can help prevent burnout.

Topics for the educational stage can relate to any aspect of the supervisee's job: orienting to agency functions, linking classroom content to practice, contextualizing case dynamics, developing new relationships, or problem-solving difficult cases. In the beginning phase, the content typically reflects needs related to starting the new job. This includes information about the agency, layout of the work environment, client population, paperwork, and expectations about such issues as confidentiality and practice orientation (e.g., cognitive-behavioral, family systems, psychodynamic). Having such information can go a long way to reduce job-related stress for new students or staff members, who are commonly anxious about being in a new setting. It also helps the supervisee feel supported and welcomed.

We and other social work educators warn against strict instructor-directed learning (Cramer 1995). Didactic instruction, used appropriately, is a helpful teaching tool, and recognized as important in social work education and supervision (Kramer and Wrenn 1994; Gitterman 1989). Information given in didactic form should be both *wanted* and *relevant*. Mini-lessons should not be imposed upon the supervisee but given in response to requests for information. Unwanted lectures are generally experienced as offensive and in the service of the supervisor's own ego. It is not an unusual mistake for supervisors, anxious to show their clinical expertise, to begin teaching on subjects their supervisees already know. For example, it was particularly insulting for Sarah to have her supervisor lecture her on transference, days after she had delivered an oral presentation on the same subject to her class. Supervisors should take time to ask what supervisees know about a topic prior to teaching it. This not only demonstrates respect for the supervisee but also helps identify and clarify misunderstandings or misinterpretations of concepts. It is also an effective strategy for assessing learning needs. Indeed, a supervisor cannot accurately perform an educational assessment without first discovering what the supervisee does and does not know.

On occasion, supervisors will identify areas for direct instruction. It is helpful for them to introduce the subject and offer to teach about it. Reluctance to hear teachings is often related to not seeing the relevance of the information. It is, therefore, important to relate the concept to a clinical issue the supervisee is encountering. Motivation for listening to mini-lessons is especially high if they believe the information will help them overcome a clinical obstacle. This is particularly true when the supervisor and the supervisee differ in what information they believe will be helpful for treating the case. The following vignette illustrates the concept of demonstrating relevance prior to offering a mini-lesson.

Dana observed that Hope, an intern, did not understand the concept of family triangulation, yet this dynamic seemed to be present in the case they were discussing in supervision. It involved a six-year-old boy who had frequent tantrums at school, disturbing his teacher and other students. During case exploration, Dana observed that Hope had not considered the role of the child's parents. Furthermore, she did not seem to understand the concept of triangulation. Dana asked, "Do you understand what I mean when I say that these parents seem to have 'triangulated' their child into their conflict?" Hope answered, "No," and immediately jumped into her interpretation of the child's problematic behaviors. She replied that the child's problems were at school and not at home, implying that the parental issues were not of direct concern. Furthermore, her clinical perspective led her to request didactic instruction on how to set up a behavior modification program for the child.

It was clear to Dana that Hope was not considering the boy's environment. In particular, she did not see the link between the parents' marital issues and the child's actions. Dana thought it important that Hope began to consider environmental (e.g., family) dynamics in her assessments. Therefore, she encouraged Hope to consider whether or not children were sensitive or reactive to their parents' emotional world, in general. Hope said they were, and added that, indeed, "Children do not grow up in a vacuum." She then recalled that she had observed the parents being openly hostile to each other and thought that it must be uncomfortable for the child. Now that the link between children and parents had been made, Hope saw the information as relevant and became very interested in the supervisor's lesson on family triangulation.

In the vignette above, it could be said that Dana and her intern, Hope, experienced a clash of perspectives in regard to the clinical issues of this case. Dana saw Hope's individual view as related to her beginning status as a practitioner, and wanted to help broaden her clinical perspective—a supervisor-identified learning objective. She wanted to help Hope begin moving to a multisystems perspective as a learning goal, not to force her to do things "Dana's way." Dana did not bulldoze Hope into hearing the "correct" way to view the situation, which would demonstrate, "I hold the only correct view, and because I am more powerful I can make you abide by it." Instead, she offered Hope the opportunity to consider another perspective on the situation. Hope was open to this only after Dana encouraged her to consider how the family was relevant to the immediate case.

Asking permission to give mini-lectures demonstrates respect for the supervisee's wishes, and allows them to set the pace and content for much of their learning. This type of behavior is an important skill in clinical work, so it is important that the supervisor model such actions. The overall process of the educational stage, including concepts of securing permission, addressing emergent information needs, and making information specific, relevant, and wanted, is demonstrated in the following vignette.

Educational Stage Vignette

As stated above, didactic instruction in the beginning phase typically has to do with educating the supervisee about the agency. Nevertheless, emergent needs identified by either the supervisor or the supervisee can be addressed. In the following vignette, the supervisor is providing the student intern with basic information about the job, which leads to an agreed-upon mini-lesson on engagement (sometimes called "relationship building" or "developing a therapeutic alliance"). We join the supervisory pair already in the educational stage. The instructor has been explaining the agency's intake process, and the intern's emergent need for additional information becomes evident. The supervisor sets aside intake process discussion in order to address the supervisee's concerns in the form of a mini-lesson.

SUPERVISOR: Once you get the referral from the teacher, you will need to contact the parents and get their permission for the child to be in our program.

INTERN: Do I call them or go to their house?

SUPERVISOR: Well, if possible, it is better to call first. We feel it is best to arrange a time when the parents are ready to hear about the program rather than dropping by unannounced. It also seems more respectful.

INTERN: Okay. Now, what happens if when I call, the parent refuses to meet with me and does not want to find out more about the program?

SUPERVISOR: Good question. Surprisingly, we have not found that happens often. I think that is because our staff spends a good deal of time engaging people prior to making requests of them—like getting their permission for their child to participate.

Note how the supervisor compliments the intern on the question. Giving compliments is an engagement technique (note how the supervisor models the technique about to be discussed) and sends the message to the intern that it is safe to ask questions and reveal a lack of knowledge. The supervisor is working to build the relationship and trust with the supervisee, while they talk about the parallel process of the supervisee's relationship to the client. Also note that the supervisor tries to minimize the intern's fear of running into a reluctant client by saying that this is something that does not happen often. If this supervisee believes that she will have to constantly "win over" clients, then her anxiety level is likely to remain high, and clients, picking up on this, may respond by being less open. Finally, note that the supervisor introduces a technique (engagement) to overcome the proposed obstacle, while informing her of a process (engage prior to requesting participation in program).

> INTERN: Engaging? We are just beginning to talk about that in our classes, but I am not sure about what exactly it is, or how to do it.
> SUPERVISOR: Would you like me to explain it to you?

Note that the supervisor asks permission before launching into an explanation. Although the supervisee has clearly said that she is not sure what it is or how to use it, she has not said that she wants a lecture on the subject at this point. Gaining her permission first allows her to voice when she is ready for new information and gives her some control over the supervision process. Moving at the client's pace is an engagement technique. Again, the supervisor is simultaneously modeling and discussing engagement behaviors.

> INTERN: That would be great.

Having gained both the intern's interest and permission, the supervisor then proceeds to give a brief description of engagement and the importance of building relationships and trust, and considers possible reasons why clients may be resistant to the program.

> INTERN: Okay, so if I understand it correctly, engagement means to begin to work toward a trusting relationship with the client. For example, if clients have had bad experiences with other social service workers, they will probably not trust me. So how I approach them may make the difference whether or not they will meet with me.
> SUPERVISOR: Right! If a mom thinks you are coming to correct her parenting, thereby accusing her of being an inadequate parent, she will probably not want to meet with you. It is sometimes necessary, but not always, to check into past experiences with social service workers. What would suggest to you that it is a good time to explore this?

Notice how the supervisor moves out of the educational stage and didactic instruction into collaborative consideration of the issues, bringing the intern back into the discussion as an active and thinking participant rather than a passive recipient of knowledge.

> INTERN: If they make a reference to past services or seem very reluctant to have me come.
> SUPERVISOR: I agree. So, what can you do if these things occur?
> INTERN: Well, it may be helpful to assure them that we are a different program, that we do not remove children, etc.
> SUPERVISOR: I like that! Very thoughtful. You have a nice way about you, I am sure you will not have too much difficulty engaging clients into the program.

The supervisor again compliments the intern on both her insight and interpersonal style. This is often useful in enhancing the supervisee's confidence about trying out new behaviors. Note how the supervisor does this just prior to suggesting this behavior (engagement) be taken on as a learning goal in supervision, attempting to move from the educational stage to the target goals stage. Also note how the intern has gone from being quite anxious about her first face-to-face meetings to being excited about "getting started."

> INTERN: Thanks. I am looking forward to getting started and trying this out.
> SUPERVISOR: Well, perhaps "mastering engagement" can be one of your target goals for this week?
> INTERN: To be fully accomplished this coming week?
> SUPERVISOR: No, probably not. But I think you could begin making great progress on that important skill. It could be an ongoing goal, until we both agree that you have it pretty well down. How does that sound?
> INTERN: Yes, I would like that.

Finally, note how the supervisor again asks for the supervisee's input into and permission on the selection of the target goal. Rather than choosing it for the supervisee, the supervisor demonstrates respect for their pace and direction by first asking for agreement. This is a useful engagement strategy, modeled by the supervisor, and can be important in the development of a positive and respectful relationship.

Supervisees generally appreciate teaching moments, and supervisors often like to teach and share their clinical wisdom. Therefore, the supervisory pair should be cautious of spending too much time on didactic instruction. When this occurs, "game playing" may be taking place (Kadushin 1992; Hawthorne 1975). For example, some supervisees would rather listen to their supervisors lecture than have their clinical work scrutinized. They learn to ask for didactic instruction as a method of preventing such examination. Alternately, supervisors who feel the need to maintain strict hierarchy may use didactic instruction as a way to maintain their position as expert and authority. In such cases, the goal of the teaching is more related to the supervisor's need for power than the supervisee's learning.

Conclusion

Upon implementing the social and didactic teaching functions of TCS, the supervisor and supervisee begin the process of selecting objectives for learning and practice. The steps of formulating supervision goals and the activities to attain them are outlined in the following chapters.

9   Target Goals

This chapter continues the presentation of the TCS stages and sequence with an in-depth discussion of the target goals stage. This stage begins the task planning and implementation sequence (TPIS), which includes generating and prioritizing target goals, selecting tasks to achieve these goals, predicting obstacles to successful implementation of tasks, revising tasks based upon consideration of potential obstacles, and clearly articulating selected target goals and tasks in the form of a written contract. TPIS is a central part of TCS, and is found in each phase of the model. It is shown below in bold.

Outline of TCS Prior to Completion of First Contract

Social stage
Explaining supervision and TCS
Educational stage
Target goals stage
    Identifying, prioritizing, and selecting tasks
    Anticipating and negotiating potential obstacles
Contracting

As discussed in chapter 3, learning is most effective when it is structured, focused, involves supervisee participation, and entails clearly defined learning objectives, activities, expectations, and criteria for evaluation. The TPIS process puts these principles of effective educational supervision into action.

Target goals represent the centerpiece of the TCS model. Through ongoing formulation of discrete goals and immediate work toward attainment, the broader objectives of supervision are actively achieved. TCS does not put forth objectives for learning or practice, but rather articulates a process for selecting and achieving them. Therefore, it can be used in almost all social work learning and practice settings (for more in-depth discussion, see chapter 12).

Target Goals Stage

This stage entails three basic steps: identifying, prioritizing, and selecting up to a maximum of three target goals for immediate work. These are carried out at each supervision meeting. Reflecting the principle of partialized learning, target goals are discrete objectives derived from more broadly defined learning and practice objectives. They are a means of working toward broad goals systematically and incrementally, providing focus for both learning and practice. Clear articulation of discrete goals helps to clarify performance expectations and reduce anxiety. Target goals are worked on between supervision meetings, generally during practice encounters. As they are attained, new ones are selected. The supervisor and supervisee agree the target goals will become the immediate focus of their work together. They are selected at each supervision meeting with the expectation that progress will made toward attaining them by the next meeting.

Most supervision does not entail explicit and ongoing use of learning objectives. Indeed, the focus is commonly problem-solving cases that need immediate attention, with little linking to learning objectives. When objectives are utilized, they are typically broadly defined, outlined only at the start of the supervision encounter, and (sometimes) revisited during formal evaluations. In contrast, TCS continues the goal selection process throughout the encounter—typically weekly in internships and biweekly or monthly in staff supervision.

This section presents a general overview of the target goal selection process, followed by a brief discussion of three issues central to understanding the implementation of this phase: partialized learning and development, types of target goals, and collaborative process. Next, the three-step target goal selection process is described in detail and illustrated with vignettes. Finally, additional considerations for implementation of this stage are considered.

Overview of the Target Goal Selection Process

Target goal selection includes three basic steps: generating a list of potential goals, prioritizing the list, and selecting up to a maximum of three. These goals, which should relate to broader agency or internship objectives, become the immediate focus of the supervisee's learning and practice. Progress toward them is generally accomplished through implementation of tasks between supervision meetings, typically with cases. Therefore, supervisees enter clinical encounters with target goals to direct their work.

Progress on goals selected during one supervision meeting is mutually evaluated at the next. For those partly or not attained, the supervisor and supervisee collaboratively determine whether to keep the target goal active, refine it, or develop a new one—e.g., putting the current one "on hold" until a more appropriate time. When goals are assessed as completed to satisfaction, supervisees are complimented on their achievement; then new goals are selected. As they are achieved, they serve as a foundation of knowledge to be drawn and built upon. This approach promotes systematic attainment of incremental goals that lead to achievement of broad objectives. Thus, the target goal selection process reflects the principle of partializing learning and development.

Partialized Learning and Development

As discussed in chapter 3, partializing learning has many advantages. Social work practice is complex and involves attention to multiple interests, dynamics, and skills. It is difficult for even seasoned professionals to actively attend to the many facets of clinical encounters. For social workers, particularly those early in their careers, the multiple areas for attention are often overwhelming, and this stress can impede both learning and good practice. Therefore, TCS was formulated to identify and work on only a few objectives at one time, and in progressive fashion. Typical supervision approaches primarily focus on case planning rather than attainment of educational objectives; learning tends to be fairly unstructured. In contrast, TCS emphasizes a highly structured educational process directly linked to case-planning activities.

In TCS, broadly defined objectives are broken down into explicit and clear target goals. Thus, the weekly selection of target goals should relate to larger objectives, such as those stated in learning agreements (Lemberger and Marshack 1991) and in job descriptions. Broad objectives are difficult to keep at the center of the supervisory process unless they are reviewed at each meeting. Because the immediate focus for most supervisees is problem-solving a particularly troublesome case, many select case-based practice aims as target goals, and the learning component of supervision is sometimes lost. TCS is designed to actively link educational and clinical experiences (theory and practice).

Types of Target Goals: Linking Learning and Practice

Learning agreements and job descriptions tend to reflect general learning or performance expectations not directly associated with specific cases or practice situations. Linking global objectives, and even specific performance competencies, to particular clinical encounters can be quite challenging, as can linking learning or performance competencies to practice experiences . Indeed, connecting theory and practice, and classroom and practicum experiences, have been long-standing difficulties in social work (Bogo and Vayda 1998; Raskin 1989). Considering various types of target goals can help actively link these components.

In TCS, target goals fall primarily into one of two categories, educational or practice, reflecting two overarching features of educational supervision: addressing *supervisee needs* related to attaining or enhancing professional social work knowledge and skills (i.e., educational objectives), and addressing *client needs* (i.e., practice objectives). Although each has a distinct emphasis, the two types of objectives are interdependent. In order to attain target goals that reflect general educational concerns, supervisees must try out new knowledge or skills in their work with clients—in practice. In turn, practice interventions should relate back to educational goals. For example, the target goal of "explore Kevin's intense anger" (example of a practice goal) could be linked to such learning objectives as "able to explore emotionally charged issues" or "able to elicit underlying feelings." In sum, educational goals can only be worked toward through clinical encounters, and practice goals should always be explicitly linked to learning.

Despite their interdependence, it is helpful to think of these components as distinct. Then, all target goals can be considered for their educational value—obviously critical in educational supervision. As stated earlier, it is not uncommon for supervision to emphasize client problem solving over professional growth. When this occurs, the danger is that all target goals will be formulated in terms of practice objectives (i.e., reflecting client needs) and that learning will not be a focus. This is particularly problematic in practicum education, where the primary concern should be student learning.

Because the constructs (educational and practice goals) are mutually dependent but aimed at different ends, explicit linking can be done fairly easily. Every clinical encounter presents the supervisee with a range of potential learning opportunities (Dea, Grist, and Myli 1982). When discussion of a case results in a practice goal (e.g., "will assess the Smith family for child abuse"), learning opportunities that underlie this clinical objective should be identified. Supervisors should remember to raise the learning component of a target goal each time a practice goal is selected. The TCS contract (discussed in chapter 10) helps by requiring clear articulation of the learning objective for each target goal. This forces a focus on learning, keeping education present and in awareness throughout supervision—a feature that makes TCS unique from other supervision approaches. When an educational objective is selected, cases in which it will be worked toward are explicitly identified. Thus, supervisee goals and client goals are linked, promoting progress for both.

Other Types of Target Goals

Some target goals are not directly associated with either educational or practice objectives, but include such things as idiosyncratic agency initiatives (e.g., learning a new filing system), school requirements (e.g., completing the formal evaluation), or supervisor activities (e.g., assisting in a supervisor's research project). These types of goals also present opportunities for learning.

Supervisee self-awareness is an area that may not be formally identified as an educational or practice objective in job descriptions or on evaluation tools, particularly in employment settings. It is an important skill that entails active monitoring of one's emotional, cognitive, and behavioral responses to stimuli, particularly during clinical encounters. Self-awareness enables deliberate choices about how to behave. Conversely, lack of self-awareness risks behaving according to one's own feelings and thoughts rather than the interests of others (e.g., clients). Knowing one's reactions and making deliberate choices about how to handle them during clinical interactions is in the clients' best interest. Informed and intentional employment of behaviors related to subjective reactions is often referred to as "conscious use of self" (Baldwin 1987; Kerson 1994; Minuchin and Fishman 1981). Skills of self-awareness and conscious use of self can both be formulated as target goals, as demonstrated in the following example:

> Trudy, a supervisor, noticed that Timothy, a usually highly compe-
> tent worker, was behaving quite differently with one client than
> usual. After she pointed this out to Timothy, he agreed that he was
> behaving oddly but said he did not know why. They both felt that it
> would be helpful for Timothy to examine what he was feeling when
> he was with that client. After some discussion, he admitted to being "a
> little afraid" of the client. Trudy inquired what it was that he feared.
> Timothy shared that he felt, because the client was a large, tattooed,
> motorbike-riding man, he might be "volatile" (an unfortunately com-
> mon negative stereotype). Timothy was avoiding raising important
> issues, fearing this would anger the client. In response to an inquiry
> from Trudy, he denied that the client had ever shown signs of volatil-
> ity. Both agreed that Timothy needed to be more aware of his subjec-
> tive reactions to people who were different from him, so that he could
> effectively work with people from diverse backgrounds. Timothy
> decided that he wanted to continue to explore his affective reactions
> as a target goal. Therefore, a goal they selected for immediate work
> was, "increase self-awareness of feelings and beliefs about clients."
> One task Timothy selected for work toward this target goal was to
> keep a journal of his feelings and beliefs. He felt that he could better
> explore his feelings when alone and that journaling was a "safe" way
> to do this. A second task involved reading more about groups of peo-
> ple different from himself. (Task development is discussed in the next
> chapter.)

Collaboration and Target Goal Selection

The selection of learning objectives and corresponding tasks can be a highly complex and stressful process. Deciding on the tasks to be completed by the supervisee at a particular point in time requires consideration of multiple factors including agency, school, supervisor, client, and supervisee learning needs. Despite social work's emphasis on andragogy and student-led learning (Knowles 1970) and suggestions that supervisees' formulation of their own learning objectives is necessary for a "most effective" supervision experience (Wodarski, Feit, and Green 1995:121), there is evidence that the majority of supervisors, specifically practicum instructors, do not involve supervisees in "thoughtful planning of the learning experience" (Abramson and Fortune 1990:284). The selection of learning activities is, unfortunately, often viewed as the job of the supervisor. This has a negative impact on both supervisee satisfaction (Fortune et al. 1985) and supervisor stress (Gitterman 1989). Instead, it should be a collaborative venture that includes both supervisor and supervisee input.

A collaborative supervisory approach has many advantages, particularly for adult learners, and is central to the target goal selection process. Although they feel obligated to direct student learning (Gitterman 1989), supervisors should be careful not to take full responsibility for the selection of target goals. As discussed earlier, enabling supervisees to participate in planning their own learning increases motivation for work, models productive use of power in a "helping" relationship, allows them to acquire skills in self-instruction, and helps build a positive and productive supervisory relationship.

When supervisees actively contribute to their own learning, target goals take on greater relevance. This is because they typically choose goals that relate to specific clinical situations—often those that are generating the most anxiety. This feeling was captured by one intern who stated that she was happy that she was able to choose "stuff I wanted to work on and that pertained to the cases which I wanted to [focus on]."

An additional benefit of supervisee participation in target goal selection is that they can help set the pace of their learning. Areas can be addressed as thoroughly as they need (e.g., until basic competency in a skill has been achieved) before they move on to other, perhaps more complex learning goals. When supervisors select goals, they risk developing assignments that are not to the level of the supervisee. If perceived as too simple, supervisees may feel insulted and disrespected. Conversely, if the assignment is too advanced, they may feel overwhelmed. In both cases, the supervisory relationship may be negatively affected. Much can be done to reduce this risk by discussing and developing target goals together.

Supervisor Leadership in Collaborative Context

Supervisors should be cautious about selecting goals for supervisees, but they should not abdicate their role in the selection of target goals, for they possess greater expertise than supervisees and are expected to take the lead in the learning process (Bogo 1993). Supervisees, particularly novice clinicians, often lack sufficient knowledge to suggest next steps for learning or practice. For example, a supervisee could not select the goal of "identifying cognitive distortions," if unfamiliar with cognitive theory. Supervisors may have the expertise to know when to choose cognitive interventions and for which cases they are most appropriate. They can introduce concepts to supervisees and discuss with them the advantages and disadvantages of utilizing such interventions in a particular case. Afterward, the supervisee is better able to evaluate such a target goal.

While this position of expertise may feel good and be ego-boosting, supervisors should attempt to maintain an authentically collaborative process, not a relationship in which supervisees feel they must always defer— e.g., proposing target goals they know the supervisor wants selected. The risk of pseudo-collaboration is particularly high if supervisees believe their ability to generate target goals is a factor in formal performance decisions (e.g., grades, merit raises). We recommend that supervisors periodically check in with supervisees about the target goal stage, exploring experiences and, if needed, ways to improve the process.

Finally, a collaborative process enables supervisees to learn how to be learners. When they are invited to select their own target goals, they are forced to think about the content, direction, and level of complexity of their own education. This engages them in self-evaluation. When target goals they have formulated are either too difficult or too easy, they must assess how they misjudged their selection. This avoids a less-than-productive focus on how well the supervisor is able to choose appropriate learning assignments for them. Self-evaluation is an important clinical and learning skill. It allows supervisees to more accurately judge their level of clinical sophistication, evaluate how informed they are about a particular area of practice, and calibrate learning pace. Indeed, even when supervisors are certain that their supervisees are making poor choices about target goals, giving them room to select goals that are either too easy or too difficult can be highly educational. If the supervisor intervenes to modify goals prior to the supervisee's work, this opportunity to learn to self-reflection and self-evaluation is lost.

Evaluating Selection of Target Goals

We believe that a supervisee's ability to generate target goals is a learning process in and of itself. Therefore, ongoing, mutual evaluation of goals should take place. In many settings, an overriding supervisory objective is to promote autonomous practice and learning. The greater their ability to select target goals, the more independent a supervisee can be. This raises an important question: "What is a *good* target goal?" This largely depends on the supervisee's level of development. A novice practitioner is doing well by simply generating ideas for target goals. More advanced clinicians, should be able to generate a range of possibilities that make sense for the cases they are carrying. In addition, they should be able to actively and independently link practice ideas to learning objectives.

Target goal selection ability has five different dimensions, each with its own continuum of complexity: 1) ability to generate target goal ideas (ranging from inability to ability to generate multiple ideas); 2) ability to generate ideas that make sense for particular cases (ranging from inappropriate to sensible); 3) ability to generate ideas independently (ranging from supervisor-directed to autonomous); 4) ability to prioritize target goals; and 5) ability to make links between learning and practice (ranging from focus on only one component to active linking). Supervisors and supervisees can use these dimensions to evaluate target goal ability.

Supervisees must develop their goal-selection ability just like any other skill. Therefore, evaluation of target goal selection ability should be ongoing. However, such assessment should be a mutual and supportive process. If supervisees are overly anxious about formal evaluations, they may feel they cannot make honest choices and take necessary risks for their own learning. For example, they might not want to admit that they need to achieve certain goals if it means paying the price down the road. Or they may continually select overly simple target goals, fearing that taking risks that might lead to failure and negative consequences. The supervisory setting should be a place where supervisees feel safe to ask questions, take risks, and share vulnerabilities (Gitterman 1989).

Mutual and collaborative evaluation of target goal selection ability enables the supervisee to learn to accurately assess their practice abilities and learning pace, to calibrate misjudgments, and to be self-reflective and independent thinkers. We recommend candid and reassuring discussion of supervisees' levels of sophistication in target goal selection and active consideration of methods for improving this skill.

The Target Goal Process: Identifying, Partializing, and Selecting

As stated earlier, the target goal process involves three distinct steps: identifying possible target goals, determining the order in which they should be addressed, and selecting a maximum of three for immediate focus. This section describes the process in greater detail, presenting various mechanisms for generating target goals, prioritizing strategies, and finalizing selections.

Identifying Target Goals

Target goals for both education and practice can originate from multiple sources, including the school, practice setting (i.e., social service agency, elementary school, hospital), funding sources, supervisee, and supervisor. Through a mutual process of exploration, the supervisor and the supervisee generate target goal ideas. The supervisor generally asks what goals for learning or practice the supervisee would like to work on, shares their own ideas, and puts forth school, agency administration, and funding source needs for consideration. Together, the supervisory pair list all identified potential target goals. They then review the list in order to determine which goal or goals (up to three maximum) will be taken up for immediate work.

The distinction between educational and practice objectives is helpful in the target goal identification process, as they entail somewhat different approaches. In general, practice goals emerge from specific cases and reflect objectives *for the supervisee* to work toward with those cases. As will be discussed later, supervisee objectives should also serve to advance, not hinder, case work. Educational goals are identified through ongoing determinations of gaps in supervisee knowledge and skill—by exploring what supervisees already know, what they must learn to satisfy school or job expectations, and what they want to learn for themselves.

Agency administrators may want the supervisee to take a particular course of action with one or many clients, or a mandating institution (e.g., courts, social services) may require certain interventions. However, it is more common for case objectives to be identified solely between the supervisor and the supervisee, within the context of larger constraints (e.g., agency, funding organizations).

The process usually entails the supervisee raising a challenging case for examination and problem-solving. The pair (or group) then collaboratively consider case dynamics and identify possible ways to proceed—possible target goals to guide the supervisee's next steps. Objectives can reflect any part of social work practice. Indeed, target goals can range from rebuilding a deteriorated clinical relationship to performing a suicide assessment to implementing a complex psychodynamic intervention to organizing the development of a new grassroots organization.

It is important to note that target goals are objectives for the supervisee, not the client—although the two should be linked. Discussion of possibilities should include consideration of whether or not supervisee objectives help or impede case progress. Because they emerge from case discussion, supervisee target goals typically relate to case problem-solving strategies, so the danger of developing case-impeding goals is low. Nevertheless, this possibility should be explored.

In the initial phase of this model, practice target goals tend to involve preparing for first meetings with clients, becoming familiar with agency case-handling procedures, and learning about community resources. Because the supervisee has not yet met with any clients, the goals are not as case-specific as those formulated in later phases. Beginning goals are fairly similar for all supervisees, because their work with clients largely involves the same activities (e.g., engagement, completing intake assessments, and paperwork). As they become more familiar with general agency practice procedures and develop individual relationships with clients, their practice goals become more case-specific and idiosyncratic. For example, after they have mastered the general intake process, supervisees should be able to formulate target goals that reflect specific intake strategies for particular types of dynamics (e.g., taking a client report of alcohol use as a cue to assess for abuse/dependence).

Because of the rather generic nature of beginning-phase practice goals, they are not easily distinguished from educational target goals. For example, the goals "perform a complete intake with Mr. Jones" and "perform a complete intake with Ms. Smith" are not much different. They both relate to the educational goal of "perform complete intakes." As the supervisee progresses in supervision and with cases, the distinction will become clearer. The following illustrative vignette demonstrates the practice target goal identification process. As you will see, the target goals relate to specific practice objectives that must be met in upcoming clinical encounters, but not yet to any individual case.

Illustrative Vignette

Mary, a new psychiatric hospital employee, meets with her supervisor, Nick. Having gone through the previous TCS stages (social, explaining supervision, educational) they are ready to begin the TPIS and the target goals stage. They begin identifying target goal possibilities by considering a topic discussed during the educational stage, performing risk-of-harm assessments, which is an important part of intakes in psychiatric settings. If the client does not pose an immediate risk to self or others, they are generally not admitted. This topic was selected because Mary's first assignment at the agency was to work at the intake desk. Note that target goal possibilities largely come from the supervisee, in a process of mutual exploration. Ideas are generated in response to the requirements of the practice environment, and direct attention to these needs helps to reduce supervisee anxiety.

NICK: So, do you feel okay with the suicide and harm to others assessments?

MARY: I think so. I understand them in principle, but don't know how well I will be able to do them when I have my first intake. I think you said that I would be at the intake desk tonight, and I will probably have an opportunity to try it out.

NICK: Well, there are slow nights, but it is likely. Do you feel ready?

MARY: I guess so.

NICK: When we talked about using the task-centered supervision model earlier, I explained that we would be choosing up to three target goals for you to work toward this week. Well, we are at the target goals stage, and the first step is to identify and list possibilities. Do you think we should list "perform intake assessments" as a target goal for you to work toward this week?

MARY: Yes, that is an important one, because before I can do anything else with clients I have to be able to tell if they pass that admissions standard.

NICK: Yes, that's right. But there are other components of the intake process. For example, you will have to ask for medical histories, past history of hospitalization, family members, resources, etc. Perhaps you would like to select one of these other areas as a potential target goal?

MARY: No, I don't think that is necessary. I had to ask those kinds of questions in my last job. And I believe that is all on the forms.

NICK: Yes, there are questions on the forms for each area.

MARY: That's pretty straightforward. But what I have never had to do is ask people about suicide or homicide.

NICK: Okay. Let's list that. If we choose that as a target goal, which I think we probably will, we will then talk about what tasks go into performing a risk-of-harm assessment.

MARY: Sounds good!

NICK: What other things do you feel you would like to select as potential target goals?

MARY: Mmm (thinking) . . . well, I think it is important for me to begin learning about community aftercare places—such as case management programs and group homes—now, so when I do discharges I will be all set to go.

NICK: That makes sense. Good thinking ahead. Let's put that down on the list.

MARY: I also would like to learn more about the team meetings. I understand the social worker coordinates and leads these? Maybe I could observe another social worker's meeting.

NICK: Yes, another good one to put on the list . . . running team meetings. How do you feel about working with people who might be actively suicidal?

MARY: I'm a little worried. I used to work in a nursing home, and every once in a while we would have a resident tell someone they were going to kill themselves. One person even tried it. But I never had to work with them directly.

NICK: What worries you?

MARY: Well, I guess that I might miss something because the person does not want to tell me the truth.

NICK: Well, that does happen. But you are worried that if client does not tell you the truth that it is a reflection of something you did?

MARY: Yes. I am afraid that because I don't have any relationship with the client, they will be less willing to participate and answer intake questions.

NICK: Okay. You would like to learn strategies for encouraging client participation during intakes?

MARY: Yes, I think that's it. I am not sure that all clients will want to be here, particularly if they are brought to us by the mobile crisis unit or police. I want to help them feel that I am working in their best interest despite the circumstances.

NICK: I am glad to hear you say that. Why don't we list that as a target goal—"implement engagement strategies to encourage client participation during intakes"?

MARY: Yes, that is a good one! I was worried that I would just have to get used to it. I am so happy that we are talking about this and will do something about it!

NICK: Should we list any others?

MARY: No, I can't think of anything else right now. I have to learn how filing is done here, but I don't think that needs to be a target goal.

NICK: Okay, great. You have identified some terrific ideas for target goals! Now let's talk about which ones you feel are priorities and decide if you can take on all three or would like to focus on only one or two for now.

Nick and Mary then transition to the prioritizing step of the target goals stage.

Educational Assessment

As stated above, educational objectives are identified by determining gaps in knowledge or skills. This is often done through an individualized educational diagnosis (Kadushin 1992) or assessment (Lemberger and Marshack 1991), which puts the supervisor "in a better position to fit the learning situation to the learner rather than the learner to the learning situation" (Kadushin 1992:196). Potential target goals can then be generated.

Educational assessments are an ongoing process and cannot be completed prior to the supervisee's start of clinical work. For internships, some schools have a "learning contract" (e.g., a statement of broad objectives and methods for meeting them) at the start of the practicum. Completing these types of assessments often necessitates supervisee self-reports about what they know and what they want to learn. This approach has obvious limitations for understanding the supervisee's position as a learner. First, it is not uncommon for supervisees to claim they are competent in an area when, in actuality, they are not—e.g., during an interview to try to win the job, to make a good first impression on their supervisor, because they do not accurately understand the concept. Second, it is important to maintain a distinction between knowledge and skill. The supervisee may be able to articulate theory and demonstrate a solid cognitive understanding of a skill, but not be proficient at it in practice. It is difficult to make determinations about skill through self-reports. Third, skills do not automatically translate across populations. For example, supervisees who have substantial experience working with children may not realize that certain behaviors (e.g., engagement techniques) may need to be modified for working with adults. They may report that they are proficient in an area in which they need some development. This is illustrated in the following example:

> Jim, a supervisee who had spent the last four years working in an elementary school, was assigned to a nursing home, which housed predominantly elderly residents, for his internship. During their first meeting, Jim and his supervisor were mutually performing an initial learning assessment based on Jim's prior practice experiences. Jim told his supervisor that he was "very good at building relationships quickly." His supervisor accepted this self-assessment and did not ask whether Jim felt his skills would apply to working with a different population. Jim had also not considered that the skills used to engage children might differ from those with older adults. Based upon this initial discussion, which assessed Jim as fully competent in this area, "relationship building" was not identified for future learning. At a subsequent meeting, Jim told his supervisor that he was having difficulty carrying on conversations with the residents. He felt awkward and worried that the residents did not find him to be, as he put it, "genuine." At this point, the supervisor and Jim reassessed "relationship building," and selected it as an area for development.

The above example demonstrates that accurate determinations about practice skill are best made through observations, explorations, and direct experiences of clinical interactions, rather than by relying on supervisee reports of previous work experiences. Initial learning assessments should be viewed as temporary and explicitly include methods for assessing areas in which the supervisee is thought to be skilled. Indeed, it is best to assess both areas of existing knowledge and skill and areas for learning *as supervisees perform their work*. Through shared observations, supervisors and supervisees can mutually evaluate performances, existing skills, and gaps in knowledge.

Viewed in this way, educational assessment is an ongoing process, which at no point should be considered "complete." As supervisees become proficient in a skill, initial assessments must be modified. Indeed, when gaps in knowledge and skill are closed, new areas for work are identified. Clinical practice is a complex endeavor that constantly challenges even seasoned clinicians. Indeed, as new, more potent treatment technologies are developed, practitioners are compelled to learn new practice theory and behaviors. This often requires "unlearning" behaviors, rethinking theoretical orientations, and acquiring new ones.

Special emphasis should be placed on identification of strengths—i.e., existing knowledge and skills (some of which may be located in the supervisee's personality, such as sense of humor or flexibility). Ongoing discovery of what they know is of great importance. Supervisees do not come to work settings as "blank slates" or "empty vessels," but with a body of existing professional and life experiences that should be drawn out and built upon. Existing skills and knowledge should provide the foundation for future learning. To use a metaphoric example, if a supervisee knows how to play guitar, many of these skills (e.g., ability to read music, understanding of how notes line up on a stringed instrument, fingering techniques) will be of great benefit in learning the violin. In practice, to use an earlier example, clinical skills for working with children, such as listening, validation, limit setting, and assessment of strengths, are also useful with older populations.

Finally, understanding what the supervisee knows is helpful in developing learning assignments in which they can succeed and feel competent. This said, it is important to remember that initially, discovery of what the supervisee can and cannot do is to some degree "a trial by fire," or experiment. It is through direct engagement in clinical work that competence can be best identified. Indeed, much discovery of what the supervisee does not know is made through "mistakes" or by experiencing difficulties. Identification of strengths can help buffer feelings of incompetence and low self-efficacy. Successes build confidence and increase motivation for learning.

Strategies to Assist Target Goal Identification and Educational Assessment

During the beginning phase, the supervisory pair focus on assessing the supervisee's levels of knowledge and skill, preferred learning style, strengths, and areas for learning. However, these educational appraisal activities should continue throughout supervision. Target goals reflect two purposes, learning and evaluation of the supervisee's capabilities. To aid in the identification process, sources for potential target goals are presented here. These include utilizing formal evaluation forms, formalizing areas discussed during the educational stage, and using information acquired through classroom education or attendance at alternative learning encounters (e.g., conferences, workshops, agency in-services).

Utilizing Formal Evaluation Forms

Many work and internship settings use a form or list of competencies for formal evaluations. In employment situations, these competencies typically reflect job performance requirements developed by agency administrators. In internship arrangements, competencies represent objectives for learning and are determined by the school.

Such an evaluation form with listed competencies is quite helpful for identifying and selecting target goals, particularly if viewed as a "menu" of possible goals. At each supervision meeting, the form can be reviewed and competencies selected to be addressed directly and in progressive fashion. Then, at times of formal evaluation, supervisees and supervisors can be clear about which objectives have been worked toward, achieved, or designated for further work, and which ones have not yet been considered.

Whether or not the evaluation instrument is selected for use as a source of target goals, we recommend reviewing it at the start of supervision for a number of important reasons. First, this allows the supervisee to see how and by what criteria they will be evaluated. Second, the review can be used to formulate a preliminary educational assessment. Supervisees can be collaboratively evaluated on individual competencies, which can provide guidance on how to proceed with learning and practice assignments. Third, review of the instrument may reveal that supervisees are not familiar with particular language or concepts, suggesting areas for didactic explanation. Fourth,particularly when competencies are defined by the school, review may demonstrate that the agency does not provide adequate opportunities to work toward the stated objective. Discovering this early allows for discussion of creative ways to achieve particular competencies. For example, the evaluation might list, "Student facilitates group process," but the agency may not currently offer any groups. The supervisor and student can then consider alternatives, such as starting a group or partnering with another agency.

Supervisors and supervisees should keep in mind that evaluation instruments tend to be generic and quite broad in their articulation of competencies; greater specificity of objectives may be needed. They may need to break down broad objectives into discrete statements. Additionally, the instrument should not be considered as a "final" menu but as a reference list. Areas for learning not includedshould be explored. For example, school evaluation forms are not designed to reflect specific treatment models or practice situations, but generalist practice skills. Interns and supervisors may wish to develop objectives that are specifically related to an individual model. For example, one student expressed a desire to learn to practice from an ego-psychology framework. He was currently taking a course on the approach and wanted to apply the theory. The supervisor and intern then developed target goals for assessing (e.g., ego defenses and coping mechanisms) and intervening (interpretation of identified defenses) using the ego-psychological approach.

Often, a well-articulated evaluation instrument is not available, particularly in employment situations. Job descriptions, if available, can serve as an alternative source for generating and formulating target goal possibilities. If no clear descriptions of job or learning requirements exist, we recommend that supervisors and supervisees take time at the start of their work together to clearly identify and list the areas for evaluation and learning. This self-generated list can be used as a menu of potential target goals. Finally, evaluation instruments should be used as a guide, not a final list of choices—in other words, not in rigid fashion.

A condensed sample evaluation form that identifies broad areas for practicum learning is presented below. Staff evaluations contain some of the same competencies but are often more specific to job requirements.

The following illustrative vignette demonstrates the use of formal evaluation forms for target goal identification and educational assessment. Tanika, a supervisor, has just handed the new student intern, Bob, a copy of his school's evaluation instrument. Note that she takes time to explain the purposes of form review and offers to clarify concepts, and that Bob's anxiety about how he will be evaluated is lessened by the review.

TANIKA: This is a copy of your school's practicum evaluation form. As you can see, it lists a bunch of skills. I think it is good for you to take a look at it, since this is what you will be graded on.

BOB: Wow . . . there are a lot of things on here!

TANIKA: Yes, there are. Do you have any questions about them?

BOB: No, not yet. I know what most of these mean. Some of these we are talking about now, in my class.

TANIKA: Great. If we run across any terms or concepts that are unfamiliar to you, let me know—I will try to explain them. If it's okay with

SUPERVISEE EVALUATION FORM

1   Describe supervisee's assignment for this past evaluation term. Include case-load, types of activities (e.g., individual treatment, group work, educational presentations, administrative) and target population.

2   Describe supervisee as a learner and use of supervision (e.g., ability to respond nondefensively to feedback, motivation for learning, self-directed discovery).

3   Describe the supervisee's development of professional values (e.g., sensitivity and integration of cultural diversity issues, confidentiality, maintaining nonjudgmental stance).

For items 4–7, rate the supervisee according to the following scale. Give examples in the comments section that are reflective of the ratings.

RATING SCALE:

    1 = needs improvement
    2 = satisfactory
    3 = outstanding
    9 = no opportunity to rate at this time
    N/A = not appropriate to placement setting

RATING

4   Supervisee's agency-related work

    completes paperwork on time   _____
    acts as a responsible representative of the agency   _____
    can describe the agency's mission   _____
    understands the structure of the agency   _____
    understands funding sources   _____

5   Supervisee's communication skills

    can communicate ideas clearly   _____
    utilizes listening skills with clients   _____
    uses empathy appropriately   _____
    attends to clients' nonverbal behaviors   _____
    recognizes impact of own nonverbal behaviors on clients   _____
    is able to facilitate communication between group members   _____

RATING

6   Supervisee's assessment skills

   integrates knowledge of life-cycle development   _____

   utilizes multiple sources of data in formulating assessments   _____

   can organize information from various sources into
coherent assessments   _____

   integrates issues related to diversity and oppression when
formulating assessments   _____

   considers biological, psychological, and environmental
factors in formulating assessments   _____

   can clearly identify the problem for focus of work   _____

7   Supervisee's intervention skills

   formulates intervention plan based on assessment
information   _____

   is able to partialize and prioritize client problems   _____

   includes and takes direction from clients about direction
of work   _____

   can perform interventions on multiple systems levels   _____

   consistently evaluates impact of interventions   _____

   deliberately utilizes self as an instrument of change   _____

   can perform crisis intervention   _____

8   Provide a summary or overall evaluation of supervisee's performance. Identify strengths and areas for improvement.

9   Identify goals for next evaluation period (use back of form if needed).

you, I would like to take a few minutes to go through the evaluation
form so that we can talk about these skills. That way, we can see which
competencies you feel you already know and can do well and which
you do not think you know or can do. That will give us an idea where
you stand, what strengths you have, and which areas we can choose to
work on as target goals.

BOB: Okay. Well, looking at this form, I have already done a few of
these things in the past. I did case management at my last job.

TANIKA: Yes, I know. Of what you see on the form, which kinds of
things did you have experience with?

BOB: Well, I had supervision in the past and I think that I was a good
supervisee. I always had my paperwork done on time, I never called in
sick, and always asked for feedback about how I was doing. Let's see.
. . . (Reviews form.) I worked with individuals and families, but I don't
think I did "counseling." I really just met with them to check up on
how things were going, but I did have to run some family meetings
that were kind of tough.

TANIKA: Sounds like you already know quite a bit. That's great, that
means you have some real strengths to draw on. You know, running
family meetings can be difficult, and many people are frightened of
that level of expressed conflict.

BOB: No, not me . . . fighting does not scare me, but sometimes I
don't know how to make it stop or make something good come out of
it for the family.

Tanika and Bob continue to review evaluation form competencies and
explore his understanding and experience with each. As they progress, Bob's
knowledge and skill level become clearer.

TANIKA: Okay, now that we have gone through most of the evaluation
form, we have a better idea about what you can and cannot do. However, I would like to continue to evaluate these skills as we go. For example, you said that you were good at drawing out clients' underlying feelings. I think it would be helpful to, at some point, select this as a target
goal to see how it goes with the population of clients you will have here.

BOB: Okay. I never have worked with mandated clients before, so
maybe it's different.

TANIKA: Now, let's consider what target goals you would like for
immediate work. An advantage to using the evaluation form to select

target goals is that when we do the evaluation for real, we will both know which ones were worked on directly and which were not.

BOB: I have to tell you, being evaluated is very intimidating. Knowing that I will know each skill and what I have done with it by the evaluation makes me feel less stressed about it.

TANIKA: Me too. We will both be clear about it. Before I did it this way I used to sit with the intern and try to remember when certain things were done and how they were performed. It was confusing. Sometimes the intern would say that they did or did not do something and I would remember it differently, so we were both left having to justify our perceptions—which did not help.

BOB: That exact thing happened with me and my last supervisor! She said that I was not good at something—making timely referrals—and I said that I was. One time I forgot about a call I was supposed to make, but remembered the next day and made it first thing in the morning, which was late. My supervisor never forgot that, and did not recognize the 400 times I made referrals correctly!

TANIKA: Things like that can be very frustrating. Using the evaluation form to select skills as target goals each week should make clear what we worked on and what we did not. Are there any objectives on the form that you think would be good to work on right now?

BOB: Well, I think we should go through them all, maybe do a few each week. So how about we choose the first three?

TANIKA: Okay. Let's put them on the target goal possibility list, and then we can discuss which we can do right now, and if there are any other pressing things that need to be addressed. We might identify issues with a specific client. When this happens, we should review the form and see which competency relates most closely to what we plan to do with that client.

BOB: Okay. Well, I did get a call from one client who told me that he was angry about having to come to treatment. I would like to learn how to deal with anger, since he is probably going to be that way when he comes in.

TANIKA: That's a great idea, and a great suggestion for a target goal. Do you see an objective on the evaluation form that matches this kind of goal?

BOB: Let's see . . . I think both "uses active listening skills" and "uses appropriate empathy" both apply.

TANIKA: Interesting! How?

BOB: Well, if he is angry, it would probably help to allow him to vent his feelings. That requires good active listening, and empathy should also help to decrease his anger. If he feels understood or "heard," then he probably will not feel he needs to say things so assertively.

TANIKA: I like that! Okay, how about we start with the active listening objective?

BOB: Sounds good!

Using Content from the Educational Stage

Because the educational stage typically involves the supervisee acquiring new information, this knowledge can be put into practice (i.e., tried out as a skill) if it is formulated as a target goal. Indeed, it is not unusual for discussion at the educational stage to naturally transition into the target goal identification stage. Supervisors should inquire whether any of the information presented during didactic instruction could be taken on as target goals. The process of utilizing educational stage content for learning goals is illustrated in the following vignette. Tonya's supervisor, Ricardo, is teaching her how to assess problems according to the task-centered practice model (Reid 1992). They are at the end of the educational stage and moving to the target goal stage.

RICARDO: To sum it up, one of the important parts of this assessment is gathering baseline information about problems. In addition to asking about the duration of the problem, when it occurs, and who is involved, it is necessary to capture its frequency.

TONYA: So, if I understand it, you want me to find out how often the problem happens?

RICARDO: Yes, exactly. So, for example . . . remember Linda the bed-wetter?

TONYA: Yes. I should find out how many times each week she wets the bed.

RICARDO: Yes! You see, if you know how often things happen, then you will more clearly know how how what you are doing, your intervention, is working. For example, if in one month she should go from wetting the bed five days a week to only once each week, you have made great progress. If you don't count, then when you evaluate in one month how things are going, the parents will tell you that she is still wetting the bed, and you will not be able to clearly see that there has been progress.

TONYA: That makes sense! I am going to meet them again this coming Monday. I will ask the problem assessment questions we talked about—especially the frequency!

RICARDO: I think that is a great idea! In a minute, we will start identifying possible target goals to start working toward. Should we list "problem assessment" as a possible target goal?

TONYA: Yes, I would like that.

Using Content from Other Instructional Settings

As stated earlier, linking classroom and textbook knowledge to real-life encounters with clients (i.e., field experiences) has been a long-standing struggle in social work education (Raskin 1989). Supervisees acquire new information from a variety of different sources, including school, readings, conference presentations, and colleagues. Often, they are anxious to try out this information in their work with clients. At such times, motivation for learning these skills is high, so they should seriously be considered as target goals.

In the following vignette, James has just returned from a workshop on brief solution-focused therapy (Nunnally 1993) and is anxious to try the techniques he learned about with his clients. His supervisor, Elsa, thinks this is a good opportunity to make use of James's enthusiasm, and helps him plan how to implement his new knowledge as a target goal. Note that as she does this, she helps James consider appropriate use of the model. It is not uncommon for practitioners to be so excited about new techniques that they are quick to use them without fully considering the client's situation. Supervisors can help them plan so that new techniques are not imposed onto clients but are instead consistent with the client's needs.

JAMES: I am so excited. I just went to a conference on solution-focused therapy and think it is a great approach. It has given me so many ideas for how to work with my clients. I can't wait to try it out!

ELSA: Wonderful. It is so nice to see you so excited about your work. How were you thinking of using it?

JAMES: Well, I think it would work with all my clients. Tomorrow I am meeting with Mr. Chen, and I think that he will really respond to this approach.

ELSA: What in particular do you plan on doing with him?

JAMES: I am going to do the whole thing—solution talk, the miracle question, identifying exceptions, scaling questions. . . .

ELSA: That sounds like a lot. Do you think Mr. Chen will be surprised by your sudden change in approach?

JAMES: Huh. I had not thought of that. I guess it might seem strange to him, since we were working toward resolving a particular problem. He might wonder why I stopped asking about the problem we were working on and changed to solutions.

ELSA: Perhaps. It is not unusual for people to be excited about new information and want to try it out right away. I think it is a good idea for you to do that, but at the same time, I think slowing down a bit to consider appropriate use of the model, slowly mastering all of its techniques, and taking the client into consideration are also important.

JAMES: I see what you mean. I was so excited about doing what *I* wanted to do, I almost forgot about the clients. I still want to try it, but perhaps I should slow down.

ELSA: I have done the same thing in the past—learned some strategies at a conference that I thought were great and rushed back to try them out. I must tell you, the techniques were usually not as successful as was described by the presenter. I think that was because the strategies were new, I was awkward about using them, and I did so inconsistently. It probably would have been better to become adept at a few techniques at a time, rather than trying to do it all first time out.

JAMES: Maybe instead of jumping in with full force, I could try and master one technique at a time.

ELSA: That sounds good to me. Which do you think you would like to work on first?

JAMES: Well, I really liked the miracle question.

ELSA: Okay. Do you think that "implements miracle question" would be a good target goal to list?

JAMES: Yes. I definitely want to try that one.

ELSA: You know, I think it is more difficult than it sounds. Once you ask the question, there are follow-up kinds of questions that are important to keep it going. It involves using solution talk. Perhaps we can also list that as a possible target goal.

JAMES: Great. That is what we were told by the presenter—that the technique involves more than a simple question. I would like to list it as a target goal.

Partializing Target Goals

In the beginning, most target goals reflect the immediate needs of getting started in a work setting: becoming familiar with agency procedures, practice orientations, and personnel, as well as preparation for first meetings with cases. The goals generally relate to first meetings: performing initial assessments, introducing the program, completing intake forms, and using relationship-building skills. Work at this phase is mostly anticipatory in nature, focusing on planning for upcoming encounters. This is different from the middle and ending phases, which entail exploration of recent encounters and planning for future work. As the supervisee becomes more familiar with the setting, goals become more reflective of idiosyncratic needs and specific encounters with clients.

In order to collaboratively generate target goal possibilities, supervisees should be asked about their initial learning desires. Example of supervisor questions include, "What would you like to learn first?" "What goals would you like to achieve during your year as an intern (or first term as employee)?" "What do you hope to learn from this job?" Many new supervisees will have difficulty answering these questions and thus, identifying target goals at the start of supervision. Indeed, it is not uncommon for them to lack enough knowledge about agency work to offer areas for learning. They may wonder, "How can I select goals before I know what I am supposed to do?" Others may think, "I thought the supervisor was supposed to tell me what to do," or, "I am still not completely sure about what the agency has to offer." Supervisors must be very active in proposing and instructing supervisees about possible target goals. The degree of directiveness should lower once supervisees have enough knowledge to begin suggesting their own learning and practice objectives.

Prioritizing and Selecting Target Goals

Once the target goals are identified and listed, they are collaboratively prioritized, and up to three are selected for immediate work. Prioritizing means placing the identified target goals in the order in which they should be addressed. This entails consideration of a number of factors, including weighing the needs of the multiple sources of target goals discussed earlier (e.g., agency, funding sources, school, supervisor, supervisee) as well as the needs of cases. If the three most pressing target goals are easily identified, then there is no need to order the entire list. However, sometimes decisions need to be made about which objective takes precedence. This should be done collaboratively, identifying the pros and cons of selecting one over the other. In our experience, this is a relatively rare occurrence. Because up to three target goals can be chosen, multiple urgent situations are generally accommodated.

It is not unusual for supervisees to select target goals to address areas that create the most anxiety for them. For example, Jane, upon learning that she was assigned a family intake, became quite concerned about facilitating the meeting and gathering the "correct" information. Although many other target goal possibilities were generated, Jane chose "perform a family assessment" as the one she felt was most critical for immediate work. Supervisors should permit prioritization of stress-producing cases; in such situations, the supervisee's motivation for learning and attempting new behaviors is high.

Prioritizing is often done in accordance with partializing for skill development. There is a hierarchy to educational target goals—some basic areas need to be understood in order to fully integrate more complex knowledge. For example, the skill of empathy can only be learned once the supervisee has mastered the skill of listening. Theories that guide assessment precede understanding of intervention selection. Prioritizing, particularly in the beginning phase, typically reflects the practice sequence.

Supervisors provide guidance as to which areas need to be addressed first in order to achieve more advanced target goals. Should a supervisee select an intervention target goal prior to meeting the client, the supervisor can assist by exploring how the proposed intervention relates to assessment information and, even more fundamental, whether the supervisee truly has the relationship with the client to successfully implement the plan. Helping supervisees explore their intervention decisions promotes a greater understanding of thoughtful practice.

Finally, learning assignments should attend to the supervisee's preferred learning style (see chapter 3 for a more in-depth discussion). Because students have varied learning style preferences, formulation of target goals should reflect these, even if not favored by the supervisor. For example, if a supervisee favors cognitive understanding prior to doing, goals can relate to reading about theory, techniques, or population considerations prior to implementation with clients. In contrast, those who learn best through direct experience that is then retrospectively related to theoretical knowledge should develop target goals that require "doing" (e.g., trying out new behaviors) as a way to understand theory. The distinction between learning and practice objectives is helpful in this endeavor. For example, it makes sense for cognitive learners to use educational objectives and for experiential learners to choose practice goals.

Formulating Target Goals

Once target goals have been prioritized and selected, final target goal statements must be formulated. This requires determining the level of complexity of each goal, and how many are to be worked on prior to the following supervision session. While the recommended number is three, at times it may be necessary to select fewer or more.

Level of Complexity

Target goals can be articulated at levels of complexity ranging from broad to narrow (or abstract to concrete). In TCS, efforts are made to break down broad objectives into subgoals that can be achieved or partly achieved by the next meeting. Because supervisees enter supervision with various degrees of knowledge and experience, target goals should be formulated accordingly.

As supervisees gain knowledge, skill, and confidence, the level of complexity of their selected goals generally increases. Selecting seemingly simple target goals in order to familiarize them with the process is encouraged in the beginning phase. For example, a beginning target goal might be "learn names of staff and their job titles." While this is not complex, it demonstrates the target goal process, focuses the immediate work of the supervisee, and allows for initial successes. In addition, it illustrates the clarity of performance and evaluation expectations attained by using target goals. This lessens supervisees' anxiety about their own role and responsibilities. They can experience first-hand how partializing allows for incremental progress toward attainment of a larger objective (e.g., "is knowledgeable about agency resources").This fairly simple and straightforward target goal represents an important learning step in terms of agency work, professional development, and the TCS process.

As a general rule, it is better to begin with goals that are too simple and increase complexity as needed than to overestimate a supervisee's skill and have to simplify goals later. Such "scaling back" can negatively affect the supervisee's confidence and motivation for work, as well as the supervisory relationship.

Number of Target Goals for Immediate Work

Based on our experience and supervisee feedback, we recommend a maximum of three target goals. This number should be used as a guide. The "appropriate" number largely depends on cases and external needs at the time (e.g., if the intern is in school, midterms and finals are highly demanding and diminish their ability to focus on practicum activities). Some target goals are more complex than others and therefore require more time to address. On occasion, the supervisory pair may decide to select only one target goal, particularly if it is complex and time-consuming. Conversely, there may be times when the three selected goals are fairly straightforward and the supervisee is able to handle a fourth. Supervisors and supervisees should use their judgment about what the student can handle in any given week. The objective is to encourage them to take risks and move forward, without overloading them. If they feel overwhelmed, learning and practice are likely to be compromised.

Limiting the focus to three discrete goals may seem questionable. This is done with the understanding that clinical work is unpredictable, and target goals cannot be rigidly adhered to in the face of emergent needs. Nevertheless, case planning is an important function of supervision. Areas for assessment and intervention can usually be identified and used to guide the supervisee's work (if this were not the case, the role of supervision would be quite limited). Focused work based upon a limited number (three) of agreed-upon target goals is legitimate and highly beneficial.

Indeed, utilizing up to three target goals for work between each supervision meeting has advantages over the use of singular, broadly defined goals (as when initial learning contracts are periodically reviewed) and unstructured approaches in which the supervisee is expected to focus on all the dynamics of a case at one time, with no explicitly articulated learning objectives. Using three goals allows attention to multiple objectives and environmental needs, and paradoxically, also provides focus and clear expectations. There are advantages to using both a multiple and a limited number of target goals.

The availability of multiple target goals minimizes potential conflict due to competing interests (e.g., agency, school, supervisor, supervisee, client).

Utilizing multiple goals enables the supervisory pair to accommodate most interests. It is rare that more than three sources will present competing needs at the same time.

Utilizing a limited number of target goals promotes focused learning, direction for practice, and clear expectations. Targeting only three immediate areas for attention reduces anxiety related to practice complexity and feelings of having to "do it all." An additional benefit is that the supervisee does not feel that they are expected to be an immediate master clinician, able to handle and attend to all aspects of the case. This can be a relief. As one intern put it:

> Before I meet with a client, I often feel overwhelmed by all that I have to think about. I then remind myself that there are only three things I have to do successfully right now. If I can just do those three . . . it keeps me focused, which helps me feel more relaxed. It also helps me feel more confident about addressing additional or unexpected issues if they come up.

Another supervisee stated: "If I am successful with only three things, that is better than doing poorly with everything, which is how I usually feel when I don't have a clear plan."

As you can see by these comments, the focus on three goals promotes greater confidence that the supervisee will do well in practice encounters. It also assures them that their learning needs will be consistently and systematically addressed. Finally, a limited number of target goals makes it clear to both the supervisee and the supervisor what the supervisee will do and on what objectives they will be evaluated. This allows for immediate feedback about learning progress and practice behaviors.

Conclusion

TCS is built around a process of identifying objectives for immediate work, which are referred to as target goals. This process typically begins with the wishes of the supervisee. Often, supervisees want to discuss challenging cases in hope of learning ways to overcome obstacles. At other times, they may request the opportunity to learn specific skills. Target goals can be formulated to reflect these wishes, and should be designed to address both case needs and supervisee learning.

Once they have selected target goals, the supervisor and supervisee consider actions, or tasks, to attain them, then organize the goals and their tasks in the form of a contract. The next chapter presents the TCS stages that follow the target goals stage: identifying, prioritizing, and selecting tasks; overcoming obstacles to task implementation; and contracting.

10 Tasks, Obstacles, and Contracting

This chapter continues presentation of the task planning implementation sequence (TPIS). After target goals are selected, tasks to attain them are identified, potential obstacles to successful task implementation are considered, and a contract stating what will be accomplished by the next supervision meeting is completed. This sequence is carried out in every meeting, throughout the supervision encounter. This chapter describes the stages of identifying, prioritizing, and selecting tasks; anticipating and negotiating obstacles; and contracting. These stages are listed in bold in the TCS sequence below.

Outline of TCS Prior to Completion of First Contract

Social stage
Explaining supervision and TCS
Educational stage
Target goals stage
Identifying, prioritizing, and selecting tasks
Anticipating and negotiating potential obstacles
Contracting

Identifying, Prioritizing, and Selecting Tasks

This stage involves three steps. First, task ideas are generated from multiple sources, including the literature, personal and professional experience, supervisor expertise, classroom learning, and brainstorming. Second, task ideas are prioritized in order of what is believed to be most appropriate. This includes consideration of the supervisee's capabilities, case needs, and which tasks will most likely result in successful achievement of target goals. Third, up to three tasks are selected for each target goal. The result is a maximum of nine discrete tasks for the supervisee to focus on in practice before the next supervisory meeting.

Tasks

Tasks are planned activities undertaken to attain target goals in systematic fashion. Most are carried out by the supervisee between supervisory conferences, during work with clients. Within the context of the TCS model, tasks represent clearly articulated, mutually agreed-upon statements of what will occur between meetings. They are stated in action-oriented, or behavioral, terms. Because target goals reflect both educational and practice objectives, task assignments promote purposeful, systematic, and action-oriented learning.

Called by many different names ("homework," "directives," "behavioral assignments"), tasks are important in clinical practice (deShazer 1982; Haley 1976; Minuchin 1974; Reid 1992). Since they are effective for deliberately and systematically promoting change, supervisees can use them to facilitate their own development (Storm and Heath 1985). Indeed, numerous educators conceptualize supervisory process in terms of "tasks" (Dea, Grist, and Myli 1982; Fox and Zischka 1989; Gitterman 1989; Jenkins and Sheafor 1982; Judah 1982; Neugeboren 1988; Nisivoccia 1990; Pettes 1979; Selig 1982; Siporin 1982). Task ideas can be derived from many different sources, but in TCS, task development is a collaborative process that encourages and utilizes supervisee suggestions.

Advantages of Using Tasks

Using clearly articulated tasks in supervision has many advantages: it provides focus and direction for the supervisory process and learning; enhances motivation; fosters momentum, monitoring of progress, and evaluation; allows observation of direct effects of practice behaviors; increases confidence that goals will be met; addresses issues related to accountability; utilizes supervision discussion in clinical work; and links theory and practice. After discussing each of these advantages, this section considers potential limitations of using tasks in supervision.

Provides Focus and Direction

Supervisees appreciate the focus tasks provide for clinical work and learning. Having a specific number of discrete activities to undertake minimizes the disorganization and confusion that can come with overwhelming practice responsibilities. This is demonstrated by the following statements from students who have utilized TCS:

> Having tasks . . .
> - "prevented me from running off on tangents"
> - "helped me keep track of things"
> - "helped to keep me focused—this was such a wacky case"
> - "was very helpful because it gave me somewhere to go . . . as far as what to accomplish next"
> - "helped . . . keep me so that I was not all over the place."

Limiting the number of activities (a maximum of nine) to do between supervision meetings provides added focus, particularly true when supervisees feel challenged by complex cases. As one commented, "I start off feeling I have five million things to do with the client, so having three tasks to focus on is helpful."

Enhances Motivation

A benefit of feeling focused was identified by two supervisees who independently suggested that it increased their motivation for learning and work with clients. Having tasks "helped to mobilize me when I felt frustrated and unmotivated," one explained. A benefit of increased motivation for another was greater productivity: "[having] weekly tasks gives me direction and helps me complete things, so I get more done."

Fosters Momentum, Monitoring of Progress, and Evaluation

Developing tasks forces discussion of the direction of supervision, making it clear to both the supervisee and the supervisor. In addition, it help create momentum and the sense that learning is "moving forward." Indeed, this same group of supervisees reported that the process of implementing new sets of tasks after each supervision meeting made them feel they were making progress in their work. While supervision that focuses primarily on problem-solving new cases at each meeting can be helpful, supervisees of this approach often feel that they are not advancing in any systematic way.

Furthermore, having well-articulated tasks enables supervisees to clearly monitor their progress with cases and learning goals as tasks are successfully completed and new ones are selected. Observing progress can greatly raise the supervisee's confidence as a practitioner. In addition, monitoring task completion serves an evaluative function. Supervisees can observe, and thereby assess, their own ability to perform a variety of tasks. By noting which skills they do well and which they struggle with, they can take active steps to improve their work.

Indeed, using tasks results in action-oriented learning. Rather than being passive receivers of knowledge (e.g., as when reading a textbook or listening to a lecture), supervisees can be proactive—go after learning rather than waiting for it to come to them. Furthermore, the process of selecting tasks can aid the development of critical thinking about their practice and learning. Supervisees must actively consider what steps to take next in their work with clients and in their learning. This is important for thoughtful, deliberate practice behaviors and helps to minimize impulsive decisions.

Allows Direct Observation of Effects of Supervisee Behaviors

Utilizing discrete tasks enables the supervisee to more easily see the effects of their actions. Even when assessing client progress, supervisees are frequently unsure which of their actions brought about the change. By focusing on a specific intervention (task), they can more directly trace its results and thus be clearer about its appropriateness and effectiveness and more confident about using it. By observing how well selected tasks address various challenges, supervisees can learn about the effectiveness of specific interventions.

Increases Confidence That Learning Goals Will Be Met

It is common for learning goals to be identified at the start of the supervisory encounter (practicum) without discussion of how supervisees will go about achieving them. The process of selecting goals for immediate work and breaking them down into discrete tasks clarifies how the goals will be incrementally and systematically achieved. As a result, supervisees gain confidence that learning objectives will be met.

Addresses Issues of Accountability

Having tasks provides clarity of expectations. Indeed, explicitly defining activities to be carried out confirms responsibilities (Fox and Zischka 1989). Both the supervisor and supervisee knows what is and is not expected of the supervisee, and on what behaviors they will be evaluated.

Supervisees are often worried about how and for what they will be evaluated, and whether they are "doing the right thing." Using clearly defined and mutually agreed-upon tasks can clarify expectations and reduce anxiety about which behaviors to use in their work in the field. This can be seen in the following reports from supervisees who have used TCS:

- "I know what I am physically supposed to do. Whether I am getting it accurately or not—I don't always know . . . but technically, I know exactly what I'm supposed to do."
- "Having tasks was very helpful because I knew what had to be accomplished."
- "Having tasks . . . keeps me in line with what [I] am supposed to do."
- "I like having specific tasks . . . clarifies my role."

Utilizes Supervision Discussion in Clinical Work

Despite long discussions and case planning, it is not uncommon for supervisees to either forget or be unclear about what was agreed upon in supervision when sitting face to face with clients. In TCS, developing tasks with the explicit objective of implementing them with cases is a significant part of the supervision meeting. Thus, there is an ongoing utilization of what was talked about in the conference in practice with clients.

Links Theory and Practice

The difficulty in linking theory and practice has been an ongoing concern in social work education (Raskin 1994; Walden and Brown 1985). In TCS, task development should be explicitly tied to theory—that is, knowledge about social work practice, human behavior, research, and policy. Additionally, when tasks are selected for intervention, they should be traceable to a theoretical base. The theory-practice link is supported during target goal formulation. The TCS contract calls for both educational and practice objectives, related to discrete target goals. Discussion of how to implement the tasks related to these educational objectives encourages consideration of theory. This method of connecting theory and practice can be useful in linking classroom and field experiences, also an ongoing concern in social work supervision (Raskin 1989; Vayda and Bogo 1991).

When Tasks Are Not Advantageous

Despite the many advantages of tasks in supervision, three cautionary statements are in order. Two concern two "supervision F-words," "fake" and "forced," and the third has to do with the danger of task development crowding out other aspects of the supervisory relationship.

Fake Tasks

When supervisees are unable to generate task ideas, they may feel pressure to come up with something in order to satisfy the supervisor. They may then offer "fake" tasks—activities that they are not genuinely interested in implementing and are only suggesting to appease the supervisor. It is likely that such tasks will not be valued and that there will be low motivation to complete them. This problem is most likely to occur at the start of the supervisory relationship, when the student is concerned with gaining their supervisors' approval and work with clients has not yet begun.

Supervisors can take steps to lessen the risk of fake tasks. First, they should normalize the potential for fake task development by explicitly discussing this dynamic. Second, they should periodically explore supervisees' perceptions of the "genuineness" of the tasks developed. This is particularly important when the intern seems to be giving clues that the tasks are fake (nonverbal behaviors, resistance to developing tasks, suggesting overly simple ideas). Third, they should encourage supervisees to express when they are unable to generate authentic tasks, not construct a relationship in which supervisees feel they will be penalized either overtly (e.g., through the grade) or covertly (e.g., the supervisor relaying disgust through nonverbal responses).

Forced Tasks

A second concern (and supervision F-word) is forced tasks. Tasks are likely to feel forced when they have not been developed in collaborative fashion. It is important that supervisors take care not to unilaterally assign tasks. Perhaps more subtle, they must watch that they are not setting up a relationship that appears collaborative—where in reality, the supervisee is suggesting tasks that he or she knows the supervisor wants implemented. Then the supervisee is focusing on their supervisor and on learning skills to appease them, rather than on their own growth.

The supervisor is ultimately responsible for formally evaluating the supervisee's performance. Therefore, interns may not feel safe to disagree or to suggest tasks that they know will be looked upon with disapproval. Supervisors must take care to establish and maintain an open and trusting learning environment.

Task Development Overriding Affective Experiences

The third caution relates to the instrumental functions of task development overriding the supervisee's affective experiences. Clinical practice can be an emotionally intensive endeavor, particularly for novice practitioners. They experience strong affective responses to clients, agency policy and procedures, school requirements and course discussions, personal matters, and supervision itself. It is often necessary to process affective responses before supervisees are able to actively engage in practice and supervision activities. For example, a supervisee will have difficulty concentrating on task development if preoccupied with thoughts of a recent personal loss.

When supervisors ignore the affective aspects of supervision in favor of completing its instrumental functions, they put the relationship at great risk. Such an approach conveys to the supervisee that they are considered less important than the tasks to be implemented. It is not surprising, in such situations, that students resent the neglect of them as "human." Furthermore, they may imitate their supervisor's neglect of affective responses in favor of instrumental functions in their work with clients. Although TCS includes the social stage to address affective reactions, they should be attended to throughout the supervisory meeting.

The process of generating task ideas is ripe for affective reactions. Supervisees may have strong feelings about how clients should be treated, based upon personal values or rigid loyalty to a philosophical orientation. Left unaddressed, emotional reactions may be an obstacle to agreeing on or implementing tasks. Therefore, supervisors need to provide opportunities for processing affective responses throughout the meeting. However, this does not mean changing the nature of supervision to psychotherapy. Supervisees should not be treated but rather given opportunities to vent, express their emotionally based reasons for wanting to take certain actions, and develop strategies to successfully engage in practice or supervision activities.

Generating Task Ideas

For each target goal, the supervisee and supervisor work together to generate task ideas. It is a collaborative process in which both make suggestions. In general, the supervisor will begin the process by asking the supervisee for their ideas. As both make suggestions, they list them. When no more ideas are generated, they review the list and critique each idea in terms of its appropriateness to the situation.

Ideas can emerge from multiple sources of knowledge such as readings, prior clinical successes, personal experiences, agency requirements, course assignments, and brainstorming. For the most part, potential tasks are generated by partializing target goals into the discrete behaviors that go into achieving them. The following scenario illustrates this process:

Susan, a supervisee, believed that her client, Mr. Thompson, was struggling with feelings of anger about the recent death of his mother. Although Mr. Thompson said he was "okay" with the loss and that "life goes on," Susan observed behaviors that suggested otherwise. For example, when she asked Mr. Thompson about his mother, he would quickly change the conversation. Later in her meeting with him, Mr. Thompson told a story about how, after being "cut off" by another car, he followed the driver until he stopped (about an hour later) "to curse him out." Susan had also observed that Mr. Thompson seemed to be more easily agitated than prior to his mother's death. During Susan's review of this case with her supervisor, they selected the target goal "address Mr. Thompson's underlying anger." They then generated a list of possible tasks that included:

- convey to Mr. Thompson that anger is a normal reaction to loss
- share with Mr. Thompson observations of behaviors that suggest he is not "okay" with the loss
- point out to Mr. Thompson that he quickly changes the subject when asked about his mother
- inquire about how others in his family are handling the loss
- ask whether his supports (e.g., family, friends) have noted a change in his behavior since his mother's death
- ask him for his *thoughts* about his loss (rather than directly about his *feelings*)
- confront Mr. Thompson, telling him that he is angry, despite his claim that he is not
- tell Mr. Thompson that people often feel "orphaned" or "abandoned" when a parent dies, and ask if he has these feelings
- tell Mr. Thompson a story of another person who denied anger about a recent job loss and also had "road rage" (i.e., explosive anger at other drivers when in his car), which dissipated after he recognized he was angry about his job
- disclose Susan's own temporary experience of anger when her grandmother died
- suggest that Mr. Thompson "journal" (write in a journal about his experience of his mother's death)

As can be seen, multiple task possibilities can be generated for this fairly narrowly stated target goal. The number identified depends upon how broadly or narrowly each goal is stated. For target goals stated in extremely broad terms, an overwhelming number of task ideas can be generated. In such cases, it may be necessary to further partialize the goals (revisiting the target goal stage) prior to generating task ideas. For example, for the target goal "can assess family process," hundreds of task ideas could be generated. Breaking this goal down into separate family assessment areas would be helpful—e.g., observing communication patterns, hierarchy, alliances and triangles, parenting behaviors, multigenerational transmissions, and emotional expressiveness (to name just a few).

When Supervisees Are Unable to Generate Ideas

Identifying potential tasks should be a collaborative process to which both the supervisee and the supervisor contribute. However, there may be situations (e.g., when the supervisee is new to the TPIS process) when the supervisee is unable to come up with suggestions. Indeed, even if they are able to generate target goal ideas in the previous stage, they may not know how to go about achieving them. Three basic approaches can be taken, with varying degrees of supervisor directiveness: the supervisor providing task ideas for the supervisee; the supervisor putting forth task ideas and asking the supervisee for feedback about each; and the supervisor offering suggestions for supervisee independent activities (e.g., reading) to discover possible ideas. Each approach has benefits and drawbacks.

Supervisor Providing Ideas

It is not uncommon for supervisees to lack knowledge about how to proceed in particular situations and look to their supervisors for strategies. They particularly appreciate when supervisors offer a range of practice options and then discuss the strengths and weaknesses of each. This sounds easier than it is in actual practice. Rather than offering task alternatives for collaborative evaluation, supervisors may wish to give supervisees answers directly because of time considerations or their own need to be seen as expert (Wilson 1981). Although this may be faster, it is less helpful to the supervisee's learning. It may also foster dependency and require supervisors to provide direction on an ongoing basis.

This said, there are times when supervisor-provided tasks may be helpful. For example, many novice social workers do not have enough experience and thus feel unqualified to offer ideas. Taking a developmental perspective on supervisee learning, it may be necessary to use a directive approach at first and move toward a more collaborative (and eventually supervisee-directed) process as knowledge increases. Supervisors can teach how to generate task ideas by modeling. We recommend that this be done explicitly (i.e., the supervisor should openly state that they are modeling this process) and only for a short time. Supervisees should become active in the process as early as possible. Helping them to learn early how to generate and critique their own task ideas will likely reduce requests for limited supervisor time in the future.

Finally, some supervisors may be tempted to immediately provide task ideas because it gives them an opportunity to show off their expertise. We encourage them to keep a watchful eye to prevent their own wishes to be viewed as experts taking precedence over opportunities for supervisee learning.

Supervisor Suggesting Ideas for Critique

A second approach entails the supervisor making suggestions that are then collaboratively critiqued. The supervisor should first challenge the supervisee to draw upon their own knowledge base and previous experience, using prompts such as, "What did your textbook say goes into performing a family assessment?" or "What have you done in past similar situations?" It is not uncommon for supervisees who initially are stumped to be able to generate ideas with minor prompts.

If the supervisee is still unable to generate task ideas of their own, the supervisor should put forth task suggestions. Each should be evaluated by the supervisory pair for strengths and limitations. As the list of task ideas grows, the critique should include what makes the most sense for the particular situation. While this process is more time-consuming than the supervisor providing task ideas, it benefits supervisee learning. They observe how to critique potential interventions and generate task ideas, and know that their responses to suggestions are valued. Furthermore, they learn first-hand that a range of task possibilities exist for most situations — that there are rarely fixed, singular, or "right" behaviors to implement in any given circumstance.

Supervisee-Generated Task Ideas

The third approach is to arrange for supervisees to take on activities aimed at helping them discover task possibilities on their own, such as consulting readings, talking with instructors, or engaging in role play. The supervisor does not offer any suggestions, instead challenging the supervisee to take complete responsibility for generating task ideas. Supervisees may be asked to research what tasks are involved in addressing a particular clinical issue raised in supervision. For example, a supervisee working with a young woman with bulimia went to the library and reviewed literature on eating disorder assessment and intervention techniques.

This approach is particularly helpful when supervisors are also unable to generate task ideas, such as when a case presents challenges that are outside their own range of experience. The following example illustrates this approach:

> Brandon, a supervisee, wanted to learn how to perform an assessment using the task-centered practice model (Reid 1992). From his course readings, he knew that the first step involved problem identification,

and he chose this as a target goal. However, when his supervisor asked about task ideas, Brandon was unable to articulate the steps that make up the problem identification process. Rather than providing Brandon with task possibilities, the supervisor asked him if he felt that revisiting his readings would clarify potential activities. Brandon responded that he remembered that his readings clearly spelled out the practitioner behaviors that went into performing problem identification. He added that the readings would allow him to list these behaviors and enable him to better "put them to memory" for future encounters. Therefore, Brandon proposed two immediate tasks for attaining the target goal: read about task-centered problem identification and generate a list of activities that go into performing this technique.

By taking on tasks aimed at discovering the activities that further practice and educational objectives, supervisees develop the skill of independently generating possible "next steps" in their own learning and practice. In short, they learn how to be self-sufficient learners and practitioners.

The disadvantage of this approach is that it can be highly time-consuming. Indeed, because many target goals reflect pressing case needs, there may not be enough time for supervisees to take on such activities. One way to handle this problem is to schedule a brief supervision meeting for the next day in order to review the supervisee's self-generated task ideas. These can then be collaboratively critiqued prior to implementation with cases.

Prioritizing and Selecting Tasks

After task ideas have been generated and listed, the list is reviewed and prioritized, and up to a maximum of three tasks per target goal are selected for immediate work. This way, supervisees devote themselves to a maximum of nine discrete tasks to be carried out between supervision meetings, and both supervisee and supervisor have a clear understanding of what is expected. The following example illustrates the prioritizing and selecting tasks process, continuing the earlier example of Susan and Mr. Thompson and utilizing the list of possible tasks they generated.

After generating a list of task ideas, Susan and her supervisor prioritized the list and selected tasks for implementation, based upon which were more appropriate at this point in Mr. Thompson's treatment. For example, they agreed that the idea of "disclose Susan's own temporary experience of anger when her grandmother died" was inappropriate at this time. Mr. Thompson had suggested in past conversations that he believed it was acceptable for women to express emotions but not for men. Since Susan was female, it was unlikely that he would feel her experience applied to him. This task would probably not benefit Mr. Thompson as much as others on the list.

Because Mr. Thompson did not seem ready to discuss his own feelings about the loss at this time, tasks that challenged him to directly discuss his experience were temporarily prioritized lower than those that aimed to reduce his anger through normalization and other indirect techniques. The supervisor and Susan agreed that the target goal would be met incrementally, by creating an environment in which Mr. Thompson felt safe to explore his feelings in the future. Therefore, they selected the following three tasks from the original list:

- convey to Mr. Thompson that anger is a normal reaction to loss
- ask whether his supports (e.g., family, friends) have noted a change in his behavior since his mother's death
- after completing the first two tasks, suggest to Mr. Thompson that people often feel "orphaned" or "abandoned" when a parent dies, and ask if he has these feelings

Note that none of these tasks directly or immediately addresses the selected target goal, "address Mr. Thompson's underlying anger." It is not uncommon for multiple steps to be required in attaining a goal. Mr. Thompson not being ready to recognize his anger requires that Susan take steps to create the environment in which he can do this. This target goal will be kept for ongoing work, even after these three initial tasks have been successfully implemented. Three new tasks will be selected in each subsequent supervision meeting to work toward this goal until it has been met.

You may have also observed that a statement of when to implement the last task—"after completing the first two"—has been included. This was done because the third task was assessed as more confrontational than the first two; it directly asks Mr. Thompson about his feelings. While Susan and her supervisor liked this task, they felt that it could not be implemented without some prior steps (i.e., the first two tasks). Giving an order to the tasks is the kind of specificity in task formulation that can be helpful for both learning and practice.

Levels of Task Specificity

Tasks can be formulated at different levels of specificity ranging from broad to concrete. Broad tasks lack procedural details related to specific actions, such as when and how they will be carried out. For example, the broad task, "confront Mr. Smith about his drinking," does not detail how this confrontation is to take place—with family members present?—or when—as the subject comes up? at the start of the session? Does it mean directly stating, "You have a drinking problem"? Or should the supervisee first ask Mr. Smith to describe his drinking behaviors and perceived consequences?

Broadly stated tasks offer a direction for intervention but leave much to the supervisee to determine. This approach is particularly suited to advanced practitioners, who are able to intervene effectively with minimal direction. However, the lack of procedural detail risks confusion about expectations. For example, even seasoned practitioners are concerned about whether or not their supervisors will consider their approach "correct." Therefore, particularly at the beginning of the supervisory relationship, we encourage constructing task statements that are as specific as possible. The greater the specificity, the clearer the expectations, and the more likely it is that the tasks will be implemented.

Unless both the supervisee and the supervisor agree that broad tasks are appropriate (e.g., the supervisee is an advanced practitioner), they should be broken down into concrete tasks. These clearly spell out how and when they are to be implemented. This high degree of specificity minimizes confusion about expectations. The difference between broad and concrete tasks is illustrated by an example stated in both formats:

Broad task: Tell Ms. Hernandez about community resources.
Concrete task: Call Ms. Hernandez today at 4:30 and tell her about day care programs in her neighborhood. If she is unreachable at 4:30, call again tomorrow morning, before she goes to work.

As can be seen, the broad task does not give details about when or how to tell Ms. Hernandez, or which resources to inform her about. The concrete task spells this out.

Again, how tasks are stated largely depends upon the supervisee's abilities and their agreed-upon degree of autonomy in making choices. Because task specificity can be viewed on a continuum ranging from broad to concrete, the detail in which activities are stated can be increased or decreased as needed. For example, as supervisees gain clinical sophistication, their tasks may be stated more broadly.

The level of task specificity should be worked out by the supervisory pair. This said, we prefer the use of concrete tasks for all practitioner levels because they make expectations clear. However, supervisors should be cautious about utilizing concrete tasks with advanced practitioners without first explaining the benefits of this approach. These supervisees may perceive the greater specificity as insulting, patronizing, or punitive.

Preference for Level of Task Specificity

Supervisees will differ in the degree of task specificity they prefer, depending on developmental concerns, learning styles, and the supervisory relationship. As supervisees progress in their work or practicum settings, they commonly go through developmental changes. For example, at the start, they are often focused on themselves—e.g., what they are doing wrong or right. As their gain knowledge of the agency and become more confident about their skills, their focus becomes more client-centered (Dawson 1975). Novice social workers are likely to prefer concrete tasks, appreciating the clear directions. As they increase their knowledge and skill and are more able to participate in the task selection process, they are likely to feel more confident about taking on broadly defined tasks, in which they have greater flexibility in implementation.

Supervisee specificity preferences also depend upon learning style. Some learners prefer structured, clearly spelled out assignments, while others favor less direction and greater flexibility. As one supervisee put it, "It's like in school, some people like assignments that say, 'write a paper about anything,' and some people like the instructor to say, 'I want A, B, C, D, and E, in this order . . . with these headings'." The supervisory pair should discuss preferences for structure in their learning assignments.

Supervisors should also consider that degree of task specifity may be related to the supervisory relationship. Since concrete tasks are more straightforward, supervisees may feel more secure selecting them, particularly in untrusting relationships. For example, an intern made the following statement about "playing it safe" with his supervisor: "Because she expects things to be done exactly the way she wants, I select mostly concrete tasks. When I try things out that are a little different, she becomes angry with me and tells me that I am 'stubborn' and 'passive aggressive'." Conversely, when supervisees feel positively about the relationship, they may be willing to select abstract or more broadly defined tasks. Because it is easier to clearly demonstrate that concrete tasks have been implemented rather than abstract ones, the selection may relate more to issues of accountability than to learning.

Number of Tasks

Although the recommended maximum for work between supervision meetings is nine tasks (three for each target goal), the actual number may vary according to such considerations as the complexity of the task, the case in which it is to be implemented, and the supervisee's current work demands.

The total number selected often has to do with the perceived time each will take to carry out. Some tasks take longer than others, depending upon the complexity of the cases in which they are to be implemented. For example, the task of contacting the parent of a child can be a highly time-consuming process in one case and rather simple and quick in another.

The supervisee's current workload may influence the final number of tasks. When a worker has a case "blow up" into active crisis, there may not be time to focus on tasks related to other cases. Also, school requirements can affect the student's workload and amount of time available for task implementation. There may be occasions (e.g., when midterm and final assignments are due) when they are unable to handle nine tasks.

Allowing Supervisees to Select "Wrong" Tasks

The task selection process is collaborative and promotes supervisee input. There will likely be times when supervisors feel that certain tasks suggested by their supervisees are wrong (e.g., ineffective, ill-timed) and should not be selected for implementation. However, allowing supervisees to try out their ideas can be beneficial, even when the tasks seem unhelpful or strange. Supervisors who do this often find themselves pleasantly surprised by how well some odd-sounding supervisee ideas work. For example, Shawna, an intern, told her supervisor that she wanted to help a particularly talkative seven-year-old child stay more focused in school. She generated the task idea of having him watch the second hand on the classroom clock for one minute whenever he felt like talking. Privately, the supervisor thought this was an odd idea—that the child was incapable of independently redirecting his attention. He shared his concerns, but because Shawna felt that this task would be effective, he went along with it. Much to his surprise, it went quite well. Supervisors can learn different ways of intervening (i.e., task possibilities) by allowing their supervisees to take on activities that they perceive as odd.

Allowing supervisees to take on "wrong" tasks depends, of course, upon the potential risk to the client. In cases where clients are in danger (e.g., suicidal, actively abusing alcohol), supervisors should step in to prevent certain task ideas from being implemented. For example, a supervisee who was a big fan of Jay Haley's strategic family problem-solving model (Haley 1976) wanted to try a paradoxical intervention with a compliant client who was struggling with a serious eating disorder and concordant health problems. The supervisor told the him that he was not permitted to use this situation for experimentation.

However, as a rule, supervisors should not rigidly reject supervisee-suggested tasks that they feel are problematic. This reaction is likely to be related to concern about the effect on clients, or to a different theoretical (or cultural) orientation. Instead, supervisors should explore with supervisees the expected outcome of potential tasks. This often helps supervisees realize that certain tasks may not be beneficial. When insistent about selecting particular tasks, they should be permitted to try them out (provided there is no serious client risk involved). Supervisees can learn through experience about the effectiveness and timing of certain interventions; this is likely to be more effective and lasting than a supervisor's preventative explanation why a task may not work. For example, an intern is more likely to remember a client's negative reaction to a selected task (e.g., giving the client an ultimatum) than the supervisor's saying prior to implementation, "I don't think you should give your client an ultimatum—it will make him very angry."

Finally, there is a relational danger to consistently restricting what supervisees are allowed to do: they may implement what they want, regardless of what they agree to in supervision. It is not uncommon for supervisees to pretend to go along with their supervisor's suggestions, due to the power differential in the relationship, and implement their own ideas when with clients. Giving them freedom to choose, and to make their own mistakes, enables them to be more open.

Empirically Based Practice

Some interventions have been shown to more effective than others for various human challenges. Therefore, when possible, each task to be implemented by supervisees with cases should be evaluated for its empirical support. This teaches thoughtful selection of intervention behaviors based upon evidence of the most effective practice currently available. In short, it teaches supervisees to engage in empirically based practice. While we believe that much can be learned by experiencing so-called "wrong" tasks, we strongly encourage preference be given to tasks related to empirically validated interventions.

Anticipating and Negotiating Obstacles

This stage consists of two steps: anticipating potential obstacles to carrying out the selected tasks and formulating a plan for negotiating them. The supervisee and supervisor work together to predict possible obstructions to implementation of the tasks selected in the previous stage. These may include negative client reactions, environmental factors (e.g., client's phone out of service, lack of social service agency cooperation), collateral family members' resistance, and supervisee personal reactions (e.g., countertransference). In short, supervisees are asked to look ahead and consider ways to ensure successful task implementation.

When possible obstacles have been identified, options for overcoming them are discussed. There are three general ways to negotiate obstacles: abandon and replace the task, revise it , or keep it and formulate a backup plan in case difficulties arise.

If selected tasks are deemed overly problematic after consideration of potential obstacles, they may be abandoned and replaced. This is likely to occur when a selected task is based on information that has yet to be confirmed. For example, many novice practitioners are quick to suggest ideas to "fix" client problems without having taken the time to fully understand them. Their tasks designed to intervene may need to be replaced with assessment tasks.

On occasion, selected tasks are found to be sensible but may need to be modified to minimize glitches. For example, a task may originally involve a supervisee telling a client to take a certain action. After discussion, this may be modified to asking the client to consider the proposed action. This is a small revision, but the task of telling is likely to encounter more obstacles than asking.

Finally, the original task may be kept and modified. Strategies for dealing with potential obstacles are developed as a backup plan—should problems arise, the supervisee will be prepared to address them. This is illustrated in the following example:

> Kendra, a case manager, was responsible for helping elderly patients continue to take their medication after their release from the hospital. She made home visits to monitor medication compliance. One of her patients struggled with memory loss, but was certain that she would remember correctly which pills she had to take and when. Kendra selected the task of asking the patient to allow a family member to take over keeping track of her pills. During the identification of obstacles process, Kendra predicted that the patient might refuse anyone else's help with this matter. If this obstacle arose, Kendra was prepared with backup strategies she had developed with her supervisor. One of these involved exploring with the patient whether her refusal was related to a fear of losing independence. Kendra was prepared to change the nature of the home visit from concrete matters (i.e., pill taking) to providing emotional support.

Anticipating possible events that might make tasks irrelevant, insufficient, or problematic minimizes the chance that the supervisee will encounter difficulties performing them. Having anticipated various problematic scenarios, supervisees will run into fewer surprises, feel less overwhelmed when obstacles arise, and have greater confidence in implementing tasks.

The following section discusses the process of generating potential obstacles and developing plans for negotiating them. An illustrative vignette demonstrates this stage in action. Suggestions to assist identification of potential obstacles are given, and the educational and practice benefits of engaging in this process are discussed.

The Process

The process of generating potential obstacles begins with the supervisor asking the supervisee to try to predict possible problems that might block the successful implementation of selected tasks. The supervisor and supervisee then enter into a collaborative discussion in which they share their ideas. As they identify potential obstacles, they develop strategies for overcoming them. At times, they will discover that selected tasks need to be modified or replaced. Then they may revisit the task selection stage, and after selecting new tasks, reenter the discussion of potential problems. Indeed, consideration of obstacles may result in frequent movement between the two stages.

The following scenario illustrates the process of generating potential obstacles, exploring ideas for negotiating them, and revising originally selected tasks:

Sue was working with a twelve-year-old girl and her mother. The girl was in danger of expulsion from school because of a large number of absences. After exploration of the problem, Sue discovered that because the child's mother was at work during the early morning hours, the girl was responsible for getting herself up and off to school. Sue asked the child how she got herself up each morning. The girl replied that she "just woke up" when she was no longer tired. Therefore, Sue selected the task, "suggest setting an alarm clock each night before child goes to bed."

In the following dialogue between Sue and her supervisor, Jeanne, note how the supervisor both asks the supervisee for potential obstacles and contributes her own suggestions. Also note that the supervisor's questions are future-oriented, asking Sue to think ahead so that she will be prepared for a variety of roadblocks. Finally, note how discussion of possible obstacles leads to discussion of how to negotiate them, which results in revision of the initial task.

SUE: What a great idea! It's so simple. She really just needs an alarm clock by her bed. I am going to suggest it to her.
JEANNE: Sounds good. What potential obstacles do you think you might run into when implementing this task?
SUE: Mmm . . . I am not sure. Maybe they don't own an alarm clock.
JEANNE: Yes, that would be a big obstacle! If you suggest it and she does not own one, what will you do?

Note that the supervisor asks about obstacles rather than immediately suggesting them. In this case, the supervisee is able to easily predict a possible problem. The supervisor asks for the supervisee's backup plan so that the task will be successful even if roadblocks are encountered.

SUE: Well, I guess I should include the mother in the discussion of the alarm clock. It is not likely a twelve-year-old will buy an alarm clock on her own.

JEANNE: So, including the mother in this discussion may make the task go more successfully. And you will suggest that they buy one. What obstacles might you encounter to this suggestion?

SUE: Maybe they can't afford to buy one. They do not have much money.

JEANNE: Not being able to buy one may be an obstacle indeed. Another potential problem is that they could pretend to go along with the idea but not tell you that, in reality, they cannot afford to buy a clock. For some people, admitting that might be embarrassing. That happened to me once. The family I was working with kept making excuses week after week about why they had not yet bought an alarm, and then I realized that it was probably related to money—and not resistance, as I had originally thought!

SUE: I never thought of that. Perhaps I should first ask if they have an alarm clock, and if not—should I ask them if they are able to buy one? Should I raise the question of whether or not they can afford it?

JEANNE: How would you ask about that?

SUE: Well, maybe I could normalize by acknowledging having to spend money in order to deal with this.

JEANNE: Perhaps. Be prepared with how much alarm clocks cost, or with places they can buy used ones. Or, if necessary—because they are not able to buy one—be prepared with another suggestion . . . that is, modifying the present task.

Until this point, discussion has been about identifying obstacles and trying to come up with strategies for handling them. However, the process of making predictions demonstrates that the selected task should be modified or changed.

SUE: That makes sense. If they do not seem thrilled by the idea of buying one, I will offer another idea. I could suggest to the mother that she call her daughter from work at a specified wake-up time.

JEANNE: That does not cost any extra money. You have very good ideas, but perhaps you should ask them what they think would get the child to wake up on time?

SUE: That's really where I should start. It is best if the ideas come from them. I want so much to help them, I forgot about asking them first. If they do not seem to be able to come up with a solution on their own, then I will suggest my ideas and ask them what they think.

JEANNE: That sounds like a good approach. So let's change the original task from "will suggest setting an alarm clock each night before child goes to bed" to "will ask the family for their ideas about how to have child wake up on time for school each morning."

SUE: Yes. That sounds much better.

JEANNE: Can you anticipate any obstacles to this task?

Note that discussion of obstacles has resulted in a modification of the originally selected task. Now the supervisor and supervisee move back into the anticipating and negotiating obstacles stage. The prior discussion of obstacles remains important in formulating a backup plan: even after Sue implements the new task, she may still need to offer her suggestions (e.g., setting an alarm, mother calling from work). She may encounter the obstacles identified earlier. Having discussed possible complications, she is now more prepared for them.

SUE: Well . . . they may not be able to think of anything. Maybe they have tried a bunch of things, and nothing has worked.

JEANNE: This may indeed be the case. Have you asked them what they have tried in the past?

SUE: No. I guess I should add this as a task for me, before I ask them for their ideas about how to get her up on time. If I were in the same situation, and I had already tried setting an alarm clock and it didn't work, I would be irritated that the idea was being suggested. It would make me think the person thought I was stupid.

JEANNE: I agree that adding the task of "ask what they have tried in the past" is a good plan. Can you foresee any obstacles to this?

Again, from discussion of potential obstacles, initial tasks have been revised in order to make progress toward a target goal. Note how the discussion of potential obstacles forces the supervisee to be self-reflective and modify her initial instincts. Indeed, through this brief exploration of obstacles, Sue has learned how to adjust her practice so that it is more client-centered. Many new social workers are anxious to be helpful; however, this often interferes with client input and self-determination. By generating possible obstacles, supervisees can learn to develop interventions that are most helpful without the supervisor first telling them that their ideas are problematic.

> SUE: No. They might end up fighting about why past things failed, but otherwise no.
> JEANNE: Okay.

Discussion continues until the supervisee and the supervisor agree that there are few, if any, remaining obstacles that can be realistically foreseen. Identified obstacles that are unlikely or do not pose real problems do not require active development of strategies to negotiate them. This said, it has been our experience that obstacles that seem easily negotiated to supervisors may be quite challenging to supervisees.

Although it is impossible to predict the future, it is important to be prepared for what might happen in impending encounters. This can reduce surprises and increase supervisees' confidence that they can implement tasks successfully.

Asking About Potential Obstacles

How the supervisor asks the supervisee for ideas about potentially challenging events is important, because it concernsproblems that may come up with tasks often generated by the supervisee. If not stated properly, the question may come across as insulting—as though the supervisor expects the student's suggestion to fail.

We recommend that the supervisor raise the question of obstacles by asking about the possible effect or consequences of carrying out a particular task. Furthermore, the supervisor should consider the context when posing the question. In other words, the discussion should be framed in terms of how the situation might pose particular challenges to implementation of the proposed task. The focus should be on the appropriateness of a task given certain circumstances, not on the supervisee's ability (or inability) to generate problem-free tasks.

Finally, some supervisees may feel this questioning is overly negative. In such situations, there are alternative ways to initiate the discussion of obstacles. Rather than asking, "Do you see any obstacles that might interfere with your success in carrying out the task?" the issue could be raised in other ways: "What needs to happen for the task to be implemented successfully?" "What challenges might this situation pose as you implement this task?" "What do you expect will happen when you implement this task?"

Assisting with Identification of Potential Obstacles

Supervisees are not always able to predict possible challenges in tasks they select. This section offers suggestions for improvng their skills in this area and presents strategies for helping supervisees identify obstacles when they are unable to generate their own ideas.

Temporal Considerations

One strategy for helping supervisees generate obstacles is to consider problems in temporal fashion, that is, in terms of when they might occur during task implementation. Those that arise before implementation prevent the supervisee from being able to carry out the selected task as planned. For example, an intern might enter a family meeting with a task to address a particular problem identified in an earlier session, only to discover that the family is now focused on a different concern. If properly prepared, the supervisee has a backup plan that includes asking the family which issue takes priority. Should the family select the immediate problem, the supervisee can either postpone the task until the family wants to address the earlier issue or abandon it entirely.

Obstacles that arise during task implementation typically reflect negative client reactions to the task. A supervisee might enter a client meeting with high hopes that their task will go well and be surprised to discover the client reacting angrily to the intervention. If they have anticipated this possibility, the supervisee is unlikely to feel surprised and unprepared to handle the negative response. They will be ready with a backup plan.

Supervisors and supervisees should also consider obstacles that may arise after the implementation of selected tasks. Tasks may appear to be successful upon completion but encounter problems later. This is of particular concern when the selected task is to give a client a directive. For example, Tom, a supervisee, successfully implemented a task that entailed suggesting to a passive female client that she start "standing up for herself." This included practicing saying no to demands she did not want to fulfill. The client, following Tom's directive, refused a request from her boss and was subsequently "written up" for an "attitude problem." The client was horrified and angry that she had followed Tom's advice. This obstacle could have been prevented had Tom and his supervisor anticipated possible results from implementing the directive. Indeed, the task could have been modified to involve discussion with the client about "safe" encounters in which practice this behavior.

Clinical Sequences

Potential obstacles to task implementation can be identified by looking at how clinical practice is typically ordered. Although it is often a nonlinear endeavor, certain activities are usually required before others can be implemented. As discussed earlier, it is not uncommon for novice practitioners to propose interventions before completing a thorough assessment. The proposed interventions, out of clinical sequence, may be well intentioned but are inherently problematic.

For example, Jan, a supervisee about to meet with a new client for the first time, proposed the task of telling a depressed young man that his depression was related to parental rejection of his life choices. While this may or may not have been true, telling the client this before a working relationship had been developed and before Jan knew more about his situation made the task highly problematic—fraught with potential obstacles. Taking time to consider activities that should occur before implementing an intervention minimizes difficulties. At the same time, the supervisee learns how to order and pace their practice.

When Supervisees Are Unable to Identify Potential Obstacles

At the beginning of TCS supervision, the supervisor may need to identify potential obstaclesbecause the supervisee is not yet able to generate ideas of their own. While supervisor-provided ideas are important, we recommend the use of "What if . . . ?" questions and role play as preferable alternatives. A short discussion of supervisor-provided potential obstacles is followed by an overview of these two alternative strategies. Finally, the role of didactic education and exploration of supervisee emotional obstacles are briefly considered.

Supervisor Providing Potential Obstacles

Like the process of generating target goal and task ideas, generating potential obstacles should include the supervisor's input, particularly when students are unable to proceed. Supervisors can draw upon and share their own practice experiences related to encountering obstacles. However, they should be careful not to become the sole source of potential ideas. As with their other input, obstacles should be put forth for collaborative consideration. Supervisors should challenge supervisees to critique the ideas as they apply to the situation in which the selected task is to be implemented. Additionally, supervisor-provided suggestions may suggest additional possibly challenging scenarios. In other words, the supervisor's provision of ideas can serve to both model the process and "prime the pump" for the supervisee.

"What if . . . ?" questions. An effective strategy for helping the supervisee to think of potential obstacles involves the supervisor presenting scenarios the supervisee might encounter when implementing a selected task through the use of "What if . . . ?" questions. This is, ultimately, the same as the supervisor providing suggestions, except that as the potential obstacles are posed, the supervisee is challenged to consider how they would handle them. The obstacle becomes a "real" potential problem.

The "What if . . . ?" technique consists of asking, "When you do X, *what if* Z were to happen?" (either implied or stated: "rather than Y"), as illustrated in the following example.

Jim, a social worker at a family service agency, and his supervisor formulated an intervention plan that included "ask each family member for their perception of the problem that brought them to seek treatment." When asked about potential obstacles, Jim was not able to foresee any. To challenge him to consider possibilities, the supervisor asked, "*What if* as one family member is talking, others are constantly interrupting?" Jim recognized this as a potential obstacle and strategized with the supervisor ways to negotiate it. He said that when interruptions occurred, he would politely but directly request that the family members not interrupt. At this point Jim thought of another potential obstacle: they might disregard his request. After some further brainstorming, Jim felt that he should add the task of discussing rules—which included not interrupting—for family meetings at the start of the session.

Note how the process stimulated Jim to think of a second potential obstacle on his own. Before his supervisor used the "What if . . . ?" prompt, he had been unable to identify any.

Supervisees appreciate this approach because it challenges them to both think on their feet and consider the possible consequences of their actions. Pushing them to think beyond implementation of interventions to potential reactions reduces impulsive decision making. The process of anticipating possible scenarios promotes the development of thoughtful and deliberate practitioners.

Role play. Role play is a widely used teaching technique in supervision. While not always supported as an educational tool (Munson 1993), it is quite helpful as a strategy for identifying potential obstacles. The process consists of acting out the parts of a typical clinical encounter. There are two common approaches. In the first (supervisor as client), the supervisor takes on the role of the client, while the supervisee "plays" him- or herself. This gives the supervisee opportunity to practice behaviors before meeting with the client. The second approach (supervisor as practitioner) entails the supervisor playing the role of clinician and the supervisee acting as the client. In some cases, the client is known and the supervisee attempts to replicate their behavior. In this approach, the supervisor, acting as the clinician, demonstrates how he or she would interact with that client. The purpose is often to show the student different ways of handling a difficulty with a client. In other situations, the client is not known, and the emphasis is on demonstrating a technique.

Engaging in role play is a particularly effective way to demonstrate potential obstacles when supervisees cannot foresee them. At the beginning of TCS, the first (supervisor as client) is particularly useful. When the supervisee is unable to identify potential obstacles to successful implementation of a selected task, the pair can enter into a role play in which the supervisor as client creates obstacles. The supervisee then experiences first-hand what may lie ahead and has the opportunity to consider and try out ways of negotiating the obstacles. The supervisor can share how certain supervisee behaviors come across, which may provide insight about "invisible" consequences. This is illustrated in the following example:

Lloyd and his supervisor, Brenda, entered into a role play in which Lloyd played himself and Brenda played his client. Lloyd was to carry out a selected task that involved telling Brenda to be "less controlling with her son." Brenda responded to the statement by pretending to be hurt, saying that Lloyd had insulted her as a mother. When the role play ended, Lloyd said that he wanted to revise the task because of Brenda's reaction. He added that his client would probably not openly express the hurt, but would feel it—and hurting her was not his objective.

The second approach (supervisor as clinician) is also useful for identifying potential obstacles. Being on the receiving end of the selected task, supervisees are able to directly experience its emotional impact. In addition, they may be challenged to consider a variety of ways of responding to the task. They can then begin to identify how some pose difficulties for the practitioner and can be considered obstacles to successful task implementation.

Role play is also useful for evaluating skills and understanding of concepts. Supervisees may be able to conceptualize and articulate a skill but not have a solid grasp of how to implement it. In other words, they may be able to produce a well-formulated and suited task but be unable to apply it in practice. The role play enables both supervisors and supervisees to *see* how supervisees implement various behaviors.

This insight allows for an accurate assessment of what the supervisee can and cannot do, so the supervisory pair can more easily determine and formulate tasks of appropriate complexity. It also demonstrates a major obstacle to carrying out the task—the supervisee's skill level—that is difficult to anticipate without direct observation of supervisee performance.

Finally, role play is helpful for supervisees who are able to readily identify obstacles; they can try out their skill at negotiating them.

Didactic education. It is common for supervisees to be unable to generate their own potential obstacles because they lack the requisite knowledge and experience. Therefore, it is important for supervisors to provide information that will help them anticipate obstructions. For example, a supervisee may select the task of asking the "miracle question" (Nunnally 1993), believing that the entire intervention consists of asking this one question. They will quickly run into difficulty if they do not know how to continue to work with the theme. In such cases, the supervisor may need to teach the supervisee what to do next. The supervisee is better able to identify their lack of knowledge as an obstacle if the supervisor asks them to anticipate what needs to happen directly after implementation of the task.

Emotional Obstacles

Because social work is often an emotionally laden endeavor, supervisees must consider their own reaction to tasks. For example, they may feel uncomfortable selecting a task that involves confronting a client about a drinking problem, performing a suicide assessment, or asking a sexually abused child for information about the abuse. Such activities are difficult to carry out if they trigger an emotional response in the supervisee. The response may become an obstacle to successful task completion. It is important for supervisors to inquire, particularly for emotionally challenging tasks, about the supervisees' emotional response to and capacity to perform them.

Such inquiry also demonstrates that the supervisor acknowledges the difficulty of the supervisee's work, and prevents the focus from remaining solely on the instrumental functions of supervision. It is an opportunity to model empathy and support. Furthermore, discussion of emotional responses is an important part of assisting the development and presence of self-awareness in practitioners.

Danger of Skipping the Anticipating Obstacles Stage, Even with Simple Tasks

At times, supervisors and supervisees may want to bypass the process of anticipating potential obstacles, particularly if selected tasks appear to be simple or straightforward. However, our experience is that even simple tasks are more likely to fail if possible problems are not discussed. Many supervisors have expressed frustration when a supervisee does not follow through on a task because of an unexpected obstacle. The task of completing a home visit provides a good example: it is not uncommon for (usually novice) supervisees to report that they went to the client's residence, found no one at home, but took no further steps. Had the obstacle of the client not being at home when the supervisee arrived been anticipated and discussed, it is likely that the supervisee would know what to do next—and feel compelled to do it. The supervisor could have used the "What if . . . ?" strategy and asked, "What if no one is at home when you get there?"

Many supervisors do not take the time to ask about obstacles when a seemingly straightforward task is selected, because to them it may appear obvious what should be done if simple obstacles, such as an empty house, arise. However, the supervisee may not feel secure enough to act independently or be sophisticated enough to know to visit the house again. Therefore, it is strongly recommended that all tasks, even simple ones, be discussed in terms of anticipated obstacles.

Learning and Practice Advantages of Anticipating Obstacles

This stage is extremely beneficial to supervisees because it helps them learn to predict and assess the potential consequences of the interventions they are considering for use. Impulsive intervention choices are reduced, and students develop the ability to be thoughtful practitioners and to create sound treatment plans. Finally, anticipating what may occur with the client minimizes the chance that the supervisee will feel caught off guard and gives them more confidence in handling complications.

However, the ability to think ahead and consider what may occur in upcoming encounters is a skill that needs to be learned. In our experience, many supervisees do not enter the profession with it. They cannot anticipate encounters when they have not yet experienced the practitioner role. Engaging in this stage of TCS at each supervision meeting directly promotes acquisition of this skill.

Contracting

The contracting stage is the last step of each supervision meeting and of the task implementation sequence, and it is a feature of each phase. The end of the meeting involves writing a contract for the target goals and tasks selected. The purpose of this stage is to review what has been agreed to, clarify any misunderstandings, and ensure a mutual understanding of what learning and practice behaviors the supervisee will undertake by the next supervision meeting. As target goals and tasks are reviewed, they are listed on the contract. Some may prefer to fill out the contract as each goal and task is selected, and use the contracting stage as a time to review, clarify, and verify responsibilities. At the end of the meeting, the supervisee and the supervisor should each have a written contract in hand. (Note: Usually one form is completed during the supervision meeting and a second copy is made immediately after.)

As discussed in chapter 3, written contracts have many advantages over verbal contracts, but both are preferable to no contract. Although we highly endorse the written contract, the supervisory pair should consider the strengths and limitations of both types. We recommend this because the written version may feel to some, who don't understand its advantages, like "more paperwork," and more like an imposition than a help. The option of a verbal contract should be considered.

Supervisees have found that having a written contract in their possession is advantageous when meeting with clients.Some use it to independently review their tasks just prior to a clinical meeting. The contract helps them remained focused and reduces anxiety about what they are supposed to accomplish. They may also find the written contract a helpful reminder of what they agreed to in supervision. As one employee who began using a written contract midway through the encounter put it, "I used to leave supervision feeling really focused about what I was going to do, but by the time I met with the client I had forgotten what we had discussed. Having the written contract has been a great reminder." He added, "You know, I used to be embarrassed when I had supervision and my supervisor asked me how something we had discussed went with a client, and I had to say that I didn't do it. [My supervisor] used to get really angry with me and ask me why. I would say that I forgot, but she thought I was trying to aggravate her on purpose." In the beginning phase, supervisors should take time to explain these advantages and additional uses of written contracts.

It is also important to periodically take time to inquire about supervisees' perceptions of the contracting process. They may participate in contracting but not feel it is helpful. Continued exploration and brainstorming may make the process more beneficial.

Time Management to Promote Contract Completion

Supervisors and supervisees may discover that they run out of meeting time before they have completed the contract. Theoretical discussions and solving highly complex case problems can be time-consuming. Because the written contract can be of great value in the learning process, some recommendations for time management to ensure it is included in the supervision meeting follow.

During the meeting, supervisors and supervisees should avoid entering into lengthy discussions of general theory or global philosophies that are not explicitly connected to client problem-solving. Instead, they should be case-specific and purposeful—focusing on generating target goals and tasks. This does not mean that supervisors should disallow theoretical explorations but that such discussions should be kept brief, and kept directly relevant to immediate case problem-solving or learning objectives.

The process of completing the contract may trigger new questions, concerns, and areas for exploration. While conversational tangents may be interesting to pursue, particularly when the supervisor thinks that they have educational merit, the supervisee and supervisor should maintain focus on completing the contract. This will help keep discussions case-specific and purposeful and general theoretical arguments and philosophical abstractions brief. If material emerges that both wish to pursue, it is recommended that they write it down and return to explore it at another time.

It is important to watch the clock. We recommend that the last ten to fifteen minutes of each supervision meeting be designated for completion of the contract. (This period could be shorter if the contract has been completed throughout the meeting and only needs to be reviewed at the end.) The approach to contracting and time management depends on the styles and preferences of the supervisor and supervisee.

The Contract

An example of a completed contract follows. Note how it guides application of the steps of the TCS model (identifying target goals, selecting tasks, anticipating potential obstacles). The contract asks for up to three target goals and the educational or practice objective of each—encouraging active linking; indication of the supervisee's participation in the target goal selection and prioritization process, which encourages collaborative supervisory practice; up to three tasks for each target goal; whether or not obstacles to tasks have been considered; and any additional agreements, such as time estimates for goal attainment.

Such estimates promote active work toward target goals. However, they should be used only as guidelines. Target goals vary in complexity, and some may require more work than others. When they have been completed, new ones can be selected. If target goals need continued work, they should be kept and the agreed time limits extended.

CONTRACT

DATE: *Nov. 4*

A. Target Goals

List in order of priority the goals (up to three) that you and the student agreed to work on. Identify goals in a single word or phrase. Include the date the goal was first formulated. On the line below each identified target goal, provide the related practice or educational objective.

GOAL #1: *1st meeting with Smiths* date form. *Nov. 4*
Related practice or educational objective: *Perform family assessment*

GOAL #2: *Address Ms. Jones's anger* date form. *Oct. 23*
Related practice or educational objective: *Explore underlying feelings*

GOAL #3: *Distinguishing process and content* date form. *Nov. 4*
Related practice or educational objective: *same*

B. Prioritization Processes

___ a. student agreed on selection and priorities of goals
___ b. student disagreed on selection and priorities of goals
If "b" was checked, explain disagreement (use back if necessary)

C. Task Formulation

List three tasks the student will do to achieve each target goal:

GOAL #1
task #1: *ask each member for their perception of the problem*
task #2: *observe who speaks first and members' reactions*
task #3: *inquire about possible history of physical abuse*

GOAL #2
task #1: *point out nonverbal aspects that suggest she is angry*
task #2: *validate that anger is OK and part of grief process*
task #3: *ask if others have noticed anger*

GOAL #3
task #1: *notice WHEN Bill C. changes topic of conversation*
task #2: *with all clients—observe changes in body language as content changes*
task #3: _____

D. Were potential obstacles to task implementation considered?
Circle one: Yes No

List any additional agreements (e.g., time limits): *Goals #1 and #2 will be completed in one week; #3 will be maintained for next 3 weeks.*

Recording weekly target goals on a contract enables supervisees to clearly monitor their progress. They can look back at earlier contracts and see how far they have come. As one intern using TCS put it, "I liked having something to work on" because it "felt like I was always moving forward."

Conclusion

The supervisee implements the contracted tasks prior to the next supervision meeting, typically in work with cases, although as discussed earlier, some may reflect activities that do not involve direct (i.e., face-to-face) practice (e.g., management of a program, writing a grant). At the next meeting, task implementation is reviewed, using a task implementation evaluation form on which the supervisee has rated their performance. The task review stage is presented in the next chapter.

11   Task Review

This chapter presents an important component of the task-centered model for educational supervision (TCS): the task review stage. This stage begins the task planning and implementation sequence (TPIS), covered in the previous chapters. After implementation of contracted tasks, the supervisee and supervisor enter into a collaborative appraisal of how well the tasks were completed. This generally follows the social stage, toward the start of each supervision meeting. Task review and the TPIS sequence continue throughout the supervisory encounter after the completion of the first contract.

Outline of TCS Sequence After Completion of First Contract

Social stage
Task review
Educational stage
Target goals stage
Identifying, prioritizing, and selecting tasks
Anticipating and negotiating potential obstacles
Contracting

The task review process is a distinctive feature of TCS. This deliberate, joint review of supervisee performance of discrete behaviors is not found in most supervision arrangements. It has many benefits: ensuring linking of content from supervision to practice, promoting flow of learning from one supervision meeting to the next, and providing a mechanism for systematic and continuous feedback about performance. Its systematic and ongoing assessment of performance assists formal evaluations. Finally, because this process forces supervisees to assess their own performance, it aids in the development of self-awareness.

This chapter presents an overview of the task review process, including the optional task implementation review form. Finally, the many benefits and few limitations of this stage are discussed.

Task Review

Typically, supervisees implement contracted tasks in their field work between supervision meetings. Then collaborative assessment of the supervisee's performance takes place, usually near the start of the supervision conference, after the social stage. When tasks have been implemented successfully, the supervisee is commended for a job well done. If tasks have not been completed, an effort is made to identify obstacles that interfered with their accomplishment.

The task implementation evaluation form can facilitate this assessment. Supervisees use a numerical scale to rate how well they performed each task. Special consideration is given to the supervisee's criteria for determining their scores. Such inquiry enables supervisor insight into the supervisee's understanding of tasks and expectations about their work. Task review recognizes three possible outcomes: task successfully executed, task partially completed, and task not implemented.

For tasks that have been implemented successfully, the supervisee is complimented. Progress toward target goal attainment is then assessed. If successful task implementation results in goal attainment, new target goals are formulated during the target goal stage (which immediately follows). If tasks have been only partly completed, obstacles encountered during implementation are identified and plans for handling them are considered. Similarly, obstacles are identified when tasks have not been attempted. In such cases, target goals are usually kept for continued work.

The Task Review Process

Following the social stage, the task review process usually begins with supervisors asking supervisees how they did with the contracted tasks. A common approach is to take out the contract completed during the previous supervision meeting and run through the list of selected tasks. Since most are carried out with cases, task review tends to include a discussion of case progress. The task review should be a collaborative process in which both the supervisee and the supervisor have input, not a unilateral judgment by the supervisor of the supervisee's work. Indeed, the student's own critique of their performance is critical.

As stated earlier, it is important for supervisors to compliment supervisees on successful task execution. However, the review should cover more than just task outcomes. Perhaps of greater importance is exploration of *process* — how the task was implemented. Asking the supervisee for a detailed account of what they did enables the supervisor to give positive feedback about specific behaviors. In addition, the supervisor can ask about client reactions to task implementation, allowing the supervisee to analyze and appreciate the positive consequences of their behaviors. Supervisors may be tempted to move on to another area after a report that a task has been successfully completed. However, because it clarifies and instructs about actual supervisee practice behaviors, we recommend exploring task implementation even when no obstacles were identified and the supervisee has reported successful completion.

Such exploration can also reveal that the task did not go as well as initially reported. Supervisees may state their task execution was successful, but the review can reveal that the task was not fully understood. For example, one beginning social work intern had the task "employ empathic responses," which she selected because she was learning about it in class. During review she reported that the task went well. When asked to describe when and how she implemented it, it became clear that the student was not employing empathy but was instead using reflection. Discussion of process helped to identify and resolve her confusion over the concept. Furthermore, it promoted the skill of critical self-evaluation and demonstrated the challenge of applying classroom theory to practice.

If the selected tasks went well, the next step should be assessment of target goal attainment related to their successful implementation. If a task has not been carried out or only partly achieved, then the supervisor and the supervisee should discuss obstacles encountered and ways to overcome them. It may be necessary to create tasks to address an encountered obstacle.

The supervisor should ask the supervisee to describe in detail *how* tasks were implemented when they are rated as only partly achieved. This will reveal the supervisee's knowledge about the social work technique and the skill needed to apply it, helping the supervisor to identify misconceptions about practice behaviors and provide clarification and education when needed. Indeed, it is not uncommon that supervisees report that they did not do well with a task, but the supervisor, having obtained details, learns that they did quite well. The discussion also enables the supervisor to identify productive parts of task implementation in order to give positive feedback. If tasks have been partly completed, some aspects went well. It is helpful to identify these.

Some supervisees may indicate that "things went well" in order to keep the supervisor from seeing perceived flaws. Asking for details disables this protective strategy. Anxiety about sharing faults is likely at play when the supervisee resists responding to detailed inquiry. Resistance also suggests that the supervisee does not feel safe in the supervisory relationship. Supervisors should raise this and consider ways to support the supervisee and develop an open and trusting relationship. Supervisors should also consider their role in this development.

Using a Variation of the Agreed-Upon Task

During the task review, it may be discovered that the supervisee chose to implement a variation of the contracted task. This happens for a variety of reasons, including these four possibilities.

First, unpredicted obstacles may have been encountered during task implementation, requiring the supervisee to creatively modify tasks in order to meet treatment or target goals. A second possibility is that the task was broadly defined, leaving the supervisee and supervisor with different understandings of what it should look like in action.

Third, the supervisee may have been attempting to demonstrate their independence. Considering supervision in its developmental context, it can be expected that the supervisee will want to differentiate from the supervisor at some point in the relationship. Making creative decisions about implementing tasks in their own style rather than mimicking the supervisor's is understandable. It allows the supervisee to make independent decisions within the context of the contract.

Fourth, variations on contracted tasks may reflect a power struggle in the supervisory relationship. Supervisors should evaluate whether supervisees feel that tasks are being forced upon them or that they do not have enough say in their practice and learning decisions. Assessment of a power struggle should include an exploration of the supervisory process. In addition, if a supervisor suspects that a supervisee is doing what he or she wants in reaction to supervisor suggestions, they should share that perception with the student in order to jointly evaluate the situation.

Supervisors should be careful not to negatively judge variations for this reason: the modified tasks may be better than the original formulations. They should first explore the result of the modified task. They may be surprised that the task went well. In addition, supervisors can learn from supervisee choices about new approaches and differing styles.

Caveat: Don't Rush to Judgment

As supervisees give the details of task implementation, supervisors may hear things that disturb them. Their initial impulse may be to disapprove. However, before making a negative judgment about their supervisee's behavior, they should first ask, "What happened after you did the behavior?" This allows both to learn about the impact of the action. Asking for the client's response may reveal that the behavior had a surprisingly positive effect. Based on our experience using TCS, we have found that supervisee creativity in implementing tasks is helpful to supervisor learning. Supervisors who are open to deviations from original task formulations often discover new ways to approach situations. Growth and learning by both members of the instructional relationship (supervisory pair) is a goal of feminist pedagogy (Dore 1994).

Using the Task Implementation Rating Form

An option for aiding the task review process is the task implementation rating form. It includes a four-point scale that ranges from 4 (completed) to 1 (not completed). Supervisees are encouraged to score their performance of tasks immediately after carrying them out. They typically take the form with them into the field, and discuss the ratings with the supervisor when they return to supervision.

The four-point scale may not be appropriate for all types of tasks. For example, it is often hard to know when abstract tasks have been "completed." Tasks such as "perform problem exploration" and "ask about family history" frequently have no clear ending point. Hence, we recommend that supervisors not be as concerned with the actual rating as with how supervisees came up with it. In other words, they should ask the supervisee to describe the criteria used to formulate the rating, particularly with abstract tasks.

As discussed earlier, emphasizing how the score was determined rather than the score itself provides greater insight into the supervisee's understanding of the task. Such inquiry can be helpful for identifying misconceptions about practice behaviors. The following example illustrates this point.

A supervisee stated that he had successfully implemented tasks for "restructuring" a family he was working with. When the supervisor asked him to explain the details, it became clear that although the supervisee had done some interesting things that might have been beneficial to the family, restructuring was not one of them. The supervisor informed the supervisee of this, discussed the technique further, and then explored the impact of the supervisee's actions on the case.

By exploring how the supervisee came up with his score, the supervisory pair were able to address a misconception. Had the focus remained on the score, the supervisor would have congratulated the supervisee on a job that had not been accurately performed. In addition, the supervisor's evaluation of the supervisee's skill would have been erroneous.

Again, supervisors may be tempted to move on after a supervisee's report that a task has been successfully completed. Because of the benefits discussed here, they are urged to explore task implementation even when no obstacles were identified and the supervisee reports successful completion.

We present the task implementation rating form as an option because the use of scores may be overly threatening for some supervisees, particularly when a safe supervisory relationship has yet to be established. Another reason for anxiety may beinterpreting ratings as overall evaluations of one's self rather than reflections of learning behaviors. Therefore, it is helpful to clarify the purpose and focus of the rating, and in some cases, wait until the supervisee feels they are in a safe learning environment before using them.

It is not necessary to give a numerical rating to task implementation in order to use TCS. What is important is reviewing perceptions of how the task went and the criteria used in deciding on a particular score. Therefore, we recommend that supervisors emphasize the process of establishing a score rather than the score itself—using the task implementation rating form. However, should this raise such anxiety that it impedes the supervisee's learning, the form should be set aside until the supervisee is more ready to use it.

TASK IMPLEMENTATION RATING FORM

Immediately following the implementation of one of the contracted tasks, evaluate your progress with tasks using the following scale:

4 = Fully completed
3 = Mostly completed
2 = Partly completed
1 = Not completed
N = No opportunity

Note: Some concrete tasks (e.g., call client's teacher, change meeting time) can only be rated either "fully completed" or "not completed."

Contracted tasks are often formulated to be implemented multiple times (e.g., with different clients, in different situations). Also, some may require a few attempts to complete. Therefore, space is provided for rating the task each time it is implemented. If the task is developed to be carried out only once and is "fully completed" after the first attempt, then disregard spaces for 2nd, 3rd, 4th, and 5th ratings.

	Rating of 1st implementation	2nd	3rd	4th	5th
GOAL #1					
task #1	_____	_____	_____	_____	_____
task #2	_____	_____	_____	_____	_____
task #3	_____	_____	_____	_____	_____
GOAL #2					
task #1	_____	_____	_____	_____	_____
task #2	_____	_____	_____	_____	_____
task #3	_____	_____	_____	_____	_____
GOAL #3					
task #1	_____	_____	_____	_____	_____
task #2	_____	_____	_____	_____	_____
task #3	_____	_____	_____	_____	_____

Comments: Use the space at the bottom of this page or the back of this sheet to make any comments you think would be useful to yourself or to your supervisor—changes you made in the task, what you did, problems/obstacles encountered, etc.

Identification of Actual Obstacles

When tasks have been evaluated as not completed or partly completed, efforts should be made to identify obstacles to implementation: "real" roadblocks encountered while attempting to implement selected tasks, referred to here as "actual obstacles." These differ from "anticipated obstacles," which are problems that the supervisor and supervisee imagine might occur. (For more on anticipated obstacles, see chapter 10.)

As supervisees experience and take note of actual practice obstacles, they learn to better predict future difficulties. In other words, the knowledge they gain through direct experience can be drawn upon when formulating future tasks and considering potential problems (e.g., during the anticipating obstacles stage). The supervisee thus becomes more thoughtful and sophisticated about developing tasks and predicting possible obstructions.

Another benefit of encountering and identifying actual obstacles is that it enhances self-evaluation skills. It is a good way for supervisees to identify their own practice deficits and learning needs. When they encounter and identify an actual obstacle, the supervisor and supervisee can explore its origins, which could include task formulation, inadequate assessment, practitioner behaviors, and contextual factors. Identifying the obstacle can illuminate which areas of the supervisee's practice need bolstering and allow them to reformulate the original task and "take another crack at it"—with greater insight about obstacles and how to negotiate them when they arise.

Advantages of Task Review

The task review stage is a systematic process for assessing supervisee performance. As such, it has a number of benefits for both learning and the supervisory encounter. Task review provides ongoing feedback, assists monitoring of supervisee progress, aids the formal evaluation process, promotes focus on learning, promotes self-awareness, links content of supervision meetings, and facilitates case review.

Provides Ongoing Feedback

Ongoing, timely, and specific feedback is an important part of educational supervision (Freeman 1985; Kadushin 1994). It provides the supervisee with the necessary information to take corrective action and continually improve practice. Although supervisors should give direct and ongoing feedback, the task review process teaches supervisees how to critique their own performance—to generate their own feedback. It encourages them to be self-reflective, observe the impact of their behaviors, and correct their actions based on their own cognitive appraisals. Whether the source of the feedback is the supervisor, the supervisee, or collaborative critique, the systematic and structured review of task performance ensures it will be useful.

Assists Monitoring of Supervisee Progress

Because task review provides a mechanism for ongoing feedback, it facilitates monitoring supervisees' progress as learners and practitioners. As they demonstrate competence in discrete skills (tasks), new tasks are selected and added to the written contract. Each completed contract marks progress the supervisee can observe; the contracts together form a portfolio of accomplishments. This visible evidence of advancement increases supervisee confidence and enhances motivation for learning to work with cases. Finally, because tasks are explicitly tied to learning and practice objectives, the task review process systematically monitors progress toward target goals. This is particularly useful during formal evaluations.

Aids the Formal Evaluation Process

Through task review, supervisees and supervisors are able to monitor successful task implementation and target goal achievement at each meeting. This is helpful in preparing for formal evaluations. With ongoing feedback, supervisees should be well aware of how they are doing with various skills and social work knowledge—what they have and have not accomplished, and how well they have been able to implement discrete activities. Therefore, they should not be surprised during formal evaluations. This is particularly true if evaluation forms or job descriptions are used as a primary source for target goal generation and selection. Indeed, using these instruments as menus makes it easy to identify which skills have been addressed directly and which have yet to be covered. When tasks are not taken from such specific sources, it can be a challenge to match target goals and tasks with listed competencies.

The evaluation instrument can be used as a checklist for recording successful completion of each competency (task). This is, obviously, easier on paper than in practice, which is rarely linear or limited to a narrow range of activities. Once a supervisee has demonstrated that they can perform a skill competently, it need not be selected as a task at each supervision meeting— even if it is repeatedly required in practice. The supervisee is recognized as already possessing that skill, and the focus is on accomplishing others. That said, if the supervisory pair feel the supervisee should reselect a task because a current situation presents new challenges, they should do so. Otherwise, only skills that have not been addressed directly through task selection or tasks that have not been successfully completed should be chosen.

Promotes Focus on Learning

The ongoing and direct feedback obtained through task review enables supervisors and supervisees to maintain a focus on learning. Evaluation of the supervisee's work, rather than case dynamics, is at the center of this process. Reviewing tasks and target goals also maintains an ongoing focus for the supervisory encounter as a whole—i.e., achieving target goals. As one supervisee put it, "With the task review, the goals do not get lost from one week to the next" but are instead systematically worked toward.

Promotes Self-Awareness

A critical part of supervision is the supervisee's development of self-awareness (Atwood 1986; Sweitzer and King 1999). Because the task review process challenges the student to examine their own performance, it promotes this skill. As one supervisee said, "it forces you to reflect and critique yourself." Another supervisee commenting on this aspect of the task review said, "it is good and helpful to evaluate your own practice . . . it makes it easy to see if what I did was helpful or not and whether I should do it again or not."

Self-critique is important in enhancing self-awareness. For example, when actual obstacles to his task implementation were reviewed, Frank, a social work intern, discovered that it was not unusual for them to be related to personal issues. He gave the example of not following through with a task that involved consultation with a client's teacher. During the task review, Frank identified that he did not carry out the task because he became aware of negative feelings toward the teacher. The supervisor praised Frank for engaging in self-critique, which led to this self-awareness. Subsequently, they addressed Frank's negative feelings and considered alternative ways of interacting with that teacher. Without a process that requires self-critique, it is unlikely that supervisees will consider their behaviors so explicitly. Frank reflected, "I learned a lot about myself as a practitioner by reviewing what things I did worked and which ones did not."

The supervisor can maximize the self-evaluation benefits of task review by asking the supervisee how they came up with their ratings of task performance. One supervisee said, "I liked it when I scored myself too low [on the task evaluation form] and we talked about it. . . . I could see that I'm too hard on myself . . . and after talking to my supervisor, I see that I did pretty well considering the circumstances." It is not uncommon for supervisees, particularly beginning ones, to have high standards for themselves. Some expect to be able to quickly "cure" clients with long-standing problems, and others are upset when an intervention does not turn out as perfectly as it did in their textbooks. Developing self-awareness is important for maintaining realistic expectations for practice.

Links Supervision Meeting Content

Systematic review of task implementation promotes continuity of content and learning from session to session, which is often lacking in unstructured approaches, that consist of problem-solving the "case of the week." In this type of supervision process, it becomes difficult to clearly identify how learning objectives are achieved. By contrast, when ideas discussed in one supervision conference are revisited in the next, learning is consistent and ongoing. As one supervisee put it, "I knew what was coming from week to week." Mutual understanding of a clear agenda for the supervision meeting is a feature of quality supervision (Munson 1993; Shulman 1993).

Supervisees appreciate when cases are discussed on an ongoing basis. They are able to see the effects of certain tasks and monitor client progress as well as their own. As one intern noted, it is helpful to discuss cases in context rather than in isolation: revisiting the tasks and case situations made "talking about cases like an ongoing story."

Facilitates Case Review

An additional benefit of task review is that it ensures that the case in which the tasks were implemented is also reviewed. Thus, the task review process typically segues into more in-depth case exploration. One supervisee called it a "natural transition"; they appreciated that the review was not limited to discussion of whether tasks had been implemented successfully but extended to the tasks' relationship to the overall case. Another supervisee added that "having the task review makes you [the supervisee] automatically go over cases." This enables monitoring of case progress from one supervision conference to the next. In contrast, supervision arrangements that use the CW approach are unlikely to track ongoing progress with cases. Supervisor awareness of supervisee caseload progress is important for learning, making sound practice decisions, and administrative oversight.

Using Task Review in Short-Term Settings

The task review process can be useful in short-term practice settings, such as crisis centers, where practitioners may only meet with clients once. In such situations, the task review is more concerned with supervisee performance than case progress. In extended practice settings, the supervisor and supervisee have ongoing cases from which prior interactions can be used to develop tasks, but in crisis work it is difficult to predict what the supervisee will encounter. One intern who had crisis intervention duties and typically met with clients only once reported that while she was unable to set up and review tasks targeted for client progress, she was able to select tasks for her skill development. Reviewing her actions with a client in crisis with her supervisor, they were able to identify areas for future work—to select tasks that were more global and reflected the supervisee's educational level and goals. The point is well illustrated in the following example.

> A supervisee had just finished working with Mark, a client in crisis. During their discussion of her interactions with Mark, she and her supervisor identified that although Mark had stayed angry throughout the entire encounter, she had not addressed his emotional state. In an ongoing case, the supervisee would likely set up a task such as "explore Mark's anger" (a practice objective). Since it was unlikely that she would see this client again, the supervisee and her supervisor developed tasks for future crisis encounters, including "explore the client's emotions"—thus targeting the supervisee's learning a practice skill, rather than forwarding a particular case. This skill can be implemented with each new client the supervisee works with during the coming week.

In settings where ongoing work with clients is not possible, supervision can feel chaotic—moving rapidly from one case to the next with no connection between them. Using the task review process, content from each supervision meeting can be reviewed in the next. Supervisees state that this helps to provide a "flow" to their work and learning.

Cautions

While task review offers many advantages, two cautions should be considered. First, used in rigid fashion, task review only discusses those behaviors that have been contracted. It is helpful to keep the process flexible so that supervisees are able to review other aspects of their interactions. Second, some supervisees may not feel comfortable reviewing their behaviors, particularly when the results may be tied to job promotions or school grades. Indeed, performance review is central to formal evaluations. However, during the task review we recommend the supervisor focus on supervisee learning and progress rather than on deficits. In addition, it is important to consider the supervisee's ability to examine their own practice and take corrective action. A supervisee may continually give low ratings to their task performance yet be learning rapidly. Another may rate their task implementation highly and not be accurate or be advancing their learning. Thus, we recommend that scores not be the sole means of evaluation. This helps supervisees to be less concerned about the numbers and more focused on the process of evaluation.

Conclusion

The task review stage has many advantages, including the provision of mechanisms for ongoing feedback, self-critique, linking supervision meeting content, assisting case review, monitoring supervisee progress, and maintaining a focus on supervisee learning. Upon completion of the task review, the task implementation and planning sequence (TPIS) is carried out and a contract is completed. This process continues throughout the supervision encounter.

This completes presentation of the steps of TCS. Special considerations for application of the model are taken up in the following chapter.

12 Applications of TCS

TCS offers a process for conducting educational supervision. It does not prescribe particular learning content (i.e., educational objectives) or structures (e.g., one-to-one, group, peer). Therefore, the model can be applied for an array of purposes and in a variety of settings. This chapter provides an overview of the various applications of TCS, demonstrating the model's flexibility and practicality. It begins with a presentation of how TCS handles varied learning content, then discusses the use of TCS in supervision with different theoretical and practice orientations. The adaptability of TCS for use within varied structures is demonstrated, and the differences in using the model with staff and interns are considered.

Content

TCS offers a process for selecting and achieving educational objectives in supervision but does not delineate specific areas for learning. Thus, the model is adaptable for teaching a broad spectrum of educational content. The ultimate choice of target goals is up to the supervisor and supervisee, within the context of the larger learning environment (e.g., agency, funding sources, school). Indeed, the supervisory pair can use TCS to articulate learning content (as target goals) that reflects almost any area of social work practice. They may choose topics that reflect mastery of agency procedures, interventions with specific populations (AIDS patients, homeless people,

people with schizophrenia), work in varied settings (school, hospital, mental health agency), particular practice orientations (cognitive, psychodynamic, family systems), and objectives related to self-awareness. They can even choose to develop tasks to enhance the supervisee's ability to be a supervisee (e.g., becoming less defensive about receiving feedback)!

As stated earlier, in chapter 9, agencies and schools of social work often outline content for learning in their evaluation instruments. Many supervisors and supervisees use these as guidelines for selecting educational content. TCS enables them to address either agency- or school-required objectives as well as individualized goals. It offers a process for educational supervision in both direct (micro) and indirect (macro) practice settings.

TCS and Macro-Centered Settings

Social workers practice in a wide variety of settings and at multiple systems levels. While many work face-to-face with clients, others work to ameliorate social problems through program development, community organization, and policy work. Those whose activities target larger numbers of people, and who do not (for the most part) engage in face-to-face work are often referred to as *macro*-practitioners (Kirst-Ashman and Hull Jr. 1999). Many schools of social work offer "concentrations" in administration, community organization, or management, in which practicum work focuses on learning macro-practice skills.

Although this book has emphasized supervision in direct (micro-) practice contexts, TCS is ideal for macro-practice supervision as well. The process of formulating educational and practice objectives as target goals is identical. Although the learning content may differ, the task planning and implementation sequence is the same: identify and select target goals, formulate tasks to attain them, consider potential obstacles that might hinder successful task implementation, contract, execute tasks in the field, and review tasks and evaluate performance at the following supervision meeting.

In macro settings, the supervisor and supervisee collaboratively select areas for learning that reflect those types of interventions. For example, a graduate student concentrating in community organization had an internship at an urban, economically disadvantaged elementary school. She found that parent-teacher relations in the school district were poor and thought it important to work to improve them. There was no parent-teacher association (PTA), so she and her supervisor selected starting a PTA as a target goal. They formulated tasks to systematically attain this objective while the intern developed skills in community organization.

The TCS process of partializing work into target goals and tasks is useful in educational supervision in a broad variety of macro-practice settings requiring knowledge and skills in such areas as policy development (e.g., performing needs assessments, lobbying for the passage of bills), program administration (e.g., writing policy and procedures manuals, managing budgets, evaluating program success), grant writing, and creating and presenting psychoeducational workshops.

Theoretical and Practice Orientations

Although TCS is a modification of the task-centered practice model, it should not be considered for teaching only task-centered practice. TCS can be used to provide educational supervision for most, if not all, practice orientations. Target goals and tasks can readily be developed to teach cognitive-behavioral, psychodynamic, and humanistic approaches, as well as family systems, solution-focused, and task-centered practice.

For example, a supervisee in an agency with a psychodynamic orientation can select target goals that reflect this practice approach. Assessing ego defenses and coping mechanisms, uncovering feelings tied to early parent-child relationships, and articulating intrapersonal conflicts can allbe target goals. Related tasks could include implementing interpretations and linking present interpersonal struggles to relationships with significant figures from the past (Malan 1979).

In humanistic practice, learning might include acquiring skills in employing empathy, using silence, and inquiring about affective responses to events. Family systems goals might include identifying patterns of triangulation, identifying complementarity in couples, and helping families communicate more effectively. Supervisors and supervisees using a cognitive-behavioral approach might formulate target goals related to identifying automatic thought responses, monitoring internal dialogues, and teaching editing skills. Scaling questions, identifying exceptions, employing compliments, and using the miracle question are possible goals for learning solution-focused practice (Nunnally 1993).

Some practice orientations that rely heavily on personal affective reactions as the primary source for learning and decision making, such as experiential and Gestalt, may be difficult to supervise using TCS. These approaches typically do not articulate discrete skills to be applied in future interactions but posit learning how to respond in the "here and now" — which makes target goal and task planning more challenging. Nevertheless, supervisors and supervisees using these practice orientations may be able to develop target goals that reflect their principles.

As stated earlier, TCS was not designed as a model primarily for teaching task-centered practice. It is a flexible educational supervision model that can be used to supervise across a broad spectrum of practice approach settings. This said, using TCS does "teach" supervisees about task-centered practice procedures. In our view, this both offers advantages and presents some possible dilemmas.

Supervising in a Task-Centered Setting

As discussed in chapter 3, supervision and clinical work represent parallel processes with many similarities that both complicate and assist supervisory work. Thus, special attention should be paid to parallel process issues. TCS can be used to provide educational supervision to supervisees learning task-centered practice as well as other models. A few considerations should be kept in mind for each.

Utilizing TCS with workers learning and using task-centered practice offers a few advantages. Supervisees have the opportunity to learn the procedures through direct experience: how to partialize objectives, develop activities (i.e., tasks) that lead toward goal attainment, consider practice obstacles, and monitor progress through rating completion of agreed-upon tasks. Indeed, in two studies practicum interns reported that using task-centered procedures for supervision helped them learn about the task-centered practice model (Caspi and Reid 1998; Larsen 1980). As one student stated, "I reflect on what the supervisor does with me . . . as an example . . . for when working with clients."

TCS also teaches how to engage in a collaborative "helping" process and provides insight about the client's experience on the receiving end of a task-centered model. This increased awareness can help practitioners be more aware of how certain behaviors may come across — i.e., which are helpful and which are not. For example, a supervisee in one study (Caspi and Reid

1998) reported that the model helped his work with clients because "I know what it feels like to be on the other end . . . so I can be more sensitive." Another intern appreciated the organization of TCS and felt that clients would also enjoy task-centered procedures: "it [TCS] helps me feel more structured, so I know that it also makes clients feel structured . . . in a positive way."

Attempting to replicate behaviors experienced in supervision in their practice with clients is recognized as an important part of supervisee learning (Shulman 1994). However, when models with almost identical processes are being utilized for both supervision and practice, some dilemmas are raised. As stated throughout this book, supervisees observe their supervisors' behaviors closely and often attempt to replicate them in their clinical work. Therefore, supervisors using task-centered procedures to supervise task-centered practice must pay particular attention to how they behave. Their implementation of task-centered procedures in supervision will demonstrate to supervisees how to act with clients. Those who give their supervisees room to self-direct their learning tasks will likely have supervisees who enable their clients to self-determine their treatment goals and how to achieve them. Conversely, supervisors who "give" supervisees tasks, rather than developing tasks collaboratively, will likely discover that their supervisees are assigning tasks for clients.

One potential problem of concurrent use of task-centered procedures for supervision and practice is supervisees feeling "caseworked" or "therapized." On the receiving end of the model, it is not difficult for supervisees to picture themselves as, and feel like, clients. As one explained, "I can sometimes see what the supervisor is trying to do . . . and it makes me feel like I am a client." Although she also reported that she did not feel therapized, such an experience highlights the challenge of maintaining a clear supervision-therapy boundary when using similar models in supervision and clinical work. As stated in chapter 4, this boundary can, at times, be tenuous. Using TCS to supervise task-centered practice can make the distinction even more difficult, particularly when supervisors are working with students on building skills of self-awareness and conscious use of self.

There are advantages and dilemmas in using TCS to supervise in settings that do not use task-centered pratice. Using TCS models a highly collaborative approach that enables supervisees to be self-directed in their learning and teaches about measuring task performance, generating ongoing feedback, and evaluating practice—skills that are increasingly necessary in today's practice. However, these benefits can represent potential obstacles if the principles greatly differ from the practice model being utilized. For example, some practice orientations (e.g., psychodynamic) believe that problems are solved through insight development and emotional catharsis (Malan 1979). TCS puts forth a more action-oriented approach for achieving goals. Nevertheless, it can still be used to teach psychodynamic skills. For example, upon identifying the task "will inquire about client's underlying feelings," the supervisor and supervisee can role play, with the supervisor taking the role of the clinician to model how this skill may look in action. Furthermore, using a supervision process that differs from the clinical model, particularly when the latter is centered on affective insight, decreases the risk of transgressing the supervision-therapy boundary.

Structure

As discussed in chapter 2, the predominant structure for social work supervision is the traditional model: one supervisor and one supervisee, meeting face to face, usually for one hour each week (Rothman and Jones 1971). Other common arrangements include group, secondary, peer, and consultation supervision. Supervision also occurs in nontraditional settings such as training centers (e.g., teaching laboratories, field units), where it often involves multiple supervisors and supervisees. There are a wide array of supervision structures, often highly individual and idiosyncratic arrangements. Furthermore, innovative structures are continually being developed and introduced. TCS was created so that it could be employed in most arrangements, as it does not prescribe a specific structure but rather outlines a process that is readily and easily adapted.

Group Supervision

Group supervision usually entails one supervisor working with two or more (usually a maximum of eight) supervisees. Although the supervisor provides leadership, group members are actively responsible for giving each other support and feedback. TCS procedures are easily implemented in this setting, following guidelines for task-centered practice with groups (Tolson, Reid, and Garvin 1994). The supervisees take turns presenting cases and sharing their thoughts about possible target goals. The group gives both positive and critical feedback and offers suggestions for target goals, tasks, and potential obstacles. The supervisee then contracts with the group to implement the agreed-upon tasks. At the next supervision meeting, the group reviews task implementation and discussed successes and encountered obstacles.

The group structure offers opportunities for learning that are not present in the traditional structure. Supervisees have a chance to receive ideas from multiple sources (rather than only from the supervisor), listen to others' presentations, enter into critical assessment of their work, and share feedback. In essence, they have the opportunity to experience supervision at both ends—providing and receiving. Another advantage is that in settings with only limited time for supervision, one supervisor can work with multiple supervisees simultaneously.

Group approaches have some drawbacks. Members must devise rules for turn-taking, interrupting, and "crisis" cases, and each member receives less individualized time. We recommend that group rules for time allocation be discussed and agreed upon early in the supervisory encounter. Finally, because groups involve a larger number of supervisees, we recommend that group meetings be scheduled for longer blocks of time (a minimum of an hour and a half) in order to accommodate the many needs of members.

Secondary Supervision

As discussed in chapter 2, secondary supervision (including "task" and "team" supervision) is becoming increasingly common, particularly in practicum settings. This approach entails a supervisee working with a designated and a secondary supervisor. The designated supervisor performs as the "supervisor of record" and oversees assignments and evaluations. This person may only meet with the supervisee weekly for an hour at a time, and is typically not available between meetings. The secondary supervisor works directly with the supervisee, is accessible during the workday, and assists the supervisee in performing tasks between meetings with the designated supervisor. This includes providing education and support. This arrangement is commonly utilized when the designated (or primary) supervisor is not able to provide direct supervision due to work demands, limited time, or lack of expertise in the area the supervisee is practicing. It is sometimes considered when an agency does not have staff that meet the requirements to serve as a social work practicum supervisor. The agency may contract with a qualified "outside" person to perform as the designated supervisor while staff provide secondary supervision to interns.

TCS works well for secondary supervision arrangements, helping to promote clear communication about work to be accomplished. For the sake of clarity, we recommend that, if possible, all three (the designated and secondary supervisors and the supervisee) meet and participate in the formulation of target goals and tasks. If this is not possible, communication of objectives can still be enhanced by using TCS. Contracts developed between designated supervisors and supervisees can be shared with secondary supervisors, informing them of the specific activities to be implemented each week. This helps both supervisors maintain consistency in their work. In any case, we recommend that primary and secondary supervisors meet occasionally to assess their work, clarify confusions, discuss disagreements, and consider ways to improve the supervisee's experience. We also recommend that secondary supervisors participate in ongoing evaluation (i.e., ratings) of task implementation as well as formal evaluation processes.

Advantages of Conjoint Meetings

We strongly recommend that supervision meetings include the secondary supervisor. This offers a few distinct advantages. First, it helps to promote clear communication among the three "players" and to clarify the work to be done. Not being included is likely, at times, to create confusion for the secondary supervisor about why certain activities, interventions, or objectives were selected. When all three work together, the secondary supervisor does not have to rely on the supervisee's report of what was discussed and agreed to during meetings with the lead supervisor.

Second, working as a threesome minimizes the development of covert coalitions. For example, if the secondary supervisor is not directly involved, the lead supervisor and supervisee may collude by minimizing the secondary supervisor's authority. Indeed, a secondary supervisor may report that a supervisee's work is inadequate, while the designated supervisor tells the supervisee that their work is fine, or worse, that the secondary supervisor's own work is below par. This can result from the desire to demonstrate authority by dismissing or minimizing the expertise of the secondary supervisor.

Third, conjoint meetings are likely to promote greater investment by secondary supervisors. They can participate in teaching, offer ideas, share
observations, and provide feedback. Inclusion validates their roles as supervisors and as authorities who have valuable information to offer, and
removes the designated supervisor as the only source of expertise. Indeed, it
supports a "team spirit." Additionally, it teaches secondary supervisors about
supervision, enabling them to take on lead supervisory activities in the
future.

Fourth, meeting together lessens opportunities for "creative" supervisees
to misrepresent their lead supervisors' wishes. Although we believe this
rarely occurs, when anxiety is high, supervisees may rely on deceit as a way
to minimize their stress. For example, a student very worried about their ability to confront an angry client may tell the secondary supervisor that the lead
supervisor stated that confrontation was not warranted at this time.

Peer Supervision

Peer supervision differs from the traditional approach in that there is no
distinct supervisor and supervisee. In this arrangement two or more colleagues (i.e., peers) meet to give and receive case consultation, education,
and support—without the anxiety of hierarchical relationships and formal
evaluations. Members of equal status (peers) take turns presenting cases to
each other. The one presenting voluntarily takes on the role of supervisee.
Members listening to the presentation become temporary supervisors, sharing their thoughts and giving feedback—providing case consultation.

Because TCS offers a collaborative process for the systematic development of learning and practice objectives, it is well suited for peer supervision
structures. A hierarchy is not necessary to implement the process. As each
member takes on the role of supervisee, the others assist with the selection of
learning and practice goals and tasks to achieve them. For example, a practitioner (i.e., temporary supervisee) might identify to peers that he wished to
improve his ability to make accurate diagnoses using the *DSM-IV* (American Psychiatric Association 1994). The peers would then offer strategies for
accomplishing this objective. They might suggest that the presenter partialize the *DSM-IV* into subgroups, and subsequently suggest tasks, such as
practicing application of selected diagnostic categories to clients, identifying
which clients fit the categories and which do not. At the following meeting,

the presenter would then report on task implementation, in accordance with the task review step of TCS. By contracting, peers are accountable to each other. Perhaps the greatest advantage of using TCS for peer supervision is that it a consistent and clear process for all to follow. When peers get together to provide each other with supervision, they may have differing beliefs about how to go about it. One may have a strong family systems orientation while the other primarily utilizes a cognitive approach. When in the role of supervisor, each may use their practice orientations to try to assist the other. While this may have some learning benefits—e.g., helping each other to see things from a different perspective—it may also may hinder reaching their individual goals. Using TCS, each is able to self-identify target goals in accordance with their practice approach. They are clear about how supervision is to proceed, and what is expected in terms of participation.

Consultation

Varying uses of the word "consultation" exist in the supervision literature. Here, the term refers to the provision of independently contracted supervision. In this arrangement, a worker "hires" a supervisor (who is not associated with the worker's agency) to address (usually self-determined) professional needs. Although some agencies will demand that struggling workers seek assistance to improve, most consultation arrangements are initiated by motivated learners who want to maximize their professional development. Consultation can be either continuous or "as needed."

Social workers seek out private consultation for a variety of reasons. Some agencies do not provide supervision, and others may only give administrative direction and not address clinical or educational concerns. A worker may feel that the agency-provided supervision is inadequate for their learning needs. Additionally, agency supervisors may not possess the required qualifications to help the worker obtain or maintain licensing. Although consultants can be of great help in such circumstances, they must take care not to collude with the supervisee against the agency supervisor. Finally, private practitioners often seek out consultation.

Consultation typically is a more egalitarian relationship than traditional, agency-based supervision. Formal evaluations are not necessarily tied to promotion, raises, or grades. The supervisee is more able to take the lead in expressing what they want out of the supervisory experience. Thus, the nature of consultatory supervision can vary greatly according to the supervisee's wishes. The focus may be on improving knowledge and skills, problem-solving situations (without attention to learning), or obtaining emotional support. Also, the emphasis may change as the consultant and supervisee work together. For example, it is not uncommon for social workers to initially seek out consultation because of frustration with agency-related concerns. Many do not feel safe sharing negative reactions with their agency supervisors, and they may feel it unfair to continue "unloading" their frustrations onto their friends and families. Using consultation to "vent" feelings about their workplace may be necessary in the beginning, to safely express difficult emotions. Supervisees may then be ready to consider solutions for agency-related difficulties, engage in case planning, and set educational objectives.

Because consultants are hired for a wide variety of needs, it is critical that the goals of the encounter be clearly articulated from the start. It is not uncommon for the consultant and supervisee to be working toward different purposes, particularly since the process is not governed by agency or university constraints. The challenge of this aspect of consultation is illustrated in the following example. Note that attending to the supervisee's affective responses is useful in identifying where the consultant should start and addressing the power struggle that has emerged between them.

Don sought out consultation because of overwhelming frustrations he felt with his agency. His aim was to have a place to vent feelings, receive support, and learn how to use his affective reactions more effectively in practice. Don told Anne, the consultant, on the phone that he "wanted to do better at work." She did not ask for clarification, and assumed that this meant he wanted to improve his clinical practice knowledge and skills. As Don shared his negative *feelings* about his work setting, the consultant focused on critiquing his *behavior*. Don became frustrated that his feelings were not being acknowledged and validated. The consultant became confused because each time she inquired about his behaviors, Don would change the conversation to what she saw as complaints about his work administrators. She felt they were playing out a power struggle in which she was attempting to "pull" Don away from negative complaints—to get him to take action on them—and Don was becoming "more firmly planted" in his wish to complain. She shared her perspective of having entered into a power struggle and asked Don what he wanted from supervision. He replied that he too had become frustrated with the process and only "wanted help dealing with all the stress of work." This helped Anne review the direction of her work. She focused more on providing emotional support. After only a relatively brief time, Don reported feeling relief about being able to share his feelings, and was more ready to discuss techniques for resolving work frustrations.

TCS is quite useful in consultation arrangements, as it emphasizes supervisee-directed selection of objectives, which promotes clarity of expectations. However, the primary aim of TCS is educational development. Because supervisees seek private consultation for varied reasons, it is important that TCS be used flexibly. There may be times (e.g., when affective reactions seem to be impeding work) when it is necessary to emphasize the social functions of the model prior to entering the task planning and implementation sequence, although the process of exploring possible target goals will likely highlight the supervisees' aims for consultation. However, most supervisees who hire consultants do so because they want to improve their practice abilities.

For educational purposes, TCS does not have to be modified for use in consultation. It is particularly well suited to ongoing arrangements—e.g., meeting every week, two weeks, or monthly. The process of selecting target goals and the tasks to achieve them, considering potential obstacles, and clearly articulating work to be accomplished between meetings in the form of contracts keeps the encounter focused and productive. In "as needed" arrangements, the consultant and supervisee meet infrequently—e.g., at times the consultee is overwhelmed by their work. Typically, the focus of the meetings is to problem-solve immediate concerns, not necessarily to promote learning. TCS offers a process for developing tasks to address concerns in systematic fashion. However, because the intermittent work is captured in the written contracts, events can be tied together for identifying patterns in the supervisee's work that lead to times in which they feel "stuck." Educational objectives can then be developed and worked toward.

Colluding Against Agency Supervisors

Consultants must take care not to collude with supervisees who contract with them privately—e.g., without the knowledge of the supervisees' agency administrators. Such supervisees may complain about perceived inadequacies of their supervisors or administrators, seeking support in making decisions that challenge agency policy. We strongly encourage that consultants inquire whether supervisees have hired them without the knowledge of their agency, explore concerns about sharing this information with their agency, and consider methods of working with the agency's support. Agencies are responsible for the welfare of their clients and have the right to know when "outsiders" (i.e., consultants) are participating in developing interventions. By opening up this discussion, consultants are better able to make decisions about how to support supervisees, with both agency and supervisee needs in mind. Furthermore, we encourage agencies that do not provide educational supervision for their employees to pay for consultation—particularly in states where supervision is a requirement for professional licensing.

Using TCS in Staff vs. Internship Supervision

While the primary aim of internship supervision is education, staff supervision can have different emphases, including administration, case problem-solving, support, and education. Supervision that focuses on administrative aspects commonly involves monitoring staff work, particularly its concrete aspects (e.g., number of home visits each week, status of paperwork). When the central aim is to assist with cases, supervision helps staff manage challenging cases in order to promote "best possible practice" for clients. Although learning often accompanies this type of supervision, it is usually not explicitly addressed through active links to educational objectives. Supportive supervision emphasizes the provision of resources to ensure that supervisees are able to best carry out their jobs, including emotional support. Finally, some staff supervision arrangements emphasize education and professional development directly.

Because the focus of staff supervision varies, it is necessary to openly discuss the central function of the encounter at the start. As in consultation arrangements, it is helpful to inquire of supervisees what they want from the encounters. Surprisingly enough, we have found that some staff supervisees do not want to use supervision for education but rather for accountability purposes or emotional support. If supervisors attempt to focus on goals for professional development, they are likely to enter into a power struggle related to the central aim of the encounter. Seasoned workers in particular may not wish to focus on education. They often have a choice about how to use supervision, so it is important to openly discuss its function early in the relationship.

TCS is a model for educational supervision. It can also be employed for administrative purposes, with some modification, reflecting a change of emphasis from achieving educational objectives to getting the job done. In administrative supervision, "getting the job done" typically means completing concrete activities, such as updating progress notes, making timely referrals, and doing a minimum number of home visits each day. Using TCS, the instrumental work to be done is partialized into target goals and discrete tasks are formulated to attain them.Potential obstacles to implementing these tasks are considered, in order to promote greater success in carrying them out. However, there is no in-depth discussion of how these activities relate to educational needs or objectives. Each week the supervisor and supervisee can rate progress during the task review process. As certain areas are mastered, they move on to new ones until they feel that the supervisee can autonomously carry out these work activities. Then the supervisory pair can decide whether continuing supervision is necessary.

TCS Across Disciplines

Because TCS offers procedures for systematic attainment of learning and practice objectives, the model has applications for disciplines beyond social work. Many professions teach practice by having the new worker learn through direct experience. For example, prospective schoolteachers enter into student teaching arrangements in which they work directly with cooperating teachers in real classrooms. The classroom teachers, typically in conjunction with university supervisors, are responsible for educating the prospective teachers, helping them to achieve the competencies required to demonstrate they can be successful on their own. TCS could be utilized in this setting to ensure that these competencies are systematically worked toward and attained.

Other professions (e.g., medicine, nursing, counseling psychology) use mentoring, tutoring, and preceptoring to teach new practitioners. With some minor modifications (e.g., not using process recordings, adjusting number of tasks to be selected each week), TCS offers these professions a tool for educating in the field.

Conclusion

TCS is a structured process that offers flexibility while maintaining a clear focus on supervisee development. It can be utilized in a wide variety of supervisory settings and for a range of educational objectives. In addition, it provides measures for accountability—not usually contained in a supervision model. Because TCS targets ongoing, specific, explicit (often written) goals, the work that has taken place behind the usually closed doors of supervision can be easily identified and clearly monitored by supervisors, supervisees, agency administrators, and university officials (e.g., field liaisons), if necessary.

Additionally, the TCS process can be empirically evaluated. Because supervisees and supervisors numerically rate the success of actions at each meeting, it is possible to empirically determine if supervision is productive. This should appeal to agencies and social work programs concerned with issues of accountability and objective methods for evaluating supervisee progress. In addition, it should appeal to supervisees and supervisors who want to clearly demonstratethat supervision is working.

While experts have stated many principles for good supervisory practice, clear, discrete steps for achieving these ideals are not generally offered in the form of a coherent model. TCS provides structure and ongoing immediate feedback, partializes learning, promotes class-practicum integration by linking tasks to theory, and addresses both the instrumental and the affective components of the supervisory relationship. Additionally, the guidelines put andragogical principles into practice, outlining a collaborative, supervisee-centered framework. The ability to direct their learning allows supervisees to gain experiential insight into issues of self-determination, a core social work value.

In addition, the model's emphasis on empowering supervisees to become independent learners by helping them acquire skills for self-directed learning is consistent with principles of feminist pedagogy. In the TCS setting, supervisees are empowered by experiencing and integrating skills for goal achievement. This promotes their ability to engage in independent practice, an ultimate goal of the practicum (Livingston, Davidson, and Marshack 1989) and a skill increasingly necessary for agency staff given shrinking resources for supervision activities. Finally, TCS is readily applied for a variety of educational purposes (e.g., teaching clinical models) and in a variety of settings (e.g. hospital, school, mental health agency) as well as a broad spectrum of supervisory arrangements (e.g., peer, group, consultation). TCS is adaptable and practical, and offers advantages over other supervisory approaches.

Appendix

TCS Guidelines

Introduction

The task-centered model for educational supervision (TCS) provides an ordered series of steps for systematic attainment of learning objectives. It approaches educational development in social work much like learning to play a sport. For example, to become a competent skier, capable of safely managing terrain of varying difficulty, one must master an array of skills involving proper body movements. During formal ski instruction, the teacher may shout out many commands as the skier is attempting to make it down the hill: "Keep your weight forward! Bend your knees! Knees should be over your toes! Keep your arms forward! Shift your weight on the turns! Keep your upper body still! Keep your shoulders pointing downhill!"

Trying to attend to and implement so many directions simultaneously can be quite overwhelming. For many, learning is much easier when the focus is on only a few specific objectives at a time. This enables incremental mastery of skills; proficiency in basic maneuvers is achieved before complex ones are attempted. A solid grasp of basic skills is often necessary for carrying out more difficult endeavors. The TCS model guides this type of learning process—focusing on a few discrete areas at a time, incrementally building skills, beginning with more basic tasks and increasing complexity as supervisee competence grows.

TCS enables supervisors and supervisees to break down the many areas of social work practice into goals and specific tasks. It provides a well-defined series of activities (stages) to be carried out during and between supervision meetings, so the supervisee can systematically work toward and attain educational objectives. What follows is a brief overview of the TCS process.

Overview of TCS

Each supervision meeting begins with a "social" period to assist the transition into supervision activities, provide support for the supervisee, and tend to the supervisory relationship. This step is designed to develop the affective components of the supervision experience and to prepare supervisees to actively engage in the instrumental functions of the model (i.e., those aimed at achieving educational objectives). The social stage is followed by time set aside for direct instruction. Supervisees typically have many questions, and this allows supervisors to provide requested information. Subsequently, the focused work of identifying and working toward objectives begins.

During each meeting, supervisees and supervisors collaboratively identify learning and practice objectives for immediate, targeted work. These objectives are evaluated, prioritized in order of perceived importance, and formulated as "target goals". Actions, or tasks, for attaining the target goals are then selected. Potential obstacles to task implementation are considered, and supervisees are asked to predict problems they might encounter when attempting to carry out the selected tasks. When potential obstacles are identified, selected tasks may be changed, modified, or kept with "backup plans" for handling problems that arise. At the end of each meeting, the supervisor and supervisee review the selection of target goals and tasks and agree to them in the form of a contract. The supervisee then implements the agreed-upon tasks before the next meeting, typically in work with cases.

At the start of the next supervision meeting, task implementation and target goal attainment are evaluated. If target goals have been successfully attained, the supervisee and supervisor select new ones. If not, they are kept for continued work or modified based upon the evaluative discussion. The process of continually identifying goals, tasks, and obstacles and then implementing, reviewing, and evaluating tasks and progress toward goals encompasses the major activities of TCS. These steps are carried out during each supervision meeting.

The model is tailored for three phases of supervision: beginning, middle, and ending. The beginning phase is brief and concludes at the completion of the first contract. It contains a stage specifically to inform supervisees about the social work supervision process and TCS procedures (which includes copying these guidelines and sharing them with supervisees). The middle phase contains the sequence of activities that will continue until the end of the supervisory encounter. Although the ending phase is not marked by a different sequence, it represents a unique time in the supervision experience. During this phase, target goal and task selection reflect the process of ending relationships and attending to the issues that commonly arise during terminations (see chapter 6 for a discussion of these issues). The stages of TCS provide a road map for conducting the educational supervision meeting.

Outline of the TCS Sequence

Beginning phase (from the initial meeting until completion of the first contract)
Social stage
Explaining supervision and TCS
Educational stage
Target goals stage
Identifying, prioritizing, and selecting tasks
Anticipating and negotiating potential obstacles
Contracting
Middle and ending phases (from completion of the first contract through the final encounter)
Social stage
Task review
Educational stage
Target goals stage
Identifying, prioritizing, and selecting tasks
Anticipating and negotiating potential obstacles
Contracting

Please note that the following guidelines provide an overview of the model's process, giving only cursory descriptions of each step. Refer to the main part of this book for thorough discussion of the principles that underlie these steps, the nuances and complexity of actual implementation, and the educational benefits of each stage. The chapter in which each stage is discussed in depth is noted throughout these guidelines.

Social Stage

The social stage is the first part of the supervision meeting and is a feature of each phase. It is usually brief (about five minutes of a one-hour meeting, longer depending upon need) and generally consists of welcoming sequences and "small talk" to help make the transition from outside interests to supervision activities. During this stage, the supervisor is particularly concerned with attending to supervisee anxiety and any strong emotional reactions, in order to process them and ensure a productive supervisory encounter. The social stage can be facilitated by adapting the clinical skill of "starting where the client is" to "starting where the supervisee is." The supervisor should temporarily set aside their own agenda to allow the supervisee to express any pressing concerns. This demonstrates that supervision is a safe place to voice fears and expectations related to their work. Attending to emotional experience helps to develop an open and trusting supervisory relationship, which maximizes supervisee learning. See chapter 8 for an in-depth discussion and illustrative examples of the social stage.

Explaining Supervision and TCS

This stage consists of three steps. First, if necessary, supervisees are taught about the unique characteristics and expectations of social work educational supervision. This may include discussing how it differs from other supervision arrangements (e.g., retail management). After this general overview of supervision, more specific discussion of how it is typically conducted at the agency should occur. This enables the supervisory pair to reach mutually agreeable expectations for the encounter.

Second, the TCS procedures are shared, explained, and considered for use. This process includes giving the supervisee a copy of these guidelines for review and reference. Third, the supervisory pair come to a working agreement about the schedule, frequency, duration, and location of meetings. Although the explaining supervision and TCS step only occurs during the beginning phase, sporadic review of supervision expectations may be needed later in the encounter. See chapter 8 for more information.

Educational Stage

The educational stage is an important step of each phase. Although teaching moments can occur at any point in the supervisory meeting, time specifically set aside for didactic instruction is profitable. Supervisees appreciate receiving "mini-lessons" (approximately two to five minutes long) about various components of their job. However, these supervisor-delivered lessons should be both relevant for and wanted by the student. The instruction is typically given in response to supervisee requests for information. Chapter 8 provides more comprehensive discussion of this stage.

Target Goals Stage

Target goals represent discrete learning and practice objectives that supervisors and supervisees agree will become the immediate focus of their work together. These goals are selected at each supervision session, with the expectation that progress will be made toward attaining them by the next meeting. This stage begins the process of identifying and working toward educational objectives in incremental fashion. It involves three basic steps: identifying, prioritizing, and selecting up to a maximum of three target goals for direct undertaking. As goals are attained, new ones are selected.

Supervisors may begin this step by asking supervisees what they would like to learn. They should also share their ideas about which skills and knowledge they view as important for supervisees to competently perform their jobs. Review of performance evaluation forms and job descriptions can help identify areas for learning. Using such forms clarifies expectations of the encounter, gives direction and purpose to the learning, and reduces surprises during formal evaluations. For a more in-depth discussion of this stage and using these forms, see chapter 9.

Identifying, Prioritizing, and Selecting Tasks

Once target goals have been selected, tasks—the actions (or behaviors) to be carried out in order to attain them—are collaboratively identified. Supervisee tasks are usually implemented between supervisory conferences, during work with clients.

This stage involves three steps. First, task ideas are generated from multiple sources, including the literature, personal and professional experience, supervisor expertise, classroom learning, agency requirements, and brainstorming. Second, the ideas are prioritized in order of appropriateness after consideration of the supervisee's capabilities, case needs, and which tasks will most likely result in successful achievement of target goals. Third, up to three tasks are selected for each target goal. The result is a maximum of nine discrete tasks for the supervisee to focus on between supervisory meetings. For an in-depth discussion of tasks, the task selection process, and examples of this process in action, see chapter 10.

Anticipating and Negotiating Obstacles

Before finalizing the selection of tasks, supervisors and supervisees consider potential challenges to successful task implementation: negative client reactions, environmental factors (e.g., client's phone is out of service, plan is contingent on social service agency cooperation), collateral family members' resistance to the treatment plan, and supervisee personal reactions (e.g., countertransference). In short, supervisees are asked to look into the future and consider ways to ensure that their planned interventions go as well as possible.

When possible obstacles have been identified, options for overcoming them are discussed. Tasks can be abandoned and replaced, revised, or kept with the formulation of a "backup plan" to be used if the potential problems arise. The process of anticipating obstacles has many benefits, including helping the supervisee learn anticipatory skills (e.g., considering the impact of planned interventions prior to carrying them out) and reducing surprises during clinical encounters. See chapter 10 for a thorough examination of this stage, its process, educational advantages, and examples.

Contracting

The contracting stage is the last step of the supervision meeting, and is a feature of each phase. It entails reviewingthe selected target goals and tasks and constructing a written contract. The aim is a clear and mutual understanding of the focus of the work and of what specific actions should be accomplished by the next meeting. Both the supervisee and the supervisor should leave with a copy of the written contract in hand. After this stage, the supervision meeting ends and the supervisee goes off to implement the agreed-upon tasks. For a discussion of the advantages of contracting and an example of a completed TCS contract, see chapter 10.

The completion of the first contract marks the end of the beginning phase and the start of the middle phase of the supervision encounter. The middle phase involves all but one of the stages (explaining supervision and TCS) discussed above, and includes a new step, the task review stage.

Task Review

The task review stage is utilized from the start of the middle phase until the end of the supervision encounter, and is a central feature of TCS. It appears directly after the social stage in the TCS sequence. Task review entails collaborative assessment of task implementation, and often begins with supervisors asking supervisees how they did with the contracted activities. A common approach is to take out the contract completed during the previous supervision meeting and run through the list of selected tasks. When tasks have been implemented successfully, the supervisee is commended for a job well done. If tasks have not been completed, an effort is made to identify obstacles that interfered with their accomplishment. Since most tasks are carried out in work with cases, it is typical for task review to be accompanied by a discussion of case progress.

The task implementation evaluation form can facilitate the assessment of task performance. The supervisee uses a numerical scale to rate their performance of each task. Special consideration is given to their criteria for determining the scores. Such inquiry enables insight into the supervisee's understanding of tasks and expectations about their work.

The task review should be a collaborative process in which both the supervisee and supervisor have input, not unilateral judgment by the supervisor of the supervisee's work. The supervisee's own critique of their performance is critical. It builds skills of self-awareness and self-evaluation. For a thorough examination of the task review stage, its process, considerations, and educational benefits, see chapter 11.

After completing the task review stage, the supervisor and supervisee return to the educational stage and repeat the sequence of steps, including selecting target goals and tasks, identifying potential obstacles, and contracting. This cyclical process is repeated throughout the supervisory relationship. These guidelines are not meant as rigid prescriptions, but should be used flexibly in accordance with the needs of supervision.

References

Abramson, J. S. and Fortune, A. E. (1990). Improving field instruction: An evaluation of a seminar for new field instructors. *Journal of Social Work Education* 26 (3): 273–286.

Akin, G. and Weil, M. (1981). The prior question: How do supervisors learn to supervise? *Social Casework* 62 (8): 472–479.

Alperin, D. E. (1998). Factors related to student satisfaction with child welfare field placements. *Journal of Social Work Education* 34 (1): 43–54.

American Psychiatric Association. (1994). *Diagnostic and Statistical Manual of Mental Disorders.* (4th ed.). Washington, DC: American Psychiatric Association.

Aponte, H. J. and Winter, J. E. (1987). The person and practice of the therapist: Treatment and training. *Journal of Psychotherapy and the Family* 3 (1): 85–111.

Arlow, J. A. (1963). The supervisory situation. *Journal of the American Psychoanalytic Association* 11:574–594.

Atwood, J. D. (1986). Self-awareness in supervision. *The Clinical Supervisor* 4 (3): 79–96.

Baker, D. R. and Smith, S. L. (1987). A comparison of field faculty and field student perceptions of selected aspects of supervision. *The Clinical Supervisor* 5 (4): 31–42.

Baldwin, M. (1987). The use of self in therapy: An introduction. *Journal of Psychotherapy and the Family* 3 (1): 7–16.

Basso, R. V. J. (1987). Teacher and student problem-solving activities in educational supervisory sessions. *Journal of Social Work Education* 23 (3): 67–73.

Becherman, A. and Burrell, L. (1994). A rock and a hard place: Trying to provide culturally sensitive field experiences in rural, homogenous communities. *Journal of Multicultural Social Work* 3 (1): 91–100.

Beless, D. W. (1993). Foreword. In L. Schulman, *Teaching the Helping Skills: A Field Instructor's Guide*. Alexandria, VA: Council on Social Work Education.

Benavides, E., Lynch, M., and Velasquez, J. (1980). Toward a culturally relevant field work model: The community learning center project. *Journal of Education for Social Work* 16:55–62.

Berengarten, S. (1957). Identifying learning patterns of individual students: An exploratory study. *Social Service Review* 31:407–417.

Berkun, C. (1984). Women and the field experience: Toward a model of nonsexist field-based learning conditions. *Journal of Education for Social Work* 20 (3): 5–12.

Bernard, J. M. (1989). Training supervisors to examine relationship variables using IPR. *The Clinical Supervisor* 7 (1): 103–112.

Blake, R. and Peterman, P. J. (1985). *Social Work Field Instruction: The Undergraduate Experience*. Lanham, MD: University Press of America.

Bogo, M. (1993). The student/field instructor relationship: The critical factor in field education. *The Clinical Supervisor* 11 (2): 23–36.

——. (1983). Field instruction: Negotiating content and process. *The Clinical Supervisor* 1 (3): 3–13.

Bogo, M. and Power, R. (1992). New field instructors' perceptions of institutional supports for their roles. *Journal of Social Work Education* 28 (2): 178–189.

Bogo, M. and Taylor, I. (1990). A practicum curriculum in a health specialization: A framework for hospitals. *Journal of Social Work Education* 1:76–86.

Bogo, M. and Vayda, E. (1998). *The Practice of Field Instruction in Social Work: Theory and Process*. New York: Columbia University Press.

——. (1991). Developing a process model for field instruction. In D. Schneck, B. Grossman, and U. Glassman (Eds.), *Field Education in Social Work: Contemporary Issues and Trends*, 59–66. Dubuque, IA: Kendall/Hunt.

Brannon, D. (1985). Adult learning principles and methods for enhancing the training role of supervisors. *The Clinical Supervisor* 3 (2): 27–41.

Brown, A. and Bourne, I. (1996). *The Social Work Supervisor*. Philadelphia: Open University Press.

Bruck, M. (1963). The relationships between student anxiety, self-awareness, and self-concept and student competence in casework. *Social Casework* (March):125–131.

Carroll, D. and McCuan, P. (1975). A specialized role function approach to field instruction in social administration. In Council on Social Work Education (Ed.), *The Dynamics of Field Instruction: Learning Through Doing*. New York: Council on Social Work Education.

Caspi, J. (1997). *The task-centered model for field instruction*. Ph.D. diss., School of Social Welfare, State University of New York at Albany.

Caspi, J. and Reid, W. J. (1998). The task-centered model for field instruction: An innovative approach. *Journal of Social Work Education* 34 (1): 55–70.

Catalano, S. J. (1985). Crisis intervention with clinical interns: Some considerations for supervision. *The Clinical Supervisor* 3 (1): 97–102.

Chambers, D. E. and Spano, R. (1982). Integration of learning in field instruction. In B. W. Sheafor and L. E. Jenkins (Eds.), *Quality Field Instruction in Social Work: Program Development and Maintenance*, 226–234. New York: Longman.

Clancy, C. (1985). The use of the andragogical approach in the educational function of supervision in social work. *The Clinical Supervisor* 3 (1): 75–86.

Collins, D. and Bogo, M. (1986). Competency-based field instruction: Bridging the gap between laboratory and field learning. *The Clinical Supervisor* 4 (3): 39–52.

Collins, P. (1993). The interpersonal vicissitudes of mentorship: An exploratory study of the field supervisor-student relationship. *The Clinical Supervisor* 11 (1): 121–135.

Conklin, J. J. and Borecki, M. C. (1991). Field education units revisited: A model for the 1990s. In D. Schneck, B. Grossman, and U. Glassman (Eds.), *Field Education in Social Work: Contemporary Issues and Trends*, 122–130. Dubuque, IA: Kendall/Hunt.

Council on Social Work Education, ed. (1975). *The Dynamics of Field Instruction: Learning Through Doing*. New York: Council on Social Work Education.

Cramer, E. P. (1995). Feminist pedagogy and teaching social work practice with groups: A case study. *Journal of Teaching in Social Work* 11 (1/2): 193–215.

Curiel, H. and Rosenthal, J. A. (1987). Comparing structure in student supervision by social work program level. *The Clinical Supervisor* 5 (2): 53–67.

Davenport, J. A. and Davenport, J. (1988). Individualizing student supervision: The use of androgical-pedagogical orientation questionnaires. *Journal of Teaching in Social Work* 2 (2): 83–97.

Dawson, B. G. (1975). Supervising the undergraduate in a psychiatric setting. In Council on Social Work Education (Ed.), *The Dynamics of Field Instruction: Learning Through Doing*. New York: Council on Social Work Education.

Dea, K. L., Grist, M., and Myli, R. (1982). Learning tasks for practice competence. In B. W. Sheafor and L. E. Jenkins (Eds.), *Quality Field Instruction in Social Work: Program Development and Maintenance*, 237–261. New York: Longman.

DeJong, C. R. (1975). Field instruction for undergraduate social work education in rural areas. In Council on Social Work Education (Ed.), *The Dynamics of Field Instruction: Learning Through Doing*. New York: Council on Social Work Education.

De Shazer, S. (1982). *Patterns of Brief Family Therapy: An Ecosystems Approach*. New York: Guilford Press.

Dewey, J. (1938). *Experience and Education*. New York: Macmillan.

Dore, M. M. (1994). Feminist pedagogy and the teaching of social work practice. *Journal of Social Work Education* 30 (1): 97–106.

Dore, M. M., Epstein, B. N., and Herrerias, C. (1992). Evaluating students' micro practice field performance: Do universal learning objectives exist? *Journal of Social Work Education* 28 (3): 353–362.

Dorfman, R. A. (1998). *Paradigms of Clinical Practice*. New York: Brunner/Mazel.

Dunn, R. (1982). Teaching students through their individual learning styles: A research report. In National Association of Secondary School Principals (Ed.), *Student Learning Styles and Brain Behavior*, 142–152. Reston, VA: National Association of Secondary School Principals.

Eisikovits, Z. and Guttman, E. (1983). Toward a practice theory of learning through experience in social work supervision. *The Clinical Supervisor* 1 (1): 51–63.

Elliot, R. (1986). Interpersonal process recall (IPR) as a psychotherapy process research method. In L. Greenberg and W. Pinsof (Eds.), *The Pscyhotherapeutic Handbook: A Research Handbook*, 503–528. New York: Guilford Press.

——. (1984). A discovery-oriented approach to significant change events in psychotherapy: Interpersonal process recall and comprehensive process analysis. In L. Rice and L. Greenberg (Eds.), *Patterns of Change: Intensive Analysis of Psychotherapy Process*, 249–286. New York: Guilford Press.

Elliot, R. and Shapiro, D. (1992). Client and therapist as analysts of significant events. In S. Toukmanian and D. Rennie (Eds.), *Psychotherapy Process Research: Paradigmatic and Narrative Approaches*, 132–155. Newbury Park, CA: Sage Publications.

Ellison, M. L. (1994). Critical field instructor behaviors: Student and field instructor views. *Arete* 18 (2): 12–21.

Fellin, P. A. (1982). Responsibilities of the school: Administrative support of field instruction. In B. W. Sheafor and L. E. Jenkins (Eds.), *Quality Field Instruction in Social Work: Program Development and Maintenance*, 101–115. New York: Longman.

Fine, M. (1992). *Disruptive Voices: The Possibilities of Feminist Research (Critical Perspectives on Women and Gender)*. Ann Arbor: University of Michigan Press.

Fortune, A. E. (2000). Initial impressions and performance in field practica: Predictors of skill attainment and satisfaction among graduate social work students. Unpublished paper. School of Social Welfare, University at Albany, State University of New York.

——. (1994). Field education. In F. G. Reamer (Ed.), *The Foundations of Social Work Knowledge*, 151–194. New York: Columbia University Press.

Fortune, A. E. and Abramson, J. S. (1993). Predictors of satisfaction with field practicum among social work students. *The Clinical Supervisor* 11 (1): 95–110.

Fortune, A. E., Feathers, C., Rook, S. R., Scrimenti, R. M., Smollen, P., Stemerman, B., and Tucker, E. L. (1985). Student satisfaction with field placement. *Journal of Social Work Education* 23 (3): 92–104.

Fortune, A. E., McCarthy, M., and Abramson, J. S. (In press). Student learning processes in field: Relationship of learning activities to quality of field instruction, satisfaction, and performance among MSW students. *Journal of Social Work Education*.

Fox, R. (1983). Contracting in supervision: A goal oriented process. *The Clinical Supervisor* 1: 37–49.

Fox, R. and Guild, P. (1987). Learning styles: Their relevance to clinical supervision. *The Clinical Supervisor* 5 (3): 65–77.

Fox, R. and Zischka, P. C. (1989). The field instruction contract: A paradigm for effective learning. *Journal of Teaching in Social Work* 3 (1): 103–116.

Frank, J. D. and Frank, J. B. (1991). *Persuasion and Healing: A Comparative Study of Psychotherapy.* 3rd ed. Baltimore: Johns Hopkins University Press.

Freeman, E. M. (1985). The importance of feedback in clinical supervision: Implications for direct practice. *The Clinical Supervisor* 3 (1): 5–26.

Freeman, S. C. (1993). Structure in counseling supervision. *The Clinical Supervisor* 11 (1): 245–252.

Freeman, I. and Hansen, F. C. (1995). Field instructors' perceptions of the social work field education process. In G. Rogers (Ed.), *Social Work Field Education: Views and Visions.* Dubuque, IA: Kendall/Hunt.

Galassi, J. P. and Trent, P. J. (1987). A conceptual framework for evaluating supervision effectiveness. *Counselor Education and Supervision* 26:260–269.

Galm, S. (1972). *Issues in Welfare Administration: Welfare—An Administrative Nightmare.* Subcommittee on Fiscal Policy of the Joint Economic Committee, U.S. Congress. Washington, D.C.: U.S. Government Printing Office.

Gantt, A., Pinski, S., Rosenberg, E., and Rock, B. (1991). The practice research center: A field/class model to teach research, practice and values. In D. Schneck, B. Grossman, and U. Glassman (Eds.), *Field Education in Social Work: Contemporary Issues and Trends,* 149–154. Dubuque, IA: Kendall/Hunt.

Gardiner, D. (1989). *The Anatomy of Supervision.* Philadelphia: Open University Press.

Gelfand, B., Rohrich, S., Nevidon, P., and Starak, I. (1975). An andragogical application to the training of social workers. *Journal of Education for Social Work* 11 (3): 55–61.

George, A. (1982). A history of social work field instruction: Apprenticeship to instruction. In B. W. Sheafor and L. E. Jenkins (Eds.), *Quality Field Instruction in Social Work: Program Development and Maintenance,* 37–59. New York: Longman.

Gitterman, A. (1989). Field instruction in social work education: Issues, tasks and skills. *The Clinical Supervisor* 7 (4): 77–91.

Gizynski, M. (1978). Self-awareness of the supervisor in supervision. *Clinical Social Work Journal* 6:202–210.

Gladstein, M. and Mailick, M. (1986). An affirmative action approach to ethnic diversity in field work. *Journal of Social Work Education* 22 (1): 41–49.

Glassman, U. (1995). Special issues in the education of field instructors. In G. Rogers (Ed.), *Social Work Field Education Views and Visions,* 185–196. Dubuque, IA: Kendall/Hunt.

Glassman, U. and Kates, L. (1988). Strategies for group work field instruction. *Social Work with Groups* 11 (1/2): 111–124.

Gordon, M. S. (1982). Responsibilities of the school: Maintenance of the field program. In B. W. Sheafor and L. E. Jenkins (Eds.), *Quality Field Instruction in Social Work: Program Development and Maintenance*, 116–135. New York: Longman.

Gordon, W. E. and Gordon, M. S. (1989). George Warren Brown's field instruction research project: An experimental design tested by empirical data. In M. S. Raskin (Ed.), *Empirical Studies in Field Instruction*, 15–28. New York: Haworth Press.

Gray, S. W., Alperin, D. E., and Wik, R. (1989). Multidimensional expectations of student supervision in social work. *The Clinical Supervisor* 7 (1): 89–102.

Grossman, B. (1980). Teaching research in the field practicum. *Social Work* 25 (1): 36–39.

Grossman, B. and Barth, R. P. (1991). Evaluating a delayed-entry model of first-year field work. In D. Schneck, B. Grossman, and U. Glassman (Eds.), *Field Education in Social Work: Contemporary Issues and Trends*, 131–140. Dubuque, IA: Kendall/Hunt.

Grossman, B., Levine-Jordano, N., and Shearer, P. (1990). Working with students' emotional reactions in the field: An educational framework. *The Clinical Supervisor* 8 (1): 23–39.

Hagen, B. (1989). The practicum instructor: A study of role expectations. In M. S. Raskin (Ed.), *Empirical Studies in Field Instruction*, 219–236. New York: Haworth Press.

Hale, M. P. (1969). Innovations in field learning and teaching. In B. L. Jones (Ed.), *Current Patterns in Field Instruction in Graduate Social Work Education*. New York: Council on Social Work Education.

Haley, J. (1976). *Problem-Solving Therapy: New Strategies for Effective Family Therapy*. San Francisco: Jossey-Bass.

Halgin, R. P. (1985/1986). Pragmatic blending of clinical models in the supervisory relationship. *The Clinical Supervisor* 3 (4): 23–46.

Hamilton, N. and Else, J. F. (1983). *Designing Field Education: Philosophy, Structure, and Process*. Springfield, IL: Charles C. Thomas.

Hartman, C. and Wills, R. M. (1991). The gatekeeper role in social work: A survey. In D. Schneck, B. Grossman, and U. Glassman (Eds.), *Field Education in Social Work: Contemporary Issues and Trends*, 310–319. Dubuque, IA: Kendall/Hunt.

Hartman, W. R. (1990). *The effect of evaluation on learning in graduate social work direct practice field instruction*. Ph.D. diss., Rutgers, The State University of New Jersey, New Brunswick.

Hawthorne, L. (1975). Games supervisors play. *Social Work* 29 (3): 179–183.

Henry, C. St. G. (1975). An examination of field work models at Adelphi University School of Social Work. *Journal of Education for Social Work* 11 (3): 62–68.

Hepworth, D. H. and Larsen, J. (1990). *Direct Social Work Practice: Theory and Skills*. Belmont, CA: Wadsworth.

Hess, A. (1986). Growth in supervision: Stages of supervision and supervisee development. *The Clinical Supervisor* 4 (1–2): 51–67.

Holtzman, R. F. (1994). Letter to the editor. *The Clinical Supervisor* 12 (2): 143–149.

Jacobs, C. (1991). Violations of the supervisory relationship: An ethical and educational blind spot. *Social Work* 36 (2): 130–135.

Jenkins, L. E., and Sheafor, B. W. (1982). An overview of social work field instruction. In B. W. Sheafor and L. E. Jenkins (Eds.), *Quality Field Instruction in Social Work: Program Development and Maintenance*, 3–20. New York: Longman.

Johnston, N., Rooney, R., and Reitmeir, M. A. (1991). Sharing power: Student feedback to field supervisors. In D. Schneck, B. Grossman, and U. Glassman (Eds.), *Field Education in Social Work: Contemporary Issues and Trends*, 198–204. Dubuque, IA: Kendall/Hunt.

Judah, E. H. (1982). Responsibilities of the student in field instruction. In B. W. Sheafor and L. E. Jenkins (Eds.), *Quality Field Instruction in Social Work: Program Development and Maintenance*. New York: Longman.

Kadushin, A. E. (1992). *Supervision in Social Work*. New York: Columbia University Press.

———. (1991). Introduction—Field education in social work: Contemporary issues and trends. In D. Schneck, B. Grossman, and U. Glassman (Eds.), *Field Education in Social Work: Contemporary Issues and Trends*, 11–12. Dubuque, IA: Kendall/Hunt.

———. (1974). Supervisor-supervisee: A survey. *Social Work* 19:288–298.

———. (1968). Games people play in supervision. *Social Work* 13 (3): 23–32.

Kagan, N. and Kagan, H. (1990). IPR—A validated model for the 1990s and beyond. *The Counseling Psychologist* 18 (3): 436–440.

Kahn, E. M. (1979). The parallel process in social work treatment and supervision. *Social Casework* 60 (9): 520–528.

Kaiser, T. L. (1997). *Supervisory Relationships: Exploring the Human Element*. Pacific Grove, CA: Brooks/Cole.

Kanter, J. S. (1983). Reevaluation of task-centered social work practice. *Clinical Social Work Journal* 11 (3): 228–244.

Kaplan, T. (1991). A model for group supervision for social work: Implications for the profession. In D. Schneck, B. Grossman, and U. Glassman (Eds.), *Field Education in Social Work: Contemporary Issues and Trends*, 141–148. Dubuque, IA: Kendall/Hunt.

———. (1988). Group field instruction: Rationale and practical application. *Social Work with Groups* 11 (1/2): 125–143.

Kerr, M. E. and Bowen, M. (1988). *Family Evaluation: An Approach Based on Bowen Theory*. New York: Norton.

Kerson, T. S. (1994). Introduction: Field instruction in social work settings: A framework for teaching. *Clinical Supervisor* 12 (1): 1–31.

Kilpatrick, A. C. (1991). Differences and commonalities in BSW and MSW field instruction: In search of continuity. In D. Schneck, B. Grossman, and U. Glassman (Eds.), *Field Education in Social Work: Contemporary Issues and Trends*, 167–176. Dubuque, IA: Kendall/Hunt.

Kilpatrick, A. C., Turner, J. B., and Holland, T. P. (1994). Quality control in field education: Monitoring student performance. *Journal of Teaching in Social Work* 9 (1/2): 107–120.

Kirst-Ashman, K. K. and Hull Jr., G. H. (1999). *Understanding Generalist Practice*. Chicago: Nelson-Hall.

Kissman, K. and Tran, T. V. (1990). Perceived quality of field placement education among graduate social work students. *Journal of Continuing Social Work Education* 5 (2): 27–30.

Knappe, M. E. (1975). The training center concept: Educating social workers for a changing world. In Council on Social Work Education (Ed.), *The Dynamics of Field Instruction: Learning Through Doing*. New York: Council on Social Work Education.

Knight, C. (1996). A study of MSW and BSW students' perceptions of their field instructors. *Journal of Social Work Education* 32 (3): 399–414.

Knowles, M. S. (1972). Innovations in teaching styles and approaches based upon adult learning. *Journal of Education for Social Work* 8 (2): 32–39.

———. (1970). *The Modern Practice of Adult Education*. New York: Association Press.

Koerin, B. B., Harrigan, M. P., and Reeves, J. W. (1990). Facilitating the transition from student to social worker: Challenges of the younger student. *Journal of Social Work Education* 2:199–207.

Kolb, D. (1984). *Experiential Learning: Experience as the Source of Learning and Development*. Englewood Cliffs, NJ: Prentice-Hall.

Kolb, D. A. (1985). *The Learning Style Inventory*. Boston: McBer and Co.

Kramer, B. J. and Wrenn, R. (1994). The blending of andragogical and pedagogical teaching methods in advanced social work practice courses. *Journal of Teaching in Social Work* 10 (1/2): 43–64.

Lambert, M. J. (1992). Implications of outcome research for psychotherapy integration. In J. C. Norcross and M. R. Goldfried (Eds.), *Handbook of Psychotherapy Integration*, 251–276. New York: Basic Books.

Lammert, M. H. and Hagen, J. (1975). A model for community-oriented field experience. In Council on Social Work Education (Ed.), *The Dynamics of Field Instruction: Learning Through Doing*. New York: Council on Social Work Education.

Larsen, J. (1980). Competency-based and task-centered practicum instruction. *Journal of Education for Social Work* 16 (1): 87–94.

Larsen, J. and Hepworth, D. H. (1982). Enhancing the effectiveness of practicum instruction: An empirical study. *Journal of Education for Social Work* 18 (2): 50–58.

Latting, J. L. (1992). Giving corrective feedback: A decisional analysis. *Social Work* 37 (5): 424–430.

Laughlin, S. G. (1978). *Use of self-instruction in teaching empathic responding to social work students.* Ph.D. diss., Universtiy of California, Berkeley.

Lazzari, M. M. (1991). Feminism, empowerment, and field education. *Affilia* 6 (4): 71-87.

Lemberger, J. and Marshack, E. F. (1991). Educational assessment in the field: An opportunity for teacher-learner mutuality. In D. Schneck, B. Grossman, and U. Glassman (Eds.), *Field Education in Social Work: Contemporary Issues and Trends,* 187–197. Dubuque, IA: Kendall/Hunt.

Livingston, D., Davidson, K. W., and Marshack, E. F. (1989). Education for autonomous practice: A challenge for field instructors. *Journal of Independent Social Work* 4 (1): 69–82.

Lowy, L. (1983). Social work supervision: From models toward theory. *Journal of Education for Social Work* 19 (2): 55–62.

Lynch, V. J. (1987). Supervising the trainee who treats the chronically suicidal outpatient: Theoretical perspectives and practice approaches. *The Clinical Supervisor* 5 (1): 99–110.

MacLean, M. (1986). The neurolinguistic programming model. In F. J. Turner (Ed.), *Social Work Treatment: Interlocking Theoretical Approaches,* 341–374. New York: Free Press.

Malan, D. H. (1979). *Individual Psychotherapy and the Science of Psychodynamics.* London: Butterworth.

Manis, F. (1979). *Openness in Social Work Field Instruction: Stance and Form Guidelines.* Goleta, CA: Kimberly Press.

Manoleas, P. and Carrillo, E. (1991). A culturally syntonic approach to the field education of Latino students. *Journal of Social Work Education* 27 (2): 135–144.

Marshack, E. F. (1986). Task supervision: A quiet revolution in field teaching of MSW students. *Arete* 11:45–50.

Marshack, E. F. and Glassman, U. (1991). Innovative models for field instruction: Departing from traditional methods. In D. Schneck, B. Grossman, and U. Glassman (Eds.), *Field Education in Social Work: Contemporary Issues and Trends,* 84–95. Dubuque, IA: Kendall/Hunt.

Martin, M. L. and Alper, S. (1989). Mutual responsibility in supervision: A student workshop. *Arete* 14 (q): 52–56.

Marziali, E. and Alexander, L. (1991). The power of the therapeutic relationship. *American Journal of Orthopsychiatry* 61 (3): 383–391.

Matorin, S. (1979). Dimensions of student supervision: A point of view. *Social Case-work* 60 (3): 150–156.

May, L. I. and Kilpatrick, A. C. (1989). Stress of self-awareness in clinical practice: Are students prepared? *The Clinical Supervisor* 6 (3/4): 303–313.

Mayers, F. (1970). Differential use of group teaching in first-year field work. *Social Service Review* 44 (1): 63–74.

McClelland, R. W. (1991). Innovation in field education. In D. Schneck, B. Grossman, and U. Glassman (Eds.), *Field Education in Social Work: Contemporary Issues and Trends,* 177–184. Dubuque, IA: Kendall/Hunt.

McCroy, R. G., Freeman, E. M., and Logan, S. (1986). Strategies for teaching students about termination. *The Clinical Supervisor* 4 (4): 45–56.

McCroy, R. G., Freeman, E. M., Logan, S., and Blackmon, B. (1986a). Cross-cultural field supervision: Implications for social work education. *Journal of Social Work Education* 22 (1): 50–56.

Minuchin, S. (1974). *Families and Family Therapy.* Cambridge: Harvard University Press.

Minuchin, S. and Fishman, C. (1981). *Family Therapy Techniques.* Cambridge: Harvard University Press.

Minuchin, S. and Nichols, M. (1993). *Family Healing: Tales of Hope and Renewal from Family Therapy.* New York: Touchstone.

Mishne, J. (1983). Narcissistic vulnerability of the younger student: The need for non-confrontive empathic supervision. *The Clinical Supervisor* 1 (2): 3–12.

Mokuau, N. and Ewalt, P. L. (1993). School-agency collaboration: Enriching teaching, scholarship, and service in state hospital placements. *Journal of Social Work Education* 29 (3): 328–337.

Moore, L. S. and Urwin, C. A. (1991). Gatekeeping: A model for screening baccalaureate students for field education. *Journal of Social Work Education* 27 (1): 8–18.

Munson, C. E. (1993). *Clinical Social Work Supervision.* New York: Haworth Press.

——. (1989). Editorial: Trends of significance for clinical supervision. *The Clinical Supervisor* 7 (4): 1–8.

——. (1987). Field instruction in social work education. *Journal of Teaching in Social Work* 1 (1): 91–109.

——. (1984). Stress among graduate social work students: An empirical study. *Journal of Education for Social Work* 20 (3): 20–29.

Neugeboren, B. (1988). Field practica in social work administration: Tasks, auspices, selection criteria and outcomes. *Journal of Social Work Education* 24 (2): 151–158.

——. (1971). Developing specialized programs in social work administration in the master's degree program: Field practice component. *Journal of Education for Social Work* 7 (3): 35–47.

Nisivoccia, D. (1990). Teaching and learning tasks in the beginning phase of field instruction. *The Clinical Supervisor* 8 (1): 7–21.

Norberg, W. and Schneck, D. (1991). A dual matrix structure for field education. In D.Schneck, B. Grossman, and U. Glassman (Eds.), *Field Education in Social Work: Contemporary Issues and Trends*, 96–121. Dubuque, IA: Kendall/Hunt.

Norman, J. S. (1987). Forum: Supervision: The affective process. *Social Casework* (June):374–379.

Nunnally, E. W. (1993). Solution-focused treatment. In R. A.Wells and V. J. Giannetti (Eds.), *Casebook of the Brief Psychotherapies*, 288–300. New York: Plenum.

Parihar, B. (1984). *Task-Centered Management in Human Services*. Springfield, IL: Charles C. Thomas.

Patti, R. J. (1980). Field education at the crossroads: Exploring alternatives for administration practica. *Administration in Social Work* 4 (2): 61–104.

Payne, M. (1991). *Modern Social Work Theory: A Critical Introduction*. Chicago: Lyceum.

Pettes, D. E. (1979). *Staff and Student Supervision: A Task-Centred Approach*. London: George Allen and Unwin.

Pilcher, A. J. (1982). The development of field instruction objectives. In B. W. Sheafor and L. E. Jenkins (Eds.), *Quality Field Instruction in Social Work: Program Development and Maintenance*, 63–75. New York: Longman.

Pilcher, A. J. and Shamley, D. A. F. (1986). Practice-research unit: A fieldwork model at La Trobe University in Melbourne, Australia. *Australian Social Work* 39 (3): 29–35.

Rabin, C. (1985). Matching the research seminar to meet practice needs: A method for integrating research and practice. *Journal for Education for Social Work* 21 (1): 5–19.

Rabin, C., Savaya, R., and Frank, P. (1994). A joint university-field agency: Toward the integration of classroom and practicum. *Journal of Social Work Education* 30 (1): 107.

Raschick, M., Maypole, D. E., and Day, P. A. (1998). Improving field education through Kolb learning theory. *Journal of Social Work Education* 34 (1): 31–42.

Raskin, M. (1982). Factors associated with student satisfaction in undergraduate social work field placements. *Arete* 7 (1): 44–54.

Raskin, M. S. (1994). The Delphi study in field instruction revisited: Expert consensus on issues and research priorities. *Journal of Social Work Education* 30 (1): 75–89.

———. (1989a). Introduction. In M. S. Raskin (Ed.), *Empirical Studies in Field Instruction*, 1–13. New York: Haworth Press.

———. (1989b). Adelphi study in field instruction: Identification of issues and research priorities by experts. In M. S. Raskin (Ed.), *Empirical Studies in Field Instruction*, 29–46. New York: Haworth Press.

——. (1989c). Factors associated with student satisfaction in undergraduate social work field placements. In M. S. Raskin (Ed.), *Empirical Studies in Field Instruction*, 321–331. New York: Haworth Press.

Raskin, M. S., ed. (1989). *Empirical Studies in Field Instruction*. New York: Haworth Press.

Real, T. (1990). The therapeutic use of self in constructivist/systemic therapy. *Family Process* 29:255–272.

Reid, W. J. (1997). Research on task-centered practice. *Social Work Research* 21 (3):132–137.

——. (1992). *Task Strategies: An Empirical Approach to Clinical Social Work*. New York: Columbia University Press.

——. (1986). Task-centered social work practice. In F. J. Turner (Ed.), *Social Work Treatment: Interlocking Theoretical Approaches*, 267–295. New York: Free Press.

——. (1984). Towards a generic model. In B. Parihar, *Task-Centered Management in Human Services*. Springfield, IL: Charles C. Thomas.

——. (1978). *The Task-Centered System*. New York: Columbia University Press.

Reid, W. J. and Epstein, L. (1972). *Task-Centered Casework*. New York: Columbia University Press.

Reynolds, B. (1942). *Learning and Teaching in the Practice of Social Work*. New York: Farrar and Rinehart.

Rhodes, S. L. (1986). Family treatment. In F. J. Turner (Ed.), *Social Work Treatment: Interlocking Theoretical Approaches*, 432–453. New York: Free Press.

Rich, P. (1993). The form, function, and content of clinical supervision: An integrated model. *The Clinical Supervisor* 11 (1): 137–178.

Rogers, G. and MacDonald, P. L. (1992). Thinking critically: An approach to field instructor training. *Journal of Social Work Education* 28 (2): 166–177.

Rompf, E. L., Royse, D., and Dhooper, S. S. (1993). Anxiety preceding field work: What students worry about. *Journal of Teaching in Social Work* 7 (2): 81–95.

Rosenblatt, A. and Mayer, J. E. (1975). Objectionable supervisory styles: Students' views. *Social Work* 20 (3): 184–189.

Rosenfeld, D. J. (1989). Field instructor turnover. In M. S. Raskin (Ed.), *Empirical Studies in Field Instruction*, 187–218. New York: Haworth Press.

Rothholz, T. and Werk, A. (1984). Student supervision: An educational process. *The Clinical Supervisor* 2 (1): 14–27.

Rothman, J. and Jones, W. C. (1971). *A New Look at Field Instruction: Education forApplication of Practice Skills in Community Organization and Social Planning*. New York: Association Press.

Rothman, J. and Thomas, E. J., eds. (1994). *Intervention Research: Design and Development for Human Service*. New York: Haworth Press.

Saari, C. (1989). The process of learning in clinical social work. *Smith College Studies in Social Work* 60 (1): 35–49.

Satir, V. (1987). The therapist story. *Journal of Psychotherapy and the Family* 3 (1): 17–25.

Schmidt, D. M. (1976). The development of self-awareness in first-year social work students. *Smith College Studies in Social Work* 46:218–235.

Schneck, D. (1991a). Part I: Conceptual foundations for field education. In D. Schneck, B. Grossman, and U. Glassman (Eds.), *Field Education in Social Work: Contemporary Issues and Trends*, 13–16. Dubuque, IA: Kendall/Hunt.

——. (1991b). Integration of learning in field education: Elusive goal and educational imperative. In D. Schneck, B. Grossman, and U. Glassman (Eds.), *Field Education in Social Work: Contemporary Issues and Trends*, 67–77. Dubuque, IA: Kendall/Hunt.

——. (1991c). Ideal and reality in field education. In D. Schneck, B. Grossman, and U. Glassman (Eds.), *Field Education in Social Work: Contemporary Issues and Trends*, 17–35. Dubuque, IA: Kendall/Hunt.

Schneck, D., Grossman, B., and Glassman, U. (Eds.). (1991). *Field Education in SocialWork Contemporary Issues and Trends*. Dubuque, IA: Kendall/Hunt.

Selig, A. L. (1982). Responsibilities of the field instruction agency. In B. W. Sheafor and L. E. Jenkins (Eds.), *Quality Field Instruction in Social Work: Program Development and Maintenance*. New York: Longman.

Serok, S. and Urda, L. V. (1987). Supervision in social work from a Gestalt perspective. *The Clinical Supervisor* 5 (2): 69–85.

Shafer, C. (1982). The methods of field instruction. In B. W. Sheafor and L. E. Jenkins (Eds.), *Quality Field Instruction in Social Work: Program Development and Maintenance*. New York: Longman.

Shapiro, C. H. (1989). Burnout in social work field instructors. In M. S. Raskin (Ed.), *Empirical Studies in Field Instruction*, 237–348. New York: Haworth Press.

Shatz, E. O. (1989). Preface. In M. S. Raskin (Ed.), *Empirical Studies in Field Instruction*. New York: Haworth Press.

Sheafor, B. W. and Jenkins, L. E., eds. (1982). *Quality Field Instruction in Social Work: Program Development and Maintenance*. New York: Longman.

Showers, N. (1988). *Factors associated with graduate social work student satisfaction in hospital field education programs*. Ph.D. diss., City University of NewYork.

Shulman, L. (1994). *Teaching the Helping Skills: A Field Instructor's Guide*. Alexandria, VA: Council on Social Work Education.

——. (1993). *Interactional Supervision*. Washington, DC: NASW Press.

Siddle, S. and Wilson, J. (1984). Mapping murky waters: Describing content and techniques in student supervision. *Australian Social Work* 37 (1): 6–12.

Siporin, M. (1982). The process of field instruction. In B. W. Sheafor and L. E. Jenkins (Eds.), *Quality Field Instruction in Social Work: Program Development and Maintenance*, 175–197. New York: Longman.

Skolnik, L. (1985). *Final Report: Field Education Project*. Washington, DC: Council on Social Work Education.

Smith, N. J. (1981). Fieldwork education: Substance or myth. *Contemporary Social Work Education* 4 (1): 21–29.

Sowers-Hoag, K. M. and Harrison, D. F. (1991). Women in social work education: Progress or promise? *Journal of Social Work Education* 27 (3): 320–328.

St. John, D. (1975). Goal-directed supervision of social work students in field placement. *Journal of Education for Social Work* 11 (3): 89–94.

Star, B. (1979). Exploring the boundaries of videotape self-confrontation. *Journal of Education for Social Work* 15 (1): 87–94.

Storm, C. L. and Heath, A. W. (1985). Models of supervision: Using therapy theory as a guide. *Clinical Supervisor* 3 (1): 87–96.

Strean, H. S. (1986). Psychoanalytic theory. In F. J. Turner (Ed.), *Social Work Treatment: Interlocking Theoretical Approaches*, 19–45. New York: Free Press.

Strom, K. (1991). Should field instructors be social workers? *Journal of Social Work Education* 27 (2): 187–195.

Stuyvesant, R. (1980). *Study of an integrative teaching approach in social work education*. Unpublished master's thesis, University of Utah, Salt Lake City.

Sweitzer, H. F. and King, M. A. (1999). *The Successful Internship: Transformation and Empowerment*. Pacific Grove, CA: Brooks/Cole.

Tendler, D. and Metzger, K. (1978). Training in prevention: An educational model for social work students. *Social Work in Health Care* 4:221–231.

Thomlison, B., Rodgers, G., Collins, D., and Grinnell, R. M. (1996). *The Social Work Practicum: An Access Guide*. Itasca, IL: F. E. Peacock.

Tolson, E. R. (1987). The systemic skill training model. *The Clinical Supervisor* 5 (4): 5–18.

Tolson, E. R. and Kopp, J. (1988). The practicum: Clients, problems, interventions and influences on student practice. *Journal of Social Work Education* 24 (2): 123–134.

Tolson, E. R., Reid, W. J., and Garvin, C. D. (1994). *Generalist Practice*. New York: Columbia University Press.

Turner, F. J., ed. (1996). *Social Work Treatment: Interlocking Theoretical Approaches*. 4th ed. New York: Free Press.

——, ed. (1986). *Social Work Treatment: Interlocking Theoretical Approaches*. 3rd ed. New York: Free Press.

Van Soest, D. and Kruzich, J. (1994). The influence of learning styles on student and field instructor perceptions of field placement success. *Journal of Teaching in Social Work* 9 (1/2): 49–69.

Vayda, E. and Bogo, M. (1991). A teaching model to unite classroom and field. *Journal of Social Work Education* 27 (3): 271–278.

Vonk, E. and Thyer, B. (1996). Evaluating the quality of supervision: A review of instruments for use in field instruction. Paper presented at the 42nd

Annual Program Meeting of the Council on Social Work Education, Washington, DC.

Walden, T. and Brown, L. N. (1985). The integration seminar: A vehicle for joining theory and practice. *Journal of Education for Social Work* 21 (1): 13–19.

Wall, J. C. (1994). Teaching termination to trainees through parallel processes in supervision. *The Clinical Supervisor* 12 (2): 27–37.

Walther, V. N. and Mason, J. (1994). Social work field instruction in a perinatal AIDS setting. *The Clinical Supervisor* 12 (1): 33–52.

Watson, K. W. (1973). Differential supervision. *Social Work* 18 (3):80–88.

Webb, N. B. (1988). The role of the field instructor in the socialization of students. *Social Casework* 69 (1): 35–40.

——. (1983). Developing competent clinical practitioners: A model with guidelines for supervisors. *The Clinical Supervisor* 1 (4): 41–51.

Wijnberg, M. and Schwartz, M. (1977). Models of student supervision: The apprentice, growth and role systems models. *Journal of Education for Social Work* 13 (3):107–113.

Wilson, S. (1981). *Field Instruction: Techniques for Supervisors.* New York: Free Press.

Wodarski, J. S., Feit, M. D., and Green, R. K. (1995). Graduate social work education: A review of two decades of empirical research and considerations for the future. *Social Service Review* (March):108–130.

Zayas, L. H. (1989). Data collection in child assessment: Approaches to student supervision. *The Clinical Supervisor* 7 (1): 75–88.

Zimmerman, N., Collins, L. E., and Bach, J. M. (1986). Ordinal position, cognitive style, and competence: A systemic approach to supervision. *The Clinical Supervisor* 4 (3): 7–23.

Name Index

Abramson, J. S., 38, 45, 50, 65, 82, 92, 95, 97, 98, 127, 131, 137, 143, 153, 158, 204, 217
Akin, G., 132
Alexander, L., 130
Alper, S., 101, 104, 120, 127, 134, 154, 195
Alperin, D. E., 37, 43, 82
American Psychiatric Association, 297
Aponte, H. J., 128, 129
Arlow, J. A., 85
Atwood, J. D., 65, 67, 104, 154, 285

Bach, J. M., 52
Baker, D. R., 65, 92, 98, 204
Baldwin, M., 130, 216
Barth, R. P., 41
Basso, R. V. J., 53, 58, 82, 174
Becherman, A., 131
Beless, D.W., 85, 127, 170
Benavides, E., 51
Berengarten, S., 136
Berkun, C., 5–12
Bernard, J. M., 150
Blake, R., 139

Bogo, M., 32, 34, 36, 41, 43, 45, 47, 48, 51, 80, 83, 84, 87, 95– 97, 99, 101, 103, 126–128, 131–133, 136, 153, 170, 175, 178–179, 214, 218, 247
Borecki, M.C., 42
Bourne, I., 81
Bowen, M., 143
Brannon, D., 34, 48
Brown, A., 81, 83, 246
Bruck, M., 134, 179
Burrell, L., 131

Carrillo, E., 51
Carroll, D., 45
Caspi, J., 2, 37, 54, 59, 65, 67, 84, 150, 173, 204, 292
Catalano, S. J., 51, 135
Chambers, D. E., 179
Clancy, C., 34, 47, 48
Collins, D., 175
Collins, L. E., 34, 41, 51, 52, 87
Conklin, J. J., 42
Cramer, E. P., 50, 74, 75, 204
Curiel, H., 44, 135, 137, 143

Davenport, J., 34, 73, 74, 81
Davenport, J. A., 34, 73, 74, 81
Davidson, K. W., 303
Dawson, B.G., 45, 87, 256
Dea, K. L., 43, 46, 131, 215, 243
DeJong, C. R., 40, 84
De Shazer, S., 243
Dewey, J., 48, 74
Dhooper, S. S., 93
Dore, M. M., 34, 43, 50, 75, 102, 181, 280
Dorfman, R. A., 36
Dunn, R., 80

Eisikovits, Z., 36, 48
Elliot, R., 150, 175
Ellison, M. L., 35, 50, 65, 97, 98, 127, 128, 131, 133, 176, 204
Else, J. F., 43, 51, 75, 139
Epstein, B. N., 353–362
Epstein, L., 43, 53, 76
Ewalt, P. L., 45

Feathers, C., 92–104
Feit, M. D., 34, 217
Fellin, P. A., 132
Fishman, C., 129, 216
Fortune, A. E., 33, 37, 40, 43, 46, 50, 65, 82, 92, 95, 98, 127, 131, 135, 137, 143, 153, 157, 175, 204, 217
Fox, R., 34, 50, 51, 75–78, 80, 81, 127, 131, 154, 158, 170, 180, 195, 243
Frank, J. B., 130
Frank, P., 41, 51, 130
Freeman, E. M., 45, 51, 58, 59, 61, 84, 127, 128, 131, 153, 170, 180, 283

Galassi, J. P., 152
Galm, S., 143
Gantt, A., 45
Gardiner, D., 80
Garvin, C. D., 294

Gelfand, B., 34, 48
George, A., 31, 34, 180, 197
Gitterman, A., 96, 131, 133, 136, 179, 205, 217, 219, 243
Gizynski, M., 35, 104, 127, 130
Gladstein, M., 51
Glassman, U., 34, 39, 45, 48, 144, 149, 175, 201
Gordon, M. S., 41, 142
Gray, S. W., 43
Green, R. K., 34, 217
Grist, M., 43, 46, 131, 215, 243
Grossman, B., 41, 45, 51, 134
Guild, P., 80, 81
Guttman, E., 36, 48

Hagen, B., 124, 132
Hagen, J., 41, 42, 45, 84, 175
Hale, M. P., 35, 40
Haley, J., 52, 85, 105, 243
Halgin, R. P., 53
Hamilton, N., 43, 51, 75, 139
Hansen, F. C., 84, 127, 128
Harrigan, M. P., 127, 132, 170
Harrison, D. F., 74
Hartman, C., 161
Hartman, W. R., 161, 180
Hawthorne, L., 95, 99, 102, 121, 122, 139, 179, 194, 200, 210
Heath, A. W., 52, 85, 105, 142, 243
Henry, C. St. G., 39, 42, 201
Hepworth, D. H., 37, 49, 53, 57, 58, 65, 76, 174, 179
Herrerias, C., 43
Hess, A., 87, 88, 105
Holland, T. P., 40
Holtzman, R. F., 138, 144, 153
Hull Jr., G. H., 290

Jacobs, C., 75, 139
Jenkins, L. E., 32–35, 83, 84, 131, 144, 177, 243

Johnston, N., 75, 92, 98, 139
Jones, W. C., 39, 45
Judah, E. H., 43, 45, 99, 101, 119, 134,
    183, 243

Kadushin, A. E., 2, 3, 35, 51, 57, 59, 61,
    62, 65, 67, 71, 72, 80, 81, 85, 87, 92,
    95, 97–99, 106, 120–122, 127, 133,
    134, 136, 140, 142, 143, 158, 160,
    178, 183, 184, 194, 198, 200, 210,
    224, 283
Kagan, H., 150
Kagan, N., 150
Kahn, E. M., 52, 85, 86, 105, 109, 122,
    125, 142, 170, 179
Kaiser, T. L., 59, 76, 80, 95, 117, 138
Kanter, J. S., 173
Kaplan, T., 37, 41, 53, 155, 179, 201
Kates, L., 45
Kerr, M. E., 143
Kerson, T. S., 87, 90, 99, 104, 127, 128,
    130, 131, 134, 138, 142, 154, 170,
    178, 179, 216
Kilpatrick, A. C., 17, 33, 40, 43, 44, 134
King, M. A., 80, 138, 285
Kirst, Ashman, K. K., 290
Kissman, K., 157
Knappe, M. E., 42, 48
Knight, C., 204
Knowles, M. S., 34, 47, 73, 74, 79, 139,
    178, 217
Koerin, B. B., 127, 132, 170, 179
Kolb, D., 48, 74, 80, 81
Kopp, J., 34, 35, 41, 51, 84, 95, 126,
    127
Kramer, B. J., 47, 50, 205
Kruzich, J., 80, 81

Lambert, M. J., 130
Lammert, M. H., 41, 42, 45, 84, 175
Larsen, J., 37, 43, 48, 49, 53, 57, 58, 65,
    76, 174, 175, 179, 292

Latting, J. L., 51, 59, 61, 67, 73
Laughlin, S. G., 45
Lazzari, M. M., 34, 50, 51, 75, 76, 102,
    139
Lemberger, J., 177, 214, 224
Levine-Jordano, N., 51, 134
Livingston, D., 303
Lowy, L., 46, 48, 95, 178, 181
Lynch, V. J., 45, 51

MacDonald, P. L., 136, 146, 147, 153
MacLean, M., 129
Mailick, M., 51
Malan, D. H., 291, 294
Manis, F., 34, 47–49, 75, 95, 97, 131,
    133, 179
Marshack, E. F., 34, 39, 41, 42, 48, 144,
    175, 177, 201, 214, 224
Martin, M. L., 101, 104, 120, 127, 134,
    154, 195
Marziali, E., 130
Mason, J., 87, 128
Matorin, S., 56, 93, 105, 109, 131, 133,
    136, 146, 179, 190
May, L. I., 134
Mayer, J. E., 98
Mayers, F., 33, 41, 92, 105, 134, 138,
    142
McCarthy, M., 204
McClelland, R. W., 40
McCroy, R.G., 45
McCuan, P., 45
Metzger, K., 45
Minuchin, S., 129, 216, 243
Mishne, J., 52
Mokuau, N., 45
Moore, L. S., 131, 161
Munson, C. E., 44, 59, 65, 67, 75, 84,
    102, 105, 118, 123, 127, 130, 131,
    134, 137, 149, 166, 183, 194, 195,
    268, 286
Myli, R., 43, 46, 131, 215, 243

Neugeboren, B., 45, 243
Nichols, M., 129
Nisivoccia, D., 95, 97, 131, 136, 179, 243
Norberg, W., 42, 175
Norman, J. S., 52, 65, 67, 93, 95, 97, 98, 105, 142, 179
Nunnally, E. W., 234, 269, 291

Parihar, B., 41, 53
Patti, R. J., 45
Payne, M., 128
Peterman, P. J., 139
Pettes, D. E., 48, 49, 134, 139, 243
Pilcher, A. J., 42, 46, 175
Power, R., 34, 84, 95, 127, 132, 153

Rabin, C., 34, 41, 45, 51
Raschick, M., 48
Raskin, M. S., 34–37, 39, 82, 84, 131, 143, 144, 158, 176, 214, 234, 246, 247
Real, T., 129
Reeves, J. W., 127, 132, 170
Reid, W. J., 2, 49, 52, 53, 57, 76, 84, 105, 142, 173, 174, 176, 178, 181, 204, 233, 243, 252, 292, 294
Reitmeir, M. A., 75, 92, 98, 139
Reynolds, B., 87, 90
Rhodes, S. L., 129
Rich, P., 36, 142
Rodgers, G., 136, 146, 147, 153
Rompf, E. L., 93, 180
Rooney, R., 75, 92, 98, 139
Rosenblatt, A., 33, 92, 98, 105, 134, 138, 142
Rosenfeld, D. J., 124, 132, 142
Rosenthal, J. A., 44, 135, 137, 143
Rothholz, T., 36, 38, 59, 135, 136, 139, 143, 158
Rothman, J., 35, 38, 39, 45, 173
Royse, D., 93

Saari, C., 37, 87
Satir, V., 130
Savaya, R., 41, 51
Schmidt, D. M., 104, 127, 145, 154
Schneck, D., 32, 36, 40, 42, 46, 48, 49, 143, 175
Schwartz, M., 33, 34, 48, 133, 180
Selig, A. L., 91, 133, 243
Serok, S., 52
Shafer, C., 32, 33, 35, 39, 41, 42
Shamley, D. A. F., 45, 175
Shapiro, C. H., 124, 132, 135
Shatz, E. O., 35–37, 144, 176
Sheafor, B.W., 32, 34, 83, 84, 131, 144, 176, 243
Shearer, P., 51, 135
Showers, N., 82
Shulman, L., 48, 52, 59, 63, 65, 67, 76, 79, 86, 87, 91, 105, 122, 125, 127, 130–132, 142, 143, 153, 158, 159, 164, 167, 168, 170, 179, 185, 189, 195, 286, 293
Siddle, S., 65, 92, 98, 136
Siporin, M., 46, 95, 97, 179, 243
Skolnik, L., 143, 144
Smith, N. J., 35, 65, 92, 98
Smith, S. L., 204
Sowers-Hoag, K. M., 74
Spano, R., 179
St. John, D., 48
Star, B., 149
Storm, C. L., 52, 85, 105, 142, 243
Strean, H. S., 129
Strom, K., 59, 132, 143, 158
Stuyvesant, R., 53, 174
Sweitzer, H. F., 80, 138, 285

Taylor, I., 45
Tendler, D., 45
Thomas, E. J., 173
Thomlison, B., 77, 161
Thyer, B., 151, 166

Tolson, E. R., 34, 35, 41, 51, 53, 84, 95,
    126, 294
Tran, T. V., 157
Trent, P. J., 152
Turner, F. J., 36
Turner, J. B., 36, 40

Urda, L. V., 52
Urwin, C. A., 131, 161

Van Soest, D., 80, 81
Vayda, E., 32, 34, 36, 47, 51, 80, 83, 84,
    131, 133, 136, 214, 247
Velasquez, J., 51
Vonk, E., 151, 166

Walden, T., 83, 246
Wall, J. C., 86, 170
Walther, V. N., 87, 128
Watson, K. W., 39

Webb, N. B., 33, 37, 48, 49, 53, 96, 97,
    104, 120, 127, 129, 131, 134, 136, 142
Weil, M., 132
Werk, A., 36, 38, 59, 135, 136, 139, 143,
    158
Wijnberg, M., 34, 48, 133, 180
Wik, R., 43
Wills, R. M., 161
Wilson, J., 48, 57, 98, 251
Wilson, S., 34, 46, 48, 49, 51, 57, 65,
    92, 105, 119, 128, 130, 132, 139, 142,
    145, 147, 153, 179, 183
Winter, J. E., 128, 129
Wodarski, J. S., 34, 217
Wrenn, R., 47, 50, 51, 205

Zayas, L. H., 45
Zimmerman, N., 52,
Zischka, P. C., 34, 50, 51, 75–78, 127,
    131, 170, 180, 195, 243

Subject Index

Academic approach. *See* Field instruction approaches

Accountability. *See* Field instruction

Adult-sensitive learning. *See* Field instruction approaches

Affective experiences, 56, 64–66, 92–95, 98, 119, 184–185, 187, 194, 248–249

Alternative structural approach. *See* Field instruction approaches

Andragogical approach. *See* Field instruction approaches

Andragogy, 34, 47–49

Apprenticeship approach. *See* Field instruction approaches

Articulated approach. *See* Field instruction approaches

Autonomy and independence, 89–90

Blended teaching. *See* Field instruction approaches

Block placements, 40

Boundary of supervision and therapy, 105–114, 141–142

Consultation, 192, 298–300; defined, 4

Contract: defined, 76; example of, 12, 274–275; prioritization process of, 12, 28, 273–274; target goals of, 11, 28, 274; task formulation, 12, 28, 275; time management of, 272–273

Contracting, 271–275; collaborative process of, 79; defined, 76; goal-oriented style of, 77; phases of, 5, 271–275; written vs. oral style of, 78

Delayed-entry approach. *See* Field instruction approaches

Didactic instruction, 203–206

Diversity, 114–118, 138

Educational supervision: affective responses in, 159; approaches to challenging aspects of, 5; beginning phase of, 5, 156–162; boundary of supervision and therapy in, 105–114, 141–142; case review, 164–165; content of, 43, 46, 289–290; defined, 2–3; developmental process of, 87–89; dimensions of, 38–40; education about, 195–196; encountering diversity in, 114–118, 138; ending or

Educational supervision (*continued*)
termination phase of, 162–170; environmental factors of, 90–92; expectations for supervisee and supervisor, 135–136; functions of, 2, 97–99; history of, 31–54; learning assignments in, 136; links between clinical encounters and learning objectives during, 82; links of classroom and field during, 83–84; middle phase of, 5–8, 182; modifying practice models for, 52; opportunities for learning, 82; power struggles in, 140–141, 185, 190–194; preparation for, 156; principles of effective, 55–95; retrospective processing of, 167; resources and support for, 157–158; triangulation in, 143–144; *see also* Field instruction; Task-Centered Model of Educational Supervision (TCS)

Empirically based practice, 176–177

Evaluation of performance, 159–162, 166–167, 229–233

Feedback: adult learning principles in, 58–59, 73–74; by supervisee, 66–67; complimenting as, 63; evaluating quality of, 69; example of, 68; principles of, 59–60; providing positive, 62–64; purposeful questioning as a strategy of, 67; specific behaviors and, 60; timeliness of, 77

Feminist pedagogy, 49–50, 75–76, 176, 181, 280

Field instruction: accountability and quality concerns, 37, 78, 139, 174, 177, 244, 246, 257; challenging aspects of, 51; dimensions of, 38–46; educational objectives of, 43, 53, 71–72, 77, 168, 214, 224–225, 289–290, 302; history of, 31–54;

models of, 36–37; modifying models for, 52; principles of effective instruction, 55–95; *see also* Educational supervision

Field instruction approaches: academic, 33; adult-sensitive learning, 48; alternative structural, 40–42; andragogical, 34, 47–49; apprenticeship, 32; articulated, 33–34; blended teaching, 51; contemporary, 35; delayed entry, 41; feminist pedagogy, 49–50, 75–76, 176, 181, 280; group, 41; learner focused process, 47–48; learning and teaching centered, 46–47; secondary, 39, 41–42, 149, 201, 295–297; therapeutic and growth, 33; team, 41–42; traditional, 39–40

Field units, 33

Group supervision, 294–295

Intern, defined, 4

Learning: feminist pedagogy and, 49–50, 75–76, 176, 181, 280; opportunities for, 82; partialized learning and development of, 56–57; principles of, 55–96; principles of adult learning, 48; self-directed style of, 74–75

Learning agreements, 51, 77, 214; *see also* Contracting

Learning assignment, 136–137, 157, 176, 226, 237–238

Learning objectives, 3, 8, 43–45, 58, 71–95, 172, 177–178, 180, 211–212, 214, 286

Multidiscipline use. *See* Task-Centered Model of Educational Supervision (TCS)

Obstacles, 242–275; anticipating and negotiating, 259–260, 271; emotional, 269; identification of, 265

Parallel process, 56, 68, 88–89, 170, 179, 207, 292
Peer supervision, 297
Personal issues, 108–112
Phases of supervision, 182–211
Power struggles, 140–142
Principles of effective instruction, 55–95
Process, defined, 46
Process recording. See Recording

Questioning, purposeful, 67

Recording, process, 39, 91, 149; tape, 149–150
Relationship. See Supervisory relationship
Role play, as supervisory technique, 268–269

Secondary supervision. See Task-Centered Model of Educational Supervision (TCS)
Self-directed learning, 74
Settings for educational supervision, 3, 40, 44–45, 175, 185, 195–197, 202, 234, 287–288, 290, 292–298
Staff, defined, 4
Staff supervision, 301
Supervisee: affective experiences and reactions of, see Affective experiences; anxiety of, 118, 124, 133–136; autonomy and dependence, 89–90; evaluation of, see Evaluation of performance; expectations for, 135; orientation of, 157; resources and support for, 157–158; responsibilities of, 118–119

Supervision: administrative, 2–3; defined, 2–3; educational, 2–3; supportive, 2–3; purpose for, 179–199; see also Educational supervision, Field instruction, Task-Centered Model of Educational Supervision (TCS)
Supervisor, 126–155; anxiety of, 12–124, 130–131, 153–154; as role model, 40, 84; authority of, 138–140; competence of, 132–133; dealing with personal issues, 127–128; education of, 132; expectations of, 135–136; influential role of, 126; positive attributes of, 127–128; roles and educational tasks of, 131; selecting learning assignments, 136; self-awareness of, 145–150; use of self by, 128–130
Supervisory relationship, 96–125; as a teaching tool, 103–104; boundary of supervision and therapy in, 105–111; functions and responsibilities, 28, 147, 123–124, 127–128; interactional process of, 99, interdependence in, 100; overview of, 97; parallel process of, 56, 68, 88–89, 170, 179, 207, 292; triangulation in, 143–144; working with individual differences, 114, 138
Support, modeling of, 270

Target goals: complexity of, 238; example of selecting, 222–226; evaluation of, 227–241; formulation of, 238; identification of, 220–226, 242–243, number of, 239–240; partialized learning and development of, 213–214, 236; prioritization and selection of, 12, 216–220, 236, 242–243, 253; target goal stage, 212–213, 242; types of, 214–216

Task-Centered Model of Educational Supervision (TCS): beginning phase of, 156–162; conjoint meetings and, 296–297; collaborative relationship using, 178–179; consultation and, 192, 298–300; defined, 1, 4; development of, 172–176; didactic instruction using, 203–206; education assessment using, 274–277; educational stage of, 5, 18, 183, 197, 203–304, 209–211, 233, 242, 276; empirical orientation of, 176–177; ending or termination phase, 242; example of supervision meeting using TCS, 7–28; explaining supervision using, 194, 199–200; functions of, 182–210; group supervision using, 294–295; learning content in, 175–176; middle phase of, 182; macro–centered setting and, 290–291; multidiscipline use of, 302–303; obstacles in, 242–275; overview of, 5, 397; peer supervision and, 297–298; phases of, 5–6, 228, 240, 324; power struggles in, 140–141; principles of, 176–181; process of, 6–7; reluctance to use, 200–201; secondary supervision and, 295; social stage of, 5, 8, 18, 183–194, 22, 242, 276; structure of,

49, 73, 225, 247, 360; staff supervision and, 301–302; tasks, 242–275; theoretical and practice orientations of, 291–292; structure of, 294–295; see also Obstacles; Target goals; Tasks

Task planning and implementation, 242–258; anticipating and negotiating obstacles in, 259–260; temporal considerations of, 265

Task review, 276–288; advantages of, 282–287; caution in use of, 288; task rating form for, 281–282; in short-term settings, 287; link between supervision and content in, 286; process of, 277–278

Tasks, 242–275; advantages of, 243–247; defined, 243; disadvantages of, 248; formulation of, 247–248; goal-achieving actions of, 180–181; identification, prioritization, and selection of, 253, 357–359; levels of specificity, 255–257; linking theory and practice using, 246–247; number of, 257; variation of, 279

Team approach. See Field instruction approaches

Triangulation, 143–144; and conjoint meetings, 296–297